GUIDE TO
NATIONAL
PARKS
OF THE UNITED STATES

EIGHTH EDITION

Redwood National Park

GUIDE TO
NATIONAL
PARKS
OF THE UNITED STATES

EIGHTH EDITION

Photography by Phil Schermeister

NATIONAL GEOGRAPHIC
WASHINGTON, D.C.

National Parks | Contents

INTRODUCTION | 6
Using This Guide 8 | Map 10

EAST | 12
Acadia 16 | Biscayne 26 | Congaree 32 | Dry Tortugas 40 |
Everglades 46 | Great Smoky Mountains 56 | Mammoth Cave 64 |
Shenandoah 72 | Virgin Islands 82

MIDWEST | 90
Badlands 94 | Cuyahoga Valley 100 | Isle Royale 106 | Theodore
Roosevelt 112 | Voyageurs 122 | Wind Cave 130

SOUTH CENTRAL | 136
Big Bend 140 | Carlsbad Caverns 150 | Guadalupe Mountains
160 | Hot Springs 166

SOUTHWEST | 172
Arches 176 | Black Canyon of the Gunnison 184 | Bryce Canyon 190 |
Canyonlands 198 | Capitol Reef 208 | Grand Canyon 214 | Great Basin
224 | Mesa Verde 232 | Petrified Forest 240 | Saguaro 246 | Zion 252

ROCKY MOUNTAINS | 260
Glacier/Waterton 264 | Grand Teton 272 | Great Sand Dunes 284 |
Rocky Mountain 292 | Yellowstone 300

PACIFIC SOUTHWEST | 312
American Samoa 316 | Channel Islands 320 | Death Valley 326 |
Haleakalā 332 | Hawai'i Volcanoes 342 | Joshua Tree 350 | Pinnacles
356 | Sequoia & Kings Canyon 362 | Yosemite 370

PACIFIC NORTHWEST | 380
Crater Lake 384 | Lassen Volcanic 392 | Mount Rainier 398 | North
Cascades 406 | Olympic 414 | Redwood 422

ALASKA | 430
Denali 434 | Gates of the Arctic 442 | Glacier Bay 448 |
Katmai 456 | Kenai Fjords 462 | Kobuk Valley 468 | Lake Clark 474 |
Wrangell–St. Elias 480

CREDITS & INDEX | 488
Acknowledgments | Illustrations Credits | Index | Map Key

Introduction

Need on occasion to get away from it all? Then this might be the book for you. Flip to pages 208–213 and you'll discover that the fantastically eroded slickrock solitudes of Utah's Capitol Reef National Park are "so remote that the nearest traffic light is 78 miles away."

And if that's too close, turn to pages 362–369: Deep within the rugged wilderness of California's Sequoia & Kings Canyon National Parks there is a "spot that is farther from a road than any other place in the lower 48 states."

There's simply no better getaway in the United States than a visit to one of the 59 national scenic parks — ranging from Alaska to the Virgin Islands, from Maine to American Samoa—profiled in this all-new eighth edition of our enduring classic. Exceptionally informative and refreshingly candid, this volume is *the* handbook to the crown jewels in our far-flung network of protected places.

This guide also draws upon a very deep legacy between National Geographic and the national parks. These two have been intertwined since 1915, when our pioneering editor Gilbert H. Grosvenor, on a two-week pack trip to California's Sierra Nevada, first sat spellbound beneath giant sequoias. There and then he determined to enlist this Society in the crusade to protect and preserve such marvels. He dedicated an entire issue of *National Geographic* magazine—April 1916's "Land of the Best"—to showcasing the glories of our natural heritage, placing a copy in each congressman's hand. Only a few months later, on August 25, 1916, President Woodrow Wilson signed the act creating the National Park Service.

Over the years National Geographic has helped establish, preserve, or restore Sequoia, Katmai, Carlsbad Caverns, Shenandoah, Mesa Verde, and Redwood National Parks—all of which appear in the following pages. It has also publicized the parks through at least 500 books, articles, and maps, not to mention dozens of television documentaries, online content, and our award-winning National Parks app.

— John M. Fahey, Jr.
Chairman of the Board, National Geographic Society
Commissioner, National Parks Second Century Commission

▶ USING THIS GUIDE

National Geographic's *Guide to National Parks of the United States* is designed as a travel planner to help you choose among the 59 scenic national parks within the National Park System. All of the parks offer fun, adventure, and splendor; your only decision is which one—or ones—to visit. What you want to experience will help guide your decisions.

The parks in this book are presented in alphabetical order within their geographical regions, so start your exploration by studying the opening map that shows each of the parks in the country, or if you already know where you want to go, check the Contents. Each chapter provides an overview of the parks in that region. Note: Some parks are in close enough proximity that you could perhaps see more than one on your trip.

Individual Park Entries

Our coverage of each park begins with a portrait of its natural wonders, ecological setting, history, and, often, its struggles with humans and alien species. You'll see why a single step off a trail can harm fragile plants and why visitors are detoured from areas that shelter wildlife. The parks are not just for people; they conserve ecosystems. Fourteen of the national parks have been designated United Nations World Heritage sites for their outstanding scenic and cultural wonders; more than 20 have international biosphere reserve status, signaling their distinctive, balanced, natural qualities.

From the historic/geologic/cultural overview, the chapter moves on to

"How to Visit." Travelers are encouraged not to rush through a park, but, instead, to take time to savor the beauty and to spend at least some time outdoors (outside the car).

Each entry continues with detailed descriptions of the park itself.

Other Guide Features

Information: This page, which follows each park entry, offers details on how to find the park, the best time to visit, locations of the Visitor Centers and headquarters, as well as camping and lodging information. Call or write the park, or visit the Park Service's website *(nps.gov)* for further details. Brochures are usually available free of charge from the parks. You can download a copy of the "National Park System: Map and Guide" at *publications.usa.gov/ USAPubs.php?PubID=1116.*

Campgrounds: The National Recreation Reservation Service (NRRS) *(recreation.gov;* 877-444-6777) handles reservations for many of the Park Service campgrounds in addition to numerous partner agencies such as the Bureau of Land Management, the Forest Service, and the Fish and Wildlife Service with campground locations near the national parks. Advance reservations are suggested.

Lodging: The Guide lists accommodations within the parks. The lists are by no means comprehensive, and listing does not imply endorsement by the National Geographic Society. The information can change without notice. Many parks maintain lists of lodgings in their areas, which they share on request. Also provided is information on communities near the parks and websites for local

American bison *(Bison bison)* in the Lamar Valley in Yellowstone National Park

chambers of commerce and tourist offices that might provide lodging suggestions.

Special Advisories:

• Do not take chances. People are killed or badly injured every year in the parks. Most casualties are the result of recklessness or failure to heed warnings.

• Stay away from wild animals. Do not feed them or try to touch them—not even raccoons or chipmunks (which can transmit diseases). Try not to surprise a bear, and do not let one approach. If one does, scare it off by yelling, clapping your hands, or banging pots. Store all your food in bear-proof containers (often available at parks); keep food out of sight in your vehicle, with windows closed and doors locked. Or suspend food at least 15 feet above ground and 10 feet out from a post or tree trunk.

• Guard your health. Know your limitations; don't overtax yourself. Boil water that doesn't come from a park's drinking-water tap. Chemical treatment of water will not kill giardia—a protozoan that causes severe diarrhea and lurks even in crystal-clear streams. Heed park warnings about hypothermia and Lyme disease. In western parks, take precautions to prevent hantavirus pulmonary syndrome, caused by a potentially fatal airborne virus transmitted by deer mice. Check with a ranger to learn whatever you can about staying safe.

• Expect RV detours. Check road regulations as you enter a park. Along some stretches of road, you will not be able to maneuver large vehicles. Listen to the park rangers and staff. They have the latest facts on road closings and dangers. Visit the park website before departing for the park for information that might influence your visit.

• Cell phone service. In many parks your cell phone navigation systems might not function, so consider alternate options.

Entrance Fees: The fees vary by park—days you visit, day/weekly passes, military status, vehicle permits, senior passes, and time of year—so do check individual park websites. In addition to daily or weekly fees and passes for seniors, most parks also offer a yearly fee, with unlimited entries.

For $80 you can buy an annual America the Beautiful Pass *(nps.gov/findapark/passes.htm),* which admits up to four people per visit to all national parks; also offered is unlimited admission to U.S. Fish and Wildlife Service, U.S. Forest Service, Bureau of Land Management, and Bureau of Reclamation sites.

OLYMPIC N.P.
NORTH CASCADES N.P.
MT. RAINIER N.P.
GLACIER N.P.
WASHINGTON
PACIFIC NORTHWEST
MONTANA
THEODORE ROOSEVELT N.P.
NORTH DAKOTA
MINN.
ROCKY MOUNTAINS
OREGON
CRATER LAKE N.P.
IDAHO
YELLOWSTONE N.P.
SOUTH DAKOTA
REDWOOD N.P.
GRAND TETON N.P.
WIND CAVE N.P.
BADLANDS N.P.
LASSEN VOLCANIC N.P.
CALIFORNIA (In both Pacific Southwest and Pacific Northwest regions)
NEVADA
WYOMING
NEBRASKA
YOSEMITE N.P.
GREAT BASIN N.P.
SOUTHWEST
UTAH
ROCKY MOUNTAIN N.P.
KINGS CANYON N.P.
PINNACLES N.P.
CAPITOL REEF N.P.
ARCHES N.P.
COLORADO (In both Rocky Mountains and Southwest regions)
BLACK CANYON OF THE GUNNISON N.P.
KANSAS
SEQUOIA N.P.
BRYCE CANYON N.P.
ZION N.P.
CANYONLANDS N.P.
GREAT SAND DUNES N.P. & PRES.
PACIFIC SOUTHWEST
DEATH VALLEY N.P.
GRAND CANYON N.P.
MESA VERDE N.P.
CHANNEL ISLANDS N.P.
JOSHUA TREE N.P.
PETRIFIED FOREST N.P.
OKLAHOMA
ARIZONA
NEW MEXICO
UNITED STATES MEXICO
SAGUARO N.P.
CARLSBAD CAVERNS N.P.
SOUTH CENTRAL
TEXAS
GUADALUPE MTS. N.P.
KOBUK VALLEY N.P.
GATES OF THE ARCTIC N.P. & PRESERVE
BIG BEND N.P.
ALASKA
DENALI N.P & PRES.
WRANGELL-ST. ELIAS N.P. & PRESERVE
LAKE CLARK N.P & PRES.
KATMAI N.P. & PRES.
KENAI FJORDS N.P.
GLACIER BAY N.P. & PRES.

0   miles   400
0   kilometers   600

Safety/Security Concerns: Given today's heightened awareness, some sites may require additional security procedures and identification.

Maps: The individual park and regional maps in this book were prepared as an orientation and aid in planning your trip. For more detail on trails and other facilities inside a park, contact the Park Service, call the park, or visit *nps.gov.* Always use detailed road and trail maps and where available, GPS.

The maps in this book note specially designated Wilderness Areas and National Preserves. The Wilderness Areas are managed to retain their natural qualities—no roads, buildings, or vehicles permitted. Some National Preserves allow hunting. For a list of map abbreviations used in this book see p. 495.

Finally, enjoy discovering and learning about all of our national parks.

East

Oconaluftee River, Great Smoky Mountains National Park

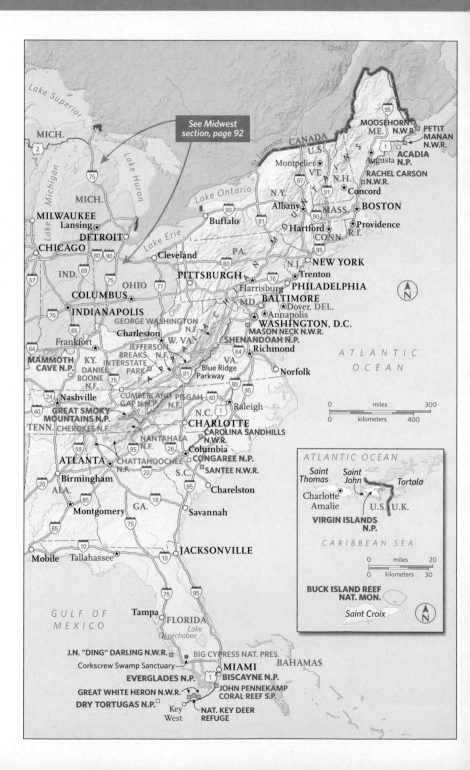

MICH.

Lake Superior

Lake Michigan

Lake Huron

See Midwest
section, page 92

CANADA

St. Lawrence

U.S.

Lake Ontario

Lake Erie

MOOSEHORN
N.W.R. — PETIT
MANAN
N.W.R.
ME.
ACADIA
N.P.
Augusta
RACHEL CARSON
N.W.R.

Montpelier
VT.
N.H.
Concord

N.Y.
Albany
MASS.
BOSTON

Hartford
CONN.
R.I.
Providence

MICH.
MILWAUKEE
Lansing
DETROIT
CHICAGO

Buffalo

Cleveland

PA.

N.J.
NEW YORK
Trenton

IND.

OHIO

PITTSBURGH
Harrisburg
PHILADELPHIA

COLUMBUS
INDIANAPOLIS

Ohio

Charleston

W. VA.

GEORGE WASHINGTON
N.F.

JEFFERSON
BREAKS
N.F.

MD.
Dover, DEL.
BALTIMORE
Annapolis
WASHINGTON, D.C.
MASON NECK N.W.R.
SHENANDOAH N.P.
Richmond

Frankfort

MAMMOTH
CAVE N.P.
KY.
DANIEL
BOONE
N.F.

INTERSTATE
PARK

Blue Ridge
Parkway

VA.

Norfolk

ATLANTIC
OCEAN

Nashville
CUMBERLAND
GAP N.H.P.
PISGAH
N.F.

GREAT SMOKY
MOUNTAINS N.P.
TENN. CHEROKEE N.F.

N.C.
Raleigh

miles 300
kilometers 400

NANTAHALA
N.F.

ATLANTA
CHATTAHOOCHEE
N.F.

Birmingham

ALA.

CHARLOTTE
CAROLINA SANDHILLS
N.W.R.
Columbia
CONGAREE N.P.
SANTEE N.W.R.

S.C.

ATLANTIC OCEAN

Saint
Thomas
Saint
John
Tortola

Charlotte
Amalie
U.S. U.K.

VIRGIN ISLANDS
N.P.

Montgomery

GA.

Charelston

Savannah

CARIBBEAN SEA

miles 20
kilometers 30

Mobile
Tallahassee

JACKSONVILLE

BUCK ISLAND REEF
NAT. MON.

Saint Croix

GULF OF
MEXICO

Tampa
FLORIDA
Lake
Okeechobee

J.N. "DING" DARLING N.W.R.
Corkscrew Swamp Sanctuary
BIG CYPRESS NAT. PRES.
MIAMI
BAHAMAS
EVERGLADES N.P.
BISCAYNE N.P.
GREAT WHITE HERON N.W.R.
JOHN PENNEKAMP
CORAL REEF S.P.
DRY TORTUGAS N.P.
Key
West
NAT. KEY DEER
REFUGE

N

Not until well into the 20th century did park planners turn their attention from the West's grand vistas to the more subtle beauties of eastern scenery. Between 1919 and 1926, Congress authorized the area's first three parks in the Appalachian Mountains. Today these parks—Acadia, Great Smoky Mountains, and Shenandoah—rank among the most visited in the nation. Six other parks round out the roster of the region's protected places.

Plants and animals that inhabit the mountains, islands, sea, and tide pools along a stretch of wild Maine coast are protected at **Acadia** National Park. The hardwood forests and flowering meadows of Virginia's **Shenandoah,** on land that had been logged, farmed, and grazed for 250 years, are studies in nature's power of recuperation. **Great Smoky** preserves large stands of virgin forest on 6,000-foot slopes along the Tennessee–North Carolina border.

Since the 1920s, the U.S. Congress has moved to safeguard other distinctive eastern biomes. The world's longest known cave network, **Mammoth Cave** in Kentucky, has some 400 miles of mapped passages. One of the newer parks in the system, South Carolina's **Congaree** nourishes 11,000 acres of old-growth bottomland forest.

Underwater wilderness awaits visitors to Florida's **Biscayne** National Park, home of the northernmost living coral reef in the continental United States. West of Biscayne lies **Everglades** National Park, established in 1947 to safeguard the unique ecosystem created by a slow-moving river, inches deep and some 50 miles wide. Endangered due to climate change and rising sea levels, Everglades provides habitat for an enormous variety of wildlife.

Off the coast of Florida and about 70 nautical miles west of Key West, on a 7-mile-long archipelago rich with birds and marine creatures, **Dry Tortugas** National Park maintains an abandoned 19th-century brick fortress, the largest in America at the time. And far to the southeast, **Virgin Islands** National Park protects much of St. John, where hillsides thick with bay, mango, and trumpet trees slope to crescent beaches rimmed by coral reefs.

Acadia

Maine

Established
February 26, 1919

50,000 acres

Acadia National Park provides proof that a park doesn't need vast wilderness to offer gorgeous scenery and the chance for immersion in the natural world. Small for a national park, composed of a patchwork of public land surrounded by towns and villages, Acadia preserves a glacier-carved landscape of rugged mountains, pristine lakes, lush forests, and long stretches of Maine's famous rocky shore. It ranks among America's most visited national parks. No one who sees it wonders why.

Most of Acadia is located on Mount Desert Island, just off the central Maine coast. Separate areas of the park lie on the Schoodic Peninsula, on the mainland to the east, and on Isle au Haut, a small island to the southwest. The Wabanaki Indians called Mount Desert *Pemetic*, "the sloping land," and it's true that flat places are scarce here. Glaciers, which retreated around 17,000 years ago, cut narrow valleys now filled with lakes and arms of the Atlantic Ocean and carved steep cliffs.

Along Park Loop Road, near Thunder Hole

Some of the wealthy part-time residents began using their influence to push for a national park on the island. Among them was oil magnate John D. Rockefeller, Jr., who donated nearly 11,000 acres to what was first called Lafayette National Park. (The name was changed to Acadia in 1929.) The first national park in the East, Acadia grew bit by bit over the years, and now it occupies 50,000 acres, including about 60 percent of Mount Desert Island.

A massive fire in 1947 destroyed Millionaires' Row and also brought about a major change in the island's ecology. Spruce-fir coniferous forest once dominated Mount Desert, but the fire created open areas that were colonized by faster-growing hardwood trees, such as birch, aspen, and maple. In fall, the many-hued foliage of these hardwoods blaze brightly, recalling the "year that Maine burned."

Glaciers also scoured granite mountaintops, leaving little soil to support forest. The lack of trees caused French explorer Samuel de Champlain, who sailed past in 1604, to call the island *Monts Desert* (barren mountains).

In the 19th century, Mount Desert Island's beauty and remoteness began attracting wealthy visitors looking for a retreat from bustling cities. Vanderbilts, Astors, Carnegies, and other illustrious families built magnificent mansions (which they called "cottages") on the island's northeast coast. The area became known as Millionaires' Row. As the 20th century arrived, the town of Bar Harbor had dozens of hotels, and people began to worry that Mount Desert was losing the qualities that had made it so attractive.

▶ **HOW TO VISIT**

The **Hulls Cove Visitor Center,** in the town of Hulls Cove—in the northernmost part of the park—marks the start of Acadia's famed **Park Loop Road.** This 27-mile scenic drive *(closed in winter)* passes many popular sites, including **Otter Cliffs** and **Jordan Pond.** A side road a quarter mile from the start of the road and another road 3.5 miles in leads to the top of **Cadillac Mountain,** with its splendid panorama of Mount Desert Island. Hike or bike a section of the park's unique and historic **carriage roads,** which offer short, easy jaunts and longer options.

If you have time, explore the park's **western side,** with its less-traveled trails and fascinating tide pools. To see many more miles of beautiful rocky shore, return to the mainland and head east to **Schoodic Peninsula,** about an hour's drive from Bar Harbor.

How best to move through the park in peak season? Don't drive into the park in July or August. Traffic can hinder your enjoyment of Acadia's beauty, so get a map to locate trailheads and attractions, and use the free **Island Explorer bus** (late June to mid-October; *exploreacadia.com; 207-667-5796*).

Eastern Side of the Park

A leisurely drive around the **Park Loop Road** is Acadia's must-do experience. It's most pleasant in the off-season or early in the morning any time of the year. No matter when you go, you'll see some of the finest scenery in the park.

Leaving the **Hulls Cove Visitor Center,** you soon reach overlooks with expansive views of **Frenchman Bay.** At

the Sieur de Monts Spring, the **Abbe Museum** *(abbemuseum.org;* 207-288-3519) focuses on the Wabanaki Native American culture. The small **Wild Gardens of Acadia** *(friendsofacadia .org)* provides a good introduction to the flora of Mount Desert Island.

A bit farther along the road is the trailhead for one of the park's most popular, strenuous, and potentially dangerous trails. The **Precipice Trail** ascends the near vertical face of **Champlain Mountain,** so steep in places that iron ladders and rungs have been set into the rock to help climbers. Less than a mile long, Precipice presents a challenge that's irresistible to many Acadia visitors. The park stresses that it's more of a "non-technical climbing route" than a trail, and anyone who attempts it should be physically fit, wear sturdy hiking boots, and have no fear of heights. (The trail is often closed in

Bass Harbor Head Lighthouse, Mount Desert Island

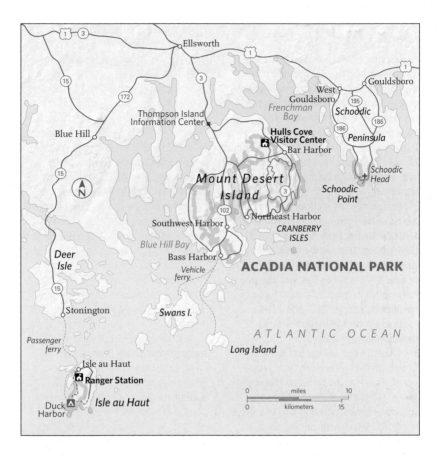

spring and summer to protect nesting peregrine falcons.)

Continue to **Sand Beach,** where the water is always cold. Even in summer, the water temperature rises to only 55°F. A lifeguard is on duty here Memorial Day through Labor Day.

Watch for the small parking area at popular **Thunder Hole.** Here, a small cave roars like thunder when the tide is just right and a large wave hits the shore, compressing the air inside the cave opening. When a powerful surge hits, water can shoot some 40 feet into the air.

Ahead lies one of Acadia's iconic sights: the 110-foot-high rock wall known as **Otter Cliffs.** The landscape architect Frederick Law Olmsted, Jr., who helped design the Loop Road in the 1930s, referred to this scenery as having "a certain bigness of sweep." His quirky phrase seems apt here; you'll certainly want to stop and admire the grand terrain. Park and maybe walk the 2-mile **Ocean Path** to **Otter Point,** find a rock, sit down, and take it all in.

About 1.5 miles past the causeway at **Otter Cove,** watch for a small, unmarked parking area. Take the

Island Excursions

You don't need a boat to visit Bar Island, less than a mile north of Bar Harbor. For 1.5 hours on either side of low tide you can walk along a connecting sandbar to the island for a fine view of the town and the Mount Desert Island highlands. As you walk around, be sure to keep an eye on the time. You don't want to be marooned by the rising tide.

In summer, the National Park Service offers a ranger-led tour *(fee)* to Baker Island, with structures of a 19th-century farm as well as the still functioning 1855 Baker Island lighthouse. A 4.5-hour cruise with the Bar Harbor Whale Watch Company *(bar harborwhales.com; 207-288-2386)* routinely comes with harbor seals, bald eagles, and ospreys.

The 2.5-hour Islesford Historical Cruise (mid-May through Oct.; *cruise acadia.com)* leaves from the Municipal Pier in Northeast Harbor and visits Little Cranberry Island and the Islesford Historical Museum, which uses ship models, tools, and photos to recall pioneer life on Maine islands. Other commercial tour boats make their way to Little Cranberry Island, where visitors can explore shops and galleries. The Cranberry Cove Ferry *(cranberrycoveferry.com)* runs regularly between Great Cranberry and Little Cranberry islands.

stairs down to **Little Hunters Beach,** a picture-perfect spot. The shore is covered in the small, rounded rocks called cobblestones. When waves come in, the cobbles make a faint tapping sound.

Thousands of rocks have been taken over the years by visitors. But it's illegal to take rocks (or any other natural feature) from a national park.

The Loop Road continues inland to reach lovely **Jordan Pond,** one of the park's most popular spots, in part because of the restaurant, which is operated by a private concessioner May to late October *(acadiajordanpond house.com; 207-276-3316)*. The view from the lawn takes in the pond and, in the distance, the twin rounded hills called **The Bubbles**. A glacier carved this valley, pushing rock debris as it moved. When it melted, the glacier left a wall of rock, called a moraine, as a natural dam. The Jordan Pond area is a great place to explore **carriage roads** (see p. 21), as several radiate out from this point.

A rewarding hiking trail, the 3.3-mile **Jordan Pond Shore Path** circles the pond, crossing wetlands and brooks along the way. As you pass **South Bubble,** near the northern end of the pond, watch for rock climbers scaling the cliff face. As the Loop Road skirts **Eagle Lake** and completes its circuit, a side road leads to perhaps Acadia's most celebrated destination. At 1,530 feet, **Cadillac Mountain** is the highest point along the North Atlantic seaboard. The vista from the pink granite summit deserves the oft-used term "breathtaking." Below, islands dot Frenchman Bay like green stepping-stones leading to the Schoodic Peninsula.

The blocky red-and-white Egg Rock lighthouse sits in the mouth of the bay. To the south, broad, low islands—Baker, Sutton, and Great and Little Cranberry— seem to float in the Atlantic like jigsaw puzzle pieces uncoupled from the ragged shore.

Lodge built by John D. Rockefeller, Jr.

From October 7 to March 6, the top of Cadillac Mountain is the first place in the United States to see the sunrise. Year-round, visitors rise before dawn to drive to the summit and greet the new day. The **Blue Hill overlook** makes a great place from which to watch the sunset. In peak season, try to avoid driving up Cadillac at midday, when finding parking can be difficult.

Of course, you can also hike to the top of Cadillac. The **North Ridge Trail** (2.2 miles) and the more strenuous **South Ridge Trail** (3.5 miles) are popular ways to the summit.

The Carriage Roads

Park donor John D. Rockefeller, Jr., loved Mount Desert Island. He had a distaste for the "garish advances of civilization," and that included motor vehicles. In 1913 Rockefeller began planning a network of what he called carriage roads through some of the island's loveliest areas. Walkers, horses with riders, bicyclists, and of course carriages were welcome; automobiles were (and remain) banned.

More than 50 miles of broad, broken-stone carriage roads were built; 45 miles are inside the park boundaries. Rockefeller also financed 16 of the 17 imposing stone bridges along carriage roads, built by local stoneworkers. As the story goes, over the years they got so good at it that Rockefeller had to remind them that he wanted a rustic look, not smoothly finished rock. (The bridges are actually steel-reinforced concrete with rock exterior.)

Carriage roads offer a wonderful way to explore the park on foot, by bike, and, in winter, by cross-country ski. Among the places with quick access to the road system are Jordan Pond, Bubble Pond, the north end of Eagle Lake, the Brown Mountain Gatehouse, and the Hulls Cove Visitor Center. You can choose routes ranging from short and easy to all-day excursions. Signposts at all intersections make navigation simple. Remember that bicycles are not allowed on carriage roads outside the park boundary, in the area south of Jordan Pond, and between Seal Harbor and Northeast Harbor.

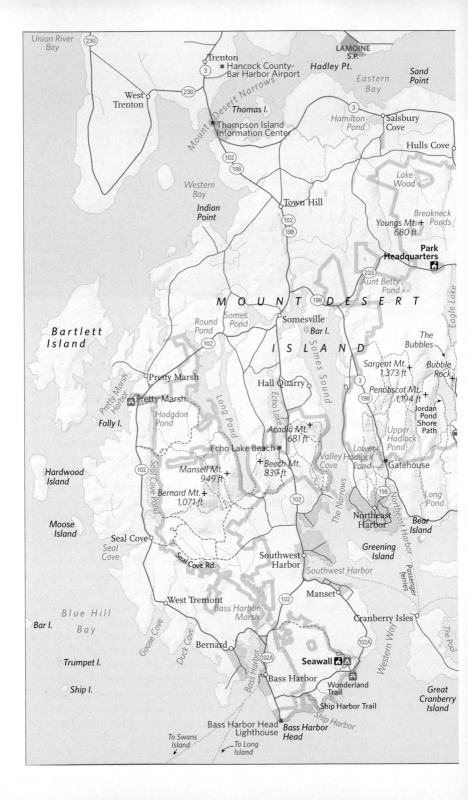

If it's your first visit to Acadia, consider the 3.3-mile **Witch Hole Pond Loop,** beginning at an impressive bridge beside Duck Brook Road. This route passes several wetlands areas and is great for wildflowers in late spring and summer.

Western Side of the Park

Somes Sound carves a long sea inlet into the heart of Mount Desert Island. To its west, the "quiet side" of Acadia National Park rewards visitors with trails that are less known, and so less crowded, than those closer to Bar Harbor.

Beech Mountain offers a fine view of Long Pond in return for 1.2 miles of moderate effort. For a challenge and another perspective on Long Pond, walk the 1.2-mile **Perpendicular Trail,** with its rock stairs, up **Mansell Mountain.** Make a 2.4-mile loop by following the Mansell Mountain and Cold Brook trails back to the trailhead. A trail with good views of Somes Sound leads to the top of **Acadia Mountain.**

The pools of water on rocky shore ledges host a fascinating array of creatures visible at low tide, from barnacles to periwinkle snails, crabs to sea anemones. Sites such as **Ship Harbor, Wonderland,** and **Seawall** offer fine opportunities to sit quietly and observe life in the intertidal zone. If the tide is out, you might want to consider tide-pooling: walking around and exploring the pools without stepping inside them. Be careful on slippery rocks, watch for the incoming tide, and leave sea creatures in place.

Sign up for a ranger-led program such as Life Between the Tides *(fee)* to learn about this diverse life zone. Make your way to or call the Hulls Cove

Visitor Center (207-288-3338) for schedules and tickets.

While you're in the area, don't miss the famous **Bass Harbor Head Lighthouse,** reached by taking Lighthouse Road south from Maine 102A. The 1858 brick structure is on the National Register of Historic Places and has been featured on countless postcards and calendars. Stay on marked paths. The lighthouse itself is private.

Continue north on Maine 102A and Maine 102, passing through several villages, to reach **Pretty Marsh,** a somewhat remote part of the national park that's also one of its nicest and most scenic picnic spots. A stairway makes it easy to descend to explore the shore of **Pretty Marsh Harbor.**

If it's a warm summer day and you feel like taking a dip, head to **Echo Lake,** the most popular swimming site on the island. A lifeguard is on duty from Memorial Day to Labor Day.

(Many Mount Desert lakes function as water suppliers and are closed to swimming.)

Schoodic Peninsula

This disjunct section of the park is reached by following Maine 3 to Ellsworth and heading east on US 1 and south on Maine 186. The trip is well worth the effort: A 6-mile road hugs the shore of the peninsula, offering views of some of the park's best coastal scenery. On a day when the waves are big, the sight of water crashing and foaming against the rocks can be spectacular, especially at **Schoodic Point**.

Several pullouts provide places from which to enjoy the views. Interpretive roadside signs lend insight on the area's wildlife, history, and geology. In places it's easy to see where black veins of magma were squeezed up into fractures in huge pink granite boulders during long-ago volcanic events.

From Schoodic viewpoints you can see Mount Desert Island to the west, as well as a variety of islands and waterbirds. Take the short, unpaved side road to the top of 440-foot **Schoodic Head** for an even better panoramic vista.

Isle au Haut

Relatively few people visit this special spot, which was given its name, High Island, by Samuel de Champlain in 1604. To reach it requires a drive of about 1.5 hours from Bar Harbor to the town of Stonington and then a ride on a private boat (isleauhaut.com; 207-367-5193) that takes passengers on a first-come, first-served basis.

Isle au Haut is about 6 miles long by 2 miles wide. Around 2,700 acres of the island belong to the national park; the rest is private property. A small year-round community grows to several hundred when the summer-only residents arrive.

Limited seasonal camping is allowed only by prior reservation, made by mail application to the park. Private lodging is also available. The number of day-trippers is limited. What this means is that visitors find wonderful solitude on the 18 miles of hiking trails that meander around the southern part of the island.

Bird-watching, picking wild blueberries, picnicking, biking, and simply reveling in the rocky coast scenery are among the favorite activities on little Isle au Haut. Walking **Western Head Road,** the **Cliff Trail,** and the **Western Head Trail** adds up to a pleasant loop of 3.7 miles.

White-tailed deer

Information

How to Get There

From Portland, ME (about 160 miles southwest), take I-95 to Bangor and then go south on I-395, US 1A, and Maine 3.

When to Go

Many park facilities are closed from around late Oct. through April or May. July and Aug. see heavy visitation and high traffic. Late June and Sept. offer pleasant temperatures and less crowding. Expect peak foliage in mid-Oct.

Visitor Center

Information is available year-round at park headquarters on Maine 233. On Rte. 3, the **Hulls Cove Visitor Center** is open daily mid-April through late Oct.

Headquarters

20 McFarland Hill Dr.
Bar Harbor, ME 04609
nps.gov/acad
207-288-3338

Camping

Blackwoods Campground (275 campsites), 5 miles south of Bar Harbor, is open May though Oct. as well as April and Nov., depending on weather conditions. **Seawall Campground** (198 campsites), 4 miles south of Southwest Harbor, is open late May through Sept. For reservations: *recreation.gov;* 877-444-6777. There is no backcountry camping in the park.

Lodging

In the park, run by a concessioner, are **Keeper's House Inn** and **Cottage Rental Robinson Point Lighthouse** (*keepers house.com;* 207-335-2990). Lodging is plentiful in **Bar Harbor** and nearby towns. The **Mount Desert** Chamber of Commerce (*mountdesertchamber.org)* can provide information. Another good source is the Bar Harbor Chamber of Commerce (*barharborinfo.com;* 207-288-5103).

Biscayne

Florida

Established
June 28, 1980

172,900 acres

Biscayne National Park serves as a popular playground for boat owners in the Miami metropolitan area, and for good reason: The beautiful blue waters of Biscayne Bay, within sight of the city skyline, offer a wealth of opportunities for cruising, fishing, and picnicking along the shore.

Yes, there are activities galore, but the park is much more than simply a sunny, fun weekend playground. Visitors who explore the park's diverse attractions discover a watery world encompassing wildlife, historic shipwrecks, and peaceful lagoons where the loudest sound is the splash of kayak paddles.

The park's colorful human history begins with the Native American Glades Culture, which left shell mounds in the area that date back more than 2,500 years. In the 19th century, farmers grew pineapples and limes on the Florida Keys; later, Adams Key was home to the Cocolobo Club, a private getaway that hosted several U.S. presidents.

There's a colorful story behind the establishment of the national park. Conservationists and developers were

Elkhorn coral

In 2014 the concessioner authorized to operate boat tours in the park ceased operations, making it difficult for most visitors to access the bay, the Keys, and the reef. At this writing, the park is going through the process required to authorize a new concessioner and resume park boat tours. Trips could start up again in 2016.

▶ HOW TO VISIT

At Biscayne National Park, exploration focuses on the water. Take in the exhibits at the **Dante Fascell Visitor Center** on the mainland and check the schedule for ranger-led paddling trips (usually December through April; 786-335-3612) along the longest mangrove forest on Florida's east coast. A snorkeling trip to the reef—another water-based activity—is a truly memorable experience.

Also consider discovering the park's watery world on your own. Rent a kayak from an outfitter outside the park and paddle around the quiet mangrove shoreline of the mainland, right near the visitor center. Beginners welcome.

Visitors who take private boats into the park should be aware of regulations applying to both personal safety and protection of the environment. It's imperative to have nautical charts and to know tide schedules to avoid running aground in shallow water. Coral reefs and other areas of the sea floor are easily damaged by anchors and boat hulls.

Mainland, Biscayne Bay, & the Keys

Begin your visit with an overview of the the park. The interpretive videos

locked in a bitter, years-long battle in the 1960s (see p. 30).

Ninety-five percent of the park area is made up of the waters of Biscayne Bay and the nearby Atlantic Ocean. The park encompasses four ecosystems:
• a narrow strip of mangrove forest bordering the shore of Biscayne Bay
• a large part of the bay itself
• the northernmost islands of the Florida Keys
• the northernmost section of the world's third largest coral reef, in the Atlantic, just beyond the Keys

Of the park's lures, what's most fascinating to many visitors is the array of colorful fish and other animal life that populates the coral reef, from sharks to sea turtles to the coral itself.

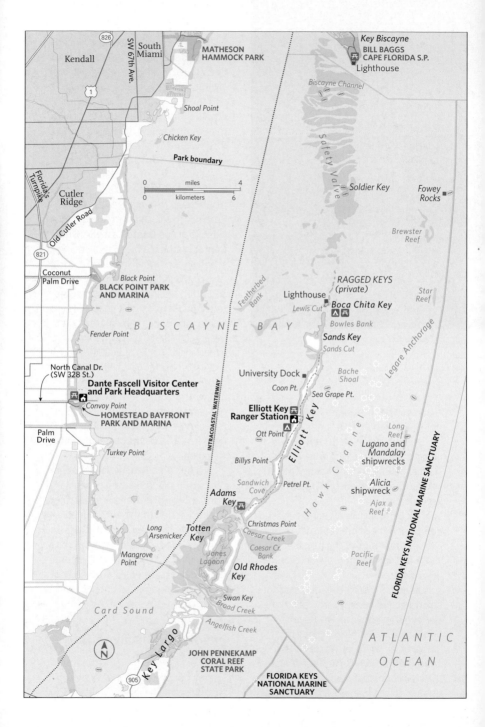

Kendall

SW 67th Ave.

South Miami

MATHESON HAMMOCK PARK

Key Biscayne
BILL BAGGS
CAPE FLORIDA S.P.
Lighthouse

Biscayne Channel

Shoal Point

Chicken Key

Park boundary

Florida's Turnpike

Cutler Ridge

Old Cutler Road

miles   4
kilometers   6

Safety Valve

Soldier Key

Fowey Rocks

Brewster Reef

Coconut Palm Drive

Black Point
BLACK POINT PARK AND MARINA

Featherbed Bank

Lewis Cut

Lighthouse

RAGGED KEYS (private)

Boca Chita Key

Star Reef

Bowles Bank

Fender Point

B I S C A Y N E   B A Y

Sands Key

Sands Cut

Legare Anchorage

North Canal Dr. (SW 328 St.)

University Dock

Bache Shoal

Dante Fascell Visitor Center and Park Headquarters

Coon Pt.

Convoy Point

HOMESTEAD BAYFRONT PARK AND MARINA

Elliott Key Ranger Station

Elliott Key

Sea Grape Pt.

Long Reef

Hawk Channel

Lugano and Mandalay shipwrecks

Palm Drive

Ott Point

Alicia shipwreck

Turkey Point

INTRACOASTAL WATERWAY

Billys Point

Ajax Reef

Sandwich Cove

Petrel Pt.

Adams Key

Long Arsenicker

Totten Key

Christmas Point

Caesar Creek

Pacific Reef

Mangrove Point

Jones Lagoon

Caesar Cr. Bank

Old Rhodes Key

FLORIDA KEYS NATIONAL MARINE SANCTUARY

Card Sound

Swan Key

Broad Creek

Angelfish Creek

N

Key Largo

JOHN PENNEKAMP CORAL REEF STATE PARK

A T L A N T I C

O C E A N

FLORIDA KEYS NATIONAL MARINE SANCTUARY

Boca Chita Key and the Miami skyline

and exhibits at the Dante Fascell Visitor Center at Convoy Point will help orient you.

A canoe or kayak trip along the shoreline could include sightings of wildlife, including manatees, the huge, gentle marine mammals that feed on underwater grasses. Manatee sightings are most likely in winter.

Birds found here include brown pelicans, gulls, terns, herons, egrets, magnificent frigatebirds, and sometimes southern Florida specialties such as mangrove cuckoos and white-crowned pigeons. You can also snorkel near the shore, although the underwater life here is not as varied and colorful as that on the coral reefs, 10 miles out to sea.

There's a short **Jetty Trail** along the shore from which visitors occasionally spot manatees, as well as a variety of birds. Rarely, an American crocodile makes an appearance.

Visitors with their own boats or those who sign up with an independent outfitter begin their trips in the shallows (4 to 10 feet deep) of Biscayne Bay. Turtle grass, shoal grass,

and similar vegetation covers the bay floor, providing protection for breeding crabs, lobsters, shrimp, and other creatures. The occasional sea turtle or barracuda may appear below, and dolphins often accompany the boat.

The portion of the **Florida Keys** that includes the national park has islands large and tiny, with histories just as widely varied. At 7 miles long, **Elliott Key** is the largest of the park's keys; primitive camping is allowed in designated areas; cold-water showers and drinking water are available.

A trail runs the length of Elliott Key, through a subtropical forest that is home to rare butterflies, including the Bahama swallowtail, and distinctive plants. (Biscayne National Park boasts several national champion trees. Indeed, many of the park's tree species are found in the United States exclusively in southern Florida.) Elliott Key was heavily homesteaded in the 19th and early 20th centuries, though most evidence of that era has disappeared.

It will require a bit of planning, but if you can arrange to take a canoe or kayak trip into **Jones Lagoon,** south of Caesar Creek, your efforts will be well repaid. (Ranger-led trips are offered here on occasion; check with the visitor center.) This quiet site, too shallow for motorboat traffic, truly is a different world. In the mangrove-ringed lagoon you may see Cassiopea jellyfish (also referred to as upside-down jellyfish), along with sharks, rays, sea stars, and spiny lobsters

Boca Chita Key, smaller and lacking drinking water, is the park's most popular island, with camping permitted. The island was once owned by businessman Mark Honeywell, who built several structures that still stand, including a 65-foot-high ornamental lighthouse. Visitors can climb the lighthouse when a park staffer or volunteer is present.

The Reefs

The **coral reefs** that stretch beyond the Keys are part of the world's third longest coral reef system, following behind Australia's Great Barrier Reef and the Mesoamerican Reef in the Caribbean Sea. Tours to the reef, which runs the length of the park's eastern edge, offer the chance for snorkelers and certified scuba divers to enjoy the diverse and colorful life of this undersea ecosystem.

Fish are the indisputable stars of the marine show. Included are such species as butterflyfish, parrotfish, damselfish, pipefish, and barracudas. Nurse sharks and loggerhead sea turtles also can be spotted. Equally colorful, other creatures of the reef include sea cucumbers, Christmas tree worms, sponges, and of course the coral itself in an array of forms such as elkhorn, brain, sea whip, and sea fan.

"Spite Highway"

In the 1950s and 1960s, developers planned a new city (to be called Islandia) in Biscayne Bay, as well as an industrial port and a deep channel to be dredged through the bay. Conservationists protested the destruction these activities would bring to the pristine environment of Biscayne Bay, and a coalition of anglers, environmentalists, writers, and politicians began promoting a plan to create a national park that would protect a long stretch of undeveloped shoreline, part of the bay, several keys, and sections of coral reef. A bitter battle ensued, culminating in the creation in 1968 of Biscayne National Monument, designated a national park 12 years later.

In the meantime, though, angry would-be developers had bulldozed a wide roadway down the length of Elliott Key, in an effort to make the environment less appealing for protection. This "Spite Highway," which has recovered somewhat through regrowth of vegetation, now serves as a hiking trail through tropical hardwood forest.

As beautiful as the reef is, it was the nemesis of the many ships that have run aground here. Biscayne National Park's **Maritime Heritage Trail,** the only underwater archaeological trail administered by the National Park Service, includes six of the dozens of shipwrecks within the park. Mooring buoys and brochures interpret such wrecks as the *Mandalay*, which sank in 1966; the *Alicia,* which sank in 1905; and the massive *Lugano,* which went down in 1913.

Family Fun Fest is a free park program held on the second Sunday of the month from December through April.

Information

How to Get There

From Miami, FL (about 35 miles north), take Fla. 821 (Florida's turnpike) south to Homestead and go east on SW 328 St. to Convoy Point.

When to Go

Dec. through April is the most popular season, with moderate temperatures and fewer mosquitoes. Water is calmer and clearer for snorkeling in summer, however.

Visitor Center

The **Dante Fascell Visitor Center** at Convoy Point is open year-round. Visitors should contact the Visitor Center before arrival for the latest information on available tours and operators.

Headquarters

9700 SW 328 St.
Homestead, FL 33033
nps.gov/bisc
305-230-7275

Camping

The park's two campgrounds, on **Elliott Key** and **Boca Chita Key,** are accessible only by boat. Elliott has toilets, showers, and drinking water; Boca Chita has only toilets. Each camping area offers some 20 sites.

Lodging

Lodging is available in the towns of **Homestead** and **Florida City**, both 9 miles west. For more information, contact the Tropical Everglades Visitor Association (*tropicaleverglades.com*; 305-245-9180).

BISCAYNE
1980

Congaree

South Carolina

Established
November 10, 2003

26,000 acres

In the early 21st century, the largest intact old-growth bottomland hardwood forest in the United States became Congaree National Park—literally shedding its ecologically inaccurate swamp designation in the process. It's among the country's least crowded parks, with just 110,000 or so annual visitors. Folks mostly stick to the northwestern corner of the park, near the visitor center, thus missing out on the moss-draped tangle of primeval floodplain forest that captivated European explorers in the 16th century.

Relative isolation has always been among Congaree's assets. Though less than 20 miles south of urban Columbia, South Carolina, the park immerses visitors in otherworldly landscapes. Park officials manage Congaree as a federally designated Wilderness, emphasizing preservation and scientific research and minimizing development. In the wilds of Congaree, beams of sunlight stream in through perforations in the dense tree canopy, giant hardwood tree trunks look like dinosaur legs, and armies

Bald cypress trees

routinely were sent off to the sawmill. Starting in the early 1950s, conservationists led a charge to prevent further logging. The U.S. Congress established Congaree Swamp National Monument in 1976 to preserve an "outstanding example of a near-virgin southern hardwood forest." This was the first step in Congaree's journey to becoming a national park.

With its seasonal flooding, Congaree may look like a swamp and feel like one, but it is characterized as a floodplain forest. Some 11,000 acres of hardwood forest thrive on the nutrient-rich alluvial soils where the Congaree and Wateree Rivers merge and frequently flood.

And what of the park's name? It refers to the native inhabitants who lived along the Congaree River. In the late 17th and early 18th centuries, the Congaree were sold as slaves, fell victim to disease (smallpox) brought by Europeans, and were killed fighting in wars with British colonists and other native peoples.

During the Revolutionary War, deep southern woods such as Congaree earned stealthy General Francis Marion the nickname "Swamp Fox." The wilderness provided him and his men a strategic and safe haven from which to outwit British troops.

of conical "knees" rise from the bald cypress tree roots like stalagmites poking up through ferns and fungi. One park ranger described them as the clenched knuckles of a vast community of trees "holding hands" underground to hold each other up.

There are bald cypress trees deep in the woods that died more than a century ago, mostly the result of logging. The stumps that remain provide refuge for prothonotary warblers as well as for insects and fungi.

Before the days of federal protection, Congaree's swamplike conditions literally protected many of its hardwood trees from ax-wielding outsiders. Still, by 1915 most of the original cypress tree population had been decimated; 500-year-old trees

▶ HOW TO VISIT

Allow a full day for hiking—and an extra day if you want to fish or paddle. Leave your car at the parking lot; there are no roadways within the park. Named for the South Carolina outdoorsman and newspaper editor who kicked off the drive to save Congaree

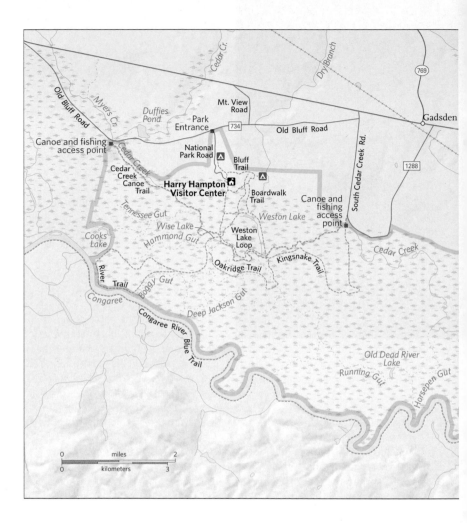

in the early 1950s, the **Harry Hampton Visitor Center** is the park's gateway. Inside, a video and exhibits reveal the history and ecology of the park.

A synthetic bald cypress holds court in the exhibit hall, soaring through the ceiling and flaring 14 feet wide, with a hollow base for kids to explore. A framed map illustrated by conservationist John Cely chronicles the lay of the land in meticulous detail. (Maps are available for sale.)

From the visitor center, more than 20 miles of established hiking trails issue from the **Boardwalk Trail,** a wheelchair- and stroller-friendly loop that links some of the park's most impressive loblolly pines and hardwoods.

Other trails that branch off from the boardwalk include the **Weston Lake Loop** (4.4 miles), **Oakridge Trail** (6.6 miles), **River Trail** (10 miles), and the more remote **Kingsnake Trail**

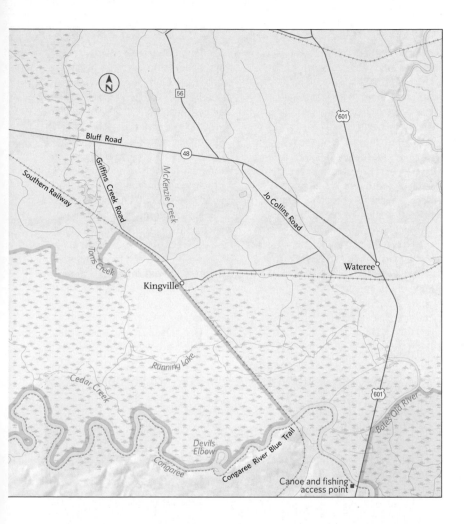

(11.7 miles). The flat terrain makes miles pass quickly.

Anglers cast for bass and yellow perch in Weston Lake, while paddlers explore the park on the marked **Cedar Creek Canoe Trail** or the **Congaree River Blue Trail,** a 50-mile paddling trail. Whether by land or water vessel, exploration of Congaree depends entirely on the water levels, which can fluctuate by 10 or more feet throughout the year.

Boardwalk Loop

This 2.4-mile loop begins on a short boardwalk that connects the visitor center to the **Low Boardwalk** (1.1 miles), which rests on the forest floor. As the path crosses a primeval swampy flat, upland pines and hardwoods transition to the old-growth loblolly pines and mixed hardwoods of the swamp.

On this walk, visitors see water

tupelos, with their smooth, swollen bases, and bald cypress trees, with fluted trunks surrounded by protruding knees. Wild grapevines drape across the path and hug the trees, many of which are covered with Spanish moss and poison ivy. Congaree's most iconic photographs are taken along this mesmerizing stretch of boardwalk. A self-guided brochure available at the visitor center interprets numbered sites along the route, including a moonshine still.

On this loop it's easy to understand why the park has picked up nicknames such as "Redwoods of the East" and "Home of Champions." The 130-foot-high tree canopy of massive oaks, cypress, tupelos, and more is impressive. Indeed, this is one of the world's tallest forests.

Among Congaree's champion trees is a loblolly pine that's as tall as a 17-story high-rise; its girth is 15 feet. There's also the tallest recorded standing sweetgum, cherrybark oak, American elm, swamp chestnut oak, overcup oak, common persimmon, and laurel oak trees. According to one contemporary biologist, Congaree harbors "acre for acre, more record trees than any other place."

But a walk through Congaree National Park is about so much more than the trees. As an international biosphere reserve and federally designated Wilderness area, Congaree supports a complex ecosystem. The daytime sounds of songbirds and woodpeckers give way to the nighttime screeches of owls and the distant squeals and grunts of wild boars.

A boardwalk through the woods

Owls and Boars and Fireflies, Oh My

Nearly 200 species of birds have been spotted in this globally important bird area. It's a particularly good place for spotting neotropical and temperate migrant birds, including 34 kinds of warblers. The prothonotary warblers—aka "swamp canaries"—migrate here each April to nest in the cavities of hollow trees and in cypress knees. During spring, Congaree's bird sounds can be likened to a symphony. All of South Carolina's woodpeckers have been spotted at Congaree and can often be heard overhead as they bore pockmarks into the tree trunks.

After nightfall in the fall and spring, rangers lead visitors toting red flashlights on "owl prowls," in search of barred owls, with their call of "who cooks for you, who cooks for you all?" On one trip, participants had a front-row view as a barred owl swooped in to snatch—and crush—a flying squirrel in mid-flight.

Around the last week of May through the first week of June, synchronous fireflies *(Photinus carolinus)* convene at Congaree—a phenomenon that occurs only at a few places on Earth, including pockets of Southeast Asia. Near dusk, visitors observe groups of fireflies "blinking on and off at the same time, like a Christmas tree," as one ranger describes it.

Weston Lake is home to alligators as well as venomous snakes and large snapping turtles. Congaree's wild boar population has grown exponentially in recent years and is wreaking havoc on the park's creek banks and vegetation.

Congaree floods several times each year, typically in winter and early spring. Floodwaters frequently cover nearly 80 percent of the sprawling parkland, sometimes submerging the wooden walkways.

Sweet gums, cherrybark oaks, water oaks, and hollies thrive in the higher, drier soil to the west. Cypresses, water tupelos, red maples, and water ashes soak up the lowlands' standing water.

Some 159 types of beetles dive, burrow, and scavenge in these waters, which also teem with bass, sunfish, perch, catfish, crayfish, and snails. Congaree is also a breeding ground for 21 kinds of mosquitoes, which may feel like a conservative count during a muggy summer day. Also crawling and slithering through the park are 20 snake species, from brown water snakes to copperheads, as well as box and snapping turtles, several species of salamanders, and a disharmonious population of frogs and toads.

At **Weston Lake,** the Low Boardwalk connects to the 0.7-mile **Elevated Boardwalk,** lofted some eight feet above ground as it courses through bottomland hardwoods and upland pines. Every four or five years, floodwaters cover the walkway, and storm damage sometimes renders this segment of the park off limits. In 1989, Hurricane Hugo made a major mark here, striking gaps in the tree canopy; this portion of the park now provides a glimpse into forest regeneration.

Elsewhere in the Park

Beyond the boardwalks, an easy-to-follow network of numbered dirt trails delves deeper into old-growth forest.

Connected to the boardwalk, **Weston Lake Loop** (4.4 miles) traces the edge of the oxbow lake, actually a channel of the Congaree River. The trail follows a channel of cypress and tupelo trees down to **Cedar Creek,** the park's largest creek. It is a nesting grounds for great blue herons and kingfishers. River otters frolic in the dark waters of Weston Lake, and an observation deck is equipped with benches that allow you to take advantage of a lake view that just might reward you with an alligator sighting.

A popular choice for those in search of a moderate hike is the **Oakridge Trail** (6.6 miles), which connects to the Weston Lake Loop and is named for the large oaks that populate the old-growth forest. The trail crosses several guts that bring floodwaters in and out of the park.

The **River Trail** (10 miles), which branches off from the Western Lake Loop, is the only hiking trail that takes in the Congaree River, the area's lifeblood. A trip through this section of the park is a walk through ecological succession.

The vegetation varies dramatically from west to east. A cypress pond on the north side of the trail appears cast in a sepia tone, with a lush jungle of vines. At the farthest point, where the trail meets the river, hikers can walk onto an exposed sandbar when waters are low.

As the most remote hike in Congaree National Park, the out-and-back **Kingsnake Trail** (11.1 miles), accessed from the Weston Lake Loop (after crossing Cedar Creek), is favored for its bird-watching and wildlife-spotting opportunities. White-tailed deer, marsh rabbits, opossums, and raccoons scamper in this backcountry where giant cherrybark oaks line the trail. The final 1.2 miles before hikers turn back follows an old logging road to a canoe put-in spot and parking area along Cedar Creek.

On the other side of the visitor center, the **Bluff Trail** makes a 0.7-mile arc north along a slight rise on the edge of the floodplain. The trail, which passes through a young forest of primarily loblolly pines and hardwoods, provides access to a primitive campground, after-hours parking area, and the boardwalk.

More Highlights

To see many of Congaree's state and national champion trees, visitors are required to leave the comfort of the marked trails—and make sure to bring along a good compass. Throughout the year, park rangers lead GPS-enhanced hikes devoted to seeing these big trees. Other free park experiences include walks that focus on bird-watching, history, the skulls and furs of resident mammals, and examples of ecological adaptations (see p. 37).

Visitors can also join an annual Christmas bird count or sign up for occasional guided canoe tours. Any day of the year when water levels are favorable, the park's waterways are open to paddlers who bring their own canoes or kayaks (available for rent in nearby Columbia). Call the park visitor center ahead of time to get information on water levels.

Though mosquitoes, wasps, spiders, and snakes lurk around its brown waters, Cedar Creek provides paddlers a rare stillness that could well be described as transcendent.

Paddling Cedar Creek

Information

How to Get There

From Columbia, SC (about 20 miles north), take US 48. From Charleston (about 115 miles south), take I-26 West to I-77 North. From Charlotte, NC (about 110 miles north), take I-77 South. All routes turn onto S.C. 48/Bluff Road; follow Old Bluff Road; park signs lead the rest of the way.

When to Go

Most pleasant is spring and fall, which coincide with bird migration seasons. During winter, bare trees afford longer views. Summer is often hot and humid; the tree canopy lends a slight cooling effect.

Visitor Centers

The **Harry Hampton Visitor Center** is open 9 a.m. to 5 p.m., Tues. through Sat. Restrooms and brochures are available around the clock. Upon arrival, check the mosquito meter over the restrooms at the visitor center. Rankings go from "all

clear" to "war zone." Headquartered at Congaree is the **Old-Growth Bottomland Forest Research and Education Center,** which focuses on riverine and forested landscapes across the Southeast.

Headquarters

100 National Park Rd.
Hopkins, SC 29061-9118
nps.gov/cong
803-776-4396

Camping

A free permit is required and campers self-register at one of two primitive campgrounds—**Longleaf** (14 sites) and **Bluff** (6 sites). Limited backcountry camping.

Lodging

There is no lodging within Congaree National Park. Hotels are plentiful in **Columbia, SC** *(columbiacvb.com).*

Dry Tortugas

Florida

Established
October 26, 1992

64,700 acres

One of America's most unusual and remote national parks, Dry Tortugas National Park is located 68 miles west of Key West, Florida, in the Gulf of Mexico. Though it encompasses 101 square miles, more than 99 percent of the park surface area is actually the waters of the Gulf of Mexico. Seven tiny islands (or six or five, depending on wave action, tides, and hurricane activity) make up the park's land area. Just getting to the park provides visitors with a feeling of accomplishment: The only way to reach it is by boat or seaplane.

So what's the attraction? Crystal-clear water abounding in healthy coral reefs and marine life, for one thing. Vast flocks of seabirds in nesting season, spring and fall, for another.

Most significant, though, is Fort Jefferson, the largest all-masonry fort in the United States. The 19th-century fortification rises on one of the park's tiny islands, Garden Key, and stands as an awe-inspiring example of sweeping military architecture. Its history is as unique as its glorious mid-water setting.

Fort Jefferson

Tortugas is Spanish for "turtles." Spanish explorer Juan Ponce de Leon came upon these specks of land in 1513 as he was sailing around Florida. He named them for the sea turtles found in the gulf. Sailors, including pirates, used the turtles as food and also took huge quantities of eggs from colonies of terns and other birds. The word "dry" was added to the name as a warning to sailors running low on freshwater that they would find none hereabouts.

The United States took control of the Dry Tortugas when it acquired Florida from Spain in 1822. A light-house was built on Garden Key, the largest of the islands, in 1825, to guide ships through the maze of reefs and shoals. (A taller lighthouse was constructed on nearby Loggerhead Key in 1857.) In 1846, the U.S. government began construction of a fort on Garden Key, intending it as a base from which to control ships trying to enter the Gulf of Mexico.

The fort was huge, with room for 1,500 soldiers and the capability to withstand a one-year siege. Construction continued through the Civil War until the U.S. Army abandoned the fort in 1874. Though some 16 million bricks had been assembled for its formidable walls, the fort was never officially finished. Despite its eight-foot-thick walls and sheer sweeping proportions, it had been made vulnerable by advances in artillery.

In addition, the structure had settled into the fine sand more than had been expected, and there were fears that adding more bricks and heavy cannons would cause the mammoth structure to sink.

Was all the effort wasted? Not really. Even though its cannons never fired a shot in conflict, its mere presence helped prevent foreign aggression.

During the Civil War and for nearly a decade after, Fort Jefferson served as a military prison. Its most famous prisoner was Dr. Samuel Mudd, who set the broken leg of John Wilkes Booth, the assassin of President Abraham Lincoln. Although Mudd said he had no idea who Booth was when he performed the work, he was convicted of conspiracy and sent to the Dry Tortugas in 1865. Mudd was pardoned in 1869, in part because he had saved many lives during an epidemic of yellow fever at the fort in 1867.

Fort Jefferson was used sporadically for other purposes over the years, including as a refuge to

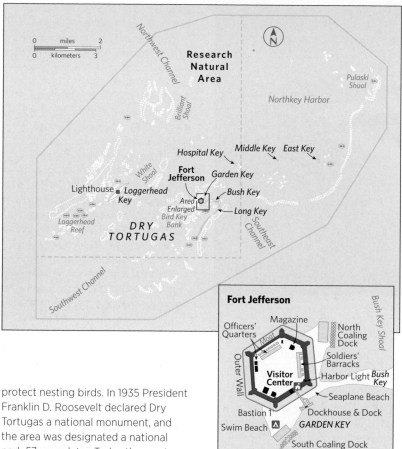

Fort Jefferson

Officers' Quarters · Magazine · North Coaling Dock · Soldiers' Barracks · Moat · Outer Wall · Visitor Center · Harbor Light · Bush Key · Seaplane Beach · Bastion 1 · Dockhouse & Dock · GARDEN KEY · Swim Beach · South Coaling Dock · Anchorage Area · Bush Key Shoal

protect nesting birds. In 1935 President Franklin D. Roosevelt declared Dry Tortugas a national monument, and the area was designated a national park 57 years later. Today the most enthusiastic visitors are history buffs, snorkelers, and bird-watchers.

► HOW TO VISIT

Most visitors are day-trippers to main island **Garden Key,** on either a half-day or full-day seaplane trip or a full-day ferry trip. On a half-day trip (2.5 hours on the island) you have enough time for a quick tour of **Fort Jefferson** and a quick snorkel around the moat wall, although it might be more satisfying to choose one or the other.

On a longer visit, you can leisurely tour the fort, walking around the terre-plein (the "roof") and the surrounding moat wall. You can do some snorkeling and perhaps visit **Bush Key** (unless it's off-limits because of bird nesting, in spring and fall).

If possible, consider an overnight at a very basic campsite *(fee).* You must bring all your supplies, including drinking water, to the site, but the solitude and chance to fully explore Garden Key offer a fine reward for the effort.

Garden Key

From the beach where seaplanes land or the dock where the ferry ties up, cross the bridge over the moat that surrounds **Fort Jefferson** and walk through the sally port (entrance). No doubt you'll want to simply pause for a few moments to marvel at the huge structure's immense interior **parade ground.**

Imagine the scene in the 1860s, when the wife of a surgeon stationed here wrote, "We numbered at that time about four hundred, and represented a busy little town. The fort at night was brilliant with lights, and the place was active with the bustle of many people."

The nearby **visitor center** offers a video presentation and exhibits that include historic artifacts. You can take a self-guided tour of the fort; interpretive signs are well placed around its grounds and halls.

The ferry operator offers a guided tour for passengers. Be sure to visit the bastion (the fort's projecting corner structure) opposite the sally port to see the fort bakery and the chapel. The ceiling of the latter features brickwork so graceful that it draws appreciation even from modern brickmasons. Look closely to find the name of the mason, Jno [John] Nolan, and the date, 1859, when the ceiling was completed.

Climb the stairs leading to the terreplein, as the top of the fort is called, to see restored cannons and enjoy

Fort Jefferson's moat

fabulous views of Garden Key, the moat, **Bush Key, Loggerhead Key,** and the gloriously blue surrounding sea. Take note of the unusual rooftop lighthouse, which was built in 1876 of metal rather than brick.

You can also walk all the way around the fort on the wall that encloses the moat. (Moon jellyfish, barracuda, butterflyfish, grouper, tarpon, and many other sea creatures flourish in these waters.)

Additional Experiences

Snorkeling is usually good around the pilings of the Garden Key's old docks, especially directly along the fort's brick moat wall. (Snorkeling is not allowed in the moat itself.) The park has designated a self-guided snorkel route with underwater signs along a portion of the moat wall.

Those who can access nearby **Loggerhead Key** will find great snorkeling on what's called the "windjammer wreck," a sunken steel-hulled sailing ship just south of the island. (There are around 200 wrecks and other remains of "maritime mishaps" in Dry Tortugas waters.) Best time for snorkeling and scuba diving is May through September.

In late March and April, Fort Jefferson is filled with bird-watchers who come to experience a grand spectacle. Birds migrating north across the Caribbean Sea or the Gulf of Mexico spot Garden Key and then drop in for a rest. At times, every tree and shrub in the parade ground as well as along the fort walls seems to be covered in birds. Flying in are thrushes, warblers, buntings, orioles, and other species of migrating birds.

Cannon Fire

The huge cannon at Fort Jefferson could fire shells up to 3 miles, which brings up the question: Why couldn't enemy ships intent on attacking U.S. interests simply sail past the fort, out of range?

They could, but a more important point is that the only safe, deepwater anchorage in the area is located less than 2 miles from the fort. Enemy ships passing nearby could be pursued by U.S. warships, which could then return to the only safe harbor in the region. Foreign vessels couldn't follow without risking traversing unfamiliar shallow water and coming within range of Fort Jefferson's cannon.

Fort Jefferson is one of a series of military structures known as "Third System forts." These forts along the U.S. coastline were authorized after the War of 1812, and by 1867 there were 42 in existence, from Maine to California. By then, more powerful artillery had been developed that could penetrate the masonry walls of the Third System forts, and new forms of coastal defense were instituted.

From spring through summer, thousands of sooty terns and brown noddies (also a type of tern) nest on Bush Key, adjacent to Garden Key. Visiting Bush Key is prohibited during the nesting season to protect the breeding colonies.

Other seabirds can be seen with some regularity around Garden Key; look out for magnificent frigatebirds, brown pelicans, and brown and masked boobies.

Diving at Dry Tortugas

Information

How to Get There

Unless you have your own boat, transportation to Garden Key is by concession-operated seaplane *(keywest seaplanecharters.com;* 305-293-9300) or ferry from Key West *(drytortugas.com;* 800-634-0939). Private charter boats can be booked in Key West.

When to Go

The park can be visited year-round. Nov. through April can see cooler temperatures and rough seas with poor visibility for snorkeling and diving. May through Oct. brings calmer water and hot weather. Hurricanes, though rare, can strike June through Nov.

Visitor Centers

There is a small visitor center within **Fort Jefferson**. Information is also available at the **Florida Keys Eco-Discovery Center** *(floridakeys.noaa.gov;* 305-809-4750), where a national park ranger is sometimes on duty.

Headquarters

P.O. Box 6208
Key West, FL 33041
nps.gov/drto
305-242-7700

Camping

Primitive camping (10 sites) is allowed on the small beach at **Garden Key.** The site has grills, picnic tables, and toilets. Campers must be completely self-sufficient; water, food, shower facilities, and supplies are not available at the park. All trash must be packed out.

Lodging

There is no lodging in the park other than the campground sites. Lodging is plentiful in **Key West** *(keywestchamber .org;* 305-294-2587).

DRY
TORTUGAS
EST 1935

Everglades

Florida

Established
December 6, 1947

1,500,000 acres

Unlike many western parks with their scenic mountains and canyons, Everglades National Park was set aside to preserve an ecosystem comprising a web of animals and plants found nowhere else. The largest wilderness in the eastern United States, Everglades shelters the endangered manatee, the Florida panther, the threatened crocodile, and others.

Drive to Everglades National Park from Florida City, along Fla. 9336, as most visitors do, and get a graphic lesson in conservation along the way. From residential and commercial areas, the highway passes by fields of squash, cucumbers, tomatoes, and strawberries, crossing canals that are part of south Florida's complex water management program.

The park welcome sign marks a sudden and stark change in the environment, with a succession of natural habitats lying to the west. The 38-mile main park road winds through subtropical hardwood hammocks, pinelands, groves of bald cypress, mangrove forest, and the great "River of Grass," the sheet of fresh water that originally flowed from the southern

Canoeing Nine Mile Pond

shores of Lake Okeechobee through sawgrass across central Florida and out to Florida Bay.

As expansive as the park is, it represents only about one-fifth of the original Everglades ecosystem. Much of the rest has been destroyed or greatly altered for agriculture, urban and suburban growth, and water supply for some six million area residents. People need places to live, food, and water, but the development of southern Florida has come at a great price.

Once, water flowed seasonally from the headwaters of the Kissimmee River, 200 miles north, down through Lake Okeechobee and the greater Everglades, continuing to Florida Bay. Water-management systems designed to protect from flooding during hurricanes disrupted this eons-old pattern, resulting in the degradation of large areas of natural landscape and the decline of wildlife populations. In addition, changes in water flow have threatened the underground aquifer that provides drinking water for Miami and other cities and towns. Concern over these issues led to the massive Comprehensive Everglades Restoration Plan (CERP), a decades-long, multibillion-dollar project to address water problems over an 18,000-square-mile area commonly called "the Everglades."

CERP has given new hope to conservationists and planners who have long worked to preserve the Everglades and protect the natural resources of the national park. Water flow has been improved, and there are signs that populations of wading birds such as wood storks are making a comeback. In 2014 the species was upgraded from endangered to threatened.

There are new threats to the greater Everglades ecosystem in the form of introduced non-native species of plants and animals. The Brazilian pepper tree, for instance, has taken over large areas to the exclusion of native vegetation, and an influx of huge, predatory Burmese pythons has caused a dismaying loss of raccoons, rabbits, and foxes. Oscars, tilapia, and other alien fish displace native species in many areas.

Despite problems, the park remains one of America's great nature experiences. From crocodiles to butterflies, palms to orchids, the subtropical Everglades environment offers rewards unique in North America.

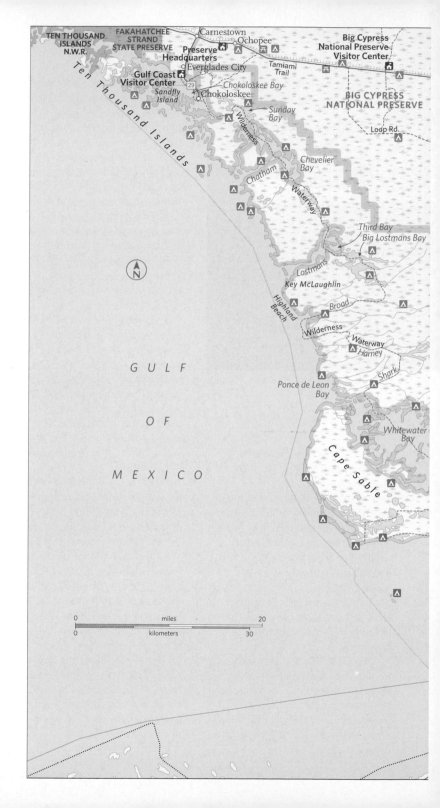

TEN THOUSAND
ISLANDS
N.W.R.

FAKAHATCHEE
STRAND
STATE PRESERVE

Carnestown

Ochopee

Tamiami
Trail

Big Cypress
National Preserve
Visitor Center

Preserve
Headquarters

Everglades City

Gulf Coast
Visitor Center

29

Sandfly
Island

Chokoloskee Bay

Chokoloskee

Sunday
Bay

BIG CYPRESS
NATIONAL PRESERVE

Loop Rd.

Ten Thousand Islands

Wilderness

Chatham

Chevelier
Bay

Waterway

Third Bay
Big Lostmans Bay

Lostmans

Key McLaughlin

Highland
Beach

Broad

Wilderness

Waterway
Harney

Shark

Ponce de Leon
Bay

Whitewater
Bay

Cape Sable

G U L F

O F

M E X I C O

N

	miles		20
0			
0	kilometers		30

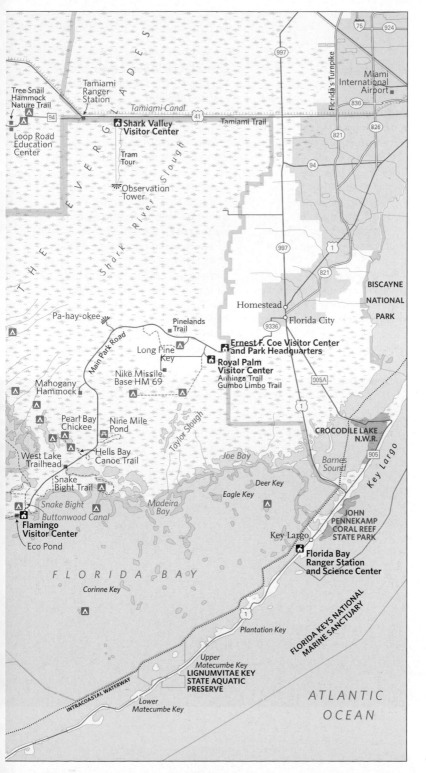

Tree Snail
Hammock
Nature Trail

Loop Road
Education
Center

Tamiami
Ranger
Station

94

Tamiami Canal

THE EVERGLADES

Shark Valley
Visitor Center

Tram
Tour

Observation
Tower

Shark River Slough

41   Tamiami Trail

Pa-hay-okee

Pinelands
Trail

Main Park Road

Long Pine
Key

Nike Missile
Base HM 69

Mahogany
Hammock

Pearl Bay
Chickee

Nine Mile
Pond

West Lake
Trailhead

Hells Bay
Canoe Trail

Snake
Bight Trail

Snake Bight

Buttonwood Canal

Flamingo
Visitor Center

Eco Pond

Madeira
Bay

Taylor Slough

Joe Bay

Deer Key

Eagle Key

FLORIDA   BAY

Corinne Key

Miami
International
Airport

75   924

997

Florida's Turnpike

830

826

821

94

821

997

Homestead

Florida City

9336

Ernest F. Coe Visitor Center
and Park Headquarters

Royal Palm
Visitor Center

Anhinga Trail
Gumbo Limbo Trail

005A

1

BISCAYNE

NATIONAL

PARK

CROCODILE LAKE
N.W.R.

Barnes
Sound

905

Key Largo

JOHN
PENNEKAMP
CORAL REEF
STATE PARK

Key Largo

Florida Bay
Ranger Station
and Science Center

FLORIDA KEYS NATIONAL
MARINE SANCTUARY

Plantation Key

INTRACOASTAL WATERWAY

Upper
Matecumbe Key

LIGNUMVITAE KEY
STATE AQUATIC
PRESERVE

Lower
Matecumbe Key

ATLANTIC

OCEAN

▶ HOW TO VISIT

Visitors explore on foot, by bicycle, or via canoe or kayak. Also available are guided tram and boat tours. The park's vastness may tempt you to rush through in an attempt to see as much as you can. Resist the urge.

Most visitors arrive sometime during December to April, when heat, humidity, and insect activity are down. Birds, alligators, and other animals are concentrated in smaller, dry-season wetlands and thus are easier to see.

Despite its huge size, the park has only three main hubs for visitation, and two of them have limited activities. If you have only a short time, you may need to choose one area to explore. The best one-day tour begins at the **Ernest F. Coe Visitor Center,** west of Homestead, and follows the main park road to **Flamingo,** where you'll find another visitor center and a roster of ranger-led activities.

Everglades National Park is a little more subtle than most parks. To get a sense of it takes time. Go to the park at dawn or stay until dusk to enjoy the best wildlife activity. Stop for a while on a quiet trail or backcountry waterway, watching and listening.

Ranger-led programs reveal aspects of life here that might otherwise be overlooked. Learn about this rich and intricate ecosystem and you'll understand why the park has been officially designated an international biosphere reserve, a World Heritage site, and a wetland of international importance.

Ten Thousand Islands mangrove trees

Everglades National Park has taken its place among the planet's greatest natural areas.

Stop along the way to walk one or more of the interpretive trails. The **Anhinga Trail** at **Royal Palm** is deservedly famous for wildlife viewing. With more time, take a boat tour at Flamingo or rent a kayak and paddle around Florida Bay.

If you have more time, consider a tram tour or bicycle ride through **Shark Valley,** in the northern section of the park (25 miles west of the Florida Turnpike in Miami, on US 41 on the Tamiami Trail). Activities offered at the **Gulf Coast Visitor Center** in Everglades City, in the far western part of the park, focus on the water, with guided boat tours and canoe and kayak rental for day trips or camping out in the **Ten Thousand Islands** area.

Eastern Entrance to Flamingo

The **Ernest F. Coe Visitor Center** provides the usual amenities, including interpretive exhibits, an information desk, a bookstore, and an introductory video. The hiking trails that issue from here offer a great way to see the park but lack the variety found at most parks. Most of the more varied backcountry is accessible only by water.

The main park road travels 38 miles to the Flamingo area on **Florida Bay,** providing access to several hiking trails along the way, as well as put-in spots for canoe/kayak trails. The road is out-and-back, not a loop.

Nearly everyone turns off the main park road to visit the **Royal Palm** area, and for good reason. The 0.8-mile **Anhinga Trail,** part paved and part boardwalk, offers some of the best wildlife viewing in the park. Wading birds such as herons and egrets (and, yes, anhingas) feed in wetlands where alligators and turtles swim. Wildlife here is so accustomed to humans that it's easy to take close-up photos. Rangers lead regular nature walks here, well worth joining.

The adjacent 0.4-mile **Gumbo Limbo Trail** winds through a hardwood hammock—the local name for a dense woodland growing on a natural rise in the surrounding marsh. The trail passes among trees such as royal palm, gumbo limbo (with its distinctive peeling red bark), mahogany, and live-oak. Ferns and strangler figs, whose exposed roots dangle after seedlings take hold in tree branches, contribute to the lushness of the vegetation. Black-and-yellow zebra longwing butterflies flit gracefully through the undergrowth, and bird-watching can be excellent.

Though not as well known as some other ecosystems, slash pine woodland is one of the most endangered environments in southern Florida. Slash pine forest is found on higher ground that's easy to clear and develop; as a result, only 2 percent of the habitat remains standing.

A few miles farther down the main park road, the 0.4-mile **Pinelands Trail** passes among bald cypress trees hardly taller than a person. These are mature trees, stunted in their growth by shallow, nutrient-poor soil. Here and there stand "domes" of tall bald cypresses crowded into areas with more water. These are favorite destinations for the activity known as "slough slogs." Join in by donning old sneakers and tromping out through the wet grassland to enjoy the magical habitat, teeming with life—right at your feet. If you're at all apprehensive about setting out to do this on your own, check for regularly scheduled ranger-led slough slogs.

Pa-hay-okee Overlook and **Mahogany Hammock** make rewarding stops along the main park road. The former is a raised viewpoint over the great River of Grass in its "vast glittering openness," as pioneer Everglades conservationist Marjory Stoneman Douglas described it. At the latter, a boardwalk passes through a dense hardwood hammock where palms, ferns, and epiphytes ("air plants" growing on tree limbs) give visitors the feeling they've been transported to a place deep in the tropics.

The road passes several spots for launching canoes and kayaks, offering the opportunity for paddling trips both short and overnight. (Bring your own boat or rent one outside the park or at Flamingo; check with the concessioner there, 239-695-3101.)

The 5-mile loop at **Nine Mile Pond** combines open marsh and mangrove forest, while the **Hells Bay Canoe Trail** passes through mangrove tunnels and open ponds en route to camping spots *(permit required).* For other boating routes, pick up a trail guide at the **Flamingo Visitor Center.**

The Flamingo area offers several hiking possibilities, although heat, humidity, and especially mosquitoes can make this activity uncomfortable from about May through November.

At **West Lake** a short boardwalk winds through the stiltlike roots of a mangrove forest to a viewpoint of the bay. The **Snake Bight Trail,** a 1.6-mile

Missiles in the Glades

The Cold War between the United States and the Soviet Union was at its height in the 1960s, especially during and after the 1962 Cuban missile crisis, when the Soviets planned to place nuclear weapons in Cuba. In response, the U.S. Army built anti-missile installations armed with Nike-Hercules surface-to-air defense missiles at four sites in southern Florida. One missile site, active from 1964 to 1979, was built inside the park, just west of the Royal Palm area.

The formerly top-secret Nike Missile Base HM 69 (also known as Site A-2-52) was opened to the public for tours in 2009. The base remains almost exactly as it was when it was abandoned, perfectly preserved as a memento of one of the most potentially dangerous eras of American history. Park rangers lead regular tours of the base, visiting missile launch areas, guard-dog kennels, barracks, control centers, and other buildings. Head over to park headquarters to make reservations for these popular guided tours.

hike from the road to a bight (small bay) on Florida Bay, is famous as one of the best bird-watching walks in southern Florida. Look for rarities such as mangrove cuckoo and white-crowned pigeon; at the bay you could be lucky and see a small flock of flamingos. (It is very easy to confuse flamingos with the more common roseate spoonbill, another large pink bird.)

Eco Pond offers another of the park's excellent short nature walks, a 0.5-mile loop circling a small pond where waterbirds roost and butterflies abound.

Flamingo, with a small store and a campground, marks the end of the park's main road, with island-studded **Florida Bay** stretching to the south and the Florida Keys reaching beyond the horizon. Rangers at the visitor center can offer assistance and advice. You can rent canoes and kayaks here for a spin around Florida Bay. Stick close to shore if you're unsure of your abilities. Landing is restricted on many of the islands; you can come to shore on **Bradley Key.**

This area of the park is the most likely place to spot a crocodile, the saltwater relative of the far more abundant freshwater alligator. The Everglades is the only place in the world where alligators and crocodiles are found together, where the salt water and fresh water meet. A croc sighting is possible along **Buttonwood Canal** as well as on a narrated **boat tour** (239-695-3101).

Snowy egret

Shark Valley

US 41, also known as the Tamiami Trail, runs west from Miami to Naples. About 20 miles of its length forms a portion of the northern boundary of the park. The Tamiami Trail provides access to two park gateways.

About 18 miles west of Miami is the entrance to the **Shark Valley Visitor Center.** The "valley" here is actually that of the Shark River Slough, one of the major slow-flowing sheets of water that comprise the Everglades "river of grass." The water here, moving at speeds that average about two feet a minute, eventually enters the Gulf of Mexico, some 40 miles to the southwest.

The main attraction at Shark Valley is a 15-mile loop **Tram Road,** which heads into the heart of the Everglades, mostly through sawgrass marsh. (Touch the edge of a leaf and you'll quickly understand why it's called "saw.") The tram road was in part built by a company exploring for oil before the national park was established. It's closed to private vehicles but can be traveled on a guided tram tour, by bicycle, or on foot.

The tram ride makes a fine introduction to the Everglades ecosystem, as trained narrators describe sites along the way. They point out, for example, how a rise or fall of just a few inches in elevation can make a difference in the vegetation, with hardwood hammocks on higher ground and cypress swamp in depressions.

Alligators are commonly seen along the road, with a wide variety of wading birds, turtles, and the occasional white-tailed deer or snake.

A highlight might be a sighting of the federally endangered snail kite, a hawk that feeds almost exclusively on large apple snails. Tours stop for a break at a 65-foot-high **observation tower,** with a rare, elevated 360-degree panorama of the Everglades.

Walking or bicycling the Shark Valley road is a great way to feel a part of this vast marsh environment. Bike rentals are available at the visitor center. Remember, as always, to maintain a safe distance from wildlife, including, of course, alligators. (Though they seem sluggish, they can move quickly on land for short distances.)

Shark Valley has two short trails, the 0.5-mile, wheelchair-accessible **Bobcat Boardwalk** and the 0.25-mile **Otter Cave Hammock Trail.** Both provide welcome shade on sunny days.

Gulf Coast Area

For a real "old Florida" feel, take Fla. 29 south from the Tamiami Trail to the town of Everglades City and the park's **Gulf Coast Visitor Center.** This facility is the gateway to the **Ten Thousand Islands** region of the Gulf Coast. Here, mangrove islands and tunnel-like passageways create a maze where land meets sea.

Activities in this area focus on the water; exploration can be rewarding for experienced boaters but sometimes daunting for beginners. Here, it's important to know your paddling ability and get advice from rangers before choosing an adventure.

Those who want to venture out on their own can bring a canoe or kayak or rent one at Everglades City. Options range from a quick paddle around the islands near the dock to a multiday camping trip into the wilderness.

The 5-mile round trip to **Sandfly Island** is popular and not too difficult, especially if you time it to take advantage of outgoing and incoming tides. Other day trips include the **Halfway Creek, Loop,** and **Turner River** water trails. These can take from four to eight hours.

The ultimate adventure for experienced boaters is the challenging 99-mile-long **Wilderness Waterway,** which follows a winding route along the coastline, all the way from Everglades City to Flamingo. Those who paddle the entire length usually allow at least eight days for the trip, camping on land, on the beach, and on elevated platforms called "chickees." Motorized boats can make the trip in one long day.

The most popular activity, however, requires no boating skill: concessioner-operated **guided boat tours** leave from the dock at the visitor center. One of the two tours travels out to the Gulf of Mexico, winding among islands and offering the chance to see bottlenose dolphins, manatees, bald eagles, ospreys, brown pelicans, and more. The other tour uses a smaller boat to travel among inland mangrove habitat, with common sightings of alligators, small mammals, and a variety of waterbirds.

Palmettos

Information

How to Get There

To reach the main park entrance from Miami, FL (about 50 miles north), take Fla. 821 (Florida's Turnpike) south to Florida City and then go west on Fla. 9336 (Palm Dr.). The Shark Valley area is on US 41 about 18 miles west of Miami, and the Gulf Coast visitor center is another 40 miles west; from there, head south 4 miles on Fla. 29.

When to Go

There are two seasons: a wet summer and a dry winter. May through Nov. the weather is hot and humid; mosquitoes can be extremely bothersome. Ranger-led tours and other activities are limited in summer. Dry-season visits are generally more pleasant (though more crowded), with a March through April visit usually best.

Visitor Centers

Three visitor centers (**Ernest F. Coe** in the east, **Shark Valley** in the north, and **Gulf Coast** in the west) are open daily year-round. The **Flamingo Visitor Center** (southern tip of the park) is staffed intermittently mid-April to mid-Nov. but fully operational the rest of the year.

Headquarters

40001 State Road 9336
Homestead, FL 33034
nps.gov/ever
305-242-7700

Camping

Long Pine Key (108 sites) and **Flamingo** campgrounds (274 sites) are reached via the main park road *(recreation.gov;* 877-444-6777). The park also offers primitive backcountry camping (permit required). Most backcountry sites can be reached only by boat, but a few are accessible to hikers.

Lodging

Lodging is plentiful in **Homestead** and **Florida City,** just east. Lodging also can be found in **Everglades City,** just northwest. Tropical Everglades Visitor Association *(tropicaleverglades.com;* 305-245-9180).

Great Smoky Mountains

North Carolina & Tennessee

Established
June 15, 1934

522,000 acres

When President Franklin D. Roosevelt dedicated Great Smoky Mountains National Park, he gave his speech with one foot in North Carolina and the other in Tennessee. It was a fitting gesture given the decades-long cooperative effort to establish a park in the southern Appalachians, an endeavor that involved not just officials in the two states but private groups and even schoolchildren, who pledged pennies to help fund land purchases.

Great Smoky Mountains now ranks as America's most visited national park. It delights millions of annual visitors who come for its ancient mountains, lush forests, diverse flora and fauna, dozens of waterfalls, and engaging history. As part of its overall interpretive mission, the park emphasizes three major themes: biological diversity, the continuum of human presence in the southern Appalachians, and scenic beauty.

The park's 814 square miles represent the largest federally protected upland area east of the Mississippi River. The elevation range of 875

The Smoky Mountains

agency created to provide work and wages for young men during very challenging economic times.

▶ **HOW TO VISIT**

If it is beauty you seek on a one-day visit, a drive up **Newfound Gap Road,** a hike to **Ramsey Cascades,** or a trip around **Cades Cave Loop Road** are certain to reveal varied aspects of the park's scenic splendor, with vast views over rolling ridges to old-growth forest to the pastoral landscapes shaped by settlers' farms.

First-timers should experience the park's most popular destinations. Newfound Gap Road (US 441) bisects the park, climbing over a ridge of the Appalachians, and **Cades Cove,** a valley, once was home to a thriving farming community.

If you have more time, less-traveled roads and hiking trails—including many easy walkways—allow you to experience the subtle features that are the essence of the park: the massive trunks of a century-old tulip trees; the fluting songs of wood thrushes; the tangy scent of a spruce forest.

Indeed, you have to get off the road to really get to know and appreciate the park. There is a wealth of opportunities for intimate discovery.

Forests in the park have suffered in recent years from non-native invasive insects, which have killed firs and hemlocks, altering the natural functions of ecosystems. Park staffers continue to seek solutions, hoping to help control or at least strike a balance with these alien pests.

Dense forests cloak the Appalachians. The moisture they release as a result of evaporation combined

to 6,643 feet within Great Smoky Mountains creates widely different life zones. Moving from the park's lowest to highest points is, in effect, like traveling from the Southeast to Maine— from post oaks and wild turkeys to Fraser firs and ravens. Fueled by up to 85 inches of rainfall annually, the park ecosystem boasts a stunning array of plants and animals.

In addition to the ongoing heritage of Cherokee Indians in and near the park, Great Smoky Mountains preserves a nationally significant collection of pioneer-era log buildings as well as structures built during the Depression. Much of the original development of facilities and restoration of early settlers' buildings was carried out by the Civilian Conservation Corps (CCC), an

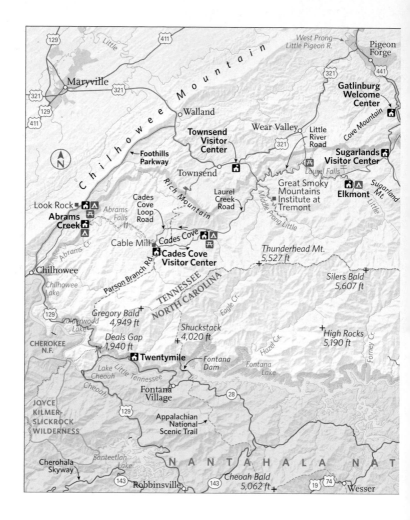

with high rainfall often creates fog—the "smoky" mist that gives this mountain range and the park their names.

Newfound Gap Road

Winding for 31 miles between the gateway towns of Gatlinburg, Tennessee, and Cherokee, North Carolina, this beautiful drive connects the park's two main visitor centers: **Sugarlands**

and **Oconaluftee.** Along the way it passes picnic areas, trailheads, and scenic overlooks as it climbs almost 4,000 feet before descending.

At the **Chimneys Picnic Area** (Mile 7) you'll find the **Cove Hardwood Nature Trail,** one of the park's best short walks, with old-growth forest. The 2-mile **Chimney Tops trail** (Mile 9) and the 2.3-mile **Alum Cave** (Mile 15), both strenuous, also are popular trails here. The former leads to rocky

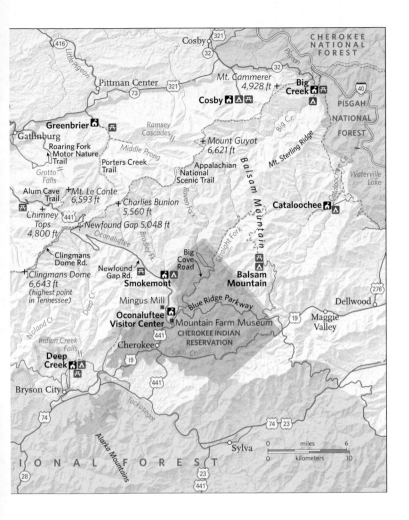

summits with great views; the latter is the shortest route to 6,593-foot **Mount Le Conte,** third highest peak in the park and the site of the park's only commercial lodging (see p. 63).

At Mile 15 is 5,048-foot **Newfound Gap,** the road's crest. Before this road was built in the 1930s, people used a wagon road at nearby Indian Gap to cross the mountains. The **Appalachian Trail** intersects the road here, and many people like to walk a

bit of this historic route that runs some 2,180 miles from Georgia to Maine.

The 4-mile, moderately strenuous hike to **Charlies Bunion** (a rocky knob with fine vistas) follows the Appalachian Trail and the Tennessee–North Carolina state line.

Nearby is the 8-mile road to famed **Clingmans Dome,** usually closed from December through March. With an observation tower reached by a 0.5-mile paved trail, the site offers a

Wild and Wet

Favorite discoveries for visitors come under the heading of "the three Ws": wildlife, waterfalls, and wildflowers. Black bears (as many as 1,500 live in the park) top the wildlife list, but elk, white-tailed deer, wild turkeys, and more than 200 species of birds are regularly seen. In addition, 30 species of salamanders make Great Smoky Mountains a center of small-amphibian diversity.

Waterfalls are nearly common-place. There's thundering Abrams Falls in Cades Cove and countless unnamed cascades on small creeks. Laurel Falls is the most popular waterfall in the park. It is accessed by a paved, fairly easy trail; other falls are reached via walks that range from short strolls to strenuous hikes.

Great Smoky Mountains is rife with blooming plants. An annual Spring Wildflower Pilgrimage highlights the peak blooming season of April, though visitors find plants in bloom from late winter well into fall. Among the most popular flowers are those of shrubs, including mountain laurel, rhododendron, and flame azalea, which splash color over hillsides from May through July, the timing dependent on the species and the elevation at which the shrubs grow.

grand panorama of the Appalachians on clear days. The "view" is just gray clouds when fog shrouds the peaks at this 6,643-foot elevation, the highest in the Smokies.

Temperatures here average more than 20°F cooler than at Gatlinburg. Spruce-fir forest, red squirrels, and dark-eyed juncos make the environment seem more like Canada than the Southeast.

As the Newfound Gap Road descends, it passes overlooks with especially outstanding views of the **Oconaluftee River** and **Deep Creek** valleys. At **Kephart Prong** (Mile 23) and **Smokemont Campground** (Mile 27), trails traverse forests regrown after intensive logging in the early 20th century.

Stop at **Mingus Mill** (Mile 30) to see a restored 1886 grist mill that uses a turbine rather than a waterwheel to turn the millstones—advanced technology for its day. A miller is on site to explain the operation.

A half-mile farther on, the **Oconaluftee Visitor Center** offers maps, books, brochures, and advice from rangers. It also includes the small but excellent **Cultural History Museum** that highlights the relationship between people and the land, from the native Cherokees and their forced removal in the 19th century up through the establishment of the national park.

Just outside, the open-air **Mountain Farm Museum** showcases a collection of historic log structures, including a farmhouse, huge barn, smokehouse, blacksmith shop, and corn crib. The easy, 1.5-mile **Oconaluftee River Trail** features displays highlighting Native American history.

Cades Cove

Located in the western part of the Tennessee side of the park, this broad, 2,400-acre valley was home to more than 130 families in the mid-19th century. Many of their homes, barns,

Vsitors along Deep Creek Trail

churches, and other buildings still dot the landscape, adding to the appeal of this portion of the park. What once were farm fields (largely corn) are now open grasslands, a boon for wildlife watchers.

So popular is Cades Cove that in summer and the "leaf-peeping" foliage season of October, it can take hours to drive the 11-mile one-way loop road. A "bear jam" could cause a lengthy traffic backup. Visitors can help ease congestion by using pull-offs to view wildlife. Consider walking or biking the loop when it's closed to motor vehicles, Wednesday and Saturday mornings from early May to late September.

Among Cades Cove highlights is the 1820s **John Oliver Place,** the oldest log house in the area, built of hand-hewn logs and split-wood shingles. About a mile farther along is the turn to the Primitive Baptist Church, built in 1887 to replace an earlier log cabin.

About halfway around the loop is the short trail to the **Elijah Oliver Place,** a homestead that includes a log house, smokehouse, corn crib, spring house, and chicken coop. Note the "stranger room" added to the porch to accommodate visitors.

A 2.5-mile trail leads to striking **Abrams Falls**—certainly not the tallest waterfall in the park but the largest by water volume. Carry plenty of drinking water, wear sturdy shoes, and take your time on this moderately strenuous hike.

The **Cable Mill** area is a must stop, encompassing a small visitor center, an operating water-powered grist mill, a striking "cantilever" barn (with a large roof overhang), a sorghum mill, an 1887 frame house, as well as several other buildings.

The last portion of the loop passes several historic structures, including the **Carter Shields Cabin,** one of the most captivating photo opportunities in the park, especially in spring when the dogwoods are in full bloom.

Elsewhere in the Park

The **Roaring Fork Motor Nature Trail,** a 6-mile loop reached from downtown Gatlinburg (turn south at traffic light 8), provides a wonderful way for people with limited mobility to experience a Great Smokies forest.

You'll pass rocky streams and several log cabins and other historic structures, as well as the trailhead for the 1.3-mile walk to **Grotto Falls,** a waterfall that provides considerable scenic reward for moderate effort.

A few miles east of Gatlinburg, off US 321, a side road follows the **Little Pigeon River** to the **Greenbrier** area.

Here you'll find the trailhead for the strenuous 4-mile hike to **Ramsey Cascades,** at 100 feet high the tallest waterfall in the park. The last two miles of this trail pass through splendid old-growth forest.

A less strenuous option is the nearby 3.6-mile **Porters Creek Trail,** which heads upstream to an old cemetery, an 1875 barn, and a healthy grove of tall hemlocks. Spring wildflowers are a special seasonal attraction on Porters Creek Trail.

The North Carolina side of the park generally sees fewer crowds than the Tennessee side, and features several appealing destinations in addition to those along **Newfound Gap Road.** The **Deep Creek** site near Bryson City offers three waterfalls along a loop hike of just 2.4 miles. Longer jaunts take hikers into some of the park's old-growth forest, untouched by 20th-century loggers.

Reached by winding mountain roads off either US 276 in North Carolina or Tenn. 32, the **Cataloochee** area was once home to the largest community in what is now the national park. Families totaling around 1,200 people farmed and raised livestock, and even developed an early tourism industry based on trout fishing. One resident said life here "was more like livin' in the Garden of Eden than anything else I can think of."

Today the Big and Little Cataloochee valleys preserve several historic structures, including houses, barns, churches, and a schoolhouse. Cataloochee increased in popularity after 2001, when elk were reintroduced. It remains an excellent place to spot these animals as well as black bear and deer.

A park volunteer plays a dulcimer at the Mountain Farm Museum.

Information

How to Get There

From Knoxville, TN (about 25 miles north), take I-40 to Tenn. 66, then US 441 to the park's Gatlinburg entrance. From Asheville, NC (about 40 miles east), take I-40 to US 19, then US 441 to the Cherokee entrance. Less traveled routes include the Foothills Parkway (Exit 443 from I-40), US 321 in Tennessee, and the Blue Ridge Parkway in North Carolina.

When to Go

The park offers year-round attractions, though the Clingmans Dome Road and some minor unpaved roads are closed in winter. Summer and Oct. weekends are the most crowded times. Winter weather occasionally closes Newfound Gap Road (US 441).

Visitor Centers

Sugarlands, on US 441 south of Gatlinburg, TN; **Oconaluftee,** on US 441 north of Cherokee, NC.; **Cades Cove,** on the scenic loop off Laurel Creek Rd. in the northwestern section of the park. All open year-round.

Headquarters

107 Park Headquarters Rd.
Gatlinburg, TN 37738
nps.gov/grsm
865-436-1200

Camping

Ten developed campgrounds (113 sites); some sites can be reserved *(recreation. gov;* 877-444-6777). Advanced reservations are required at **Cataloochee.** Backcountry camping requires a permit *(fee;* 865-436-1297).

Lodging

The only lodging within the park is the historic **LeConte Lodge** *(lecontelodge .com;* 865-429-5704), reached by a hike of about 5 miles. Seven cabins, three multiroom lodges, no electricity, shared bathrooms. Hotels are plentiful in **Gatlinburg, TN** *(gatlinburg.com;* 865-436-4178 or 800-588-1817), **Cherokee, NC** *(cherokeesmokies.com;* 828-788-0034), and other nearby communities.

Mammoth Cave

Kentucky

Established
July 1, 1941

52,830 acres

One of the world's great natural wonders, Mammoth Cave National Park sits beneath Kentucky hills and hollows. It earned its grandiose designation in the early 19th century, when tourists marveled at the enormity of its underground chambers. With more than 400 miles of mapped passageways, Mammoth Cave National Park encompasses the planet's longest known cave system, with five levels and caves yet to be discovered.

Some 12 miles of Mammoth Cave are open to the public, with tour routes offering a diversity of experiences, from strolls that focus on spectacular formations to more challenging walks that center on cave history. For the latter, visitors don protective gear and crawl through tight passageways.

Mammoth Cave's vast rooms and winding tunnels exist today because of a coincidence of geologic events. More than 300 million years ago, what is now central Kentucky was covered by a shallow tropical sea, where organic matter formed layers of limestone hundreds of feet thick. Fifty million

A Mammoth Cave lantern tour

who want to enjoy stalactites, stalagmites, columns, draperies, and other subterranean features should study tour descriptions and choose from the cave's scenic routes.

There's more to the national park than just the cave, of course. Mammoth Cave's 82 square miles encompass lush forests that teem with wildlife, as well as 27 miles of the Green River, one of North America's most biologically diverse waterways. Biking, hiking, horseback riding, boating, and fishing are active options—before or after experiencing the world belowground.

► HOW TO VISIT

Every visit should include at least one cave tour and, if you have more time, exploration above ground. Read descriptions on the park website or speak to a ranger at the visitor center when you arrive to determine which tours *(fee)* best match your interests and level of fitness. Try to make advance reservations for tours *(recreation .gov;* 877-444-6777), especially for summer and weekend visits.

Wear sturdy shoes with nonslip soles and dress for the cave temperature, in the mid-50s F year-round. Tours are led by park rangers. There are items that are prohibited on all tours, including camera tripods, large backpacks, and strollers.

You won't really know Mammoth Cave National Park without spending some time on its aboveground trails. As is the case with the cave tours, routes range from short and easy paths to longer trails that are suitable for backpackers. Also consider a canoe or kayak trip on the **Green River** or a

years later, a river system deposited sand and mud that transformed to sandstone and shale.

Over time, underground rivers cut passages through the relatively soft limestone. As the water level dropped, the cave rivers sank deeper, exposing higher channels as dry caverns. Meanwhile, the harder overlying sandstone layer served as protection for the cave system, preventing it from eroding and collapsing into sinkholes and valleys.

Cave formations are created when water seeps through limestone, dissolving minerals and redepositing them on passage ceilings, walls, and floors. Mammoth Cave's sandstone "roof" keeps this process from happening in much of the cave, so visitors horseback ride through the park; local independent outfitters offer a variety of options for boating as well as horseback riding.

Exploring the Cave

Be sure to walk through the excellent introductory exhibit in the park **visitor center,** which provides an overview of cave geology, history, and exploration. You'll learn, for example, that when the national park was established, only 44 miles of cave passages were known. Since then, dedicated cavers have expanded that figure nearly ten times, and new passages continue to be found. In perhaps the most dramatic moment of exploration here, in 1972 cavers found the long-sought connection between **Mammoth Cave** and adjacent **Flint Ridge Cave,** creating a 144-mile system.

Many visitors want to see the "prettiest" parts of Mammoth Cave, with decorative formations such as stalactites (hanging from the ceiling), stalagmites (rising from the cave floor), and columns (formed when stalactites and stalagmites join). The most direct route to scenic areas is the easy 0.25-mile Frozen Niagara Tour, named for a flowstone formation. This route has about a dozen steps up and down; an optional 49 steps reward with a close look at the **Drapery Room.**

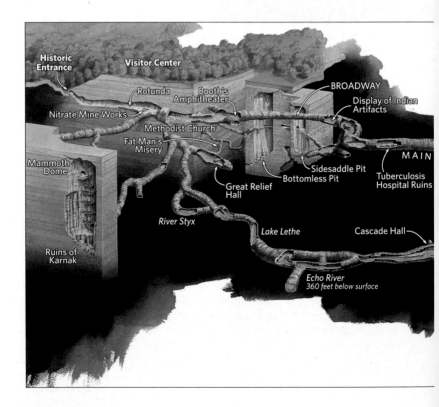

Mysterious Miners

Explorers of Mammoth Cave during the early tourism era, the mid-19th century, came across a variety of objects, including burned-out torches, drinking gourds, woven slippers, and pieces of pottery.

The explorers didn't know it at the time, but they were finding evidence of one of the interesting enigmas of the cave's history.

For 3,000 years, Native Americans entered Mammoth Cave to extract minerals, primarily salt and gypsum.

No one knows just how these substances were utilized; some experts have postulated that they were used for paint or spiritual rituals.

To seek out the gypsum, miners traveled as far as 14 miles into the cave, using only the light of cane torches and squeezing through tight passageways. The operation was, in the words of one archaeologist, "almost on an industrial scale . . . the fact that they were so systematic and so thorough."

Roughly 2,000 years ago, Native American mining of the cave abruptly ended. Modern researchers have come up with no explanation for the cessation of mining activity.

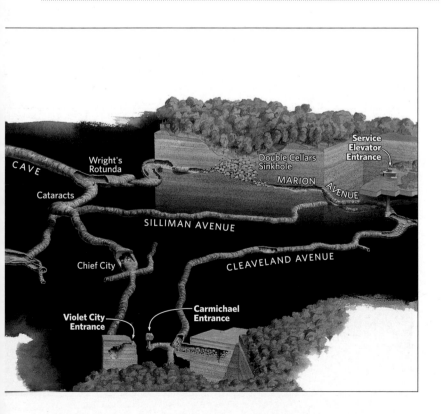

The moderately difficult 0.75-mile Domes and Dripstones Tour requires going down 300 steps, then up and down hills, to the dramatic dripstone passage of the Frozen Niagara.

Certainly one of the park's best overalll tours is the strenuous, 4.5-mile **Grand Avenue** tour. This route combines splendid scenery with information about Mammoth Cave's long and intriguing history, dating to Native American exploration of the cave as long as 5,000 years ago (see p. 67).

The moderately difficult 2-mile Historic Tour provides a detailed look at the cave's past. Long after Native Americans had discovered the cave, it was "rediscovered" around 1800 and soon found to have reserves of calcium nitrate, which could be converted into a vital component of gunpowder. During the War of 1812, enslaved African Americans worked in the cave, mining the sought-after material. Ruins of this operation, including pipelines formed from hollow logs, can still be seen.

It was shortly after this time that tourism began in earnest at Mammoth Cave, as the property passed through several owners who found ways to promote it. A legendary figure on the scene was Stephen Bishop, a 17-year-old enslaved youth who served as a guide for tourists; he ventured farther into the cave than anyone had before.

On the Historic Tour, visitors pass the **Bottomless Pit,** which acted as a barrier to exploration of Mammoth Cave until Bishop carried in a ladder or cedar pole and crossed the pit while holding a lantern in his teeth. The tour also makes stops at other famed sights discovered by Bishop during his years at the cave, including the tight passage called **Fat Man's Misery** and the 192-foot-high **Mammoth Dome.**

For a taste of what 19th-century

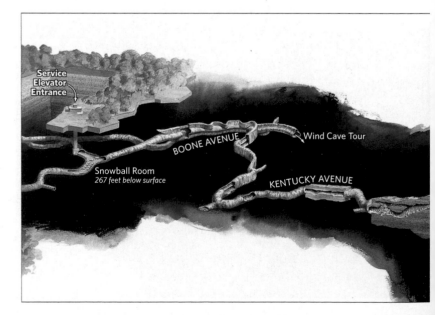

Service Elevator Entrance

BOONE AVENUE

Wind Cave Tour

Snowball Room
267 feet below surface

KENTUCKY AVENUE

Candle soot graffiti

cave tours were like, take the strenuous 3-mile Violet City Lantern Tour. Lighting is provided exclusively by old-fashioned lanterns carried by rangers as well as visitors. It's especially eerie to come upon the site where, in 1842, a doctor brought tuberculosis patients to live underground, believing that the cave air would cure them. (It had just the opposite effect.)

If you've ever wanted to know what it's like to be a caver (or spelunker), sign up for the strenuous Introduction to Caving Tour, suitable for very fit visitors ten years and older. Wearing hiking boots (above ankle height) are

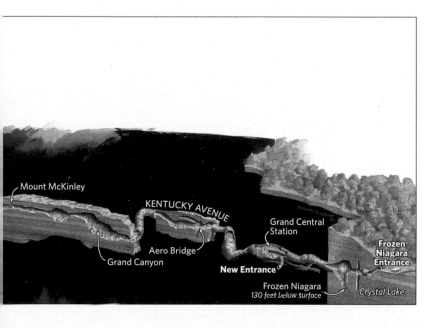

Mount McKinley

KENTUCKY AVENUE

Grand Central Station

Frozen Niagara Entrance

Aero Bridge

Grand Canyon

New Entrance

Frozen Niagara
130 feet below surface

Crystal Lake

recommended, a helmet, coveralls, and other protective gear, you'll learn safe techniques for cave exploration so you can navigate cramped passages. (If your chest or hips measure more than 42 inches around, you won't fit.) Similar, but even more strenuous and with a minimum age of 16, the Wild Cave Tour covers 5 miles. Needless to say, if you're even remotely uncomfortable in tight spaces, neither of these tours is for you.

Two specialized tours are well worth noting. For the **Trog** excursion, participants must be 8 to 12 years old. Adults are allowed to be present only as the kids suit up in coveralls, helmets, and headlamps. Then it's off through the woods and into the cave to learn how surface and cave life interact and how to crawl through passages off the regular tour routes.

The Focus on Frozen Niagara Photo Tour is designed solely for photographers. With stops at some of the most scenic parts of Mammoth Cave, this easy walk is filled with photo ops. Tripods, not allowed on regular tours, are permitted here.

On the Surface

Mammoth Cave National Park offers more than 85 miles of trails for hiking. The most extensive trails are north of the Green River, where horseback riding and mountain biking are allowed on parts of the trail system.

A favorite short trail south of the Green River is the 1-mile **Cedar Sink Trail,** which leads to a large collapsed sinkhole. Known for spring and summer wildflowers, this easy trail dips into a sinkhole where an underground river briefly rises to the surface. Also

easy, the 0.5-mile **Echo River Spring Trail** leads to an overlook with a fine vista of the Green River and one of the largest springs in the area.

The 0.4-mile **Sloan's Crossing Pond Walk** is one of three boardwalk trails in the park. Another, the 0.1-mile **Sand Cave Trail**, near the Fort Niagara entrance, has macabre historic significance. It was in Sand Cave that famed cave explorer Floyd Collins became trapped on Jan. 25, 1925, leading to a rescue effort that attracted unprecedented national publicity. Collins died of thirst and exposure after 17 days.

Near the visitor center, walk the 0.4-mile **River Styx Spring Trail** to see the point at which the underground river flows out of Mammoth Cave and into the Green River—most of the time, that is. When the Green River is high, it sometimes flows back into the cave, flooding its lower parts.

Dedicated in June 2014, the 9-mile **Big Hollow Trail** is a single-track route designed for hiking and mountain biking. The more secluded **White Oak Trail,** in the northeastern part of the park, is open for horseback riding.

When the national park was established, the **Green River** was highly polluted. It now hosts more than 80 species of fish and a globally significant 50-plus species of mussels. Canoeing and kayaking have become very popular in recent years, with boaters enjoying wonderful views of forest and bluffs.

Local outfitters can arrange trips of various lengths, and camping on sandbars and islands makes a float trip especially enjoyable. Fishing is most productive on the lower part of the river, with anglers trying their luck on smallmouth bass, catfish, bluegill, and other game species.

Historic entrance to Mammoth Cave

Information

How to Get There

From Louisville, KY (about 90 miles north), take I-65 south to Cave City, then go west on Ky. 70. From Nashville, TN (about 90 miles miles north), take I-65 north to Park City and go north on Tenn. 255.

When to Go

The cave is open all year. Tours are offered more often in summer than during the rest of the year. All activities are best Memorial Day through Labor Day.

Visitor Center

The park visitor center is open daily, year-round.

Headquarters

1 Mammoth Cave Parkway
Mammoth Cave, KY 42259
nps.gov/maca
270-758-2180

Camping

Of the park's three campgrounds, two take reservations: **Mammoth Cave** (109 sites) and **Maple Springs** (24 sites). **Houchin Ferry** (12 sites) operates on a first-come, first-served basis. Backcountry camping requires a free permit; obtain at the visitor center.

Lodging

Mammoth Cave Hotel *(mammothcave hotel.com;* 270-758-2225) is a concessioner-operated facility near the visitor center; Several hotels are located in nearby **Cave City** *(cavecity.com;* 270-773-8833).

Shenandoah

Virginia

Established
December 26, 1935

199,000 acres

Tracing the spine of some of Virginia's most striking mountains, Shenandoah National Park famously cloaks its soft slopes in yellows, oranges, and reds every fall. But this park, modeled in the 1930s after its western cousins, also launches visitors on incredible mountain adventures year-round. Take in the vast watercolor vistas, scramble over rocks to craggy summits, or simply stroll deep in the woods—all a short drive from several major cities.

Here find wilderness, but also deep layers of human history. Unlike most national parks, Shenandoah's borders were drawn around communities where hundreds of families lived and worked the land. As planners gave the East Coast a way to experience the grandeur of the national parks of the West, residents left homesteads and farm plots to be absorbed by the forest. Since then, oaks, hickories, and other trees have overtaken orchards and cornfields, but hikers still come upon stray chimney stacks and even gravestones. People continue to farm the surrounding area.

Hawksbill Mountain, the park's highest peak

Skyline Drive, winding 105 miles from the park's northern entrance to the southern exit, forms the heart of the park, which never stretches more than 13 miles across. In the 1930s, following a road engineered to hug the mountains and showcase the most scenic views, the Civilian Conservation Corps graded slopes around the road, built stone barriers, and planted thousands of trees. Now 1.2 million people cruise Skyline Drive every year. Top speed is 35 mph, a good speed for wildlife spotting. White-tailed deer, black bears, and hawks are among the 300 animal species inhabiting this piece of the Blue Ridge.

About 100 miles of the Appalachian Trail, that 2,180-mile trek from Georgia to Maine, also course through the park, forming the backbone of its 500-mile trail system. Paths lead to summits that make the trees below look like tiny toys, and deep into storybook forests carpeted by ferns, mosses, and mushrooms.

▶ **HOW TO VISIT**

Skyline Drive is its own attraction, but keep in mind that simply driving the entire road takes at least three hours. And while the dips and curves offer delights, be sure to step out of the car. Walking among the trees and up the mountains immerses one in the park's earthy scents, birdsongs, and fresh mountain air.

If you have less than a full day, drive to the most convenient of the four entrances and explore nearby trails and overlooks—ideally after getting guidance from a ranger at an entrance station or visitor center. To make the most of a visit of a day or more, consider starting in the middle of the park, near the Big Meadows and Skyland areas, where the mountains climb highest and popular trails and amenities cluster.

Spectacular sights can also be found in the north, where several trails showcase relics of mountain settlers, and in the less-visited south, where you're most likely to find solitude in the forest.

When crowds pack Shenandoah in mid-October, rangers suggest weekday visits. Many services, and sometimes Skyline Drive itself, close during winter, though the **Harry S. Byrd Sr. Visitor Center** keeps limited hours, restrooms stay open, and intrepid souls can hike in. With the trees bare and the earth wearing a blanket of snow, wildlife—and footprints—become easier to

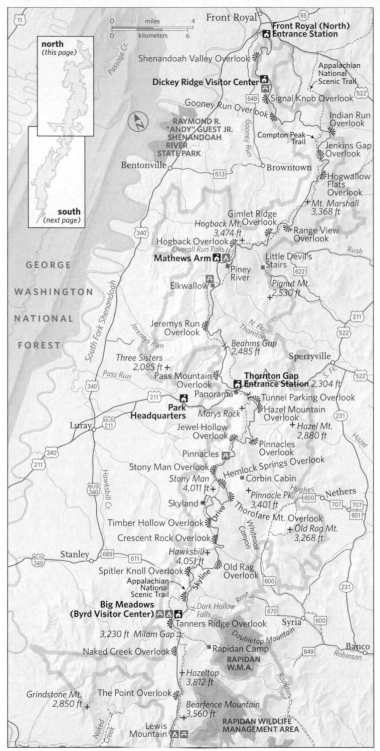

Front Royal

55

Front Royal (North)
Entrance Station

Shenandoah Valley Overlook

Dickey Ridge Visitor Center

649

Signal Knob Overlook

522

Gooney Run Overlook

Indian Run
Overlook

RAYMOND R.
"ANDY" GUEST JR.
SHENANDOAH
RIVER
STATE
PARK

Compton Peak
Trail

Jenkins Gap
Overlook

Bentonville

613

Browntown

Hogwallow
Flats
Overlook

Mt. Marshall
3,368 ft

Gimlet Ridge
Overlook

340

Hogback Mt.
3,474 ft

Range View
Overlook

Hogback Overlook

Rush

Overall Run Falls

Mathews Arm

Little Devil's
Stairs

622

Piney
River

Pignut Mt.
2,530 ft

Elkwallow

GEORGE

WASHINGTON

NATIONAL

FOREST

Jeremys Run
Overlook

N. Fk.
Thornton

211

522

South Fork Shenandoah

Beahms Gap
2,485 ft

Three Sisters
2,085 ft

Sperryville

340

Pass Run

Pass Mountain
Overlook

Thornton Gap
Entrance Station 2,304 ft

S. Fk.

522

Panorama

Tunnel Parking Overlook

Park
Headquarters

211

Marys Rock

Hazel Mountain
Overlook

231

Luray

BUS
211

Jewel Hollow
Overlook

Hazel Mt.
2,880 ft

Hazel

340

Pinnacles

Pinnacles
Overlook

Stony Man Overlook

Hemlock Springs Overlook

Stony Man
4,011 ft

Corbin Cabin

Hughes

Nethers

BUS
340

Skyland

Pinnacle Pk.
3,401 ft

600

707

601

707

Hawksbill Cr.

Drive

Thorofare Mt. Overlook

Old Rag Mt.
3,268 ft

Timber Hollow Overlook

Whiteoak
Canyon

Crescent Rock Overlook

BUS
340

Stanley

689

611

Hawksbill
4,051 ft

Old Rag
Overlook

600

231

Spitler Knoll Overlook

Appalachian
National
Scenic Trail

Skyline

Rose

Big Meadows
(Byrd Visitor Center)

Dark Hollow
Falls

670

Syria

600

Tanners Ridge Overlook

3,230 ft Milam Gap

Doubletop Mountain

Banco

Naked Creek Overlook

Rapidan Camp

RAPIDAN
W.M.A.

649

Robinson

Rapidan

Hazeltop
3,812 ft

Grindstone Mt.
2,850 ft

The Point Overlook

Bearfence Mountain
3,560 ft

RAPIDAN WILDLIFE
MANAGEMENT AREA

Lewis
Mountain

Naked Creek

11

north
(this page)

south
(next page)

miles   0   4
kilometers   0   6

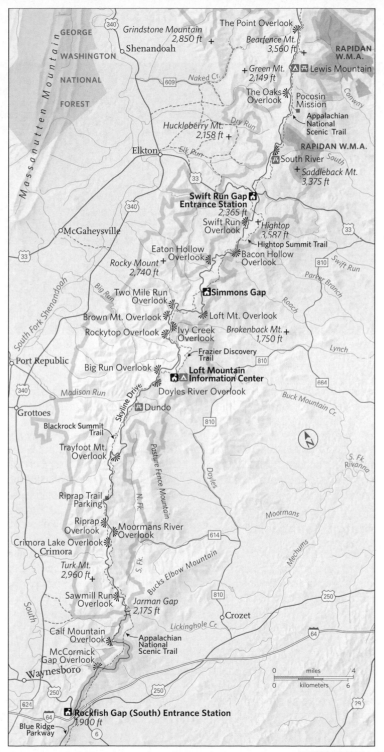

GEORGE

WASHINGTON

NATIONAL

FOREST

Massanutten Mountain

340 Grindstone Mountain
2,850 ft

The Point Overlook

Shenandoah

Bearfence Mt.
3,560 ft

RAPIDAN
W.M.A.

Green Mt. Lewis Mountain
2,149 ft

Conway

609 *Naked Cr.*

The Oaks
Overlook

Pocosin
Mission

Appalachian
National
Scenic Trail

Dry Run

Huckleberry Mt.
2,158 ft

RAPIDAN W.M.A.

South River

South

Elkton

Elk Run

Saddleback Mt.
3,375 ft

33

340

**Swift Run Gap
Entrance Station**
2,365 ft

McGaheysville

Swift Run
Overlook

Hightop
3,587 ft

33

810

Swift Run

Hightop Summit Trail

Eaton Hollow
Overlook

Bacon Hollow
Overlook

Rocky Mount
2,740 ft

Big Run

Two Mile Run
Overlook

Simmons Gap

Parker Branch

Roach

South Fork Shenandoah

Brown Mt. Overlook

Loft Mt. Overlook

Rockytop Overlook

Ivy Creek
Overlook

Brokenback Mt.
1,750 ft

Lynch

Port Republic

Frazier Discovery
Trail

810

664

Big Run Overlook

**Loft Mountain
Information Center**

Buck Mountain Cr.

340

Madison Run

Doyles River Overlook

Dundo

810

Grottoes

Blackrock Summit
Trail

Skyline Drive

Pasture Fence Mountain

Doyles

*S. Fk
Rivanna*

Trayfoot Mt.
Overlook

Riprap Trail
Parking

N. Fk.

Moormans

Riprap
Overlook

Moormans River
Overlook

614

Crimora Lake Overlook

Crimora

S. Fk.

Mechums

Turk Mt.
2,960 ft

Bucks Elbow Mountain

810

250

Sawmill Run
Overlook

Jarman Gap
2,175 ft

Crozet

Lickinghole Cr.

64

Calf Mountain
Overlook

South

Appalachian
National
Scenic Trail

McCormick
Gap Overlook

0   miles   4

Waynesboro

0   kilometers   6

250

250

79

621

64

Rockfish Gap (South) Entrance Station
1,900 ft

Blue Ridge
Parkway

6

Black bear near the Pinnacles area, along Skyline Drive

spot. Spring comes with another wash of color, when brilliant hepatica rises between fall's discarded leaves, bluets bloom alongside trails, and other flowers blossom across the park. Rangers lead wildflower walks in May. Summer weekends are popular; the park can be about 10 degrees cooler than the valley below.

Thornton Gap to the Skyland Area

Thornton Gap is relatively close to the most bustling part of the park. Just after entering Thornton Gap, off US 211, drive through the 670-foot tunnel carved into **Marys Rock** in 1932. Continuing on, the Shenandoah Valley spreads out to the west, the mountain forests eventually giving way to a quilt of rural Virginia and the town of Luray. To the east, trees undulate on the terrain of the Piedmont, which gradually slopes toward the ocean. Stop at the **Stony Man Overlook** (Mile 38) and try to find a bearded man's face in the mountain profile.

A few miles south, the **Stony Man Trail** winds 0.8 miles to the rocky "forehead" at the park's second highest point. Stony Man neighbors **Skyland,** which has eateries, an amphitheater for ranger presentations, and lodging ranging from cabins to rooms with balconies overlooking the valley.

Just south of Skyland, the **Limberlost Trail** beckons with a path paved in crushed greenstone—the rock found throughout the park. An option for those with mobility challenges, the trail is generally flat, with a boardwalk, a bridge, and plenty of benches. In June, mountain laurel blooms, making the trail a wonderland of white petals.

East of the Limberlost Trail towers **Old Rag.** The peak stuns from its overlook on Skyline Drive. To hike to it, you'll have to exit Skyline Drive and approach from Shenandoah's eastern border. This 9.2-mile trek includes a 1.5-mile scramble over giant granite boulders. The peak rewards hikers with a 360-degree view of about 200,000 acres of parkland. Back on Skyline Drive, after Mile 45, look for the trailhead to the **Hawksbill Summit,** which soars to 4,051 feet, the park's highest point.

Big Meadows Area & Points South

Popular trails are within easy reach of the Big Meadows area; keep going south for more secluded walks.

The area just north of Big Meadows is awash in options for waterfall lovers. Serious hikers might hoof it through the **Cedar Run Whiteoak Loop,** Mile 45.6, which snakes more than 7 miles through steep and rocky gorges, passing nine waterfalls. The 4-mile **Rose River Loop** leads through a dark forest before arriving at a 67-foot falls.

Still shorter, the neighboring **Dark Hollow Falls Trail** is 1.4 miles round-trip, making it the park's shortest waterfall jaunt. It runs alongside a tributary of the Rose River, down steep switchbacks, and ends where the water cascades over a mossy tumble of rocks.

At Mile 51, you will see the grassy plain that earned **Big Meadows** its name. While covering just .001 percent of the park, the meadow supports more than 16 percent of its rare plant species. Left on its own, the meadow could become a forest, but native peoples and then settlers may have maintained it with fire or grazing livestock. Today, rangers regularly burn and mow the meadow. Take in the meadow

Rapidan Camp

Before Camp David, there was Rapidan Camp, a collection of rustic cabins alongside trout-filled waters where President Herbert Hoover both relaxed and met with national and world leaders. Marines used to guard the camp, but today it's open to all. The president's home reflects Hoover's time, down to Native American rugs (gifts from the Bureau of Indian Affairs).

Today, rangers lead tours and a museum occupies the Prime Minister's Cabin. Designed by an architect known for Girl Scout camps, the retreat hardly feels presidential. Visitors will see the Town Hall site, where activities ranged from knitting to meetings of the executive committee; the Brown House, where the first couple lived; and the stone bridges over Hoover's beloved trout runs.

The Hoovers bought the land, though the Marines and Army Corps of Engineers did everything from making furniture to diverting waterways so all guests heard mountain streams. Committed to nature, the first couple left holes in some porches and roofs to accommodate trees.

After the Hoovers left, President Franklin D. Roosevelt visited, but given his disability (the result of polio), he found access difficult. He looked northeast to the mountains of Maryland, where he established what is now called Camp David.

through the large glass windows at the **Harry S. Byrd Sr. Visitor Center,** which also has a lively exhibit about the history of the park, a gift shop, and rangers quick to provide trail maps and suggestions.

Continuing south, the 4-mile round-trip **Mill Prong Trail** sets out just before Mile 53, delivering hikers to Rapidan Camp, President Herbert Hoover's summer retreat (see p. 77). The forest trail passes a small waterfall and requires hopping among large stones to cross streams.

Just before mile 57, the 1.2-mile **Bear Fence Rock Scramble** treats hikers to a 360-degree panorama of mountains and valleys. Stop at the **South River Overlook** at Mile 62.7, a great sunrise spot, and climb the **Hightop Summit Trail,** near Mile 65, in the spring to see wildflowers. After Mile 79, the **Frazier Discovery Trail** tells the park's story, highlighting how the forest reclaims pastureland over a 1.3-mile loop that includes two summit viewpoints.

At Mile 84.8, the 1-mile round-trip **Blackrock Summit** trail launches hikers onto a sky-high field of quartzite rocks. Views from the summit are superb, but even the forested parts of the trail can make hikers feel they are above it all. Skyline Drive continues through **Rockfish Gap,** where a bison path evolved into a road and, later, a highway.

Dickey Ridge & Northern Shenandoah

Front Royal, the town at the northern tip of the park, lends its name to this entrance. With a smaller **visitor center** and camping accommodations only, this part of the park is little developed. Less than 5 miles from the entrance, the **Dickey Ridge Visitor Center**

offers a small wildlife exhibit, rangers eager to give advice, and grounds with photo opportunities worthy of the family holiday card. Starting from the visitor center, trails offer glimpses of mountain life. The **Snead Farm Trail,** a 3-mile circuit, travels through a former apple orchard. The **Fox Hollow Trail,** 1.2 miles, skirts homesites and a cemetery. Combine both walks by connecting via the **Dickey Ridge Trail.**

Continuing south, **Signal Knob Overlook,** Mile 5.7, gives a clear view of "Signal Knob" on Massanutten Mountain, where Confederate troops relayed messages with flags. During the Civil War, Southern armies used the Blue Ridge as a natural screen to hide their movements.

Significantly farther back in this region's history, fast-cooling volcanic rock created curiously geometric rock formations; look for crystal-shaped rock columns. These polygonal formations can be seen at the **Indian Run Overlook** at Mile 10 or along the moderately strenuous 2.4-mile **Compton Peak Trail** (Mile 10.4). Down the road, at Mile 22.2, the **Overall Run Falls Trail** (5.1 miles) descends 1,850 feet to rocky ledges perfect for perching and observing the 93-foot waterfall—the park's tallest. But this beauty dries up before the others; go in the spring or after a big rain.

While most visitors stick to Skyline Drive, excellent trails can also be reached from the park's boundary. **Little Devil's Stairs,** best accessed from Rte. 614, west of the town of Washington, offers a classic Shenandoah workout with a 5.5-mile trip through a narrow gorge, plenty of rock scrambling, and multiple river crossings.

Dogwood (Cornus florida) along Skyline Drive

Information

How to Get There

The park is within several hours' drive from Washington, Pittsburgh, and Philadelphia. Where you come from will determine which of the four entrances you use: The most popular are at Front Royal in the north, near I-66, and Thornton Gap, closer to the middle, accessed from US 211. Moving south, the other entrances are Swift Run gap, off US 33, and Rockfish Gap, near I-64.

When to Go

Lodging books quickly for the Oct. foliage; travel during the week to avoid crowds. Most facilities close for winter and reopen in March, though the park remains open. Summers also book quickly.

Visitor Centers

Dickey Ridge Visitor Center (Mile 4.6), open daily; closed in winter. **Harry F. Byrd Sr. Visitor Center** (Mile 51), open daily; weekend hours only in winter.

Headquarters

3655 Highway 211 East
Luray, VA 22835
nps.gov/shen
540-999-3500

Camping

Reservations, recommended for weekend and holiday visits, are accepted for all sites except Lewis Mountain *(recreation.gov)*. Most of the park is open to backcountry camping *(free permit required)*. 647 campsites available at **Mathews Arm** (Mile 22.1), **Big Meadows** (Mile 51), **Lewis Mountain** (Mile 57.5), and **Loft Mountain** (Mile 79.5).

Lodging

Private concessioners offer rooms and cabins in the park, mostly at the **Big Meadows** (Mile 51) and **Skyland** (Mile 42). **Lewis Mountain** (Mile 57.5) has several cabins. The **Potomac Appalachian Trail Club** rents out primitive cabins *(patc.net)*. For more lodging information: *visitshenandoah.org.*

Shenandoah Excursions

George Washington National Forest
West Central Virginia

▷ Administratively combined with the Jefferson National Forest in 1995, the George Washington Forest borders the Shenandoah Valley. It is a recreational enthusiast's dream location with 60 miles of the Appalachian Trail, fishing, mountain biking, camping, bird-watching, cross-country skiing, horseback riding, orienteering, and camping. Open year-round. Located in west central Virginia, approximately 30 miles west of Shenandoah National Park. *www.fs.fed.us/r8/gwj;* 540-265-5100.

Wilderness Road State Park
Ewing, Virginia

▷ Featuring the reconstructed Martin's Station, an outdoor living history museum depicting life in Virginia in the late 18th century, Wilderness Road State Park offers something for history and nature enthusiasts alike. The 8.5-mile Wilderness Road Trail is good for hiking, biking, or horseback riding, while the museum offers places for picnicking. Primitive camping for groups is available. Open year-round. Located 320 miles southwest of Shenandoah National Park via I-81 S. *dcr.virginia.gov/state-parks/find-a-park.shtml;* 276-445-3065.

Sky Meadows State Park
Paris, Virginia

▷ A getaway located on the eastern side of the Blue Ridge Mountains, Sky Meadows State Park offers nature and history programs year-round as well as hiking, equestrian and biking trails, picnicking, fishing, and primitive hike-in camping *(reservations needed).* Visitor center is behind Mount Bleak House. Twenty-three miles northeast of Shenandoah National Park via Va. 638. *dcr.virginia.gov/state-parks/sky-meadows.shtml;* 540-592-3556.

Rapidan Wildlife Management Area
Stanardsville, Virginia

▷ Rapidan adjoins Shenandoah National Park. There are opportunities for visitors to partake in wildlife-related activities—photography, hunting, fishing, hiking, and horseback riding. While wildlife abounds here, evidence of the mountaineer families that once lived in the area can be seen throughout the area. Steep mountain roads, old home sites, and cemeteries are part of the landscape. Restricted primitive camping is allowed. There are 10,326 acres broken into eight separate tracts along the eastern slopes of the Blue Ridge Mountains. *dgif.virginia .gov/wmas;* 540-899-4169.

Jefferson National Forest
Western Virginia

▷ In prime Appalachia country, Jefferson National Forest is home to waterfalls, wildflowers, and Virginia's highest peak, Mount Rogers. Covering 723,530 acres, the national forest has just about every type of outdoor recreation activity: hiking, boating, fishing, horseback riding, hunting, and water sports. Plus camping. Open year-round. Information at the forest's Roanoke headquarters, about 110 miles southwest of Shenandoah National Park, via Blue Ridge Pkwy. or I-81. *fs.fed.us/r8/gwj;* 540-265-5100.

Shenandoah River State Park
Bentonville, Virginia

▷ Snaking alongside the South Fork Shenandoah River, the park covers more than 1,600 acres of land, including 5.2 miles of riverfront. In addition to a meandering river landscape, the park serves up spellbinding views of the Massanutten Mountain and Shenandoah National Park. Hiking, fishing, horseback riding, and zip-line tours. Numerous campsites include ten along the river. Open year-round. Located 14 miles southwest of Shenandoah National Park via US 340 S. *dcr.virginia.gov/state parks/find-a-park .shtml;* 540-622-6840.

Virgin Islands

United States Virgin Islands

Established
August 2, 1956

15,000 acres

The Caribbean Sea boasts scores of islands with gorgeous white-sand beaches bordered by sparkling blue water and green tropical vegetation—the stuff of a million vacation dreams. Only one, though, has more than half its land area lying within a U.S. national park, with an additional 8.8 square miles of marine habitat also inside park borders. This is St. John, part of Virgin Islands National Park and one of the most popular destinations in the Caribbean.

The Virgin Islands lie in the Lesser Antilles, 1,100 miles southeast of Miami. Several of the islands are British possessions, while others are part of the United States Virgin Islands National Park, which encompasses about 7,200 acres of St. John, a hilly island with a history as fascinating as its scenery is lovely. Humans are believed to have reached the Virgin Islands about 3,000 years ago. Archaeological finds indicate that there were settlements on St. John several centuries before Columbus arrived in the Caribbean in 1492. Denmark claimed St. John and other

Green turtle

vacation here. Among those enthralled by St. John was financier and conservationist Laurance S. Rockefeller, who bought more than 5,000 acres of land and donated it to serve as the foundation of a national park.

Snorkeling and scuba diving are highly popular in the park, which includes 5,650 acres of Caribbean Sea adjacent to St. John, as well as many small islands. To protect the marine environment, Virgin Islands Coral Reef National Monument was established in 2001. It encompasses nearly 20 square miles adjoining the national park and is administered by the staff of Virgin Islands National Park.

Today, vacationers from around the worldcome to enjoy the beaches, marine life, culture, shopping, and cuisine of the Virgin Islands. St. John, though, has neither airport nor cruise dock, and, with most of its area within a national park, it offers a less crowded, more relaxed atmosphere than do its neighbors.

islands in the 17th century, and beginning in 1718 Danes established plantations of sugarcane over most of the island. Land was cleared and the fields and sugar mills were worked by enslaved Africans, who were emancipated in 1848.

Ruins from the plantation era, among St. John's most evocative attractions, serve as reminders of the colonial period of wealth for a few plantation owners and slavery for hundreds of workers. After the plantations dwindled, St. Johnians lived by raising cattle and cultivating crops.

The United States bought St. John and several other Virgin Islands from Denmark in 1917, basically for military purposes, and by the 1930s some U.S. citizens had begun to settle and

► HOW TO VISIT

The great majority of visitors to St. John (those without their own boats) arrive by plane or ship at the nearby island of St. Thomas and take a short ferry ride to St. John. They disembark at **Cruz Bay,** on the western end of the island. Because St. John is so compact, it's possible to get a taste of scenery and history in a day by signing up for a tour that takes in one or more of the north shore **beaches** and the **Annaberg Sugar Mill** ruins.

With more time, consider hiking the **Lind Point Trail** or the strenuous **Reef Bay Trail.** Rent snorkel gear and get into the water at **Trunk Bay** or one of

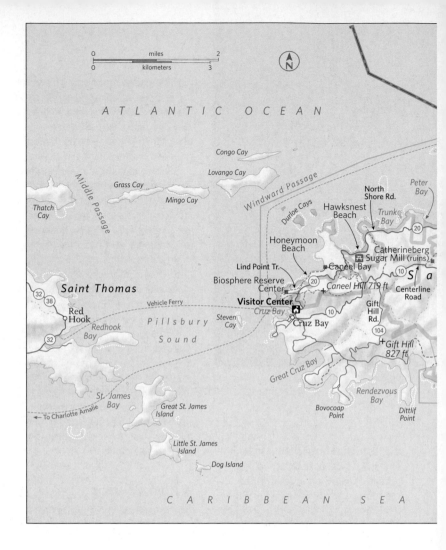

the many other island beaches. (The park offers a brochure that lists top snorkeling spots.)

Rental cars are available on St. John, but be aware that roads are narrow, steep, and extremely winding, and vehicles drive on the left-hand side of the road. Hiring a local driver is often the best bet.

Hotels are scarce on St. John; many visitors rent vacation homes for a week or more, or stay on St. Thomas and take the ferry. No passport is needed to visit the U.S. Virgin Islands, but you must have one to visit nearby British Virgin Islands such as Tortola and Jost Van Dyke.

The North Shore

The national park **visitor center** in Cruz Bay is a short walk from the ferry. Stop for maps, brochures, advice, and a schedule of ranger-led programs.

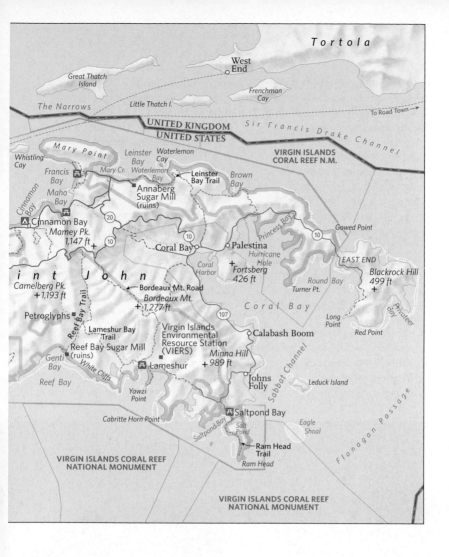

Just steps away is the beginning of the easy **Lind Point Trail.** Where the path splits, go uphill to reach an overlook (0.4 mile) with a view of Cruz Bay and the harbor. Continue to the lower trail and you'll soon reach **Salomon Beach** (0.7 mile), an inviting stretch of sand, usually uncrowded because it's not on a road; just beyond is **Honeymoon Beach.** The snorkeling can be good around the point of land between these beaches.

Here and elsewhere on the North Shore you'll almost certainly see two of the island's most common birds, the pearly-eyed thrasher (called "thrushie" by the locals) and the yellow-and-black bananaquit. With a little luck you might get to see the beautiful, iridescent green-throated carib hummingbird. You could also spot a mongoose, a weasel-like mammal.

Like many other islands, St. John has suffered from the introduction of alien species. The mongoose may be the worst. It was brought here to kill rats, but the mongoose is active mostly in the daytime and rats are nocturnal. Mongooses eat native birds, snakes, and hatchling sea turtles.

The **North Shore Road** (Rte. 20) leads to many of St. John's most popular destinations. Not far from Cruz Bay, it passes **Caneel Bay,** once a Rockefeller vacation hideaway and now a resort.

Beyond Caneel, pretty **Hawksnest Beach** is popular with locals in part because its proximity to Cruz Bay makes it convenient for a quick after-work swim.

A bit farther along North Shore road is the small parking area for the short walk to **Peace Hill,** which offers great views of the St. John coastline and islands to the north, as well as

the remains of an old windmill.

You'll want to stop at the road over-look above famed **Trunk Bay** to take in the panorama used for tourism bro-chures and postcards. The beach here *(fee)* is the most popular on St. John. (The fees collected here go to the fund-ing of lifeguards, changing rooms, and other amenities.)

Trunk Bay is also known for its 225-yard **Rivsnorkel Trail,** with under-water signs interpreting coral and other marine life. Trunk Bay is undoubtedly beautiful, but at times it can be crowd-ed with day-trippers from St. Thomas cruise ships.

Cinnamon Bay has several attrac-tions, including yet another beautiful beach (the island's longest) and the only public **campground** on St. John. Across the road are the ruins of an old sugar mill, reached by one of

Annaberg Sugar Mill Plantation

the few wheelchair-accessible trails on the island.

Cinnamon Bay is named for the Indian bay rum tree, a species of the myrtle family whose leaves provide the aromatic oil used in bay rum cologne. After the cultivation of sugarcane ended here, the production of bay rum provided income for St. Johnians.

If you're even slightly interested in St. John history, don't miss the **Heritage Education Center** at Cinnamon Bay. This small, well-done facility has displays on the island's past, including artifacts dating to prehistoric times.

Maho Beach, the next stop along the North Shore Road, may be the most popular beach among St. Johnians themselves. The water is shallow for a long way into the bay, which, combined with usually calm surf, makes it excellent for families with children.

The road continues to an intersection where a left turn leads to **Francis Bay.** The beach here is not usually crowded, and the bay itself is one of the best places on the island to spot sea turtles.

Bird-watchers like the **loop trail,** which winds through a mangrove forest around a pond where white-cheeked pintail duck swim. The path also passes the ruins of a "great house," as a plantation owner's or manager's residence was called.

A right turn at the intersection leads to one of St. John's most famous attractions, the ruins of the **Annaberg Sugar Mill.** Once part of a 1,300-acre plantation that at its peak produced 400,000 pounds of sugar a year, Annaberg is the island's best-preserved plantations. The windmill crushed cane into a liquid that was boiled to make sugar;

nearby, horses, mules, and oxen turned a wheel that crushed the cane when the windmill was not operational. A boiling house (where juice was turned into granular sugar) and an oven are among the historic ruins at the site.

Hassel Island

A little-known part of Virgin Islands National Park, Hassel Island sits in the harbor of Charlotte Amalie, the main town on St. Thomas. Covering about 135 acres, Hassel Island was originally a peninsula connected to the main body of St. Thomas but was separated by Danish authorities in the 1860s in an attempt to improve water circulation in the harbor. The island was named (with an alternative spelling) for James Hazzell, its first known owner.

The National Park Service owns about 95 percent of Hassel Island and works with a local nonprofit trust group to preserve and interpret historic sites. These include military fortifications and barracks from the early 19th-century period when Britain occupied St. Thomas during the Napoleonic Wars.

Other sites include the remains of a marine railway (used to move ships out of the water for repair), a late 19th-century wharf, the foundation walls of a British hospital, and the Hazzell family cemetery.

Interpretive trails cross the island, linking various historic sites. Several local companies offer transportation to and tours of the island. For information: *hasselisland.org;* 340-774-5541. Or check with the National Park office at Cruz Bay on St. John.

Near the parking lot for Annaberg is the beginning of the 0.8-mile **Leinster Bay Trail,** an old road from the Danish era that leads to perhaps the best-known snorkeling site on St. John. The waters along the shore here and especially around the small island called **Waterlemon Cay** abound in coral, fish, turtles, rays, and other marine life. Currents can be very strong at times, and the surf can be quite rough.

Centerline Road & the East End

Centerline Road (Rte. 10) roughly parallels North Shore Road through the island's hilly interior. Approximately 3 miles from Cruz Bay, stop to explore the partially restored ruins of the **Catherineberg Sugar Mill,** with its impressive windmill base and stone arches.

Less than 2 miles farther along is the trailhead for the popular 2.5-mile **Reef Bay Trail,** an old Danish road that begins at an elevation of 900 feet. Weaving through tropical forest, the trail is edged with some of St. John's largest trees. Note the profusions of epiphytes (plants that grow harmlessly on other plants). The trail descends to sea level at **Genti Bay,** on the island's southern shore. Along the way are several rock walls and other ruins from the island's plantation era.

A Reef Bay Trail side path leads to a lovely pool and seasonal waterfall, and ancient **petroglyphs** believed to depict Taino ancestral spirits called zemis. The trail ends at the ruins of a sugar mill that was the last to operate on St. John. Powered by a steam engine, the factory produced sugar until 1916.

National park rangers lead tours *(fee)* on the Reef Bay Trail. A boat meets participants at the bay; at the end of the tour visitors head back to Cruz Bay by boat. Those who decide to do the hike must make the steep and strenuous walk back up the trail to Centerline Road.

The road continues on to the small town of Coral Bay, which has a few cafés and shops. Continuing west on Catherine Road, you'll reach **Hurricane Hole,** a bay named for its usage as a safe harbor for boats during storms.

At **Princess Bay,** a few informal parking places are used by kayakers and snorkelers who enter the bay through breaks in the fringing mangroves. Many locals consider the snorkeling here to be as rewarding as any on the island. Mangroves serve as nurseries for dozens of species of fish, and the water around them is usually clear and calm.

South of Coral Bay, Rte. 107 leads to places that are popular with locals but little known to visitors. A short trail leads a nice beach at **Saltpond Bay,** a calm spot for swimming when seasonal waves make for rough surf on north shore beaches. A 1-mile trail continues to **Ram Head,** where viewpoints atop 200-foot-high cliffs make splendid lookouts for taking in sunsets. Note: Caution should be used on the Ram Head Trail, where a fall could be fatal. Be aware, too, that there is no shade in this area and the weather can be very hot.

A rough road winds west from Saltpond to **Great Lameshur Beach,** with a rocky but attractive shore, and sandy **Little Lameshur Beach.** Both are far less used than the north shore beaches. In between is **Yawzi Point,** which can be excellent for snorkeling.

Spotted eagle ray

Information

How to Get There

Flights to St. Thomas are available out of several American cities. Regular ferries travel from St. Thomas to Cruz Bay, on St. John.

When to Go

The weather is pleasant year-round. Nov. and Dec. are the rainiest months, and Feb. through April is the driest time of year. Hurricanes are of course unpredictable, but usually occur Aug. through Nov.

Visitor Center

The park visitor center in **Cruz Bay** is open year-round.

Headquarters

1300 Cruz Bay Creek
St. John, VI 00830
nps.gov/viis
340-776-6201

Camping

The campground at **Cinnamon Bay** (126 sites) also offers cabins. For information: *cinnamonbay.com;* 340-776-6330.

Lodging

Hotel rooms are quite limited on St. John; many visitors rent houses by the week or longer. Luxury resort accommodations can be found at **Caneel Bay** (*caneelbay .com;* 340-776-6111 or 855-226-3358). Arrange lodging as far in advance as possible during the peak season, Dec. through April. For lodging information: *visitusvi.com.*

VIRGIN ISLANDS
EST 1956

Midwest

Reconstructed Everett Road covered bridge in Cuyahoga Valley National Park

T he six parks of the Midwest offer a variety of experiences, some suburban and close-at-hand, others rugged and otherworldly. At these parks, water, in all its abundant power, nourished, built, eroded, and sculpted the diverse landscape of America's heartland.

Streams flowing from the young Rocky Mountains laid down the colorful mud that rivers would later carve into the buttes, gorges, and pillars of the Dakota badlands. The seashell-hued bluffs of South Dakota's **Badlands** National Park reveal layers of sedimentary history, the work of seas, rivers, and volcanoes. These wilds so inspired a visionary from New York that he decided to dedicate himself to conservation. His legacy endures in **Theodore Roosevelt** National Park in North Dakota.

At **Wind Cave,** bison roam and graze a 28,000-acre swath of pine forest and prairieland, with the remains of a "buffalo jump." This South Dakota cliff formation

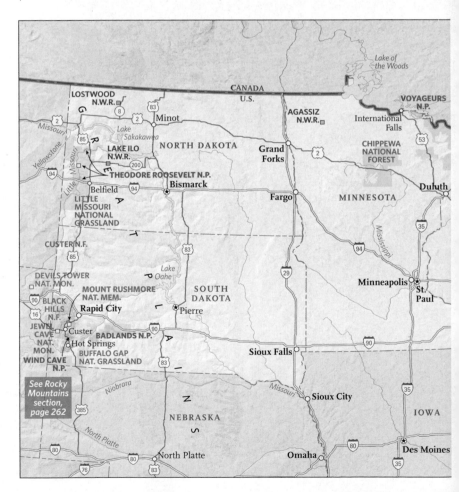

literally stopped animals in their tracks. It is a reminder of the mighty quadruped's significance to American Indian hunters. Beneath the Earth's surface lies a labyrinth of passageways that extends for miles, making Wind Cave one of the longest known underground cave formations in the world. Geological wonders abound.

Scores of lakes and streams lace the forests of Minnesota's **Voyageurs** National Park, named for the late 18th-century French Canadian fur traders who for 100 years paddled these waters. To the east, Michigan's **Isle Royale** encompasses an entire island ecosystem. In and around its lakes, thick forest, and fjordlike coast a delicate ecosystem plays out. Among the star players: wolves and their prey, moose. Ohio's **Cuyahoga Valley** National Park provides easy access to the natural world right in Cleveland's backyard. A revitalized bald eagle population coexists with human activities like hiking and biking along a 19th-century canal, farmers markets in spring, and wintertime cross-country skiing.

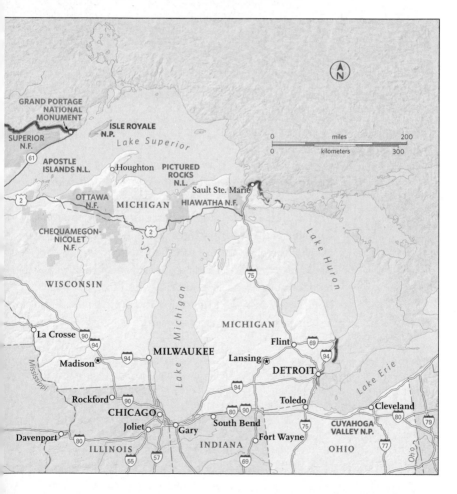

Badlands

South Dakota

Established
November 10, 1978

244,300 acres

There comes a moment when vast rolling grassland drops away to a fantastic landscape of pyramids, pillars, bluffs, knife-edge ridges, and narrow canyons. The star in these formations: water. It's been carving away at the cliffs for the past half million years or so. Badlands National Park is a place of great theatricality, an enormous stage set—colorful, dramatic, and not quite real. Architect Frank Lloyd Wright referred to it as "an endless supernatural world."

For those traveling it on foot, horseback, or in a covered wagon, this rugged terrain was certainly a bad land; for modern visitors, it's nothing short of wondrous.

Today's scenery began forming when streams (especially the White River to the south) started cutting down into a plain composed of many rock layers built up over tens of millions of years. These strata include the sediments of an ancient seafloor, silt and gravel deposited by rivers, and thick layers of volcanic ash. Exposed now, like a sliced layer cake, they create a colorful vision of buff, yellow,

Badlands landforms

is as colorful as it is varied. A drive-through park? Badlands can, and should, be so much more.

▶ HOW TO VISIT

Indeed, it's all too easy to exit Interstate 90, drive the 39-mile loop road while stopping for photos, and be back on the freeway in a couple of hours. It's much more rewarding to spend an entire day or two exploring the park: walking among the bizarre formations, driving the Sage Creek Rim Road, taking in a ranger-led program, and learning about the trove of fossils found here, from ancient alligators to the ancestors of today's dog.

Eastbound travelers on I-90 in a hurry can enter the park at the **Pinnacles (west) Entrance,** drive the scenic road, and rejoin I-90 north of the **Northeast Entrance,** where westbound drivers enter. You'll be better prepared to enjoy the park, though, if you use the latter entrance. You can stop at the **Ben Reifel Visitor Center** to get advice from a ranger and to view exhibits on geology, fossils, and natural history.

While driving the **Badlands Loop Road** you should, at a minimum, walk the 0.75-mile **Door Trail** or the 0.25-mile **Fossil Exhibit Trail.** Where the loop road turns north to exit the park, continue on unpaved **Sage Creek Rim Road** for the best chance to see bison, pronghorn, and other wildlife.

The Loop Road & Beyond

A short way from the northeast entrance is the **Big Badlands Overlook,** a parking area with an expansive view of the rugged terrain for which the national park is known. Just a couple of

pink, and brown. After a rain, the land displays a seemingly infinite spectrum of subtle tones.

The park's formations comprise a section of a geologic feature called the Wall. This 100-mile-long natural barrier ridges the landscape, dividing western South Dakota's upper and lower grassland regions. The soft rock erodes easily, at the rate of about an inch a year, which means that in another 500,000 years all this craggy country could be a flat plain.

More than half the park is grassland, where bison and pronghorn graze; bighorn sheep clamber about the steep slopes. More than 200 species of birds have been recorded in the park, and when rainfall has been sufficient, the prairie wildflower display

BADLANDS **95**

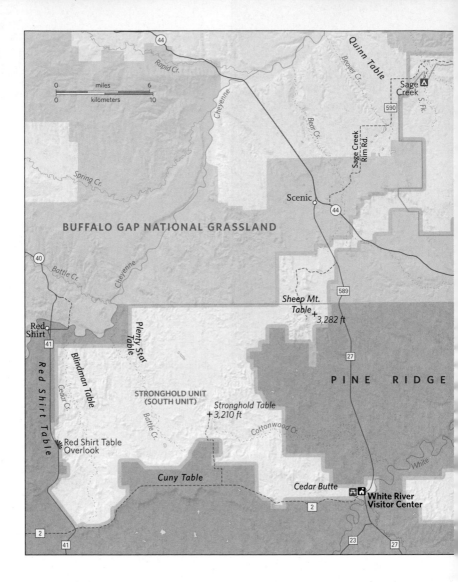

miles farther, trails offer chances to see picturesque rock formations up close. The very short **Window Trail** is wheelchair accessible, as is the first section of the 0.75-mile **Door Trail,** where the focus is on geology. The 1.5-mile, somewhat strenuous **Notch Trail** climbs to a viewpoint with a splendid panorama of the White River lowlands and the Pine Ridge Reservation. Just beyond

Cedar Pass is the 0.5-mile loop **Cliff Shelf Nature Trail.** Here, a "slump" of rock eroded from the Wall forms a flat spot where junipers and cottonwoods grow, creating a mini-haven for birds and other wildlife. The trail rises to a platform with more fine views.

The road quickly reaches the hub of park activity: the **Ben Reifel Visitor Center** and the concessioner-operated

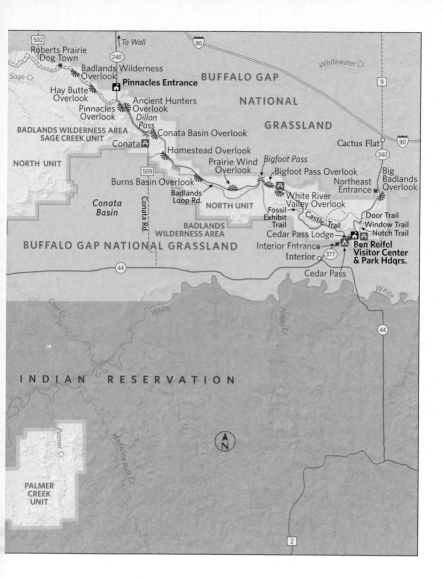

Cedar Pass Lodge, which offers lodging, camping, dining, and a small store.

Tour the exhibits at the visitor center, which interpret park geology, natural history, and the important fossil discoveries made in the park. Due to the rapid rate of erosion, new fossil finds occur frequently.

The area that is now Badlands National Park lay under an ocean during the age of dinosaurs, and so the park lacks fossils of these reptiles. What it does have is one of the world's richest collections of fossil mammals from the Oligocene epoch, about 30 million years ago, along with creatures such as turtles and alligators. About 3 miles down the road is the 0.25-mile Fossil Exhibit Trail, a good place to learn more about fossils.

The wheelchair-accessible trail passes molds of several of the finds made in the park, including that of an oreodont, a piglike animal whose fossils are the most common found here. The era of discovery continues at Badlands: In 2010, a seven-year-old girl found a significant fossil from a saber-toothed cat near the visitor center.

The loop road winds among seemingly endless rock formations, many of them displaying the varicolored layers deposited by seas, rivers, and volcanoes over tens of millions of years. The route alternately climbs up the Wall and descends again, offering fine panoramas along the way. The lovely colors of rock strata are seen at their best near **Dillon Pass,** at sites such as **Conata Basin Overlook** and **Yellow Mounds Overlook.** Dillon Pass is the only place along the road where all the park's rock layers can be seen at once.

Approaching **Pinnacles Overlook,** watch for bighorn sheep on nearby slopes. As the main loop road turns north to exit the park at the **Pinnacles Entrance,** continue west instead on **Sage Creek Rim Road** (unpaved but usually in good condition).

Badlands includes the largest expanse of mixed-grass prairie in the national park system, and in grassland areas you're likely to see black-tailed prairie dogs and larger mammals, including bison and pronghorn. Here, too, are even more vistas of intricately eroded buttes, spires, and canyons to the south.

Sage Creek Rim Road drops down off the Wall into an environment of wooded canyons and lush grass, continuing to the Sage Creek Campground. Campers in this peaceful and scenic spot sometimes awaken to the sight of bison grazing nearby.

Hiking and backcountry camping are allowed (and encouraged) in the park's 64,144-acre Wilderness area. This is where to combine beautiful vistas and solitude, but talk to a ranger and be well equipped before starting out. There are no trails in the backcountry except those made by bison, and no signs either—bison using them for scratching posts knock them down.

A New Kind of Park

As this book went to press, plans were underway to change the status of what has been the Stronghold Unit of Badlands National Park, located southwest of the main park area. Set within the Pine Ridge Indian Reservation, this remote and expansive tract has long been managed by the Oglala Lakota. Under the new agreement, Badlands would officially become the country's first tribal national park.

Details regarding ownership, management, and access were still being determined at press time, in large part because the concept of a tribal park is new to both the National Park Service and the Oglala Lakota. Special legislation had to be passed by Congress to facilitate the change, and concerns of private landowners within the proposed new park had to be addressed.

For the status of the Stronghold Unit, ask at the Ben Reifel Visitor Center, check the Badlands National Park website, or stop at the unit's White River Visitor Center (605-455-2878) on S. Dak. 27, about 20 miles south of the town of Scenic.

Buffalo grazing on prairie grasses

Information

How to Get There

From Rapid City, SD (about 60 miles northwest), take I-90 east to Wall, or continue 20 more miles to S. Dak. 240.

When to Go

Summer sees the park's highest visitation—and often very hot weather. Spring and fall offer more moderate temperatures. Winter can be beautiful in the park, but watch the forecast for occasional snowstorms.

Visitor Center

Ben Reifel Visitor Center, on S. Dak. 240, 8 miles south of I-90, is open year-round.

Headquarters

P.O. Box 6
Interior, SD 57750
nps.gov/badl
605-433-5361

Camping

Cedar Pass Campground (100 sites) is open year-round; for information on this privately managed site, contact Cedar Pass Lodge (see below). The less developed **Sage Creek Campground,** also open year-round, offers open camping. There is no water available. Both campgrounds are first come, first served. No permit is required for backcountry camping, although campers are encouraged to contact a ranger before a trip.

Lodging

Lodging is available in the park at concessioner-operated **Cedar Pass Lodge** (*cedarpasslodge.com;* 877-386-4383) and in the nearby town of **Wall** (*wall -badlands.com)*, adjacent to the park.

BADLANDS
EST 1978

Cuyahoga Valley

Ohio

Established
October 11, 2000

33,000 acres

Between Cleveland and Akron sits Cuyahoga Valley National Park. A park between two cities? Yes, one with a vast array of pleasures. In what other park can you ride a scenic railroad, stop at a roadside farm to buy fresh-picked blueberries, watch a glassblower create a decorative bowl, jog alongside a 19th-century canal, and hear a concert by one of the nation's finest symphony orchestras?

These hardly seem like typical national park activities, but they come with the territory.

Located in a suburban corridor in northeastern Ohio, Cuyahoga Valley was established as a national recreation area in 1974; it was designated a national park in 2000. Unlike traditional wilderness parks in the West, it was pieced together amid a modern landscape of towns, highways, farms, and city parks.

Over time, Cuyahoga Valley National Park has incorporated or partnered with all sorts of attractions, from historic inns to ski resorts to the Cleveland Orchestra and its summer concerts at Blossom Music Center.

Brandywine Falls

In the years since it was established, attitudes regarding the park's farms have changed. Many farmsteads were abandoned when the park opened, having sat derelict for years. Now the National Park Service, together with the local Countryside Conservancy, is offering incentives for sustainable agriculture, aiming to preserve the traditional lifestyle of the area. Today, around a dozen farms operate within the park, and a summer farmers market at Howe Meadow has become very popular.

Make no mistake, though. Cuyahoga Valley offers a wide range of rewards for lovers of the natural world. Visitors can explore geological features and enjoy some of the prettiest waterfalls in the eastern United States.

Rugged gorges are dotted with wildflowers in spring, and trails through dense forest offer a soothing escape. Beavers and otters swim in park marshes, while bald eagles and peregrine falcons nest nearby. Anglers cast for steelhead trout in the revitalized Cuyahoga River.

Linking many park sites is the Ohio & Erie Canal Towpath Trail. The Towpath Trail is truly the heart of the park, patronized by walkers, runners, bicyclists, and in winter by cross-country skiers. It traverses the park for 20 miles in its 84-mile route, which starts in Cleveland and runs south through four counties.

▶ **HOW TO VISIT**

You can experience the park in a single day, but to take advantage of the park's cultural offerings, plan on two or three days. The centrally located **Boston Store Visitor Center,** a restored 1836 building located on the **Towpath Trail,** provides information on park activities. Walking part of the Towpath Trail is a must, as are trips to waterfalls, such as **Brandywine Falls.** Check at the visitor center for activity options, including information on a trip on the **Cuyahoga Valley Scenic Railroad** *(fee; vsr.com)* and where to rent bikes. To get the most from a visit to the park, combine nature excursions to spots such as the **Ledges** with activities such as farm visits or a stroll around the village of **Peninsula,** with its shops and art galleries.

Ohio & Erie Canal Towpath Trail

Covering 20 miles, north to south, this wheelchair-accessible hike-bike

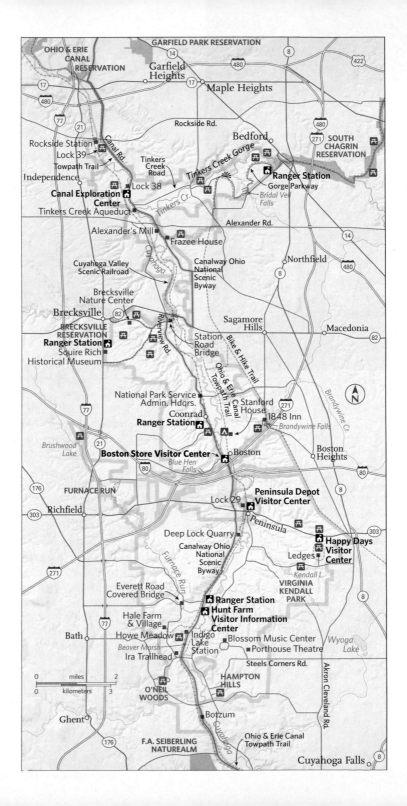

GARFIELD PARK RESERVATION

OHIO & ERIE CANAL RESERVATION

Garfield Heights

Maple Heights

SOUTH CHAGRIN RESERVATION

Rockside Rd.

Bedford

Rockside Station
Lock 39
Towpath Trail
Independence

Canal Rd.

Tinkers Creek Road

Tinkers Creek Gorge

Ranger Station
Gorge Parkway

Bridal Veil Falls

Lock 38

Canal Exploration Center
Tinkers Creek Aqueduct

Tinkers Cr.

Alexander Rd.

Alexander's Mill

Frazee House

Cuyahoga

Canalway Ohio National Scenic Byway

Northfield

Cuyahoga Valley Scenic Railroad

Brecksville Nature Center

Brecksville

BRECKSVILLE RESERVATION

Sagamore Hills

Macedonia

Ranger Station
Squire Rich Historical Museum

Riverview Rd.

Station Road Bridge

Bike & Hike Trail

Brandywine Cr.

National Park Service Admin. Hdqrs.

Ohio & Erie Canal Towpath Trail

Coonrad

Stanford House

1848 Inn

Brandywine Falls

Ranger Station

Brushwood Lake

Boston Store Visitor Center
Blue Hen Falls

Boston

Boston Heights

FURNACE RUN

Richfield

Peninsula Depot Visitor Center

Lock 29

Peninsula

Deep Lock Quarry

Canalway Ohio National Scenic Byway

Happy Days Visitor Center

Ledges

Kendall L.

VIRGINIA KENDALL PARK

Furnace Run

Everett Road Covered Bridge

Hale Farm & Village

Ranger Station
Hunt Farm Visitor Information Center

Bath

Howe Meadow

Beaver Marsh

Indigo Lake Station

Blossom Music Center
Porthouse Theatre

Wyoga Lake

Ira Trailhead

Steels Corners Rd.

HAMPTON HILLS

Akron Cleveland Rd.

miles 2
kilometers 3

O'NEIL WOODS

Ghent

Botzum

Cuyahoga

F.A. SEIBERLING NATUREALM

Ohio & Erie Canal Towpath Trail

Cuyahoga Falls

N

path combines history, nature, and recreation. It is the park's most popular attraction.

In the 1820s, a canal was excavated that roughly paralleled the Cuyahoga River, opening a route to transport goods between Lake Erie and the Ohio River. Although it operated for only a few decades, until railroads made it obsolete, the canal transformed commerce in the young United States and turned Ohio into an economic powerhouse. Today, the Towpath Trail follows the route used by mules to pull barges along the canal.

The **Canal Exploration Center,** in the northern part of the park, is housed in a historic building that, over more than a century and a half, has been a tavern, a store, a boarding-house, and a blacksmith shop. Today, the center uses innovative displays and an operational lock to bring the canal era to life. This is one of several spots in the park where you can board the **Cuyahoga Valley Scenic Railroad,** which operates along a 26.5-mile route between Rockside Station in the north and Akron, south of the park. Twenty miles of track are within the national park.

Not only is the train an engaging way to see the park, it provides hikers and bicyclists the opportunity to speedily make their way along the Towpath Trail. They flag the trains down at designated stops and ride back to their starting points. The train also offers a variety of seasonal and themed evening trips.

To the south, the Towpath Trail reaches the **Boston Store Visitor Center** and the nearby small town of **Peninsula,** with bike rentals, restaurants, galleries, and shops, including a

A River Is Reborn

When bald eagles began to nest along the Cuyahoga River in 2007, returning to the area for the first time in 70 years, it marked a milestone in the restoration of what had been one of America's most polluted waterways.

Oil slicks on the Cuyahoga River caught fire in 1969, bringing national attention to its sad history as an industrial and urban dumping ground. The fire provided impetus for the passage of the national Clean Water Act in 1972; it also inspired Randy Newman's song "Burn On."

More than 40 years of cleanup efforts and improved city sewer systems have helped revitalize nature along the Cuyahoga. Great blue herons established a nesting colony in 1985, otters raised pups in 2013, the threatened spotted turtle has returned, and the number of fish species in the national park has increased from four to more than 60.

In the words of the National Park Service: "Once a source of shame, the Cuyahoga is now an inspiration, demonstrating how people can heal a damaged river."

store operated by the nonprofit support group called the Conservancy for Cuyahoga Valley National Park *(conservancyforcvnp.org).* The village makes a great spot for a break during a walking or biking trip.

The most popular site in the park for bird-watchers, nature photographers, and anyone else interested in outdoor life is the **Beaver Marsh,** located near the railroad's Indigo

Lake station and the Towpath Trail's **Ira Trailhead.** This large wetland was once an automobile junkyard. After the vehicles were removed, beavers dammed the canal and created a marsh that's now home to muskrats, otters, waterfowl, songbirds, turtles, and a wealth of other wildlife species. The Towpath Trail crosses Beaver Marsh on a boardwalk, which is especially popular for wildlife-watching at dawn and dusk.

Waterfalls

The park's most famous waterfall, and justly so, is **Brandywine Falls,** a 65-foot cascade that makes its way down a series of sandstone ledges. Platforms provide various viewing levels, and the gorge below the falls is among the best places in the park to see spring wildflowers. A short drive west of the Boston Store Visitor Center is the trailhead for the short walk to **Blue Hen Falls,** a very pretty spot—especially in the fall when the maples and beeches turn color.

In the northern part of the national park (owned by Cleveland Metroparks) are **Tinkers Creek Gorge** and nearby **Bridal Veil Falls.** Dense hemlocks grow in this steep-sided valley among the hardwood trees, one of the reasons the gorge is a national natural landmark. Several smaller waterfalls can be seen along tributaries of Tinkers Creek. The scenic overlook on Gorge Parkway offers fine views.

Elsewhere in the Park

Donated to the public by a wealthy businessman, **Virginia Kendall Park** is a center for hiking and winter recreation, including sledding, cross-country skiing, and snowshoeing. Several historic Civilian Conservation Corps structures are located here.

The best-known Kendall Park attraction is the **Ledges,** where a 1.8-mile trail loops around striking sandstone formations that have eroded not only into ledges but also into horizontal cracks and deep vertical fissures large enough to walk through. (Be sure to read the interpretive signs about the underlying geology before walking the trail or you'll miss a large part of its appeal.)

Water evaporating from the sandstone creates a cooling effect, which in turn creates a microclimate where hemlocks, birches, and ferns flourish, as do such nesting birds as winter wren, Canada warbler, and hermit thrush, species that are rare elsewhere in Ohio.

The **Ledges Overlook** takes in a wonderful vista over the thickly wooded Cuyahoga Valley to ridges far to the west. This popular spot is famed for its sunset views.

Not far from Beaver Marsh, **Hale Farm & Village,** operated by the Western Reserve Historical Society (*wrhs.org;* 330-666-3711), re-creates 19th-century Ohio rural life through historic buildings, costumed interpreters, crafts demonstrations (such as blacksmithing and glassblowing), seasonal house and garden tours, and working farm animals.

The nearby **Everett Road Covered Bridge** is a reconstruction of an 1870s structure that was destroyed in a 1975 flood. Its appealingly nostalgic design is typical of the more than 2,000 covered bridges that were built in Ohio in the 19th century.

Living history participants demonstrate how the locks worked on the Ohio & Erie Canal.

Information

How to Get There

From Cleveland, take I-77 south and from Akron take I-77 north to I-271 and go north 3.7 miles to Ohio 303. Go east 1.8 miles to Riverview Rd. Head north 1.6 miles and turn east to reach the park visitor center.

When to Go

Late spring through fall is best for enjoying the Towpath Trail and hiking trails; colorful foliage is a bonus in autumn. Cross-country skiing and sledding are popular in winter. The Cuyahoga Valley Scenic Railroad operates year-round except for two weeks in Jan.

Visitor Center

The historic **Boston Store** is the park's main visitor center, located on Boston Mills Road, just east of Riverview Road. Open year-round.

Headquarters

15610 Vaughn Rd.
Brecksville, OH 44141
nps.gov/cuva
330-657-2752

Camping

Five primitive campsites (open Memorial Day weekend through late Oct.) are located near the historic Stanford House. For information, 330-657-2909.

Lodging

Two lodging options are located in the park. The 1848 **Inn at Brandywine Falls** (*innatbrandywinefalls.com;* 330-467-1812) offers B&B-style rooms. The **Stanford House** (330-657-2909) offers dorm-style rooms. Hotels are plentiful in nearby towns, including **Hudson** and **Independence.** Contact the Akron/Summit Convention & Visitors Bureau (*visitakron.summit.org*).

Isle Royale

Michigan

Established
April 3, 1940

571,790 acres

A fog-shrouded archipelago of glacier-scoured rock and dark coniferous forest, Isle Royale National Park comprises a main island known for its immigrant wolves and moose, and a flotilla of some 400 smaller isles set amid the clear icy waters of vast Lake Superior. Limited by a short visitor season and water-only access, this is one of the least visited parks. Yet those who see it once tend to return.

Isle Royale National Park was designed to remain a wilderness. And so it has—a wild place with no roads, few services, many foot trails, and a network of water routes for canoes and sea kayaks.

Isle Royale, 45 miles long and 9 miles wide, sports one hotel for overnighters. Rock Harbor Lodge is a homey, comfortable place at Rock Harbor. Beyond that are dozens of rustic campgrounds scattered on the shores of bays and lakes, and along the promontories.

Islands are defined by the water around them. Isle Royale includes a lot of water; its boundary stretches 4.5 miles from any exposed land. Shipwrecks ring the island as grim monuments to powerful currents and

Rock Harbor

points—**Windigo** is the other. Both have visitor centers. From Rock Harbor, trails and water routes stretch the length of the island. The **Greenstone Ridge Trail** traverses the island's rocky spine; numerous connecting trails offer a web of hiking options. Unusual for wilderness parks, some campsites feature shelters that provide relief from rain and insects.

Rock Harbor

The **visitor center,** on the ferry dock, is the place to go to get oriented and to pick up permits for wilderness trips. If you're not headed off on a multiday backpack or canoe trip, start with the **Scoville Point loop trail** (4.2 miles), a mostly level path that burrows through the forest, crosses wetlands via plank bridges, and offers oceanlike views of Lake Superior before emerging on the smooth, exposed rocky shelf of the point. Interpretive signs along the **Stoll Memorial** section of the trail (1.8 miles) touch on nature and history themes. Among the sights: abandoned mine shafts from the late 1840s, a chapter in the island's long history of copper extraction that begins with native peoples thousands of years ago. (Ancient diggings and pits have been identified in many parts of the island.) The loop trail follows the inner side of the peninsula, facing **Tobin Harbor.** The haunting cry of loons might accompany you.

In the other direction from Rock Harbor, a 3.8-mile loop follows the shore past pebbled coves and basalt headlands to **Suzys Cave,** an erosion feature caused by waves when the lake level was higher than it is now. Muddy patches of the trail can be

shifting fog. The forest, drenched by rain and frequent mist, stands in spongy carpets of moss and lichen.

Tea-colored creeks pour off the ridges, filling wetlands. Animals include, most famously, wolves, plus moose, foxes, river otters, snowshoe hares, beavers, bald eagles, and loons.

▶ HOW TO VISIT

Few visitors make it a day trip. The average stay is four days, no surprise considering the effort and preparation it takes to get here. Although private boats are allowed, most visitors arrive on ferries from Michigan, via Houghton or Copper Harbor, or from Minnesota, via Grand Portage. Activity centers on **Rock Harbor,** one of two ferry entry

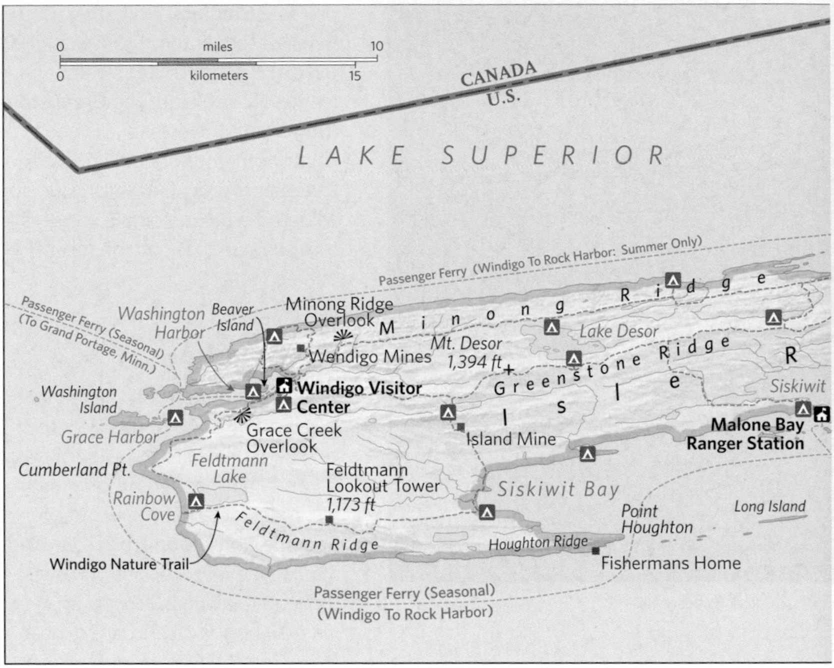
0 miles 10
0 kilometers 15
CANADA
U.S.
LAKE SUPERIOR
Passenger Ferry (Windigo To Rock Harbor: Summer Only)
Passenger Ferry (Seasonal) (To Grand Portage, Minn.)
Washington Harbor
Beaver Island
Minong Ridge Overlook
Minong Ridge
Lake Desor
Mt. Desor 1,394 ft
Wendigo Mines
Greenstone Ridge
Isle R
Siskiwit
Washington Island
Windigo Visitor Center
Grace Harbor
Grace Creek Overlook
Island Mine
Malone Bay Ranger Station
Cumberland Pt.
Feldtmann Lake
Feldtmann Lookout Tower 1,173 ft
Siskiwit Bay
Rainbow Cove
Feldtmann Ridge
Point Houghton
Long Island
Houghton Ridge
Windigo Nature Trail
Fishermans Home
Passenger Ferry (Seasonal) (Windigo To Rock Harbor)

slippery, but they are also the best places to find tracks of passing wildlife. Moose tracks are unmistakable: They look like the prints of very large deer. As for canine tracks, the small ones are fox; the large ones belong to wolves.

Other short trips near Rock Harbor require a boat, which can be rented in the park. On **Raspberry Island,** just a half-mile across from **Rock Harbor Channel,** an interpretive trail details the composition of a bog: It is a lake grown over by a floating mat of moss, orchids, sundew, pitcher plants, Labrador tea, and many other plants. Raspberry's neighboring islands also are worth exploring—but only if the water is calm.

Sheltered **Tobin Harbor** is ideal for slow exploration by canoe or kayak. Narrow channels and little islands stretching 7 miles to **Blake Point** provide endless variety. Listen for loons; this is good habitat for these denizens of the North Woods.

Stretch your legs on the 1-mile climb to **Lookout Louise.** The trail begins at a boat dock partway up Tobin Harbor. Watch for moose while skirting **Hidden Lake,** and for carnivorous pitcher plants in marshy areas along the planked walkway. The trail climbs past **Monument Rock,** a sea stack carved by the stormy lake when water levels were higher.

After winding through birch and conifers over mossy rock slabs, the path ends at a high breezy ledge, a fine place for a picnic lunch. At your

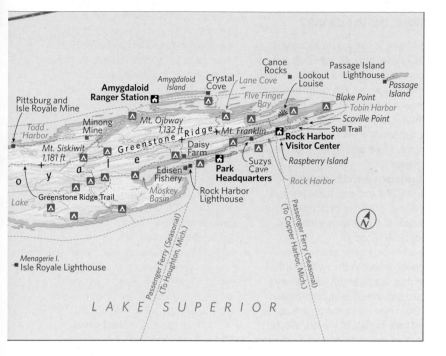

feet sprawls an intricately formed landscape of narrow bays, rocky islets, dark forest, and the gleaming expanse of Lake Superior. Ambitious hikers can walk 9.4 miles back to Rock Harbor via the **Greenstone Ridge** and **Mount Franklin.**

The **Rock Harbor Lodge,** together with the park service, combines guided boat trips with interpretive walks to several locations including historic **Edisen Fishery** and **Rock Harbor Lighthouse;** and to **Passage Island,** several miles off the island's eastern tip, with its hidden harbor and lighthouse.

Arrangements for guided boat trips, interpretive walks *(fee),* and kayak, canoe, and motorboat rental are made at the Rock Harbor Lodge office *(rockharborlodge.com).*

Windigo

A wilderness promontory, then a copper mine, a private hunting club, and back to wilderness as part of the national park, this area provides a few services at the far end of the island, including a **visitor center,** campground, camp store, and rustic cabins. Windigo is reached via ferry from Rock Harbor Portage.

Pick up a trail guide at the visitor center, and follow the 1.2-mile **Windigo Nature Trail** through a mixed forest of cedar, birch, and maple. Hike 2 miles to **Grace Creek Overlook** on Feldtmann Ridge, or 3 miles in the other direction to a lookout on **Minong Ridge.**

Paddle (in a rental boat, kayak, or canoe) the protected shoreline of Washington Harbor and, if conditions

Wolves on the Brink?

Isle Royale is famous for its wolves and moose. Virtually removed from human influence, with a limited number competing species, the island provides a unique outdoor laboratory to study the interactions of two species and their habitat. Wolves are the only large predator. There are no bears, coyotes, or cougars.

A research project, started in 1958 and still running, is the longest continuous predator-prey study ever undertaken. (For information, visit *isleroyalewolf.org.*)

Neither animal is native. Moose probably arrived in the early 1900s, swimming out from the north shore of Lake Superior. Wolves came later, also from Minnesota, loping across the frozen lake surface in the late 1940s. Since then, populations have fluctuated dramatically, with wolves peaking at 50 and moose at almost 2,400, then falling dramatically. In the face of poor forage, hard winter conditions, and abundant ticks, moose numbers collapsed to around 500 in 1996.

For wolves, fewer moose (as prey) was an issue, but their more serious problem was genetic. Given their isolation, they suffer from an absence of interaction with mainland wolves. Pup survival has fallen. Breeding opportunities have diminished.

In 2014, only about 10 wolves survived, while the moose population climbed toward 1,000. Researchers judge that without fresh genetic stock—that is, the arrival or introduction of new wolves—the current population is doomed, a fate that could have a lasting impact on the ecology of the island.

permit, explore the small islands just beyond. Float over the wreck of the passenger ship *America*, sunk in 1928. It was one of 25 ships claimed by the rocky shoals, fog banks, and storm winds of Isle Royale; its bow is visible just under the surface. This is one of ten wrecks open to scuba divers.

Backcountry

Backcountry travel is done by boat or on foot, or a combination. Crossing the island the short way, trails go up and down and up again. It appears as if the island was stroked lengthwise by a giant comb. Ridges protrude like old bones, thinly forested and often with good views of open water. Between ridges, you'll find lakes, bogs, beaver ponds, and dense forest.

To hike the entire **Greenstone Ridge Trail** is the ambition for some, but other routes can provide more variety. To camp in secluded places like **Moskey Basin** or **Lane Cove**, combined with some time high on the Greenstone, makes for a delightful trip. If you're willing to portage, you can camp and paddle on inland lakes; or loop through the intricate channels at the east end of the island, and return by crossing over inland lakes.

In planning, keep in mind that island trails are not always smoothly constructed. In many areas, they resemble game trails, following the natural terrain. They can be rocky or muddy, and walking can be slow.

It's wise to be conservative when planning distances. As for boating, Lake Superior's moods are infamously changeable and potentially dangerous. Be prudent; plan for the unexpected; allow extra time.

The park is accessible only by boat or seaplane.

Information

How to Get There

From Houghton, MI, the Park Service (*nps.gov/isro*) runs the *Ranger III* to Rock Harbor, a 6-hour trip. The Royale Line (*isleroyale.com*) runs from Copper Harbor, MI, to Rock Harbor in 3.5 hours. From Grand Portage, MN, the Grand Portage-Isle Royale Transportation Line (*isleroyaleboats.com*) reaches Windigo and Rock Harbor in 2.5 hours, with pickup and drop-off service along the way. Isle Royale Seaplanes (*royaleairservice .com*) flies seaplanes from Houghton to Rock Harbor, a 40-minute trip.

When to Go

The park is open mid-April through Oct. Weather can be unsettled in spring and fall; stormy conditions on Lake Superior can affect transport. July and Aug. are the most popular months.

Visitor Centers

Visitor centers at **Windigo** and **Rock Harbor** are open daily in season, with reduced hours outside of July and Aug. A visitor center at park headquarters in **Houghton** is open year-round.

Headquarters

800 East Lakeshore Dr.
Houghton, MI 49931
nps.gov/isro
906-482-0984

Camping

Non-fee permits are required for all camping and overnight boat docking or anchoring. Thirty-six backcountry campgrounds include 17 with group sites; many have screened shelters in addition to tent sites. Parties of 1 to 6 get permits on arrival (no reserved sites); groups of 7 to a maximum of 10 can reserve sites and must obtain permits in advance through park headquarters.

Lodging

The **Rock Harbor Lodge** (*rockharbor lodge.com;* 906-337-4993) offers rooms with private baths, plus a dining room and a dockside store. Also available are rustic one-room cabins in Windigo.

Theodore Roosevelt

North Dakota

Established
April, 25, 1947

70,467 acres

Only one of our national parks is named for a person, and Theodore Roosevelt National Park is a most fitting honor. President Theodore Roosevelt is arguably the most influential conservationist in American history. It was his experience in North Dakota—a place with "a desolate, grim beauty of its own, that has a curious fascination for me"—that set him on the path that would see him establish five national parks, 18 national monuments, and scores of wildlife reserves and national forests.

Roosevelt came to the region in 1883 to hunt, and later entered the cattle business. Though he fell in love with the area and the "strenuous life" of the frontier, he soon became dismayed by the decline of wildlife and degradation of the environment.

"It is not what we have that will make us a great nation; it is the way in which we use it," he later wrote.

What is this landscape that so inspired Roosevelt? It began to take shape about 60 million years ago, when material eroded from the Rocky

Park badlands

Mountains formed the Great Plains. Ash from western volcanoes contributed additional layers, as did vegetation that was buried and transformed into lignite coal.

Streams, including today's Little Missouri River, cut into the varied rock strata, creating an astonishing variety of canyons, bluffs, buttes, and rounded mounds in colors from pink to brown, yellowish-buff to gray. Roosevelt described the land as "so fantastically broken in form and so bizarre in color as to seem hardly properly to belong to this earth." Around these badlands stretch wide grasslands, in places giving a sense of the vast prairie where American Indians lived and hunted.

Bison are the most conspicuous and popular of the park's animals, but there are also pronghorn, elk, bighorn sheep, mule and white-tailed deer, coyotes, badgers, porcupines, and black-tailed prairie dogs.

The park comprises two main units about 70 road miles apart, plus one smaller unit. Each main unit features a scenic drive. Hiking trails, both short and long, allow a fuller exploration of this diverse and beautiful landscape.

► HOW TO VISIT

If you have very limited time, tour the **South Unit,** stopping at the **visitor center** to learn about Roosevelt's legacy. Follow the 36-mile **scenic loop drive,** pausing at overlooks and prairie-dog towns (burrows) along the way. Take time to walk at least one short trail such as **Wind Canyon.** With more time, hike a nature trail or enjoy a ranger-led walk or program.

It takes about an hour from the South Unit to reach the **North Unit,** where you'll find a 14-mile **scenic drive** (out and back) with far-reaching views of the Little Missouri River bottomlands. Consider the 1.5-mile **Caprock Coulee Nature Trail,** among the park's best short hikes. A trail brochure is available at the trailhead.

South Unit

Many people first see the park at the **Painted Canyon Visitor Center,** located just off I-94. The facility, perched at the top of a bluff, offers stunning views of the rugged, colorful badlands below; park staff can provide information and advice. The only access into the park from here is via hiking trails.

The **national park entrance** is located on Pacific Avenue, the main

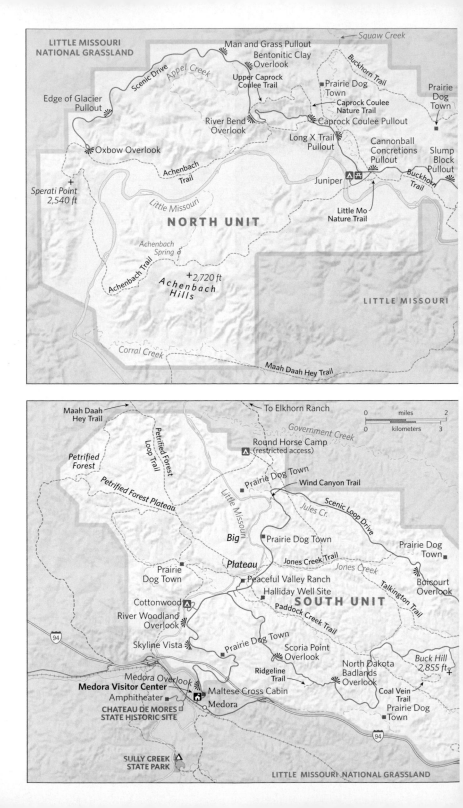

street through the historic town of **Medora.** At the **visitor center** you'll find a small but very worthwhile museum devoted mostly to Theodore Roosevelt's "free and hardy life" here in the 1880s. On display are his knife, telescope, and rifle, as well as the blood-stained shirt he was wearing during an attempted assassination in Milwaukee in 1912. (Undaunted, Roosevelt insisted on giving his scheduled 90-minute speech.) While you're in the visitor center, take time

Teddy Roosevelt's Maltese Cross log cabin, built from hand-hewn timbers and chinked with mortar

to watch the introductory video, *Refuge of the American Spirit.*

Just outside of Medora stands the small **Maltese Cross Cabin,** where Roosevelt lived for a time, beginning in 1883. Originally located about 7 miles south, the cabin contains a few of Roosevelt's personal items, including a traveling trunk. Roosevelt later built a dwelling at the Elkhorn Ranch, about 35 miles north (see p. 117).

The South Unit's 36-mile **Scenic Loop Drive** ranks as its major attraction, winding through a sampling of park terrain, from badlands to grasslands to bottomland, with tall cottonwood trees along the Little Missouri River. The route offers a number of panoramic overlooks and trailheads for short walks and longer treks. Bison can been seen anywhere along the way, as can feral horses, descendants of those that roamed the region when Roosevelt lived here. Mule deer,

A Late 19th-Century Misunderstanding

On the outskirts of Medora stands the Chateau de Mores, a house built by a larger-than-life French aristocrat named Antoine de Vallombrosa, also called the Marquis de Mores. In 1883 the marquis came to North Dakota and founded the town of Medora (named for his wealthy wife), where he built a slaughterhouse with the aim of shipping meat to eastern markets by railroad.

A haughty man who antagonized local residents, the marquis was an acquaintance of Theodore Roosevelt; the two visited each other's homes. However, when the marquis was charged with murder in the shooting of a local ruffian, he suspected that Roosevelt had been involved in the legal proceedings. The marquis sent Roosevelt a letter that ended with an offer of a duel. (It was no idle threat; the marquis fought many duels in his life and was said to have killed more than a dozen men.) Roosevelt responded that he had nothing to do with the murder charge, and the issue was dropped. The marquis was later acquitted.

white-tailed deer, and elk are seen most often at dawn and dusk; pronghorn are occasionally spotted.

You'll definitely want to stop at one of the roadside prairie-dog towns to watch the activities of these rodents and listen to their varied whistles and barks. As is the case with all wild animals (and especially with bison), don't approach or try to feed them.

The **Ridgeline Trail** is a 0.6-mile loop with displays on park geology and park environmental factors, including fire and erosion. A short side road leads to the 0.8-mile **Coal Vein Trail,** site of a true natural oddity. Here, a vein of coal burned continuously from 1955 to 1977, literally baking the adjacent sand and clay into hardened rock.

Continuing around the Scenic Loop Drive, you'll reach the **Boicourt Overlook,** with one of the finest vistas in the park. It's a great place from which to watch sunsets. A short trail leads from the road to viewpoints. The bumpy, lumpy landscape below is the result of thousands of years of erosion washing away soil and softer rock and leaving scattered small buttes and hills formed of harder materials.

Where the road reaches its northernmost point and loops around back south, be sure to make the short climb on the **Wind Canyon Trail** to a wonderful perch on a rocky bluff overlooking a bend in the Little Missouri River. This may be the most scenic spot in the South Unit and makes for another fine sunset-viewing site.

If you're looking for a longer walk that's not too strenuous, consider the **Jones Creek Trail,** which traverses the territory between the east and west sides of the Scenic Loop Drive. It's

Rock formations of eroded mud buttes

3.5 miles in total, but unless you can arrange a shuttle from one trailhead to another, it's best to simply walk the trail as far as you like and then double back to the beginning. Starting on the western end, note how the cooler, north-facing slopes on your right are more wooded than the drier, sunnier, south-facing slopes on your left.

Down in the bottomlands of the Little Missouri River, **Peaceful Valley Ranch** dates from the 1880s. It was a dude ranch from 1918 into the 1930s.

A good way to explore what is believed to be the third largest collection of petrified wood in the lower 48 states is to take a half-hour drive on Forest Service roads to a trailhead on the western edge of the South Unit visitor center, where you can get detailed directions. A high-clearance vehicle is recommended. Check with a ranger regarding weather and road conditions.

From the trailhead, it's a 1.5-mile hike out and back to reach the area with petrified wood, though you can explore more on a 10-mile loop trail if you want. Fossils have also been found on this site, which was a swamp forest around 50 million years ago. It is illegal to take or disturb petrified wood, fossils, or any other natural features in the park.

Those with a special interest in Theodore Roosevelt and his legacy might want to make the trip to the **Elkhorn Ranch Unit,** site of the retreat where he lived at times from 1885 to 1892. Roosevelt called this his "home ranch," and he spent much time sitting in a rocking chair on the veranda. Almost nothing remains of the house, but visitors can walk among the cottonwood trees just as Roosevelt did. Ask at the South Unit Visitor Center for road conditions and directions to the site, which is about 35 miles north of Medora and requires a drive of more than an hour over roads where a high-clearance vehicle is recommended.

North Unit

Only a small percentage of visitors make the drive to this part of the park, located 54 miles north of I-94. That's a shame, because the North Unit encompasses rewarding trails, picturesque expanses of prairie, and some of the best long-distance panoramas in the park.

Access to the area is via a **scenic drive** that winds 14 miles west from US 85, first following the Little Missouri River and then climbing to a grassy plateau. This is an out-and-back road, not a loop. Bison may be seen anywhere along the route.

As you enter the park, watch in the first 5 miles for longhorn cattle. The park keeps a herd of around 10 steers as a connection to the local ranching culture and the historic Long X Trail. This route was used by cowboys in the late 19th century to move cattle from southern states to the vast grasslands of North Dakota to the northern Great Plains for summer grazing.

A side road leads to the pleasant **Juniper Campground,** in the cottonwood trees beside the Little Missouri River. The 1.1-mile-loop **Little Mo Nature Trail** is a self-guided nature walk through this bottomland habitat. The first section of the trail is wheelchair accessible.

Be sure to make a stop across the main road from the campground entrance to see the collection of unusual **cannonball concretions** in the bluff. These rounded objects form when hard minerals are cemented together by water within softer sedimentary rock. The concretions becomes exposed when the surrounding material erodes away.

About 1.5 miles past the campground is the trailhead for one of the park's best short hikes. Pick up a brochure before walking the **Caprock Coulee Nature Trail.** You'll learn a lot about geology and vegetation while enjoying scenic landscapes.

A coulee is a narrow valley; the trail winds among bluffs showing seams of lignite coal, volcanic bentonite clay, and examples of petrified wood. It's 1.6 miles to the end of the nature trail and back. If you like, you can continue beyond that point to make a 4.1-mile loop, climbing to the **River Bend Overlook** before returning to the parking area.

While prairie-dog towns are easily seen in the South Unit, none are visible from the road in the North Unit. To reach one on foot, take the **Buckhorn Trail** from the Caprock Coulee trailhead and walk about a mile.

Watch for bighorn sheep in the next stretch of road as you continue to River Bend Overlook. The view here is renowned as one of the most photographed vistas in North Dakota. A historic Civilian Conservation Corps–era shelter sits on a high bluff overlooking a long bend in the Little Missouri River far below. (Note: Photographs are best taken in early morning or late afternoon rather than in the harsh light of midday.)

The scenic drive passes through prairie to reach its end at the **Oxbow Overlook,** with another splendid panorama of curves in the Little Missouri. For a different angle on this scene, walk the first mile or so of the **Achenbach Trail** down from the overlook to **Sperati Point,** the narrowest point on the Little Missouri River's route through the badlands hills.

Prairie dog

Information

How to Get There

From Bismarck, ND (about 130 miles east), take I-94 west to Medora.

When to Go

Summer is the season with highest visitation. Fall offers colorful foliage and fewer crowds. Winter brings an average of 30 total inches of snow and lows in the single digits. Portions of park roads may be closed in winter.

Visitor Centers

The park's main visitor center is located at the entrance to the South Unit in **Medora.** The **Painted Canyon Visitor Center** is on I-94, 5 miles east of Medora. The **North Unit Visitor Center** is along the scenic drive west of US 85. All visitor centers are open year-round.

Headquarters

Box 7
315 Second Ave.
Medora, ND 58645
nps.gov/thro
701-623-4466

Camping

Cottonwood Campground in the South Unit (72 campsites) and **Juniper Campground** in the North Unit (50 campsites) are open year-round and accommodate tents, trailers, and RVs (no hookups). A free permit is required for backcountry camping.

Lodging

There are no lodgings in the park. Accommodations can be found in **Medora,** adjacent to the South Unit, and in **Dickinson,** 35 miles east. Medora Area Convention & Visitors Bureau (*medorand.com; 701-623-4830*).

THEODORE ROOSEVELT EST 1978

Theodore Roosevelt Excursions

Upper Missouri River Breaks National Monument (BLM)
Fort Benton, Montana

▷ Home to a wide array of plant life, wildlife, geologic features, and recreational opportunities, the Upper Missouri River Breaks National Monument covers 375,000 acres in Montana. The 149-mile Wild and Scenic River flows through the monument. Visitors float the river, fish the waters, and marvel at the history of their surroundings—where Lewis and Clark themselves once roamed. Located 300 miles west of Theodore Roosevelt National Park via Mont. 200 W. *blm.gov/mt/st/en/fo/umrbnm;* 406-622-4000.

Little Missouri National Grassland
Dickerson, North Dakota

▷ Rugged and unspoiled, the Little Missouri National Grassland is one of four grasslands and two experimental forests that make up the Dakota Prairie Grassland. Ten area campgrounds (open late May through Labor Day) provide a base for hiking, horseback riding, and wildlife-watching. The grasslands surround Theodore Roosevelt National Park. Visitor information can be found in Dickinson, ND, off I-94. *fs.usda.gov/recarea/dpg/recarea/?recid=79469recarea/?recid=79469;* 701-250-4443.

Lostwood National Wildlife Refuge
North Dakota & Montana

▷ Ducks, marsh birds, grouse, hawks, Baird's sparrows, and Sprague's pipets as well as badgers and moose inhabit the mixed grasslands and wildflower fields of this Globally Important Bird Area. The 27,589 acres of Lostwood offer a scenic drive, grouse-viewing blind, nature trails, and cross-country skiing opportunities. Open year-round. Located off N. Dak. 8, about 135 miles northeast of Theodore Roosevelt National Park. *fws.gov/refuge/lostwood;* 701-848-2722.

Lake Ilo National Wildlife Refuge
West Central North Dakota

▷ A diverse array of wildlife and a waterfowl nesting area draw visitors to the Lake Ilo National Wildlife Refuge. As many as 100,000 birds fill the park in the fall. Nature hikes, archaeological exhibits, and scenic drives are options here; portions of the lake are open for fishing and boating. Located about 50 miles southeast of Theodore Roosevelt National Park via N. Dak. 200E. *fws.gov/lakeilo;* 701-548-8110.

Cross Ranch State Park
Center, North Dakota

▷ One of the five state parks in North Dakota officially named a Lewis and Clark National Historic Trail Site, Cross Ranch is located along the Missouri River. Comprising 589 acres of rolling grasslands and river-bottom forests, Cross Ranch State Park is the perfect venue for both summer and winter recreational activities. Offered here are boating, camping, hiking, and cross-country skiing. Open year-round. Located 130 miles east of Theodore Roosevelt National Park via I–94. *parkrec.nd.gov/parks/crsp/crsp;* 701-794-3731.

Sully Creek State Park
Medora, North Dakota

▷ Located in the heart of the North Dakota Badlands, Sully Creek State Park is one of North Dakota's smallest state's parks, but there's still lots to do: horseback riding, canoeing, hiking, biking, and camping. Get to experience the Badlands up close. Open from early April through late Nov. Surrounded by Theodore Roosevelt National Park, 2 miles south of Medora, ND, off I-94E. *parkrec.nd.gov/parks/scsp/scsp;* 701-623-2024.

Voyageurs

Minnesota

Established
April 8, 1975

218,054 acres

For a well-prepared visitor, Voyageurs National Park can be paradise. Imagine camping on your own private island, cooking freshly caught walleye for dinner, and waking in the morning to the sound of loons and the sight of a bald eagle flying over the sparkling water of a beautiful lake—all set within the legendary North Woods of Minnesota.

This scene and similar idyllic interludes await travelers to Voyageurs. The park is 40 percent water, comprising four major lakes—Rainy, Kabetogama, Namakan, and Sand Point—and dozens of smaller ones. Relatively little of the park is accessible without a boat.

Three visitor centers and a few hiking trails are found on the mainland.

Otherwise, Voyageurs is a place of water-centered attractions and activities, with 655 miles of shoreline, more than 500 islands, several historic sites, and secluded campsites on islands as well as on lakeshores. (All campsites in the park can be reached by boat only.)

Many Voyageurs visitors are Minnesotans who use their own kayaks, canoes, motorboats, and

Lake Kabetogama

location to avoid crossing the international boundary without the proper permits. (For international permits, 807-274-3655.)

As for the land, in places volcanic bedrock of the Canadian Shield has been exposed by glacial action, revealing greenstone, a type of metamorphosed basalt 2.7 billion years old. Greenstone, granite, schist, and other rocks form picturesque bluffs.

Glaciers retreated about 10,000 years ago, recently enough that only a thin layer of soil has formed atop the rock. The vast stands of white pine that once covered the land are gone, cut by timber operations more than a century ago.

The forest that has grown up represents a blend of boreal woodland and southern temperate forest. In the autumn, the green of conifers such as pine, fir, spruce, and white cedar is complemented by the colorful foliage of maple, birch, aspen, and oak.

White-tailed deer, wolves, and moose roam the woods; otters, beavers, and muskrats make homes near lakes and streams. Eagles and loons are commonly spotted on the water. Campers must use bear-proof containers for food storage to discourage visits from the plentiful black bears.

houseboats to cruise the lakes. This doesn't mean that those without a boat can't enjoy the park. Rangers lead seasonal boat tours, and local firms rent a range of watercraft, including houseboats.

Voyageurs took its name from the famed 18th-century French Canadian adventurers who paddled canoes along lakes and rivers, transporting trade goods westward and furs eastward between Montreal and the vast inland forests of Canada. So influential was this trade route that a 1783 treaty incorporated part of it as the boundary between the United States and Canada.

Fifty-six miles of the former trade route pass through Voyageurs. Boaters need to be aware of their

▶ HOW TO VISIT

Plan for at least a two-day visit. If you don't bring a boat and don't plan to rent one, check the schedule of ranger-led boat tours and programs ahead of time. (Otherwise you could arrive and find there's little to do other than hike.) Be aware that the park has three visitor centers that are separated by about 50 highway miles; boat

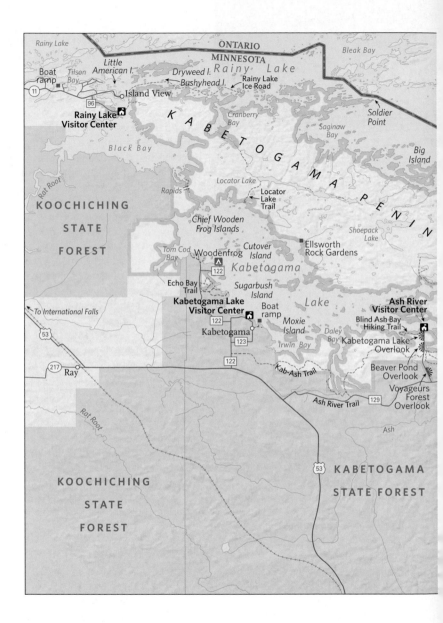

tours and other activities vary among them. If you do plan to take a boat to a campsite, remember that sites must be reserved in advance *(recreation .gov;* 877-444-6777). This ensures that everyone who sets out across a lake will have a place to stay, and eliminates the competition for sites between those in motorized craft and paddlers.

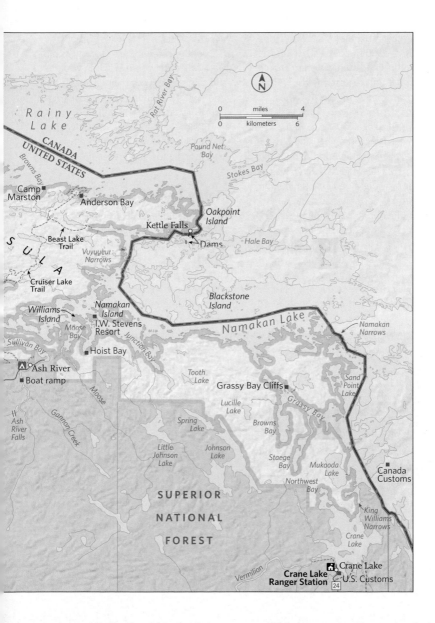

A good navigational map is vital for boating these lakes, to learn the location of submerged rocks and other hazards. Mobile phones work intermittently.

While some campsites are located on fairly protected bays, others require a trip across lake expanses where sudden bad weather can create waves up to four feet. A radio that receives weather alerts is a good idea. A marine-band radio is also helpful.

Visitors interested in history should join a boat tour to **Kettle Falls** or **Little American Island.** The **North Canoe Voyage,** a paddling trip *(fee)* aboard a reproduction of a voyageurs craft, is fun for adults and children five and older. On the mainland, the **Blind Ash Bay Hiking Trail** near the **Ash River Visitor Center** provides a good introduction to the North Woods environment.

On the Kabetogama Peninsula, the park has canoes available for rent. You must make a reservation and get a key from the visitor center. Then, in your own boat (or using a guide), you make your way to a trailhead. Next, you hike to an inland lake (trails range from very short to several miles), unlock the canoe, and paddle to a campsite. Depending on where or when you go, this can assure you of a peaceful and solitary adventure in the back-country wilderness.

(To prevent the spread of invasive species, private watercraft can't be transported to inland lakes.)

Rainy Lake

The **Rainy Lake Visitor Center,** 11 miles east of International Falls, is the only visitor center open year-round. It offers exhibits on nature and history, a bookstore, a video introducing the park, and weather updates plus advice from rangers. This is where you

A kayaker watches a rainbow arc over the lake.

Winter Fun

Although many park activities aren't an option in the often-severe winter season of northern Minnesota, the Rainy Lake Visitor Center remains open year-round. The park offers 16 miles of trails for cross-country skiing and snowshoeing; check the schedule for ranger-led snowshoe hikes. Snowshoes can be checked out for free use, and the park offers rental of cross-country skis for adults and free ski use for children.

Snowmobilers can cruise more than 110 miles of marked trails. Many anglers use snowmobiles to reach their favorite spots for ice fishing. Once the ice is thick enough, Voyageurs creates two ice roads across the lake. One begins at the Rainy Lake Visitor Center and runs to various locations depending on conditions. The other runs between the Kabetogama Lake and Ash River visitor centers.

On moonless nights, travelers can look for the shimmering colors of the aurora borealis (northern lights).

As a bonus for winter visitors to the park, this is the time when wolves are most likely to be seen, crossing the ice in packs.

sign up for a variety of ranger-led programs. In addition, this is the center for winter activities in the park (see above).

The short, easy **Ethno-botanical Garden Trail,** outside the visitor center, tells of the relationship between the Ojibwe Indians and their environment, including the plants they used for food and medicine.

The 1.7-mile **Oberholtzer Trail** begins steps from the visitor center and winds through mixed woodland to two overlooks of marsh and forest.

Several ranger-led boat tours leave from the Rainy Lake dock. The 1.5-hour Gold Mine Tour visits **Little American Island**, site of a short-lived gold-mining boom in the 1890s. Mining equipment can be seen on a short walk. About a mile east is **Bushyhead Island,** where a mineshaft is carved into the rock.

The 2.5-hour Grand Tour allows ample time for wildlife-watching (usually with views of active bald eagle nests) and also visits **Little American Island.** On the 1.5-hour North Canoe Voyage, participants help paddle a 26-foot-long reproduction of the kind of canoe used by the original voyageurs to transport trade goods, including beaver pelts. During the outing, tour leaders share details of 18th-century life here. The 2-hour Family Canoe Trip is an easy wildlife-spotting ride around calm waters. It is suitable even for beginning paddlers age five and older. Boat tours also depart on certain days from Rainy Lake to Kettle Falls.

Kabetogama Lake

Although this lake is large—60 miles long and 12 miles wide—you can safely explore it on your own.

The **Kabetogama Lake Visitor Center**, about 28 miles southeast of International Falls, on Rte. 122, is open from late May through late September, and provides interactive exhibits, a park video, a bookstore, and an information desk. Boat tours to several of the park's most interesting destinations begin here. Like all the visitor centers, this one is an embarkation point for private boaters heading to various campsites, picnic areas, and historic sites around the lakes.

One of the most fascinating historic sites in the park is **Kettle Falls,** located in the narrows where Namakan Lake flows into Rainy Lake. A small dam has taken the place of the falls here, but the main attraction is the circa 1910 **Kettle Falls Hotel.**

Now operated by a concessioner, this inn, which is on the National Register of Historic Places, offers meals and lodging in rustic rooms. The hotel underwent restoration in the 1980s, in part to correct the foundation problems that had given it the nickname "Tiltin' Hilton." (The sloping floor in the bar was left intact for old times' sake.) The 5.5-hour Kettle Falls Cruise includes time for lunch at the hotel and a short tour of the dam.

Another of the park's historic destinations is **Hoist Bay,** reached on a 2.5-hour boat tour from the Kabetogama Lake Visitor Center. Once the site of a busy logging camp, it was later rebuilt as a resort, which operated until 1973. Cabins, the kitchen, the boat house, and an ice house are among the structures still standing.

The quirkiest attraction on the shore of Lake Kabetogama is **Ellsworth Rock Gardens,** which can be visited on a 2-hour cruise. A Chicago couple spent summers here before the national park was established. Over a span of 22 years, the husband created an odd but appealing sculpture garden on a rock bluff— a charmingly random array of abstract forms where visitors can put their imaginations to good use. This makes a great spot for a picnic or just to relax for a while.

Voyageurs National Park doesn't have a large variety of loop hikes, but one can be found 3 miles west of the Kabetogama Lake Visitor Center, off Rte. 122.

The 2.5-mile **Echo Bay Trail** passes through attractive woods and reaches an overlook at a wetland that's good for wildlife-watching.

Ash River

The **Ash River Visitor Center,** about 37 miles southeast of International Falls, is open from late May through late September. The visitor center is housed in a historic lodge, and the launch area here is popular with boaters. For kayakers and canoeists, Ash River is close to an area of small bays and narrow passages between lakes Kabetogama and Namakan, providing sheltered water on which to paddle to campsites.

A popular short trail is the **Blind Ash Bay Hiking Trail,** a 2.8-mile loop through a mixed hardwood-conifer forest to a small bay lined with cattails. Not far away, a very short walk leads to a viewing platform at the **Beaver Pond Overlook,** a great place to sit, relax, and look—not just for beaver but for moose (the largest and most impressive creature here), deer, waterfowl, and other wildlife.

The 28-mile **Kab-Ash Trail**, which runs roughly parallel to the southern shore of Kabetogama Lake, serves as a hiking trail in summer and an ungroomed cross-country ski trail in winter. Several trailheads allow access to various sections for shorter hikes through forest and wetlands.

Autumn landscape

Information

How to Get There

From Duluth, MN (About 160 miles south), take US 53 north to the International Falls area.

When to Go

The main park season runs from mid-May to late Sept., when the greatest number of ranger-led programs are offered. Peak visitation comes around July 4. Many visitors enjoy mid-Sept. for the lessened crowds and beautiful fall foliage. Winters are snowy and very cold; the average low in Jan. is –8°F.

Visitor Centers

Rainy Lake, the park's year-round visitor center, is located 11 miles east of International Falls; take Minn. 11 to Rte. 96. The **Kabetogama Lake** and **Ash River** visitor centers are southeast of International Falls off US 53. These sites are open from late May through late Sept.

Headquarters

360 Hwy. 11 East
International Falls, MN 56649
nps.gov/voya
218-283-6600

Camping

All campsites (some 20 day sites and 279 campsites) require boat access; a permit is required for all camping and overnight use *(recreation.gov; 877-444-6777).* Drive-up camping is available at nearby state-run sites and at private sites.

Lodging

The only lodging in the park is the concessioner-run **Kettle Falls Hotel** *(kettlefallshotel.com),* which can be reached only by boat. There are numerous lodging opportunities in **International Falls** and **Orr,** and dozens of lakeside resorts in areas near the park boundary. For info on places to stay outside the park: *dvnpmn.com.* Also check *rainylake .org* and *kabetogama.com.*

Wind Cave

South Dakota

Established
January 9, 1903

33,851 acres

When rangers at Wind Cave National Park describe it as the "best of both worlds," they are referring to the realms below and above the Earth's surface. Underground lies one of the world's most complex and unusual caves; above is a globally significant expanse of mixed-grass prairie, home to wildlife—from massive bison to playful prairie dogs to sky blue mountain bluebirds.

It was distinctive geology that inspired President Theodore Roosevelt to designate Wind Cave America's eighth national park—the first set aside to protect a cave. In 1913, bison, elk, and pronghorn were reintroduced. (Large animals were wiped out by hunters in the 19th century.) Today, these reintroduced animals and many other wildlife species thrive in this prairie-woodland ecosystem.

The word "cave" is part of the park's name. Indeed, a subterranean tour is a must during a visit to this Black Hills site. Those who walk through the scenic subterranean passageways of Wind Cave—one of the world's longest—can admire a trove

A limestone cave's calcite crystal formations

of formations, including abundant displays of boxwork, an unusual formation composed of thin calcite structures resembling honeycombs.

But a visit to Wind Cave shouldn't end with a return to the surface.

The park's mixed-grass prairie is an ecosystem that has largely disappeared elsewhere in North America in the face of agriculture, ranching, and other development. Drive along one of the park's roads; take a walk on one of its trails, which range from easygoing to backcountry strenuous.

From many viewpoints in the park, the land seems little changed from the days when the Lakota made it their home. Bison and pronghorn graze on rolling grassland; a coyote lopes through a prairie-dog colony, hoping for an easy meal; a golden eagle soars over a distant ridge, where ponderosa pines separate the prairie and the deep blue sky. Some 60 percent of the park is open grassland, aiding wildlife-spotters.

► HOW TO VISIT

You can experience the park in one or two days. Wind Cave's **visitor center** is located off US 385, in the southern part of the park and houses exhibits on cave geology, wildlife, and park history. A film entitled *Wind Cave: One Park, Two Worlds* is shown regularly. Visitors may enter Wind Cave only on one of the many ranger-guided tours. All tours leave from the visitor center.

If you have time for a second cave tour, take the **Natural Entrance Tour,** the **Fairgrounds Tour,** or the **Garden of Eden Tour** (shortest and easiest).

For the best chance to see bison, drive Park Roads 5 and 6. Prairie dogs are usually easy to see along US 385 and S. Dak. 87. The **Rankin Ridge Nature Trail** offers fine views of the surrounding landscape, while the **Wind Cave Canyon Trail** offers an easy stroll into the park's interior.

Wind Cave

American Indians knew of the cave; some tribes continue to consider it a sacred site. The first recorded entry to the cave took place in 1881, after local settlers noticed air rushing into and out of the entrance (the "wind" of the park's name). Soon, a tourism business, the Wonderful Wind Cave Improvement Company, sprung up to guide tourists through cave

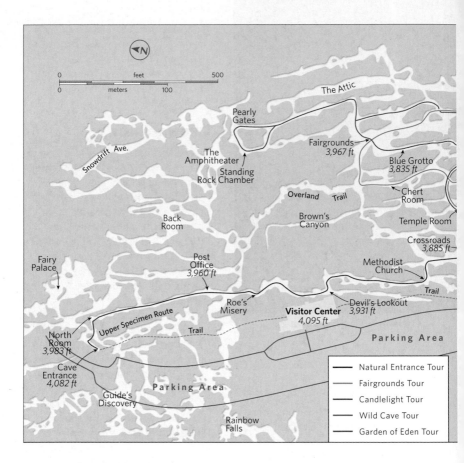

passageways. In those days, visitors could buy a piece of boxwork formation for 15 cents. (For the sake of resource management, at least, it's a good thing Wind Cave was declared a national park, where it is forbidden to remove any natural items.)

The caverns were formed in limestone deposited on a seafloor some 350 million years ago. Masses of gypsum formed within the limestone. When the gypsum swelled, small cracks formed. More gypsum filled the cracks, and mineral-rich water worked to convert the gypsum into crystal-like calcite.

This process is reflected in Wind Cave's most distinctive feature, its famed boxwork. Over time, water dissolved large passageways that form the modern cave, as well as the softer limestone between the calcite, leaving honeycomblike crystal "fins" called boxwork. These delicate formations are as picturesque as they are rare. Wind Cave contains about 95 percent of the world's known boxwood. Because Wind Cave is drier than many caves, it has few stalagmites and stalactites, which are formed as the result of water dripping through limestone.

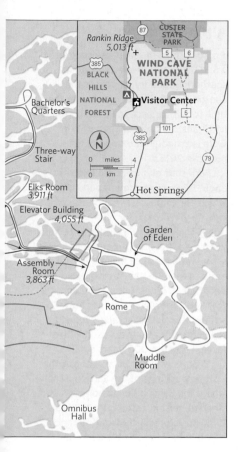

(clusters of small round formations), and flowstone (calcite deposited by a thin sheet of running water).

The Natural Entrance Tour passes by the hole in the ground where the first explorers entered before descending 115 steps to begin its 0.3-mile route. It features abundant boxwork as well as popcorn and frostwork (delicate branching crystals).

The 0.5-mile Fairgrounds Tour includes 450 steps as it passes through two levels of the cave, also with lots of typical stone formations.

Dames rocket

To get a good sense of the three-dimensional complexity of the cave, consider that 143 miles of passages lie beneath only 1.2 square miles of surface. Tour routes cover only a fraction of the cave, which twists through several different levels. Summer visitors can choose from five tour options; tours are more limited from September to Memorial Day weekend.

The Garden of Eden Tour is the least strenuous, at about 0.25 mile, with 150 steps. You enter and leave the cave via elevator and along the tour route see boxwork, popcorn

Wind Cave offers two specialized tours: the 1-mile Candlelight Tour through a less developed section, during which illumination comes from candles in buckets carried by participants, and the strenuous, 0.5-mile Wild Cave Tour, in which visitors put on helmets, kneepads, and headlamps to crawl through tight passageways.

Reservations are recommended for the Candlelight Tour and required for the Wild Cave Tour.

On the Surface

Quite often, bison (there are some 400 in the park) can be seen along US 385, which runs north-south through the park. Close to extinction in the 19th century, the result of hunting, bison were reintroduced shortly after the park's establishment.

Bison, pronghorn, mule deer, and white-tailed deer are commonly seen; elk are harder to spot. Best chances for a sighting: dawn and dusk at the edge of the ponderosa pine and aspen woodlands that are scattered among the grasslands. On a smaller note, prairie-dog towns, with their distinctive burrows, can be seen along park roads.

Two unpaved roads, numbered 5 and 6, run for several miles through the eastern part of the park and make excellent wildlife drives. Here you may be lucky and spot a coyote, badger, or porcupine, along with birds such as western meadowlark, spotted towhee, black-billed magpie, burrowing owl, and golden eagle.

Wind Cave includes about 30 miles of hiking trails, offering the chance to see its prairies and forests closely. A favorite is the moderately strenuous **Rankin Ridge Nature Trail,** a 1-mile loop that leads up to a fire tower at the park's highest point. The views are wide-ranging here; at times you can see all the way to Badlands National Park, some 40 miles to the east.

The less strenuous **Elk Mountain Nature Trail,** also about a mile,

A New Addition

In 2011, the national park acquired 5,556 acres of property along its southern boundary, known as the Sanson Ranch. Planning began at that time for visitor access, including roads and trails. This new section of Wind Cave is scheduled to open to the public in 2016.

Park staff members are excited about this new section of parkland, which encompasses what one ranger calls "a view to die for" from a high ridge. The property includes a "buffalo jump": a cliff where American Indians stampeded herds of bison over the edge to their deaths, providing a supply of meat, hides, bones, and horns for tools; sinew was used for bowstrings. Knives and scrapers found at the jump indicate it was used in this fashion about 4,000 years ago.

Visitors will also be able to see the historic buildings of the Sanson Ranch, where the Sanson family homesteaded, raising cattle from 1882 to 1987. Structures include a 1918 ranch house, a barn, and a chicken coop.

interprets the ecological zone where ponderosa pine forest meets the prairie.

An excellent longer hike combines portions of the **Centennial, Highland Creek,** and **Lookout Point Trails** for a 4.5-mile loop. The trailhead is on S. Dak. 87, about a half-mile north of US 385, and the trek passes through a variety of habitats. An easier hike, **Wind Cave Canyon** (1.8 miles), follows a road past low bluffs with scattered trees and shrubs; it's a fine walk for bird-watching.

Elk on the prairie

Information

How to Get There

From Rapid City, SD (about 60 miles north), take US 16 west to US 385 and go south to the park.

When to Go

Summer and early fall are the most popular seasons. Cave tours are on a first-come, first-served basis, and there can be waits in summer.

Visitor Center

The visitor center, off US 385, is open year-round.

Headquarters

26611 US Hwy. 385
Hot Springs, SD 57747
nps.gov/wica
605-745-4600

Camping

The **Elk Mountain Campground** (46 sites) is open year-round; in winter, services are limited and water is available only at the visitor center. Sites are occupied on a first-come, first-served basis. Backcountry camping requires a free permit from the visitor center.

Lodging

There is no lodging in the park, but lodging is available in the towns of **Custer** (*visitcuster.com;* 605-673-2244), 20 miles north, and **Hot Springs** (*hotsprings-sd .com*) 13 miles south.

South Central

Century plant *(Agave havardiana)* in Chicos Basin, Big Bend National Park

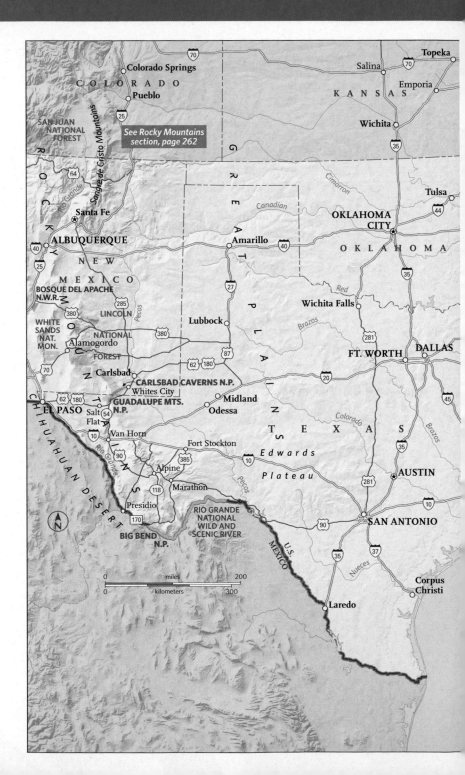

See Rocky Mountains
section, page 262

The four national parks of the South Central region offer scenery ranging from historical and underground to high and rugged ... and then there are the glorious, natural warm baths.

Water sculpted these landscapes. A reef from an ancient sea forms the 40-mile-long Guadalupe Mountain chain. Hikers can take what feels like trips back in time by climbing up to the pine-fir forests that cloak the cooler, moister peaks of Texas' **Guadalupe Mountains** National Park. This type of forest probably covered the region at the end of the last Ice Age, when early peoples hunted camels, mammoths, and four-horned antelope.

The seeping of water over millions of years created the cool, dark world of New Mexico's **Carlsbad Caverns,** with more than 30 miles of mapped passageways. The flight of bats—more than 5,000 per minute speeding out of the cave in search of insects to eat—is a thrilling nightly drama here.

Rivers etched out the dramatic Texas canyons of **Big Bend** and flash floods still tumble boulders from the steep Chisos mountaintops, continuing to rearrange the Texas scenery. Paleontologists have unearthed fossils of many creatures here, including the Big Bend pterosaur, the largest animal ever to fly.

It was the bubbling heated waters that gave rise to the health culture that surrounds diminutive **Hot Springs** National Park, which draws to Arkansas visitors in search of a restorative soak and a touch of history. In its heyday, America's Spa City counted Babe Ruth and Al Capone among its regulars. Most of the dozens of thermal springs lead into the plumbing of the Arkansas national park's bathhouses.

Big Bend

Texas

Established
June 12, 1944

801,163 acres

Vast, diverse, and remote, Big Bend National Park inspires passion among its fans. Few visit on a whim—it's not on the way to anywhere else. Those who make the journey are richly rewarded; many leave with a new favorite among the national parks.

Encompassing more than 1,200 square miles of western Texas, the park is located where the Rio Grande makes a "big bend" southward and back north again. The river forms the U.S.–Mexican border for 118 miles. Along the way it flows through some of the most spectacular canyons in North America.

Most of Big Bend is Chihuahuan Desert, a ruggedly beautiful terrain that offers a glorious display of blooming wildflowers when sufficient rain falls. In the center of the park rise the Chisos Mountains, volcanic highlands crowned by 7,832-foot Emory Peak.

It's this juxtaposition of environments—river, desert, and mountains—that gives Big Bend its broad diversity of plants and animals. Cottonwoods and willows border the Rio Grande; barrel cactus, ocotillo, and creosote bush grow in the Chihuahuan Desert; and woodlands of pine and oak cover

The Rio Grande

the slopes of the Chisos. The wildlife ranges from beaver in the riparian corridor to mule deer and javelina in the foothills to black bear in the mountains. More species of birds, bats, reptiles, butterflies, scorpions, ants, and cacti have been documented here than in any other national park.

Geologists revere Big Bend as a showcase of Earth's tumultuous past. You can see sandstone rocks 500 million years old; an outlying segment of the Rocky Mountains dating back around 100 million years; the Chisos Mountains, created by volcanic eruptions about 35 million years ago; and the Rio Grande, which took its present course less than two million years ago. Paleontologists studying the area's ancient past have discovered a

fascinating and scientifically important array of fossilized dinosaurs and other animals.

Big Bend National Park has been designated a UNESCO Biosphere Reserve; a stretch of the Rio Grande is a National Wild and Scenic River. These honors provide official recognition of the park's unspoiled wilderness and biodiversity.

▶ HOW TO VISIT

It's one thing to learn that Big Bend is a huge park. It's another thing to realize that it takes around two hours to drive from Rio Grande Village to "nearby" Santa Elena Canyon. Given its size and scope, you could easily spend a week here.

Stop at the **Panther Junction Visitor Center,** 28 miles south of the park's north entrance, to see an orientation video, study the 3-D model of the park, get maps and advice, and walk the short nature trail and learn about desert plants.

Drive to the **Chisos Basin** and admire the peaks of the **Chisos Mountains.** Then take the **Ross Maxwell Scenic Drive** to see the chasm of **Santa Elena Canyon.**

If you have more time, go birdwatching at **Rio Grande Village** and soak in the nearby hot spring. If you are equipped with the proper gear and plenty of water, walk a trail—perhaps the 3.8-mile round-trip **Mule Ears Spring Trail** in the desert or the 1.8-mile **Chisos Basin Loop Trail** in the mountains. For a wilderness river adventure, which can run from two days up to ten or more, check with local outfitters about a canoe or raft trip on the **Rio Grande.**

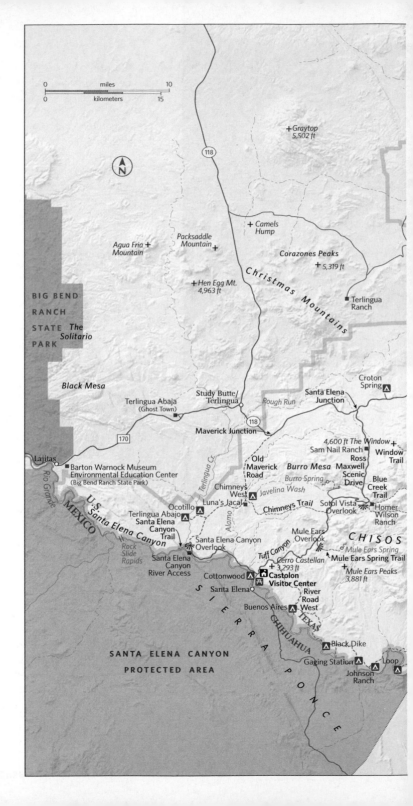

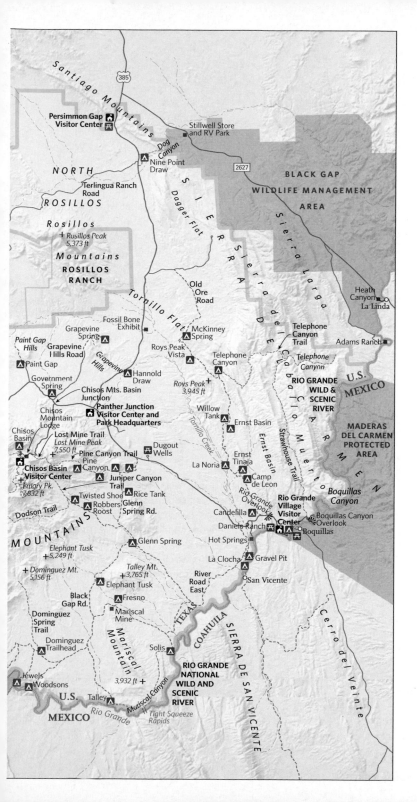

Santiago Mountains

385

Persimmon Gap
Visitor Center

Stillwell Store
and RV Park

2627

Dog
Canyon

Nine Point
Draw

NORTH

Terlingua Ranch
Road

ROSILLOS

Rosillos

+ Rusillos Peak
5,373 ft

Mountains

ROSILLOS
RANCH

Tornillo Flat

S
I
E
R
R
A

Dagger Flat

Sierra Larga

BLACK GAP

WILDLIFE MANAGEMENT

AREA

Heath
Canyon
La Linda

Old
Ore
Road

D
E
L

C
A
B
A
L
L
O

Fossil Bone
Exhibit

McKinney
Spring

Telephone
Canyon
Trail

Adams Ranch

Grapevine
Spring

Roys Peak
Vista

Telephone
Canyon

Telephone
Canyon

U.S.

MEXICO

Paint Gap
Hills

Grapevine
Hills Road

Grapevine
Hills

Hannold
Draw

Roys Peak +
3,945 ft

RIO GRANDE
WILD &
SCENIC
RIVER

Paint Gap

Government
Spring

Chisos Mts. Basin
Junction

Panther Junction
Visitor Center and
Park Headquarters

Willow
Tank

Ernst Basin

Tornillo Creek

MADERAS
DEL CARMEN
PROTECTED
AREA

Chisos
Mountain
Lodge

Lost Mine Trail

Lost Mine Peak
7,550 ft

Pine Canyon Trail

Dugout
Wells

Pine
Canyon

Ernst
Tinaja

La Noria

Ernst Basin

Camp
de Leon

Strawhouse Trail

S
i
e
r
r
a

D
e
l

C
A
R
M
E
N

Boquillas
Canyon

Chisos
Basin

Chisos Basin
Visitor Center

Emory Pk.
7,832 ft

Juniper Canyon
Trail

Twisted Shoe

Robbers
Roost

Rice Tank

Glenn
Spring Rd.

Rio Grande
Overlook

Candelilla

Daniels Ranch

Rio Grande
Village
Visitor
Center

Boquillas Canyon
Overlook

Boquillas

Dodson Trail

M
O
U
N
T
A
I
N
S

Glenn Spring

Hot Springs

La Clocha

Gravel Pit

Elephant Tusk
+ 5,249 ft

+ Dominguez Mt.
5,156 ft

Talley Mt.
+ 3,765 ft

Elephant Tusk

San Vicente

River
Road
East

Black
Gap Rd.

Dominguez
Spring
Trail

Fresno

Mariscal
Mine

M
a
r
i
s
c
a
l

M
o
u
n
t
a
i
n

Dominguez
Trailhead

TEXAS

COAHUILA

SIERRA DE SAN VICENTE

C
e
r
r
o

d
e
l

V
e
i
n
t
e

Jewels

Woodsons

Solis

3,932 ft +

Mariscal Canyon

RIO GRANDE
NATIONAL
WILD AND
SCENIC
RIVER

U.S.

MEXICO

Talley

Rio Grande

Tight Squeeze
Rapids

If you're flying to the area and renting a car, consider getting a high-clearance vehicle. This will open up opportunities to travel some of the park's primitive roads to see true backcountry and visit sites such as old villages and abandoned mines.

Gasoline is available in the park and at Study Butte on its western border, but it's a long way between stations. Make sure your vehicle is in good condition, and check your fuel gauge often.

The Chisos Mountains

Though they comprise only a relatively small part of Big Bend, the Chisos are the focus of much visitor activity. The **Chisos Mountain Lodge,** a restaurant, a campground, and a ranger station are located here, as are the trailheads of several of the park's most popular trails.

The Basin access road heads south 3 miles west of the **Panther Junction Visitor Center.** On its 6-mile route up Green Gulch, the road ascends from desert to woodland. Correspondingly, the vegetation goes from grassland dotted with cholla cactus and the tall stalks of sotol to increasingly dense woodland of oak and pine.

At Panther Pass, the **Lost Mine Trail** heads off the road to the east. It's a 4.8-mile hike round-trip, but by walking just the first mile you'll find some excellent vistas, including a view of the lava-capped mesa called Casa Grande. Interpretive signs make this hike a good introduction to Chisos Mountains ecology.

Beyond Panther Pass the road descends to the **Basin,** the focus of highland activities. The elevation here is 5,400 feet. Bluffs surround the Basin except to the west, where the V-shaped slot called the **Window** offers a perfect spot through which to see the sun set. The very easy **Window View Trail** (0.3 mile round-trip) offers a nice vista; the considerably longer **Window Trail** (5.6 miles round-trip) leads down to the spot where water drains out of the Basin.

All the peaks around the Basin, including prominent Casa Grande, resulted from volcanic activity about 35 million years ago, when ash spewed from vents and magma rose from deep within the Earth, cooling into igneous rock.

The **Chisos Basin Loop Trail,** which begins behind the Chisos Basin store, is a 1.8-mile walk requiring only moderate effort while offering good views of the Window and the rock spires called the Pinnacles. Woodland provides shade much of the way.

To climb 7,832-foot **Emory Peak,** take the steep **Pinnacles Trail** and the spur to the summit—a strenuous 10.5-mile round-trip. For a fine loop hike that captures the essence of the Chisos, take the Pinnacles Trail to **Boot Canyon** (named for a distinctively shaped rock column, like an upside-down cowboy boot) and continue via the **Colima and South Rim Trails** to descend back to the Basin via Laguna Meadow.

During this strenuous 10-mile hike you might spot the Colima warbler, which nests in the United States only in and around Boot Canyon. Avid birders come from far and wide to try to see this small gray migratory songbird, present April through summer.

In the Chisos, you could see birds such as acorn woodpecker, Mexican

Overlooking the Mexican border

jay, and western tanager; mammals include javelina, black bears, mountain lions, and the small Carmen Mountains white-tailed deer. Trees in the uplands include Texas madrone, alligator juniper, Arizona cypress, bigtooth maple, several species of oaks, and even a few aspen trees on Emory Peak. The southernmost ponderosa pines in the United States grow in the Chisos.

Visitors are bound to notice the large Havard agave, which spends most of its life as a cluster of thick, spine-tipped leaves. At maturity, the plant sends up a thick stalk that can be 20 feet tall; side branches have masses of yellow flowers, which attract hummingbirds and orioles, along with other wildlife. After flowering once, the plant dies. Havard agave is often called century plant, but it actually lives between 20 and 50 years.

Given the black bears and mountain lions that roam the uplands, hikers are cautioned to keep their distance. Park personnel at the visitor centers are at the ready to provide further recommendations regarding staying safe.

Rio Grande Village

As you drive across the desert to Rio Grande Village (20 miles east of Panther Junction), the imposing cliffs of the Sierra Del Carmen Mountains loom before you. At Rio Grande Village you'll find a **visitor center** (closed in summer), a campground, and a convenience store that sells gasoline.

Here you're more than a mile lower than the summit of Emory Peak; it can be very hot here in late spring and summer, as in other places along the river.

Bird-watchers love the area along the Rio Grande for its tall cottonwood trees and shrubby riparian vegetation, home to such notable bird species as the gray hawk, common black hawk, vermillion flycatcher, and painted bunting. Even people with little or no interest in birds can't help but notice the roadrunners hanging around the campground—sometimes running, usually walking, but seldom flying.

To see more wildlife, walk the short, easy **Rio Grande Village Nature Trail,** which in part is a boardwalk over spring-fed wetlands.

Farther east, a 4-mile dead-end road leads to **Boquillas Canyon,** where a trail enters the mouth of this impressive gorge, carved by the erosive power of the Rio Grande. The haunting song of the canyon wren echoes off the tall cliffs, and golden eagles occasionally soar overhead.

You can walk only a short distance into Boquillas Canyon; the way to see more of it is on a float trip through its entire 33-mile length—there are no take-out points along the way.

It's worth the short side trip off the main road to Rio Grande Village to visit **Langford Hot Springs,** the remains of a small resort where travelers came to soak in "healing waters" in the early 20th century, before the park was established. Healing or not, the warm spring water here feels great after a day of hiking, and locals maintain there's nothing better than to lie back and enjoy this natural hot tub under a starry sky.

For years, Big Bend visitors enjoyed crossing the Rio Grande to visit the small town of **Boquillas, Mexico,** across from Rio Grande Village. Security regulations stopped the activity for a while, but once again it's possible to take a boat across *(fee)*

Park hot springs

and have a beverage and snack in a cantina and buy souvenirs. Ask a park ranger about the border crossing, which is possible only on designated days and at limited times. You will need your passport.

Ross Maxwell Scenic Drive

This route (a portion of Tex. 118) heads south off the main east-west park road 13 miles west of Panther Junction. It winds across rugged desert landscape for 30 miles, connecting several noteworthy destinations.

Ruins at the **Sam Nail Ranch** provide a glimpse into the frontier days of the Big Bend region. Old adobe walls remain from a house built by brothers Sam and Jim Nail in 1916. When Sam married Nena Burnam two years later, it became their home, where they raised hogs, chickens, vegetables, and fruit. A windmill still turns in the breeze. The mature trees attract a wide variety of birds.

Pull off at **Homer Wilson Ranch,** where a short walk leads to buildings of what was once a large sheep ranch. A hike of a mile or so up the **Blue Creek Trail** reveals an array of red-rock pillars, spires, and hoodoos; the scenery is well worth the modest effort. (This trail was originally established as a thoroughfare for moving sheep back and forth from summer grazing areas in the Chisos Mountains to lowlands in winter.)

A little farther down the drive, take the side road to **Mule Ears Overlook** for a view of this distinctive formation, composed of solidified volcanic magma that flowed into rock fractures and was exposed by erosion. Get closer by hiking the 1.9-mile **Mule Ears Spring Trail** to an oasis-like desert spring.

Watch for the bright white volcanic material lining the road at **Tuff Canyon,** before you pass **Cerro Castellan** peak, with colorful slopes of volcanic rocks and ash deposits.

There's a seasonal **visitor center** at

Ancient Giants

There's a good reason Big Bend calls itself a "paleontological paradise." Its rock strata have yielded an amazing array of fossils, including many from the final period of the age of dinosaurs. The fossil record at Big Bend covers a continuous span of 130 million years—the most of any national park.

Among the creatures that once roamed this region is the gigantic, long-necked *Alamosaurus* (from about 70 million years ago). At more than 60 feet in length, it may have been the largest dinosaur to have ever lived in North America.

Paleontologists have found fossils of dozens of other dinosaurs at Big Bend, including agujaceratops (similar to the triceratops), duck-billed *Hadrosaurus,* and the huge sea-going predator called *Mosasaurus.*

"Super Croc" is the nickname of *Deinosuchus,* a crocodile relative that lived about 75 million years ago. With a length of nearly 40 feet and remarkably powerful jaws, it was capable of killing and eating dinosaurs, though it may have munched more often on sea turtles.

Big Bend's most famous fossil is that of *Quetzalcoatlus northropi,* one of the largest flying creatures known. With a wingspan of around 36 feet, this pterosaur (flying reptile) lived at the same time as *Alamosaurus.*

Castolon as well as a store located at the site of a frontier-era trading post and a former military station (from the days of border disputes between the U.S. and Mexico). A bit farther on is **Cottonwood Campground.** This area was once a center for cotton and vegetable farming, which continued for many years, even after the national park was established.The road winds 8 more miles through the Rio Grande lowlands to **Santa Elena Canyon,** one of Big Bend's most impressive sights. Here the Rio Grande flows through a chasm in Mesa de Anguila, with sheer cliffs up to 1,500 feet high.

A 1.7-mile round-trip trail that leads into the canyon can be reached by crossing Terlingua Creek from the parking area. The trail climbs a bit as it enters the canyon, then gradually slopes down to river level.

Limestone cliffs rise high above as you explore Santa Elena Canyon, a 7-mile-long chasm. Look down to maybe spot the rafts and canoes of river floaters below.

It wasn't the Rio Grande that sculpted this area; the river followed this route before the huge block of the Earth's surface through which it flows was uplifted. As the land gradually rose over millions of years, the sediment-filled river eroded downward, eventually carving the canyon.

Rather than retracing your route on the Maxwell Scenic Drive, you can take the 14-mile unpaved **Old Maverick Road** to Maverick Junction on the park's western border. The road passes several historic sites and lots of wide-open space with striking views.

Make a short detour west to see the ruins of the historic village of **Terlingua Abajo.** The Old Maverick Road is usually passable for regular passenger vehicles, but the going can be difficult after rains, at which time it is necessary to have a four-wheel-drive vehicle. Check with a ranger at any visitor center for weather and road information.

Rio Grande Wild & Scenic River

A 196-mile stretch of this legendary stream has been designated the Rio Grande Wild and Scenic River; 69 miles lie within Big Bend National Park.

The river flows through three awe-inspiring canyons—Santa Elena, **Mariscal,** and Boquillas. A raft, canoe, or kayak trip beneath the towering walls of the river gorges can be a wonderful experience, but it's not something to be undertaken without planning and full knowledge of possible hazards. Depending on water level, rapids can range to Class IV. Rugged terrain and limited road access mean that help could be a very long time in arriving in an emergency.

The number of people running the river is restricted; permits are required for day use and overnight outings. The park website has details.

While private trips are allowed, the easiest way to traverse the Rio Grande's canyons is by taking a float trip with an outfitter company, which will handle permits, equipment, and the often complicated necessity of shuttling river runners between put-in and take-out points.

Trips can range from one day to ten days or more, and outfitters can advise floaters about the appropriate segments for their ability levels. The park newspaper and website offer a list of companies approved to run river trips.

Balanced Rock, also known as Window Rock

Information

How to Get There

From Dallas, TX (about 550 miles northeast), take I-20 west to Monahans, then go south on Tex. 18 and US 385. From El Paso, TX (about 300 miles northwest), take I-10 east to Van Horn and then US 90 east to US 385.

When to Go

Temperatures are most pleasant from fall through spring. Summer is very hot, although cooler in the Chisos Mountains. Campgrounds and lodgings fill up quickly for Thanksgiving week, around Christmas, and during spring break.

Visitor Centers

Visitor centers at **Panther Junction** and **Chisos Basin** are open year-round. The **Persimmon Gap** visitor center is open most of the year; **Castolon** and **Rio Grande Village** are open Nov. through April.

Headquarters

P.O. Box 129
Big Bend National Park, TX
79834
nps.gov/bibe
432-477-2251

Camping

Sites at all three developed campgrounds—**Chisos Basin** (60 sites), **Cottonwood** (24 sites), and **Rio Grande Village** (100 sites)—can be reserved mid-Nov.–mid-April *(recreation.gov;* 877-444-6777) and require a permit *(fee).* For backcountry camping *(fee),* permits must be obtained in person at the Panther Junction Visitor Center.

Lodging

In Chisos Basin, the **Chisos Mountains Lodge** is a concessioner-operated facility *(chisosmountainslodge.com;* 877-386-4383). Hotels are located in **Study Butte, Terlingua,** and **Lajitas.** For more information: Brewster County Tourism Council *(visitbigbend.com).*

Carlsbad Caverns

New Mexico

Established
May 14, 1930

46,766 acres

With the words *"I shall never forget the feeling of aweness it gave me"* pioneer Carlsbad Caverns explorer Jim White recalled the time around 1898 when he first saw the newly discovered cave by the flickering light of a kerosene lantern. Carlsbad Caverns National Park continues to awe.

For more than 20 years, Jim White pushed farther into the cave, constantly trying to publicize this underground wonderland in remote southeastern New Mexico. In 1924, he guided a special National Geographic Society expedition into the caverns. The resulting report in the magazine used language a bit more formal to express a superlative judgment: "For spacious chambers, for variety and beauty of multitudinous natural decorations, and for general scenic quality, it is king of its kind."

King, indeed: Carlsbad is one of the most famous caves in the world, and the various languages heard on a walk through its passages testify to its wide-ranging appeal.

The story behind the cave's spectacular sights begins around 260 million years ago, when sea creatures formed a 400-mile-long U-shaped limestone reef along the shores of a

Left Hand Tunnel tour

broad bay. After the ocean receded, the reef was buried beneath sedimentary material. Over the past 20 million years, tectonic forces lifted, and erosion exposed, part of it as the Guadalupe Mountains, under which Carlsbad Cavern lies.

About 6 million years ago, the chambers were formed, not from underground streams as is the case for most caves, but from the dissolving power of naturally created sulfuric acid. Still later, water seeping into the cave and evaporating left behind the minerals that make up the stalactites, stalagmites, and other speleothems (cave formations).

More than 119 other caves are known within the national park boundary, including Lechuguilla Cave, the deepest limestone cave in the United States. Discovered in 1986, this cave is so pristine and scientifically important that it's open only to researchers.

There's plenty to see aboveground, too. The Chihuahuan Desert is the largest and wettest of the North American deserts. The park is one of the few places where a substantial area of this unique ecosystem is protected. Most of the park is an officially designated Wilderness, with hiking trails crisscrossing the backcountry.

► HOW TO VISIT

Begin at the park **visitor center,** which is where you buy tickets for admittance into the caverns. Ride the elevator down into the cave, and take the self-guided **Big Room** tour. This 1.25-mile walk passes many of the cave's most famous formations.

Consider traveling to the Big Room by walking the 1.25-mile route through the **Natural Entrance.** With more time, sign up for the 1.5-hour ranger-led tour of **King's Palace,** which passes through rooms known for their formations.

With an additional day or more, check out other ranger-led tours within Carlsbad Caverns or **Slaughter Canyon Cave**. Enjoy the 9.5-mile **Walnut Canyon Desert Drive,** a scenic loop through the Chihuahuan Desert. And from early spring through October, don't miss the evening bat flight (see p. 154).

Exploring the Main Cave

Walking down into Carlsbad Cavern via the **Natural Entrance** provides a real sense of how large and deep the cave truly is. This route isn't for everyone, though. It descends 750 feet in 1.25 miles, and though it's all downhill, it's also very steep.

The path is paved, but it can be wet and slippery in places. People with hip, knee, ankle, heart, or lung problems should avoid this trek, but it's fine for those of average physical ability. Visitors see creatures flying around the huge cave mouth. If it's daylight, they won't be the park's famed Brazilian free-tailed bats. Instead, May to October, they're cave swallows, birds that nest on the cave walls just inside the entrance.

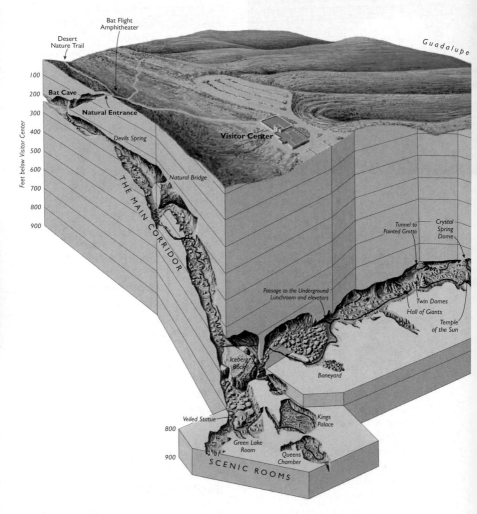

It's well worth renting a park audio guide both for the Natural Entrance walk and the Big Room tour. On the Natural Entrance walk, the audio program points out sights such as the **Bat Cave,** the **Boneyard,** and **Iceberg Rock,** a 200,000-ton boulder that fell from the cave ceiling thousands of years ago. In places, the cave roof rises more than 200 feet over the trail.

The Natural Entrance route ends at the **Big Room** loop, an easy 1.25-mile walk. The Big Room is aptly named: At 8.2 acres, it's the largest natural limestone chamber in the Western Hemisphere, and one of the largest in the world.

A stroll around this enormous space is the park's must-have experience. You walk past iconic sights such as the **Hall of Giants, Rock of Ages, Painted Grotto,** and the **Bottomless Pit.** (Early cave explorers threw rocks into the pit and, hearing no sound of impact, concluded that it was bottomless.)

Spoiling the tale, later exploration showed that the pit is about 140 feet deep. (The rocks made no noise because they struck soft soil.)

The impressive grouping of **Giant Dome** (60 feet high) and **Twin Domes** is a favorite of everyone carrying a camera (flashes are permitted in this portion of the cavern).

Some advice: Don't forget to look up! Though the eye-level sights and the walls of Carlsbad Cavern are spectacular, the ceilings here and in other

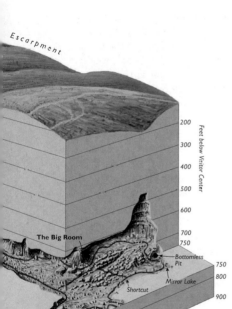

Escarpment

Feet below Visitor Center

200
300
400
500
600
700
750

The Big Room

Bottomless Pit
750
800
900

Mirror Lake

Shortcut

Top of the Cross

Lower Cave

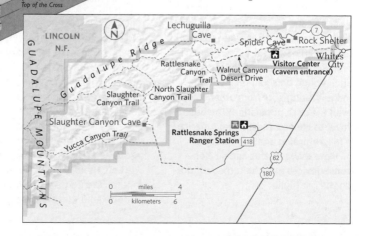

LINCOLN N.F.

Lechuguilla Cave

Spider Cave

Rock Shelter

GUADALUPE

Guadalupe Ridge

Rattlesnake Canyon

Walnut Canyon Desert Drive

Visitor Center (cavern entrance)

Whites City

Trail

North Slaughter Canyon Trail

Slaughter Canyon Trail

Slaughter Canyon Cave

Yucca Canyon Trail

Rattlesnake Springs Ranger Station 418

MOUNTAINS

0   miles   4
0   kilometers   6

chambers are often just as beautifully decorated. Changes in climate mean that Carlsbad Caverns is less wet—and therefore its formations grow less actively—than it was 10,000 years ago, when the Guadalupe Mountains received more rainfall. One stalagmite in the Big Room, **Crystal Springs Dome,** is the largest still-active formation in the cave.

Cavern Nightlife

Not all the sights at Carlsbad Caverns are underground. From mid-spring through late fall, the park holds bat-flight programs each evening, Visitors get to watch hundreds of thousands of Brazilian free-tailed bats fly out of the Natural Entrance in an immense swirling column for their nightly feeding journey.

Before the bats emerge, a ranger presents a program on this amazing natural phenomenon, explaining the bats' life history and dispelling some of the myths about these harmless mammals.

More than 300 bats can roost together in a square foot of cave ceiling. Each female returns to her pup after a night of feeding on moths and other insects.

Program time varies with sunset; call 575-785-3012 for information. The best flights happen in July and August, when young bats join their parents and migrating bats from other colonies swell the cave population. The bats travel to Mexico and Central America in fall, returning again in spring.

Note that cameras and all electronic devices must be turned off during the bat flight.

The last entry through the Natural Entrance each day is timed to allow for descent and a walk around the Big Room with time to catch the last elevator ride back to the surface. The Big Room can also be reached by taking an elevator ride down from the visitor center, avoiding the walk through the Natural Entrance.

Offered several times a day, the **Kings Palace** tour lasts 1.5 hours and visits the deepest part of Carlsbad Caverns open to the public. Often called the "scenic rooms" tour, this ranger-led walk enters the **Papoose Room, Queens Chamber,** and **Green Lake Room** in addition to Kings Palace.

Some of the finest and most intricate speleothems in Carlsbad Caverns are seen along this route. Of special note are slender "soda straws" and the delicate, curving formations known as helictites, visible in the Queens Chamber.

Once, the Kings Palace loop was part of the self-guided tour, but the delicate formations suffered too much damage from carelessness or outright vandalism.

At one point on the tour, the ranger extinguishes all the cave lighting. For many, this is the first experience of absolute darkness. The inability literally to see your hand in front of your face is eerie, to say the least.

The Kings Palace tour is strenuous; it involves descending and ascending a slope equivalent to eight stories high.

Some of the other ranger-led tours require a bit more physical and mental stamina. The moderately strenuous **Left Hand Tunnel** tour uses only candle-lit lanterns to show the way through an undeveloped section of

A Carlsbad cave's natural entrance

the cave, much of it unpaved trails. The strenuous **Lower Cave** tour passes through parts of Carlsbad Caverns toured by the 1924 National Geographic expedition.

The descent involves ladders and knotted rope. The reward for this effort: sights such as the slender Texas Toothpick formation and spherical "cave pearls."

Even more strenuous, the **Hall of the White Giant** tour requires crawling through tight passageways, climbing ladders, and negotiating slippery slopes. Participants will definitely get dirty, and this tour isn't recommended for those who can't manage enclosed places or heights.

By the way, be sure to take time to examine the three-dimensional model of Carlsbad Cavern inside the visitor center, both before and after you enter the cave. It will help you picture where you're going, and it's even more interesting when you come out and retrace the journey you've made.

Other Park Caves

Those who opt for the strenuous **Slaughter Canyon Cave** tour must make a half-mile uphill hike just to get to the entrance of the cave, which is lit only by the headlamps and flashlights of rangers and participants. This adventure tour recalls the early days of cave exploration. Sights along the way include the 89-foot-high **Monarch,** one of the world's tallest columns, and the rimstone dam known as the **Chinese Wall.** In addition, those on this tour will see ruins dating from the days when bat guano was extensively mined for use as fertilizer.

There's even more adventure awaiting those who join a tour of **Spider Cave.** The park provides participants with all sorts of gear: hard hats, headlamps, kneepads, and gloves; the four-hour trek requires plenty of crawling through narrow tunnels and scrambling up and down slopes. The reward: beautiful formations in areas including **Mace Room, Medusa Room,** and **Cactus Spring.**

It is important to keep in mind that these underground treks come with plenty of challenges and are not for everyone.

On the Surface

Known for its diversity of cacti and shrubs, the Chihuahuan Desert receives most of its rain from July to October, and usually has colder winters than do other deserts in North America.

At times the landscape is colorful with blooms of ocotillo, Mexican buckeye, mescal bean, Torrey yucca, desert anemone, morning glory, prickly pear, and claret-cup cactus. At any time of year, drive slowly on the park's unpaved scenic route and enjoy the rugged beauty of the terrain. Watch for wildlife especially early and late in the day.

There are no developed campgrounds within the park, but 50 miles of trails beckon hikers and backpackers. (A free same-day permit is required for backcountry camping.) More than 33,000 acres of the park have been officially designated as Wilderness, where trails offer the reward of solitude and the challenge of desert travel.

The **Yucca Canyon Trail,** in the southwestern part of the park, is a favorite with staffers. Following an escarpment with fine views, the 7.7-mile route leads to an isolated stand of ponderosa pines, unusual for the park. (It is always a good idea to check with a ranger about the condition of the trail.)

Much easier, and a good introduction to plant life, the **Chihuahuan Desert Nature Trail** (near the Natural Entrance) is a half-mile, mostly paved loop. A spur leads to ruins of a guano mining operation.

Located off US 62/180, 15 miles from the visitor center, **Rattlesnake Springs** is a pleasant, shaded picnic area in an outlying tract of Carlsbad Caverns, where tall cottonwoods grow near historic springs. The water here was used by Indians, pioneer travelers, and settlers, and in 1934 it became the main water source for the national park.

An oasis in the Chihuahuan Desert, Rattlesnake Springs provides a home for many species rare or unusual elsewhere in the region: snakes (including the plain-bellied water snake), amphibians (including eastern barking frog and Blanchard's cricket frog), and butterflies.

Rattlesnake Springs, a special destination for bird-watchers, has been designated an official Audubon Important Bird Area. Nesting species include yellow-billed cuckoo, Bell's vireo, eastern bluebird, summer tanager, hooded oriole, and varied and painted buntings. Wild turkeys wander the grounds among the picnic tables. Amazingly, more than 300 species of birds have been found in the vicinity of this 13-acre speck of greenery in the desert.

Stalactites and stalagmites

Information

How to Get There

To access the park's only entrance road, N. Mex. 7, turn north from US 62/180 at Whites City, which is 20 miles southeast of Carlsbad and 145 miles northeast of El Paso, TX.

When to Go

The temperature in the cave remains about 56°F year-round. In summer (late May through early Sept.) entrance hours are extended later in the afternoon.

Visitor Center

The park visitor center is located 7 miles west of Whites City, NM, on N. Mex. 7. Open year-round.

Headquarters

3225 National Parks Hwy.
Carlsbad, NM 88220
nps.gov/cave
575-785-2232

Camping

There is no developed campground in the park. Backcountry camping requires a same-day free permit, available at the visitor center. Commercial campgrounds can be found in **Whites City, NM,** and **Carlsbad, NM**.

Lodging

There is no lodging in the park. Hotels are located in **Whites City, NM,** and **Carlsbad, NM**. Carlsbad Chamber of Commerce (*carlsbad.org,* 760-931-8400).

CARLSBAD CAVERNS
EST 1930

Carlsbad Caverns Excursions

Bosque del Apache NWR
San Antonio, New Mexico

▷ The Rio Grande River bisects this refuge, where carefully maintained wetlands shelter wintering sandhill cranes, snow geese, and 18 species of ducks. Hawks, songbirds, mountain lions, mule deer, lizards, javelina, and other native wildlife thrive here. Activities include hiking, fishing, hunting, photography, and driving scenic routes. Open year-round. Visitor Center on N. Mex. 1, about 270 miles from Carlsbad Caverns National Park. *fws.gov/refuge/bosque_del_apache;* 575-835-1828.

Brantley Lake State Park
Carlsbad, New Mexico

▷ Surrounding the southernmost lake in New Mexico, Brantley Lake State Park is an oasis in the desert for boating, camping, fishing, picnicking, swimming, and hiking. Anglers can catch a variety of warm-water fish including largemouth bass, walleye, channel catfish, white bass, and bluegill. Campground facilities. Open year-round. Located 35 miles northeast of Carlsbad Caverns National Park via US 180E/US 62E. *emnrd.state.nm.us/SPD/brantleylakestatepark;* 575-457-2384.

White Sands National Monument
Alamogordo, New Mexico

▷ Undulating waves of gypsum sand, some 50 feet high, offer ever-changing vistas of the monument. Gypsum rock dissolved by rainwater from the surrounding mountains settles into the dry lake bed and alkali flats, where it crystallizes into selenite. Weathering breaks the crystals into sand, which gets piled high by scouring winds. There's a 16-mile round-trip drive, as well as a handful of hiking trails. Open daily. Entry fee. Visitor Center on US 70, 120 miles northwest of Carlsbad Caverns National Park. *nps.gov/whsa;* 575-479-6124.

Black River Recreation Area (BLM)
Carlsbad, New Mexico

▷ This 1,200-acre Chihuahuan Desert oasis is located along the Black River, a tributary of the Pecos River. The wildlife-viewing deck provides an excellent vantage point for watching waterfowl, shorebirds, and songbirds, as well as other resident wildlife. On tap are hiking, picnicking, swimming, and fishing. Open year-round. Located just southwest of Carlsbad National Park, off Washington Ranch Rd. *blm .gov/nm/st/en/prog/recreation/ carlsbad/black_river;* 575-234-5972.

Pecos River Corridor Area (BLM)
New Mexico/Texas

▷ Providing opportunities for water-based pastimes and semi-private motorized recreation, the river corridor area stretches along the Pecos, overlapping the New Mexico–Texas border. The 6,000 acres of land, with access both to the Pecos River and the areas surrounding Red Bluff Reservoir, supports fishing, boating, and swimming, as well as primitive camping and hiking. Open year-round. Located about 30 miles east of Carlsbad National Park via US 62/180 and US 285. *blm .gov/nm/st/en/prog/recreation;* 575-234-5972.

Bitter Lake NWR
Roswell, New Mexico

▷ Within the Chihuahuan Desert and the Southern Plains arena, Bitter Lake National Wildlife Refuge represents a biologically significant wetland aspect of the Pecos River watershed system. The refuge protects and provides habitats for pelicans, cranes, waterfowl, shorebirds, and stilts as well as the rare least tern. Hiking. Wildlife viewing. Open for day use only year-round. Located just over 100 miles north of Carlsbad Caverns National Park via US 285N. *fws.gov/refuge/ Bitter_Lake;* 575-622-6755.

Guadalupe Mountains

Texas

Established
September 30, 1972

86,376 acres

Though it doesn't rank among the most visited national parks, Guadalupe Mountains National Park maintains a fiercely loyal group of devotees, who return year after year to hike its rugged trails and enjoy the solitude of its uplands. With seven of the nine tallest peaks in Texas, the park offers both physical challenges and a natural diversity unique in the state—its high country is like a bit of the Rocky Mountains towering over the Chihuahuan Desert.

Guadalupe Peak, at 8,749 feet, ranks as Texas' high point, and the strenuous hike to its summit has long been among the park's most popular activities. But the park's true icon is El Capitan, the imposing limestone bluff that stands at the southern tip of the Guadalupe Mountains.

Established in 1972 at the height of the push for wilderness protection in the United States, Guadalupe Mountains maintains that ethic, with developed areas covering only a small part of its 135 square miles. No roads reach the high country, so experiencing much more than just its edges

Salt Basin Dunes

factor for safe and enjoyable hiking in the park. Many Guadalupe Mountains rangers are strong advocates of the use of trekking poles in the park. Most injuries occur during descents on steep trails when hikers lose their balance on loose rock.

Caveats aside, hundreds of visitors a year spend a day climbing **Guadalupe Peak** and are rewarded with the satisfaction of reaching the highest mountain in Texas, and (on clear days) with a panoramic vista. Other favorite destinations in the high country include **The Bowl,** known for its wildlife, and **El Capitan.**

Far less strenuous is the hike up **McKittrick Canyon,** always ranked among the most popular and beautiful walks in Texas. McKittrick is famed for the fall foliage of its maples and oaks and is often crowded at that season.

On a second day, you can visit the often overlooked **Dog Canyon,** on the park's northern edge, offering an alternative route to the Guadalupe Mountains high country, or the **Salt Basin Dunes** area, in the park's western section—new facilities make a trip to this unique landscape much easier than in previous years (see p. 164).

requires ascending 2,000 feet or more by trail. Still, there's plenty to see here with only moderate exertion.

► HOW TO VISIT

On a day trip, stop at the **Pine Springs Visitor Center** not only to learn about the park's geology, wildlife, and recreational opportunities but also to understand the challenges of hiking here. Trails to the high country are steep and rocky, making them more difficult than their mileage might indicate. There's no water available anywhere in the Guadalupe uplands. Combine that with sun, heat, and moisture-sapping wind, and dehydration and fatigue can be serious problems. Carrying enough water is the most important single

The High Country

To stand on Texas's highest point, **Guadalupe Peak,** requires an 8.5-mile round-trip hike with an elevation gain of around 3,000 feet. The trail begins in the Pine Springs campground. The first mile and a half is the steepest section. On the way up you'll pass briefly through an isolated grove of pine and Douglas fir, sheltered on a north-facing slope. Otherwise there's little shade on this hike. The pyramid

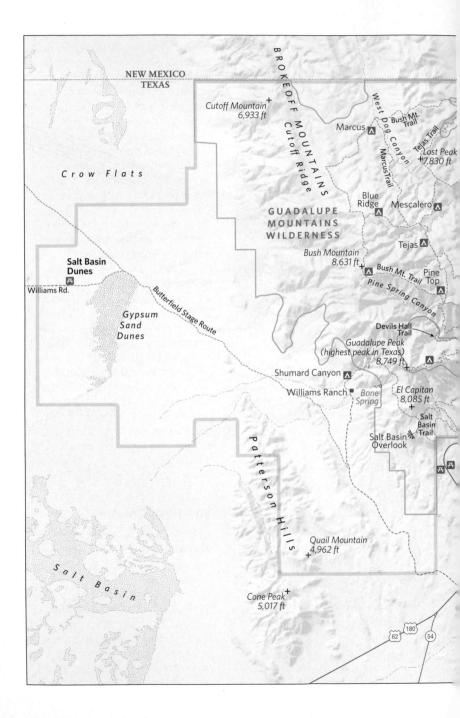

NEW MEXICO
TEXAS

Cutoff Mountain +
6,933 ft

B R O K E O F F   M O U N T A I N S
Cutoff Ridge

West Dog Canyon

Marcus ▲

Bush Mt. Trail

Tejas Trail

Lost Peak
+ 7,830 ft

Marcus Trail

Crow Flats

Blue Ridge

Mescalero ▲

GUADALUPE
MOUNTAINS
WILDERNESS

Tejas ▲

Bush Mountain
8,631 ft +

Bush Mt. Trail

Pine Top

Salt Basin
Dunes
⛺

Williams Rd.

Pine Spring Canyon

Butterfield Stage Route

Devils Hall Trail →

Gypsum
Sand
Dunes

Guadalupe Peak
(highest peak in Texas)
8,749 ft +

Shumard Canyon ▲

Williams Ranch ■

Bone
Spring

El Capitan
8,085 ft
+

Salt Basin Trail

Salt Basin
Overlook

⛺

P a t t e r s o n   H i l l s

S a l t   B a s i n

Quail Mountain
4,962 ft +

Cone Peak +
5,017 ft

62   180   54

monument at the summit commemorates the Butterfield Overland Mail stagecoach line, which passed through what is now the park in the mid-19th century. The view from here seems infinite across the desert grasslands to the east, south, and west.

Those with a hankering to stand atop **El Capitan** leave the Guadalupe Peak trail near the top, make their way down to the saddle between the two mountains, and then ascend El Capitan. At this writing there is no formal trail, though the park is planning to mark the route to minimize hikers' impact on the land.

The payoff for the strenuous 9-mile round-trip hike to **The Bowl** is a lush forest of ponderosa pine and Douglas fir, where you may spot elk, mountain chickadees, Steller's jays, and other flora and fauna reminiscent of the Rocky Mountains farther north. Mountain lions and black bears roam here, too, so hikers and campers should be aware of what to do in the presence of these predators.

McKittrick Canyon

There's not much fall foliage in western Texas, so things can get pretty hectic in this canyon when the bigtooth maples turn their dazzling shades of orange, red, and yellow (usually in late October and early November) and visitors come from long distances to see them. McKittrick Canyon makes a great hike any time of year, though, as it follows a spring-fed creek through riparian woodland.

The most popular hike is the fairly easy 2.4-mile round-trip to **Pratt Cabin,** named for pioneering geologist Wallace Pratt, who once lived here

A Dune Sojourn

Covering almost 2,000 acres on the west side of the Guadalupe Mountains, the Salt Basin Dunes area comprises the second largest expanse of gypsum sand dunes in the United States. Cresting like ocean waves and gleaming white, the dunes are a fascinating landscape to explore. For years, though, access was inconvenient, requiring checking out a key from the park visitor center (an hour's drive away) and then returning it after a visit.

It's far easier now to visit the Salt Basin Dunes, an important part of the park's natural diversity. In 2014, the park added new facilities at the dunes, improving the entrance road and constructing a parking lot, picnic shelters, restrooms, and interpretive signs. A key is no longer needed.

Make a short hike through the Chihuahuan Desert, where blooming sand verbena scents the air and black-throated sparrows sing, to reach the edge of the dunes. There you can climb the powdery gypsum or walk a section of the historic Butterfield Trail, which skirts the dunes to the east and north. The vista across the dunes with El Capitan's peak in the background makes for a striking photograph.

and who gave 5,632 acres to the U.S. government in 1957 to encourage the establishment of a national park.

The Grotto, another mile up the canyon, makes a nice picnic spot, and the trail continues (steeply) up to connect with other high-country trails. If you continue past Pratt Cabin,

watch for fossils of crinoids, brachiopods, and other ancient marine animals in the canyon walls.

Though less celebrated than McKittrick Canyon, the **Smith Spring Trail** is an excellent 1.2-mile hike to a lovely pool that forms an oasis in the Guadalupe foothills. Maidenhair ferns flourish below the maples and oaks here, and the water attracts birds and other wildlife. Crossing desert grassland before it reaches Smith Spring, the trail passes **Manzanita Spring** along the way. This section of the trail is paved, wheelchair accessible, and only 0.4 mile round-trip.

Dog Canyon

From the Pine Springs Visitor Center it's around a two-hour drive to Dog Canyon, on the northern edge of the park. The road passes into New Mexico, then back into Texas. The route comes with splendid views of wide-open spaces.

The ranger station and campground at Dog Canyon sit at the transition zone between juniper-dotted grassland and open ponderosa pine woodland. It's a quiet, less visited, and lovely site, where the whistling of broad-tailed hummingbird wings fills the air from spring into fall. Those who have discovered Dog Canyon often say it's their favorite part of the park.

In addition, visitors who want to hike into the Guadalupe Mountains high country can save 600 feet of elevation gain by beginning at Dog Canyon rather than Pine Springs. Moderately strenuous day hikes lead to excellent views at **Marcus Overlook** and **Lost Peak.**

Lower Pine Spring Canyon viewed from Hunter Peak

Information

How to Get There

From El Paso, TX (about 100 miles west), take US 62/180 east to the park visitor center. From Carlsbad, NM (about 50 miles northeast), take US 62/180 west. The closest gas station to the park is 32 miles from the visit center.

When to Go

Fall is the best time for hiking and enjoying colorful foliage. The park is often crowded then, as well as during spring break. May and June are very hot in the lowlands; late-summer rains provide some relief. In winter, the high country can see cold temperatures and occasional snow.

Visitor Center

The **Pine Springs Visitor Center** is located on US 62/180. There's a ranger station at **Dog Canyon,** in the northern part of the park.

Headquarters

400 Pine Canyon Dr.
Salt Flat, TX 79847
nps.gov/gumo
915-828-3251

Camping

Developed campgrounds are located at **Pine Springs** (39 sites) and **Dog Canyon** (13 sites). Backpackers must obtain a free permit at the Pine Springs Visitor Center or the Dog Canyon Ranger Station.

Lodging

A variety of lodgings can be found in **White's City, NM,** and **Carlsbad, NM** *(carlsbadchamber.com).*

Hot Springs

Arkansas

Established
March 4, 1921

5,550 acres

With its intriguing mix of history, geology, and nature, Hot Springs holds a unique place among America's national parks. The smallest of the parks, Hot Springs National Park wraps around a modern urban area set within a valley of the rugged Ouachita Mountains. The park and city, both named Hot Springs, developed side by side and remain intimately linked.

Congress created Hot Springs Reservation in 1832 to protect thermal springs that had become renowned for their supposed therapeutic properties. By the time it was made an official national park in 1921, Hot Springs had grown into a popular spa, attracting vacationers as well as patients seeking a cure for all sorts of illnesses.

Hot Springs became the spring-training home for several major-league baseball teams, whose players used the thermal baths to relax after workout and training sessions.

Water that fell as rain more than 4,000 years ago flows from the Earth here at an average temperature of 143°F, having been heated at a depth of about a mile belowground before

Ozark Bathhouse, built in 1922

are "in Hot Springs National Park," or imply that they are affiliated with the national park (in the federal National Park Service sense) when they are not.

▶ HOW TO VISIT

The park can be experienced in a day, though hikers might want to spend more time here. Tour the 1915 **Fordyce Bathhouse** to learn what "taking the waters" was all about. Then stroll along **Bathhouse Row** and the **Grand Promenade** to imagine the scene at the height of the bathing era.

Hike or drive up **Hot Springs Mountain** for views of the city of Hot Springs in the valley below and national park land on surrounding mountains. Then hike one or more of the many trails. Afterward, ease tired muscles by taking a traditional bath, either on Bathhouse Row or in one of the hotels that use natural spring water.

rising back to the surface. Most of the natural hot springs have been diverted into pipes flowing to hotels and to a line of spa buildings known as Bathhouse Row. The eight remaining bathhouses on the row were built between 1892 and 1923 and display a rich diversity of architectural styles.

The park's 5,550 acres encompass wooded uplands of the Ouachita Mountains, crisscrossed by 26 miles of hiking trails. Unusual for North American mountains, the Ouachitas run east–west instead of north–south, pushed up in parallel folds by an ancient collision of tectonic plates.

Note: The official name of the city adjacent to the park is Hot Springs National Park. This means that many local businesses can legally say they

Bathhouse Row

The center of many park activities is a one-third-mile-long stretch of **Central Avenue,** where **Bathhouse Row** lines one side of the street, facing private businesses. When the **Fordyce Bathhouse** opened in 1915, it was hailed as the most luxurious bathing establishment in town. It closed in 1962 but has been beautifully restored as the park **visitor center.**

Watch the park's orientation video, then take a ranger-guided tour of the Fordyce. You'll see courtyards, marble walls and staircases, fountains, a gymnasium, and the bathing area.

The nearby 1912 **Buckstaff Bathhouse** has been in continuous operation and today offers the entire

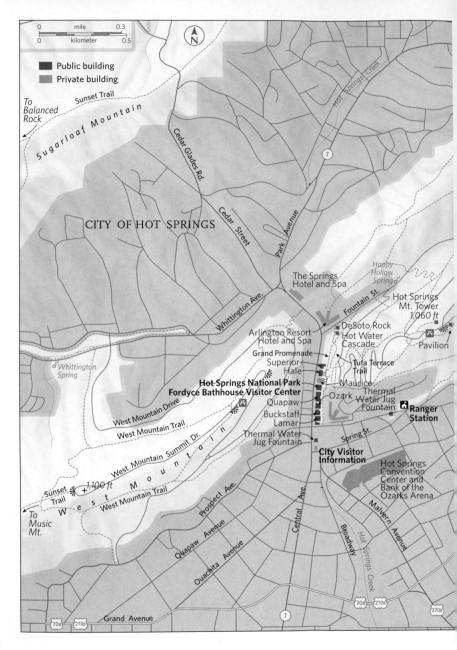

experience, from thermal water soaks to hydrotherapy sessions to massages. The 1922 **Quapaw Bathhouse**, closed for many years, has been splendidly renovated. It reopened in 2008 as a modern spa.

The National Park Service has tried, with varied success, to partner with private enterprises to find new uses for the Bathhouse Row structures. The 1923 **Lamar Bathhouse** houses park offices and the bookstore. The 1916

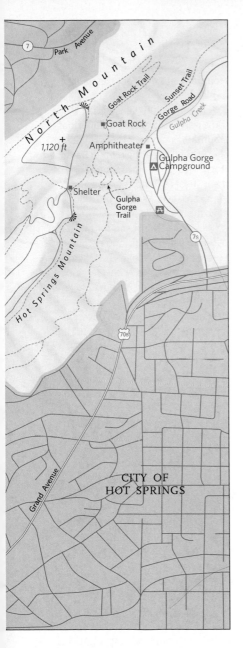

restoration. The eagles atop columns at the park's formal entrance between the Fordyce and Maurice bathhouses are the work of Edward Kemeys, who created the bronze lions at the Art Institute of Chicago.

While most spring water is piped to various bathing sites, you can see it flowing from the hillside at **display springs** near the Maurice Bathhouse. There are also several fountains where you can drink spring water that's seeing the light of day for the first time since it fell as rain some 44 centuries ago. At the spring in front of the park headquarters, cars line up so people can fill jugs with the water—either because they believe it has curative properties or because they simply want to drink some of the highest-quality water on the planet.

A stroll down the half-mile **Grand Promenade** is a must-do for all park visitors. This broad walkway, begun in the 1930s by the New Deal–era Public Works Administration, runs along the hillside behind Bathhouse Row. Look for the cascade of spring water and the built-up deposits of tufa (a form of calcium carbonate or limestone) that precipitates from the water.

Several hiking trails and a scenic road ascend **Hot Springs Mountain**, east of Bathhouse Row. There are great lookout points here, including a privately operated tower (fee) with far-reaching panoramas of the Ouachita Mountains.

The park offers 26 miles of hiking trails through pine-oak-hickory woods on the highlands around the city. Several trails can be accessed from **West Mountain Summit Drive. Sunset Trail,** at 10 miles the longest in the park, heads west from the end of

Superior Bathhouse has been repurposed as a brewery using local spring water. The 1922 **Ozark Bathhouse** is now home to the nonprofit park "friends" group and an art gallery. The 1912 **Maurice** and 1892 **Hale** await

West Mountain Summit Drive. (Other road trailheads access different sections of Sunset Trail.) In a little more than 2 miles, the path reaches **Music**

Notorious Hot Springs

In the early 20th century, Hot Springs truly deserved its nickname "The American Spa." Trains brought thousands of vacationers to the city annually, including celebrities ranging from baseball star Babe Ruth to President Herbert Hoover.

Another kind of visitor found Hot Springs an attractive retreat as well: gangsters. Al Capone was among the organized-crime figures who spent time in the spa city, playing golf, taking the waters, going to the horse races, and generally escaping the attention of big-city law enforcement.

One gangster, notorious killer Owney Madden, "retired" to Hot Springs in the 1930s, where he took part in what might well have been the largest illegal gambling operation in the country. Protected by corrupt politicians, casinos flourished until they were finally shut down in 1967—two years after Madden had died and was buried in his adopted city.

The gangsters who visited Hot Springs for the most part left their violent ways back home, sometimes even opting for good behavior. Owney Madden was locally famous for his large contributions to local charities. Al Capone, who often rented an entire floor of a local hotel to ensure privacy, was renowned as a big tipper. He once tipped a cab driver $100 to drive him from a gambling club to his hotel—across the street.

Mountain, at 1,405 feet the park's highest point.

From here, the Sunset Trail turns northeast to follow **Sugarloaf Mountain**; in about 2 miles there's a spur trail to the aptly named **Balanced Rock.** This geologic feature is one of many local outcrops of novaculite: very hard, evenly grained rock of almost pure silica.

Novaculite was used for tools by American Indians long before Europeans arrived and is still sold as "Arkansas stone," considered by many to be the finest whetstone in the world. (Its name comes from *novacula,* the Latin word for razor.) Layers of novaculite are found throughout much of the southern Ouachita Mountains from central Arkansas into eastern Oklahoma. Because it's so much harder than other rocks in these mountains, it often remains as ridges when other materials have eroded away.

Shortleaf pine is a highly abundant tree in southern Arkansas, but it has been so exploited for timber and paper products that few truly mature trees remain. You can see some fine specimens, though, in the park.

Along the **West Mountain Trail** south of Summit Drive and on Sugarloaf and Hot Springs mountains, shortleafs nearly 200 years old stand 70 feet or more above hikers, reminders of a time when forests were not managed as they are today.

Of the many other park hikes, one of the most popular is the 1.1-mile round-trip **Goat Rock Trail.** Beginning at a road overlook on North Mountain, it leads to fine views of eastern Hot Springs and Indian Mountain. Goat Rock can also be reached from the Gulpha Gorge Campground.

SUPERIOR BATHS

Superior Bathhouse, built in 1916

Information

How to Get There

From Little Rock (55 miles east), take I-30 southwest 27 miles and then continue 28 miles on US 70 and US Bus. 70.

When to Go

Year-round, although late spring and fall are the most pleasant seasons. Summers can be hot and crowded with vacationers visiting nearby lakes. The city is also quite busy during the early spring horse-racing season.

Visitor Centers

The **Fordyce Bathhouse Visitor Center,** 369 Central Ave., is open daily.

Headquarters

101 Reserve St.
Hot Springs, AR 71901
nps.gov/hosp
501-620-6715

Camping

The **Gulpha Gorge** campground (44 sites), on Gorge Rd. on the east side of the park, available daily on a first-come, first-served basis. There is no backcountry camping in the park, but the nearby **Ouachita National Forest** offers many campgrounds and primitive camping options.

Lodging

Lodging is plentiful in **Hot Springs.** Hot Springs Convention and Visitors Bureau *(hotsprings.org;* 501-321-2835, 800-SPA-CITY).

HOT SPRINGS
EST. 1921

Southwest

Walking through Bryce Canyon along Queens Garden Trail

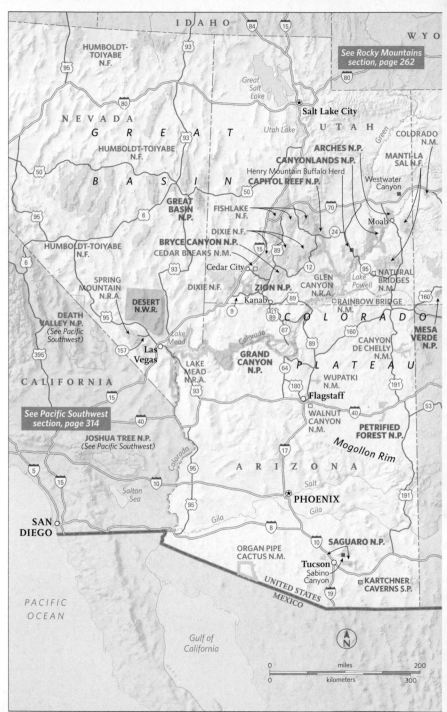

IDAHO

WYO

HUMBOLDT-
TOIYABE
N.F.

*See Rocky Mountains
section, page 262*

Great
Salt
Lake

★ **Salt Lake City**

N E V A D A

G R E A T

UTAH

Utah Lake

Green

COLORADO
N.M.

HUMBOLDT-TOIYABE
N.F.

ARCHES N.P.
CANYONLANDS N.P.
Henry Mountain Buffalo Herd
CAPITOL REEF N.P.

MANTI-LA
SAL N.F.

B A S I N

Westwater
Canyon

GREAT
BASIN
N.P.

FISHLAKE
N.F.

Moab

HUMBOLDT-TOIYABE
N.F.

BRYCE CANYON N.P.
CEDAR BREAKS N.M.

DIXIE N.F.

DIXIE N.F.

GLEN
CANYON
N.R.A.

Lake
Powell

NATURAL
BRIDGES
N.M.

SPRING
MOUNTAIN
N.R.A.

DESERT
N.W.R.

Cedar City

ZION N.P.

RAINBOW BRIDGE
N.M.

C O L O R A D O

MESA
VERDE
N.P.

DEATH
VALLEY N.P.
*(See Pacific
Southwest)*

Kanab

CANYON
DE CHELLY
N.M.

Lake
Mead

GRAND
CANYON
N.P.

P L A T E A U

Las
Vegas

LAKE
MEAD
N.R.A.

WUPATKI
N.M.

C A L I F O R N I A

Colorado

Flagstaff

*See Pacific Southwest
section, page 314*

WALNUT
CANYON
N.M.

PETRIFIED
FOREST N.P.

JOSHUA TREE N.P.
(See Pacific Southwest)

Mogollon Rim

Salton
Sea

A R I Z O N A

Salt

SAN
DIEGO

★ **PHOENIX**

Gila

Gila

ORGAN PIPE
CACTUS N.M.

SAGUARO N.P.

UNITED STATES
MEXICO

Tucson
Sabino
Canyon

KARTCHNER
CAVERNS S.P.

PACIFIC
OCEAN

Gulf of
California

N

| 0 | miles | 200 |
| 0 | kilometers | 300 |

When explorer John Wesley Powell successfully navigated the Green and Colorado Rivers on his 1869 expedition, he solidified the American fascination with the Wild West. Today many consider the Grand Canyon, core of one of 11 parks in the Southwest, an emblem of American heritage and a natural wonder of the world.

Yet the allure of the Southwest extends far beyond Arizona's **Grand Canyon** to ten other national parks. The sandstone spires, hoodoos, and fins of Utah's **Bryce Canyon** create a surreal spectacle of color and shape. Eons of wind, rain, and elements have built and broken the swooping arches of Utah's **Arches** National Park, and will continue to do so. Millions upon millions of years are quite literally on display in the multicolored sedimentary rock of Utah's **Capitol Reef**'s untrammeled canyons.

Ancient humans left an indelible mark on these lands. Ancestral Puebloans inhabited the mesa tops of Colorado's **Mesa Verde** for hundreds of years before constructing their famous cliff dwellings, including the 150-room Cliff Palace. The haunting figures of the Great Gallery, a 300-foot panel of rock art found in Utah's **Canyonlands,** offer clues to what early life was like in these desert climes.

In even the harshest of Southwest environments, life manages to thrive. In Utah's most visited and celebrated park, **Zion,** "hanging gardens" cling precariously to bald-faced rock walls. Likewise, seemingly inhospitable cliffs along Colorado's **Black Canyon of the Gunnison** teem with flora and fauna that have adapted to the vertiginous landscape. The wind-snarled bristlecone pines of Nevada's **Great Basin** rank among the oldest tree specimens on Earth, a boon for scientists studying tree-ring data. In Arizona's **Saguaro,** prickly saguaro cacti can live up to 200 years.

Then there are the long-dead trees of Arizona's **Petrified Forest,** which have evolved postmortem. Like a firsthand lesson in cell biology, the plant fossils reveal over 200 million years of chemical reactions that have resulted in a palette of eye-popping colors.

Arches

Utah

Established
November 12, 1971

76,679 acres

As the ancient Romans knew, there's something commanding about an arch, something that raises us up. Imagine more than 2,000 of them, hewn of stone, defiantly standing in the face of the erosional forces that created them. The 240 square miles of Arches National Park encompass the world's most concentrated display of these natural formations. While most arches lie hidden in the park's deepest recesses, several, such as Delicate Arch, have become icons.

Most of the park's namesake arches are made up of ancient beaches and Sahara-esque sand dunes that edged an inland sea 140 to 180 million years ago. This coral-hued Entrada layer was buried a mile deep by later sediment, whose weight cemented it into sandstone. The 300-million-year-old salt beds below shifted under the growing weight, buckling the Entrada sandstone into long accordionlike joints. After erosion carried away the sediment above, rainwater fell into these joints, widening them until they formed freestanding slabs of stone called fins. Rainwater

Delicate Arch

delicate nature is put to the test. A healthy respect for the natural forces at work only enhances appreciation of the park's awe-inspiring sights.

▶ HOW TO VISIT

Parking lots often overflow. Visit the most crowded sites—**Devils Garden, The Windows,** and **Delicate Arch**— early in the morning or late in the day. If you only have several hours, you can stroll along the 1-mile **Park Avenue Trail,** stop at **Balanced Rock,** and walk through some of the park's largest arches at the Windows.

A half day or longer allows time to add on **Landscape Arch** in **Devils Garden,** with time left over for a sunset pilgrimage to Delicate Arch. Depending on park schedules, all-day visitors could get the chance to experience a ranger-led guided walk through **Fiery Furnace** or the entire **Devils Garden Trail.**

Arches Scenic Highway

Beginning just past the **visitor center,** this 18-mile-long paved road strings together the park's most prominent sights. The road climbs from the floor of Moab Canyon to **Devils Garden,** passing through the heart of the park, with spur roads leading to The Windows, Wolfe Ranch, and the Delicate Arch area. Numerous pull-offs along the way allow for leisurely viewing of the park's major features.

Switchbacking up the steep road through the white Navajo and pinkish Entrada sandstone, you'll top out on a surreal expanse of monolithic buttes, arches, and hoodoos (natural columns of rock).

continues to erode the sandstone, forming cavities in the fins and sometimes resulting in freestanding arches.

Just as arches continue to be created, so they fall, as did Wall Arch, the park's 12th largest span, in 2008. Landscape Arch is so close to falling that no one is allowed near it. As timeless and enduring as the park appears to be, this is a surprisingly fragile environment.

It doesn't take much to upset the land's delicate balance. A misplaced footstep off-trail, where the park's soil crust is knit in knobby clumps of moss, lichen, and bacteria, can destroy decades of growth, leaving soils vulnerable to erosion.

As this small park receives more than a million visitors each year, its

Your first stop is **Park Avenue,** a narrow canyon lined with skyscraping fins and spires. Stone monuments **Nefertiti,** the **Three Gossips,** and the **Organ** can be seen along the 1-mile **Park Avenue Trail,** which slopes down through sage, rice grass, and twisted juniper. If you're going to hike it, having a driver designated to pick you up at the Courthouse Towers parking area saves having to hike back the way you came, an uphill slog.

Continue, driving across **Courthouse Wash** (the park's only year-round stream) and past the **Petrified Dunes** to gravity-defying **Balanced Rock,** one of the park's most recognizable sights. A 0.3-mile trail loops around this teardrop knob of Entrada sandstone balanced, at least for now, on a crumbling pedestal.

Turn on the spur road to **The Windows,** passing the spires and grottoes of the **Garden of Eden** along the way as you make your way up to **Elephant Butte,** the park's highest peak at 5,653 feet.

At The Windows, two trailheads link four of the park's largest arches, all within sight of each other. One gently sloping trail leads 0.25 miles to twinned **Double Arch,** the park's highest arch, with a vertical light opening of 112 feet. The other trail is the park's busiest thoroughfare: The Windows is a 1-mile gravel loop that takes in **Turret Arch, North Window,** and **South Window.** Returning via this primitive trail, you get a backside view of the two Windows framing a nose-shaped rock, aptly called the **Spectacles.**

From Balanced Rock, head to the Delicate Arch turnoff, a 2.5 mile-long spur road offering two opportunities to see the famous arch. Park at

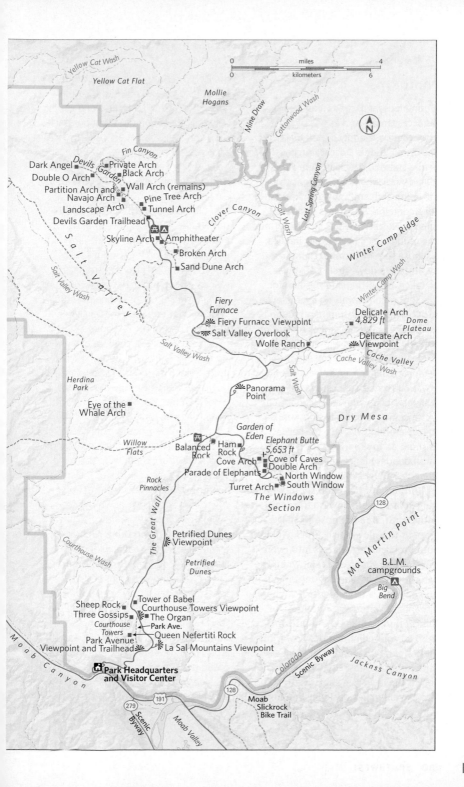

Photo Ops

Luminous landscapes and easy access make Arches one of the most camera-friendly of national parks. The classic shot is Delicate Arch just before sunset, especially from January to mid-April when the low light strikes the entire arch and snow blankets La Sal Mountains. Early birds scramble through North Windows arch to capture one of the park's most iconic images: a sunrise shot of Turret Arch framed by North Windows Arch. Care must be taken, as getting into position for this shot requires walking over uneven surfaces. From late summer through spring, the rising sun strikes the entire arch. Don't go home without a portrait of Balanced Rock. You can shoot this geologic still life from any direction and at various times: sunrise, sunset, even twilight. Not so with Landscape Arch, which comes to life only from sunrise to mid-morning. It's also the hardest to shoot as your perspective is limited by a boundary fence keeping you safe from possible rockfall.

Throughout the park, shoot when the sun is low, shadowing the rock with depth. Underexpose by half a stop, as the glowing slickrock will fool automatic camera meters into overexposing. Get out after a rain, when the saturated sandstone deepens in color. You might even catch one of Arches' ephemeral waterfalls. And look for foreground to take up the bottom third of your composition: flowering mule's ear, twisted juniper trunks, reflecting puddles. Don't limit yourself to these classic shots. With some two dozen arches easily visible in the park, you'll find one to call your own.

the Delicate Arch trailhead at **Wolfe Ranch** and hike 1.5 miles to the arch itself. (The hike is strenuous and can take an hour in and another hour back out.) Otherwise, drive another mile and cross, conditions permitting, flash-flood-prone Salt Wash to the **Delicate Arch Viewpoint** for a view of the arch, a mile away.

Four miles past the Delicate Arch turnoff, the scenic highway passes **Fiery Furnace,** a reddish pink labyrinth of narrow fins, arches, bridges, and slots that require hikers to squeeze, wriggle, and jump their way through, with no trail or cairns (stone piles) to help guide them. A permit, available at the visitor center, is required.

Unless you know the Furnace well, try to book one of the three-hour tours guided by rangers who point out what could be easily overlooked: hidden arches; potholes teeming with micro-life; and rare canyonlands biscuitroot, which grows only in sandy soil between fins of Entrada sandstone. Check the tour schedule on the park website; you also can ask at the visitor center for guided-tour information.

Four miles farther down the scenic highway from Fiery Furnace lies a short trail to **Sand Dune Arch** and a half-mile trail across a wildflower-speckled meadow to **Broken Arch.** These walks, however, are best left for another day if they keep you from driving 4 more miles to the end of the road to hike the 0.75-mile-long trail to **Landscape Arch,** at 291 feet one of the world's longest natural spans, a dramatic don't-miss park sight.

Heading through the park at sunset or during twilight, watch out for the park's furry residents, inactive during the day and now stirring to life:

coyotes, black-tailed jackrabbits, and kangaroo rats.

Delicate Arch

The strenuous 1.5-mile-long **March to the Arch** (the arch formation stands on the edge of natural amphitheater backdropped by La Sal Mountains) should be on everyone's must-do list. Give yourself two to three hours round-trip. Better yet, plan half a day.

The trail begins at **Wolfe Ranch,** a shale-chinked cabin built at the turn of the 20th century by a disabled Civil War veteran. It is the park's only evidence of ongoing human habitation. (Upon first seeing her future home, the war veteran's daughter broke into tears—and not from joy.)

A signed spur trail loops 100 yards to a Ute petroglyph panel that gives away its age: The etched figures on horseback postdate the Spanish arrival. The trail switchbacks up a steep hillside, then levels out though a field of chert boulders, a crystalline rock from which Native Americans once knapped arrowheads.

Follow the cairns up the shadeless slickrock, through pockets of piñon and juniper, and climb the 200-yard-long ramp that blasted out of a cliff. The sudden, dramatic appearance of Delicate Arch will stop you in your tracks. The 60-foot-high arch of Jurassic-era sandstone is capped by more erosion-resistant rock.

The most popular time to visit Delicate Arch is right before sunset, when the arch performs for the gathered crowd by reflecting the sun's glow in varied hues. Bring a flashlight or headlamp for the return journey.

Hikers at Deadhorse Point

If you can time an evening hike to coincide with a full moon, you may have the thrill of seeing the moon rise up over the arch.

Devils Garden Trail

The park's longest trail, **Devils Garden Trail** is a 7.2-mile loop that weaves through, around, and atop soaring fins with what might be the world's largest stockpile of natural arches. (Don't let the crowded parking area fool you. Many folks are here solely for the stroll to Landscape Arch.) From the trailhead, a groomed trail threads between fins, breaking out at 0.3 miles where a short side trail heads to **Tunnel** and **Pine Tree** arches (save these minor spans for the return trip). Pick up the pace another half mile to Landscape Arch, which is doomed to collapse in the near future (as did Wall Arch in 2008; it's now an unsigned heap of rubble 200 yards farther down the trail). Landscape Arch is a narrow ribbon of stone 306 feet long, seemingly defying gravity as it floats in a graceful span above the dunes. Beyond Landscape Arch, the trail is marked by stacked-stone cairns. (Hikers should not consider creating new cairns, which could confuse others on the trail.)

If time is short, bypass the spur trail to **Partition Arch** (0.2 mile) in favor of the trail to **Navajo Arch** (0.3 miles), whose span suggests a cave opening to an inner sanctum domed by sky.

Back on the main trail, you'll be walking atop a 10-foot-wide vertical slab with 100-foot drop-offs before coming to a short side trail to the **Black Arch Overlook,** which offers vertiginous views. Though primitive, the trail continues on another mile to **Double O Arch,** a small arch topped by a much larger one, like a double rainbow caught in stone. Here you have three options: return the way you came; continue another half mile to the 150-foot spire called **Dark Angel;** or return via the longer **Primitive Trail,** heading down Fin Canyon, which can add an extra hour of hiking time.

Elsewhere in the Park

Tower Arch, a massive 101-foot-across span wedded to a minaret-like tower, inspired the park's founding father, Alex Ringhoffer, to lobby for creation of a national monument in 1929. Yet it's the park's least visited major attraction, thanks to a remote location reached via 8.3 miles of dirt road up Salt Valley (ask at the visitor center for information on road conditions) and a 1.7-mile-long primitive trail that heads into remote Klondike Bluffs. The trail winds through an intricate landscape of sandstone formations, cresting ridge tops that offer outstanding vistas of Fiery Furnace, La Sal Mountains, and Book Cliffs.

Alongside a trail edged with claret cup cactus and leafless Mormon tea, you will see three soaring sandstone spires, nicknamed the **Marching Men.**

Perfect for a summer scorcher, the 6.2-mile **Courthouse Wash Trail** offers a wade-worthy stream under the broad-leafed shade of cottonwood trees. Pack a picnic lunch, park at the bridge along Arches Scenic Highway (11 miles from the visitor center), and head downstream (south) for lunch.

Ute Indian petroglyphs

Information

How to Get There

The park entrance is 5 miles north of Moab on US 191, which continues 25 miles to the Crescent Junction exit of I-70.

When to Go

Snowfall can glaze the slickrock from late Nov. through Feb., yet trails remain open. Blustery spring storms bring April and May wildflowers, while monsoon thunderstorms moderate scorching summer temps in July and Aug., resulting in a second wildflower bloom in early fall.

Visitor Centers

The Arches Visitor Center is open every day; hours vary by season.

Headquarters

2282 SW Resource Blvd.
Moab, UT 84532
nps.gov/arch
435-719-2100

ARCHES
est 1971

Camping

From March through Oct., plan on making reservations to secure a spot at the 50-site **Devils Garden Campground.** *(recreation.com;* 877-444-6777 or 518-885-3639). In winter, sites are available on a first-come, first-served basis.

Lodging

While there are is no lodging in the park, nearby **Moab** *(discovermoab.com)* offers a full roster of B&Bs, condo rentals, motels, hotels, and riverside resorts.

Black Canyon of the Gunnison

Colorado

Established
October 21, 1999

30,750 acres

To hear roaring rapids while peering down 2,000 feet into an abyss of dark rock is a weak-in-the-knees experience. From the canyon rim, early settlers claimed you could see "halfway to hell." Maybe not, but at Black Canyon of the Gunnison National Park you will see two billion years of Earth history on a scale that puts human life into humble perspective.

Black Canyon of the Gunnison National Park protects the most spectacular 14 miles of a 53-mile-long gorge carved by the Gunnison River, whose headwaters lie high in the Rocky Mountains. About two million years ago, after the "Gunny" had washed away the softer volcanic breccia, the river hit the dense basement rock of gneiss and schist. Trapped in a groove of its own making, the river has been carving deeper ever since, especially during the last ice age, when glacier meltwater sliced through the rock, leaving sheer cliffs in its wake.

Still one of the country's wildest canyons, it shows no evidence of human habitation. Flora and fauna, on the other hand, have adapted well to the vertical geography. Ancient

Sheer canyon walls of the South Rim of Black Canyon

the skies—golden and bald eagles, prairie and peregrine falcons—while other birds keep to the brush. Inadvertently flush one of the park's blue grouse from the sage flats and you'll know why it's called the heart-attack bird.

▶ HOW TO VISIT

You can spend the better part of a day driving the 7-mile (one way) **South Rim,** with its numerous canyon overlooks, interpretive trails, and visitor center. If you have more time, consider driving two hours to the lonesome **North Rim,** where steeper cliffs and superior river views put the canyon in full dramatic context. Only strong hikers should tred the inner-canyon routes that head to the river from the rims.

South Rim

The 7-mile **South Rim Drive** weaves through Gambel oak, serviceberry, and shrubby stands of sage (beware of roadside-grazing mule deer) before treating drivers to the first real glimpse of Black Canyon at **Tomichi Point,** one mile from the entrance.

For better views, continue 0.25 miles to the **visitor center** at **Gunnison Point,** where you can gather information before strolling out back for a grandstand view of the Gunny coursing below the snaggletoothed crags.

Consider hiking one of two trails here, either the 0.5-mile **Rim Rock Trail,** contouring the canyon's edge, or, better yet, the 2-mile **Oak Flat Loop,** which offers more biodiversity as it dips 300 feet below the rim through aspen glades and Douglas fir. This damp, shady microenvironment is more prone than the North Rim to

piñon pine groves shade the top, while Douglas fir, aspen, and blue spruce clutch the steep slopes, where "hanging gardens" flourish.

Since the 1970s, when dams were put in place to tame seasonal flooding, cottonwoods, willows, and reedy box elders have taken root along the river bottom. They are having a tough time of it now: The National Park Service won the right to flood the canyon every spring to restore the river to its pre-dam wildness.

And wild it is. Otters play, and legendary trout—rainbow, brown, and native cutthroat—lure fishermen down the steep rocky routes where yellow-bellied marmots bask on ledges. Mule deer are a common sight, elk and reclusive black bears less so. Raptors rule

A Canyon of No Return

Native Americans and early explorers traditionally avoided the formidable canyon up through the 19th century. Though early trappers knew of the canyon as early as 1809, it wasn't officially documented until 1853, when Captain John W. Gunnison passed close by. (He never entered the canyon now bearing his name.) When Ferdinand Hayden surveyed western Colorado in 1873, the closest he came to exploring the canyon's depths was to dangle a man over the North Rim on the end of a 1,000-foot rope. After getting hauled back up, the trembling man knew that the only way to reach the bottom of the canyon was to die trying.

In 1900, five men attempted to run the river in wooden boats to survey it as a possible source of irrigation. Their idea was to find a suitable site to bore an irrigation tunnel to divert river water to nearby Uncompahgre Valley. The men hiked out after three weeks, their wooden boats splintered into driftwood.

In 1903, the canyon's length was finally navigated by William Terrence and Abraham Lincoln Fellow, who took a low-tech approach, scrambling on foot, swimming underwater through the boulder-choked narrows, and riding the rapids clutching inflatable air bags.

A water-diversion tunnel was soon in the works; the four-year project, dedicated in 1909, resulted in a 6-mile-long tunnel through rock, sand, and clay. The labor it took to build this was so grueling and dangerous that the average period of employment was two weeks.

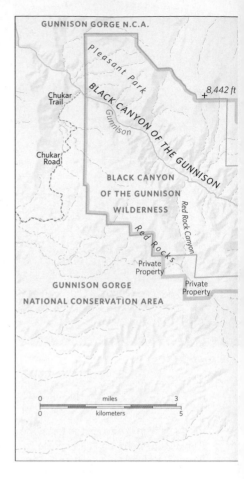

the frost-freeze cycle. This is one reason that the South Rim has eroded farther back from the river than the sun-struck cliffs of the North Rim.

For fine upstream views, drive another 1.75 miles to **Pulpit Rock,** a precipitous rock parapet crafted by the Civilian Conservation Corps in the 1930s. The real drama, however, lies farther downstream, as the river drops 480 feet in 2 miles through the **Narrows,** one of the steepest river descents in North America. From the next three viewpoints—**Cross Fissures, Rock Point,** and **Devils Lookout**—you are likelier to hear the river than

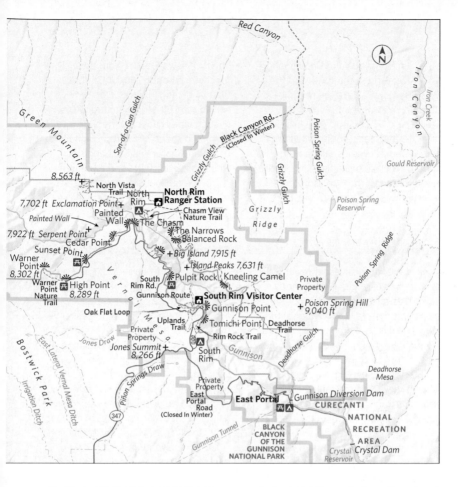

actually see it. Continue on to the **Chasm,** which is as close as most visitors get to the North Rim, 330 yards across the river. This is where the river makes a 90-degree bend to the southwest, bringing the canyon's star attraction, **Painted Wall,** into view. At 2,250 feet, this is Colorado's tallest cliff, where magma seeping into cracks in the dark gray basement rock has since hardened into pinkish pegmatite veins sparkling with crystal and mica.

Farther down the road, take the 300-yard interpretive trail to **Cedar Point** for a closer look at Painted Wall. You might spy world-class rock climbers inching up its face, though not from April through July, when the cliff is closed to allow peregrine falcons to nest undisturbed. The fastest creatures on Earth, they prey on other birds, colliding into them mid-air at 200 mph.

Sunset Point is a convenient place to watch the sun drop behind distant Grand and Monument mesas, but if you have time, head another mile to road's end at **High Point Overlook.** This is one of the park's highest elevations, at 8,289 feet, and trailhead for the 1.5-mile **Warner Point Nature Trail.** The gently descending path offers a vantage of luminous views of the

San Juan Mountains and Uncompahgre Valley farmland to the south and the West Elk Mountains to the north. In autumn, piñon jays and Clark's nutcrackers flit among 800-year-old piñon trees, taking seeds. Spring-flowering serviceberry develops purple berries in summer, a black bear staple. Trail's end reveals views of the Gunnison winding out of the canyon and onto the Colorado Plateau.

North Rim

The North Rim receives far fewer visitors. Its gravel roads, intermittently closed **visitor center,** and remoteness also contribute to the pristine solitude. While it takes two hours to drive here from the South Rim, once here you can hit the highlights in an afternoon.

Start at the campground, with **Chasm View Nature Trail.** The 0.3-mile loop, through a piñon-juniper forest, leads to two lookouts poised at the canyon's narrowest, with views of Painted Wall and upstream to the Narrows, where the roiling river cleaves a 40-foot-wide passage through 1,725-foot-high vertical walls.

For a closer look at this dark heart of the park—sunlight illuminates the abyss less than an hour a day—continue by car to the **Narrows View.** Make brief stops at the remaining overlooks: gravity-defying **Balanced Rock, Big Island View,** and **Island Peaks.** ("Island" refers to the pine-topped pinnacles rising from the river bottom.) The last stop looks out on the anthropomorphic **Kneeling Camel** formation.

Deadhorse Trail, 2.5 miles, begins at Kneeling Camel; the easier 1.5-mile **North Vista Trail** to **Exclamation Point** offers more diversity, with intermittent oh-wow views. Depart from the visitor center through sagebrush flats, then piñon and junipers. Don't miss the signed turn-off to Exclamation Point. A riveting inner-canyon panorama awaits from atop sheer 2,000-foot-high cliffs. Picnic on a natural stone bench as white-throated swifts and swallows patrol the rim, nabbing bugs. Listen for the "kee-r-r-r" of red-tailed hawks above the river's roar.

Elsewhere in the Park

Not for the faint-hearted, half a dozen routes drop to the river bottom from both rims. Figure on four hours down and back. You'll need a wilderness permit (only 15 are issued a day) for the mile-long **Gunnison Route,** leaving from Oak Flat Trail near the South Rim visitor center. Steep switchbacks give way to a straight shot down loose rock, assisted by an 80-foot chain along one daunting chute. On all routes, wear long pants to protect against poison ivy and ticks. Forget swimming. Even in summer, this rushing river is hypothermic. But you can comfort aching feet in an icy pool, and bask in the pristine inner-canyon solitude as you contemplate the climb back up.

An easier way to experience the Gunny is by car. At the park's South Rim entrance, turn on **East Portal Drive,** a 5.5-mile brake-burner wheeling down to a diversion dam, where river water is channeled through the 5.8-mile **Gunnison Tunnel.** Built from 1905 to 1909, it was the longest irrigation tunnel in the world when inaugurated by President Taft. Park downstream and hike along the river's rocky bank, watching for rising trout and gray American dippers bobbing on the rocks.

Flly fishing on the Gunnison River

Information

How to Get There

The park's South Rim lies 15 miles east of Montrose, CO, via US 50 and Colo. 347. The North Rim is 80 miles away via US 50 north to Colo. 92; you head south at Crawford, following park signs.

When to Go

At 8,000 feet above sea level, evenings cool off rapidly. High water makes for spectacular river viewing in May. Wildflowers peak in June. Brief thunderstorms add afternoon drama in July and Aug. By early fall, hiking is superb. Winter snow—possible Nov. to March—closes down both rim roads (which become cross-country ski trails). The road is plowed to the South Rim Visitor Center.

Visitor Centers

The South Rim Visitor Center is open year-round. The North Rim ranger station closes in winter and intermittently at other times.

Headquarters

102 Elk Creek
Gunnison, CO 81230
nps.gov/blca
970-641-2337

Camping

The **South Rim Campground** (88 sites; 23 with electric hookups), sequestered amid the scrub oak, can be reserved up to three days in advance. The **North Rim** provides 13 sites with vault toilets on a first-come, first-served basis.

Lodging

There is no lodging in the park. The gateway towns of Gunnison (*visit montrose.com*), **Crawford,** and **Delta** (*deltacountycolorado.com/lodging*) offer numerous hotels and B&B options.

Bryce Canyon

Utah

Established
September 15, 1928

35,835 acres

Mormon pioneer Ebenezer Bryce described the canyon as "a hell of a place to lose a cow." These days, the cows may be gone, but it's still a hell of a place to lose yourself. To gaze down on Bryce Canyon National Park's surreal amphitheaters or to hike among the sun-struck hoodoos blurs the boundary between fantasy and reality. Just like the Paiute Indians who saw the faces of their ancestors frozen in stone, here you can let your imagination roam.

Bryce Canyon is not a true canyon created by river or stream. Instead, pelting rain, melting snow, and frost wedging have eroded the eastern escarpment of the Paunsaugunt Plateau into horseshoe-shaped amphitheaters crenelated with hoodoos, fins, and spires. Bryce Amphitheater—the park's scenic heart—is the largest and most stunning of the park's 14 amphitheaters, and the reason for Bryce Canyon's national park designation.

The park was enlarged in 1931 to extend 24 miles along the plateau's eastern edge, which provides lofty views of another world-class wonder:

Hoodoos (odd-shaped pillars of rock) near Sunrise Point

the Grand Staircase. This sedimentary series of benches and cliffs begins at Bryce and descends in colorful steps —Pink Cliffs, Grey Cliffs, White Cliffs, Vermilion Cliffs, Chocolate Cliffs—all the way to the Grand Canyon, exposing 240 million years of geologic history along the way. (The oldest rocks at the bottom of the canyon date back nearly 2 billion years.)

The park's high altitude (8,000 to 9,000 feet) and pristine air allow for views of up to 200 miles. On a moonless night, the stars shine so bright they create their own shadows.

Closer at hand, endangered Utah prairie dogs keep watch over roadside meadows, where pronghorn antelope, reintroduced to the region, are commonly spotted from spring to fall.

Ponderosa pines shade the northern plateau, while Douglas fir, blue spruce, and even some bristlecone pines forest the higher southern end of the national park. Rare plants, such as Red Canyon penstemon and Bryce Canyon paintbrush, stand out like jewels alongside hiking trails that weave through the "breaks" under the plateau rim.

Though small for a national park, Bryce packs a lot into its 56 square miles, including the 1924 Bryce Canyon Lodge. This masterpiece of American national park architecture—a National Historic Landmark—is the work of architect Gilbert Stanley Underwood, who designed the lodge in National Park Service rustic style to harmonize with its surroundings. It sits between Sunrise and Sunset Points and was built by the Union Pacific Railroad.

Although it's been renovated several times, the lodge maintains its 1920s style. It consists of a large main building with a distinctive green roof (check out the handsome moiré pattern of its shingles) and log cabins set along the canyon edge.

And from here, it's just a short stroll to the world's most stunning sunrise. A dawn light washing over the hoodoos is a soul-stirring spectacle never forgotten.

▶ HOW TO VISIT

Any visit to Bryce should be a combination of two activities: visiting **Bryce Amphitheater** and taking the **Scenic Drive** to **Rainbow Point.** You can do both in five to six hours. If time is limited, forgo the scenic drive in favor of Bryce Amphitheater. Begin or end your day here for front-row views of the sunbaked hoodoos. Be sure to

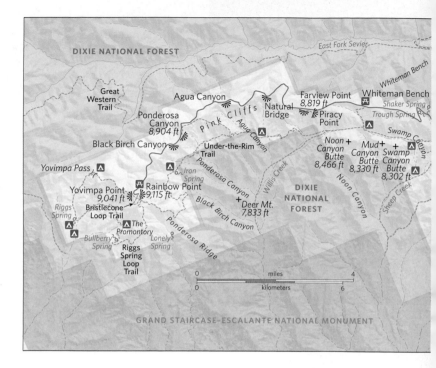

take some time to stroll the **Rim Trail.**
For a lasting impression, hike below
the rim for up close encounters with
the hoodoos.

If you don't want to hike, perhaps
join a two-hour or half-day horseback
riding trip through the hoodoos. From
early May to mid-October, ride the free
shuttle to help avoid parking-area congestion at Bryce Amphitheater. Inquire
about ranger-led moonlit hikes and
telescope stargazing.

While it might seem counterintui-
tive, given its iconic desertlike landscapes, a cold-weather visit should
be considered. Bryce Canyon can
transform into a frozen wonderland
between November and April, when
the plateau often is shrouded in snow.

Bryce Amphitheater

For sweeping vistas of the park's
marquee attraction, begin your visit
at **Bryce Point,** the highest viewpoint (8,296 feet) overlooking Bryce
Amphitheater. At sunrise, the low-
angled light animates thousands of
sherbet-colored hoodoos.

Look due north for the conspicuous **Alligator,** an eroded fin capped by
white dolomite, and northeast to the
Wall of Windows, a thin ridge punctuated by natural arches. To the east lies
the town of Tropic (pop. 520), backed
by distant **Table Cliff Plateau.** At
10,000 feet, this tectonic uplift is the
highest plateau in North America.

Now drive back 2 miles to

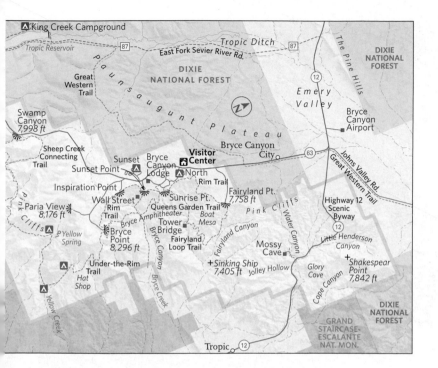

Inspiration Point. The short but steep trail to the highest of the three viewpoints, **Upper Inspiration Point** is well worth the muscle burn for its more expansive panorama of Bryce Amphitheater. On the trail back down from the point, take notice of the bristlecone pines holding fast to the retreating edge of the plateau, which erodes 1 to 4 feet every 100 years.

Consider a 15-minute stroll on the **Rim Trail** from Inspiration Point to Sunset Point instead of driving there. Along the way, you might see violet-green swallows and white-throated swifts darting along the cliffs above the dense deeply shadowed hoodoos of **Silent City.**

While you're at it, carefully scan the skies for a rare condor sighting. And ignore the Uinta chipmunks cadging handouts.

Sunset Point provides the park's most theatrical views, whether looking down on Queens Garden, the casbah-like Silent City, or the park's most illustrious hoodoo, **Thor's Hammer,** a solitary 150-foot-high limestone pinnacle brandishing a mallet-shaped capstone. Though the views are to the east, the setting sun sometimes casts a cloud-refracted glow across the amphitheater, as luminescent colors slowly coalesce into darkening shadows.

If you only do one hike in the park, begin at Sunset Point, allowing yourself two to three hours for the

e Point

moderately strenuous 3-mile round-trip trek through the heart of this hoo-doo fairyland. Begin on the **Navajo Loop Trail** through **Wall Street.** It's the Lombard Street of national park trails, with 36 steep switchbacks cutting through towering stone fins that narrow into a deep slot where centuries-old Douglas firs look like giant match-sticks caught in a bench vise.

Continue to the trail's junction with **Queens Garden Trail,** which winds through a spectacular hoodoo garden. In spring and summer, look for fuchsia-colored Bryce Canyon paint-brush, a rare plant growing only in Bryce Canyon.

Take the short spur trail to pay trib-ute to **Queen Victoria,** the most prom-inent spire, which stands in company of her stone-faced court. Continue on through a few stone passageways and ascend a ridge to **Sunrise Point,** where a half-mile stroll on the paved **Rim Trail** gets you back to Sunset Point. (When it is icy or slippery, it's best to do the hike in reverse.)

Among the embarrassment of riches in Bryce Canyon National Park, a full-moon hike through **Queens Garden** qualifies as a life list experience.

Bryce Canyon Scenic Drive

This 18-mile scenic drive edges the eastern escarpment of Paunsaugunt Plateau, offering bird's-eye panora-mas from nine lofty viewpoints amid a Douglas fir and blue spruce forest. Drive directly south to the end of the road at Rainbow Point so you can more safely pull into the overlooks on the return trip.

Rainbow Point, the park's high-est elevation at 9,115 feet, provides the

Hoodoo Magic

The Southern Paiute Indians tell a story about the Legend People, who paid no heed to this fragile land, eating all the pine nuts and drinking all the streams. When the animals complained, the trickster god Coyote invited the Legend People to a great banquet. As they feasted, Coyote cast a spell on them, turning them into the hoodoos we see today. "Hoodoo" appears to be of West African origin, a word brought to the colonies by slaves, signifying magical retribution. In early America, to have a spell cast on you was to be "hoodooed."

How eccentric columns of stone came to be known as "hoodoos" remains a mystery. Left behind by the retreating rim of the Paunsaugunt Plateau, these formations comprise sediments laid down in ancient Lake Claron and later fractured into a grid of joints and faults. When water seep-ing into these crevices freezes, it expands 10 percent, driving a wedge between the rocks.

With some 200 freeze–thaw cycles a year, the precipitation—just 16 inches a year—chisels the rock into columns, many soaring over 100 feet. Protected by caps of harder sandstone or dolo-mite, the softer layers below—lime-stone, siltstone, mudstone—erode and dissolve into undulating shapes, like geologic totem poles. Oxidized miner-als (hematite, manganese, limonite) add glowing hues of ginger, yellow, pink, and purple, as if lit from within.

On a full moon, when the Bryce Canyon hoodoos come to life, their message seems clear: Tread lightly on this land.

perfect leg-stretcher: a brisk lap on the 1-mile **Bristlecone Loop,** taking in deep lungfuls of the thin pine-scented air. The trail breaks out onto the plateau's south rim, where a few bristlecone pines have endured a thousand years or more in windswept grace.

As you make your way around the loop, detour 200 yards to **Yovimpa Point,** where most days you can see dome-shaped Navajo Mountain 90 miles to the southeast. At 10,388 feet, the mountain is the highest point in the Navajo Nation. It is a sacred peak known as Naat'tsis'aan, Head of the Earth.

Heading back north on the Scenic Drive, the first three overlooks—**Black Birch, Ponderosa Canyon, Agua Canyon**—offer views of neighboring Grand Staircase-Escalante National Monument. Agua Canyon is the most photogenic of the three, with two distinctive hoodoos, the Hunter and the Rabbit, poised on opposite sides of a steep ravine. Beyond, drifting clouds mottle an endless expanse of canyons, cliffs, and plateaus.

The next pull-off, **Natural Bridge,** provides a close-up view of the imposing natural arch, its reddish iron-oxide-rich rock in rich contrast to the deep green forest seen through its 85-foot-wide aperture.

Continue on to **Farview Point,** where you can see three of the five geologic "stairs" making up the Grand Staircase: the Pink Cliffs of the Aquarius Plateau, the Gray Cliffs of Kaiparowits Plateau, and the White Cliffs revealed on distinctive Molly's Nipple. From the parking area, a 300-yard hike continues to **Piracy Point.** Without the crowds or roadside noise, a more fitting name would be Privacy Point.

The next two pull-outs, **Whiteman Bench** and **Swamp Canyon,** are used by hikers to connect with **Under-the-Rim Trail,** which runs 23 miles from Rainbow Point to Bryce Amphitheater. This is the backpacker's version of the Scenic Drive.

If it's near sunset, end your drive at **Paria View Point,** reached via the Bryce Point Road. This is the best place to watch the last rays of the setting sun bathe the hoodoos in dramatic golden light. (Bryce Amphitheater hoodoos lose the sun illumination much earlier.) In spring and summer, there's a chance of spotting peregrine falcons here as well.

Elsewhere in the Park

Fairyland Point is often overlooked due to its approach via a mile-long spur road off Utah 63, 0.75 mile north of the park's fee station. Nor does the shuttle go here. Here you will find intimate eye-level views of some of the park's most dramatic hoodoos, and there's a good chance you'll spot wildlife, especially along the arduous 8-mile **Fairyland Loop Trail.**

Likewise, **Mossy Cave,** off Utah 12 4 miles east of Utah 63, sees fewer visitors though it's an easy half-mile stroll to reach the grotto cave. The stream riffling alongside this trail is part of a 10-mile ditch dug by Mormon pioneers across the Paunsaugunt Plateau in the 1890s, and still provides life-giving water to Bryce Valley before draining into the Colorado River.

Diverted from the East Fork of the Sevier River, this is the only water to escape the geographical sump of the Great Basin.

Cowboys lead trail rides in the park.

Information

How to Get There

From St. George, take Utah 9 east through Zion National Park, turning north on Utah 89. Turn right on Utah 12 and follow to Utah 63, the park entrance road (about 2.5 hours driving time). From Capital Reef National Park, follow Utah 12 west for 116 miles to Utah 63.

When to Go

From May to Sept., daytime temperatures are 64–80°F, cooling at night. Overlooks are crowded July and Aug. (also a time of occasional thunderstorms). In fall and spring, cooler temperatures (45–65°F) accompany fall foliage and wildflower displays. The Scenic Drive and overlooks are plowed and sanded in winter. Park rangers lead occasional snowshoe hikes through the surreal terrain. Roads are closed during and right after snowstorms.

Visitor Center

The Visitor Center is across from the fee station. It is open year-round.

Headquarters

P.O. Box 640201, Bryce
Canyon, UT 84764
nps.nps.ov/brca
435-834-5322

Camping

Two campgrounds nestle in Ponderosa pines near Bryce Amphitheater: **North** (open year-round, near the park's general store) and **Sunset** (closed winter; close to hiking trails), each with 100 tent and RV sites, available first come, first served, or by reservation, 877-444-6777.

Lodging

Within the park, **Bryce Canyon Lodge,** on the National Register of Historic Places, provides 114 rooms, suites, and historic cabins close to the canyon's rim (*brycecanyonforever.com;* 435-834-8700 or 877-386-4383). Just outside the park, five hotels, a few restaurants, and three campgrounds make up **Bryce Canyon City** (*brycecanyoncityut.gov),* while the nearby town of **Tropic** offers modest lodgings (*brycecanyoncountry.com).*

Canyonlands

Utah

Established
September 12, 1964

337,598 acres

The Green and Colorado Rivers—the original architects of Canyonlands National Park—have carved the park into three distinct districts: Island in the Sky, The Maze, and The Needles. Each could be a national park in its own right, yet the three sections combine to form something even greater: the wild red-rock heart of the American West.

In fact, Canyonlands is as wild today as when John Wesley Powell made the first documented journey down the Green and Colorado Rivers in 1869. Its 527 square miles remain the "most arid, most hostile, most lonesome, most grim, bleak, barren, desolate, and savage quarter of the state of Utah—the best part by far," according to writer Edward Abbey.

When the Colorado Plateau began uplifting 20 million years ago, its streams carved ever deeper into the sedimentary layers, creating a vast branching network of canyons feeding into the rivers.

Island in the Sky, the most visited park district, hovers 2,200 feet above the Green and Colorado Rivers. As seen from its vertigo-inducing

Mesa Arch, in the Island in the Sky district

through which churns the most intimidating white water in North America. Yet the river is lulled into submission some 14 miles downstream, beyond the park boundary, by Lake Powell and the Glen Canyon Dam. Other products of human effort are pressing in on park borders. Oil and gas wells springing up near the park have spurred controversial proposals of a Greater Canyonlands National Monument to keep this wild heartland intact.

▶ HOW TO VISIT

Each of the park's three districts must be visited separately. As the entrances to **The Needles** and **Island in the Sky** are 110 miles apart, visitors with only a half to full day usually prefer Island in the Sky for its car-friendly viewpoints and easier access to both the town of Moab and Arches National Park.

On a second day, head to The Needles for more diverse trails and fewer visitors, or get an early start en route to **Horseshoe Canyon;** hike in to view the **Great Barrier pictographs.** Exploring the rugged **Maze** section is more of an multiday expedition than an excursion, requiring a high-clearance four-wheel-drive vehicle.

Island in the Sky

Known as Isky within the park, this immense mesa brims with vast panoramas of the wild Colorado Plateau. Make sure your visit includes **Mesa Arch** at sunrise or **Grand View Point** for sunset—ideally, both.

Before dawn, make a beeline 6 miles past the visitor center to the Mesa Arch parking area and hike the groomed half-mile loop trail to

viewpoints, immense red-rock canyons stretch as far as the eye can see, with no evidence of people except the lonely track of the White Rim trail winding along the bench rock.

Ruins and rock paintings of ancestral Puebloans haunt the canyons of The Needles, where Organ rock shale and cedar mesa sandstone have eroded into colorful banded spires.

The lonely Maze district sees the fewest visitors, and not because it is any less alluring. This sandstone labyrinth of look-alike box canyons and impassable cliffs poses a supreme challenge even to veteran hikers.

The Colorado and Green Rivers join forces at the Confluence, the fluid center of the park. Their combined volume rushes into Cataract Canyon,

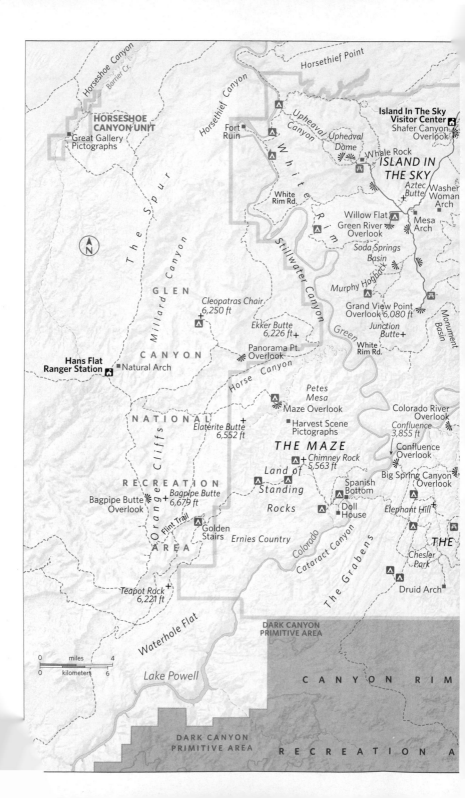

Horseshoe Canyon
Barrier Cr.
Horsethief Point
Horsethief Canyon

**HORSESHOE
CANYON UNIT**
Great Gallery
Pictographs

Horsethief Canyon

Fort
Ruin

Upheaval
Canyon

**Island In The Sky
Visitor Center**
Shafer Canyon
Overlook

Upheaval
Dome

Whale Rock

**ISLAND IN
THE SKY**

Aztec
Butte

Washer
Woman
Arch

White
Rim Rd.

Willow Flat
Green River
Overlook

Mesa
Arch

Soda Springs
Basin

Murphy Hogback

Grand View Point
Overlook 6,080 ft

Junction
Butte

Monument
Basin

Cleopatras Chair
6,250 ft

Ekker Butte
6,226 ft

White
Rim Rd.

Panorama Pt.
Overlook

GLEN

Millard Canyon

CANYON

**Hans Flat
Ranger Station**
Natural Arch

Horse Canyon

Petes
Mesa

Maze Overlook

Harvest Scene
Pictographs

Colorado River
Overlook
Confluence
3,855 ft

Confluence
Overlook

N A T I O N A L

Elaterite Butte
6,552 ft

THE MAZE

Chimney Rock
5,563 ft

Land of

Spanish
Bottom

Big Spring Canyon
Overlook

R E C R E A T I O N

Bagpipe Butte
Overlook

Bagpipe Butte
6,679 ft

Standing

Doll
House

Elephant Hill

Rocks

Flint Trail

A R E A

Golden
Stairs

Ernies Country

THE

Chesler
Park

Teapot Rock
6,221 ft

Cataract Canyon

The Grabens

Druid Arch

Waterhole Flat

**DARK CANYON
PRIMITIVE AREA**

0 miles 4
0 kilometers 6

Lake Powell

C A N Y O N   R I M

**DARK CANYON
PRIMITIVE AREA**

R E C R E A T I O N   A

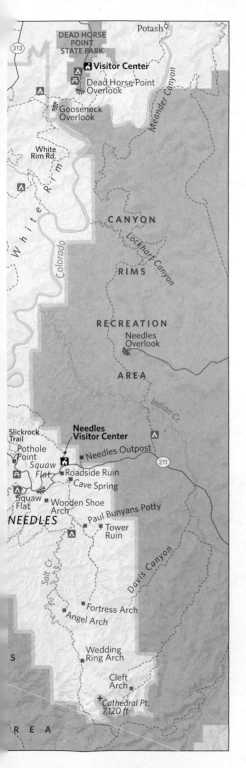

the arch, which rises from the sheer edge of a 500-foot cliff. If the light is right, you'll witness phenomenal orange colors reflecting off the 90-foot-long arch. In the basin beyond, **Washer Woman Arch** bends to its task, drawing photographers.

Trails dropping down to the **White Rim** bench or rivers below are brutal day-long affairs. There are easier plateau-top alternatives for stretching your legs. One mile from Mesa Arch, along the Upheaval Dome Road, the mile-long **Aztec Butte** trail lures you through a sandy wash and up a steep slickrock butte in search of 800-year-old granaries left by the ancient Puebloans. (Look for them under the caprock.)

A real kid-pleaser is **Whale Rock,** 3 miles farther down the same road. Reached via a half-mile trail, this 100-foot-high humpbacked dome begs to be climbed.

For a look at **Upheaval Dome,** continue to road's end and hike the rocky half-mile trail. Take some time to ponder this mysterious crater ringed with jagged spires of polychromatic rock. Geologists still argue whether this is a collapsed salt dome or rock exposed by erosion after a meteor strike some 60 million years ago.

Return the way you came, and if time permits, take the turnoff to **Green River Overlook** for austere vistas of treeless Soda Springs Basin. Edged with White Rim sandstone, the basin looks like a salt-rimmed margarita. You can glimpse the **Green River** deep in the canyon's cup. Originating in Wyoming's Wind River Range, the slow-moving Green River meets up with the muddy **Colorado River** at the **Confluence,** 47 miles from the park's northern boundary. Once back on the main road, head to its southern-most terminus at **Grand View Point,** 12 miles from the visitor center. Sync your arrival to an hour before sunset and ramble along the mile-long trail for spellbinding views of Junction Butte, Monument Basin, the Murphy Hogback, and The Needles and Maze districts. (Be sure to bring a flashlight for the return trip.)

Settle into a rocky nook and watch the rays of the setting sun splinter off the distant mesas.

The Needles

The Needles' best attribute is a net-work of diverse trails designed for day-long hiking and backpacking. If you're short on time, these four self-guided mini-hikes provide an educational sampler of the park.

Just 0.3 mile from the visitor center, park at **Roadside Ruin** and grab a trailhead pamphlet identifying native plants and how the Indians used them, as well as how they ground meal from rice grass, turned peppergrass into spice, and plucked nuts from piñon pines. The 0.3-mile trail ends at a small ancestral Puebloan **gra-nary** where this precious bounty was stored.

Continue another 0.3 mile down the road, turn left, and follow signs to **Cave Spring Trail.** The spring itself is a rarity in canyon country: a year-round water hole that has sustained life for centuries.

The crudely furnished **cowboy camp** occupying the first alcove above the trail served as a makeshift park headquarters in the early days.

Prickly pear fruit

Ancestral Puebloan paintings decorate the fire-blackened grotto next to the camp, where delicate maidenhair ferns line a mossy seep of life-giving water. Farther down the trail, ancient painted handprints on the rock seem to be reaching across the centuries.

Continue clockwise on the 0.6-mile loop trail, climbing two wooden ladders to reach the slickrock above. You'll be compensated with fine views of the banded spires of The Needles to the west.

Back on the Big Spring Overlook Road, stop at the **Pothole Point Trail,** where water-filled depressions dapple the slickrock. After a rain, these ephemeral pools burst with microlife: horsehair worms, snails, tadpoles, and fairy shrimp hatch from drought-resistant eggs. Be careful not to touch the water. The pristine potholes react immediately to chemical imbalances, in effect poisoning them.

Even if the potholes are dry, this 0.6-mile loop trail offers reward with far-reaching views of The Needles formations. Plus it is a shorter, easier version of the Slickrock Trail just down the road.

The 2.4-mile **Slickrock Trail** keeps to the high ground between Big and Little Spring Canyons, with four viewpoints serving up the park's most distant panoramas as well as your best shot at spying elusive bighorn sheep. Look for their giveaway: white rump patches.

Report all bighorn sightings to a park ranger. Because of fluctuations in the sheep population, the park tracks sightings and locations of these animals.

If you don't have two hours for the Slickrock Trail, continue on to road's

A Park Is Born

Bates Wilson (the first superintendent of Arches National Park) tirelessly wooed government bigwigs in hopes of persuading them that a Canyonlands national park would be a good idea. He took them deep into the canyons he loved, and plied them with whiskey and Dutch oven steaks. His powers of persuasion were legendary. Over a campfire in North Point, he famously inveigled Bureau of Land Management officials to sign over jurisdiction of a large part of the Maze district to the National Park Service for three shots of Jim Beam whiskey.

After President Johnson signed the park into law in 1964, Bates continued to mold the park, fighting against development of park infrastructure, arguing it wasn't the Park Service's obligation to pamper folks, even if it meant "turning away the man with the pink Cadillac."

When plans for Squaw Flat called for a regimented campground, he tore up the blueprints and designed the campground himself, tucking individual sites into rock contours and creating one of the most beautiful campgrounds of any national park in the process.

Self-reliance remains the guiding spirit of Canyonlands National Park, and Bates did everything he could to minimize the human imprint, including authoring a ban on naming any arch, tower, or distinctive landform after a person. Otherwise, there would most likely be a Bates Arch or Wilson Peak somewhere. Not that it matters. Bates's legacy is the existence of the park itself.

end at **Big Spring Canyon Overlook** for an up-close view of steep canyons crenellated by towering buttes.

This overlook is also the trailhead for a popular day trip on the **Confluence Overlook Trail,** a shadeless 5.5-mile trudge across Big Spring and Elephant Canyons and along a jeep trail to the unfenced edge of a 1,000-foot gorge where the Green and Colorado Rivers join forces.

To experience the essence of The Needles, bypass any of the above attractions to allow a half-day hike into ultrascenic **Chesler Park,** a 1,000-acre grassland meadow edged by the park's most spectacular display of these namesake spires. The 2.7-mile trail leaves from the Elephant Hill picnic area at the end of a 3-mile graded gravel road, and weaves through a narrow slot to a saddle overlooking Chesler Park. Take some time to meander through the meadow, inhaling sprigs of crushed sage, but don't get lost on the network of trails luring you deeper into Needles backcountry.

Horseshoe Canyon & the Maze

Count on a full day to visit Horseshoe Canyon, a detached section of the park that preserves a gallery of life-size figures that may have been painted as recently as 1,000 to 2,000 years ago.

The 3.5-mile-long trail (figure on 4 to 6 hours round-trip) drops 780 vertical feet to the canyon bottom and heads up Barrier Creek, past three minor pictograph panels, to the **Great Gallery,** a 300-foot-long panel displaying more than 20 shamanic effigies in red-ocher paint. Writer Edward Abbey described these ghostly figures as "apparitions out of bad dreams." Get an early start: It's a 2.5-hour drive from Moab just to reach the remote trailhead; the last 30 miles are dirt road.

To get from Horseshoe Canyon to **Hans Flat Ranger Station,** you return the way you came, turn south at the fork, and continue on. The distance from the canyon to the ranger station is 28 miles.

You'll need two things: a high-clearance four-wheel-drive vehicle and the necessary chutzpah to drive it down the hairpin turns of the **Flint Trail** to what early cowboys called "Under the Ledge," a labyrinth of fins, canyons, pinnacles, and buttes called **The Maze.** It's virtually trail-less, with some routes marked by cairns. (If you prefer to stay atop the mesa, outside park boundaries, you'll find the best Maze views at **Panorama Point,** 12.5 miles from Hans Flat.)

After descending the Orange Cliffs, the Flint Trail splits. One road heads to the **Maze Overlook** (30 miles on a bumpy road—four-wheel-drive is a must—from Hans Flat). The overlook across this curving labyrinth is a portal for multi-day backpacking adventures. The views—including a maelstrom of sandstone crested by the Organ shale Chocolate Drops, 350-million-year-old formations—are worth the bumpy ride.

A second road goes through the **Land of Standing Rocks** (more Organ shale formations) to the **Doll House,** 42 miles from Hans Flat, where you can hike down to the Colorado River at **Spanish Bottom.** Shuttle-bus pick-up at Spanish Bottom can be arranged. Jet boats connect with Moab by river—the easy way back.

Paddling the Colorado River

Information

How to Get There

To reach Island in the Sky from Moab, head north on US 191 for 10 miles to Utah 313, and drive 22 miles to the visitor center. To reach The Needles head south on US 191 to Utah 211, then west 34 miles to the park entrance. The Maze is reached via I-70, then south on Utah 24. Follow for 25 miles to a signed dirt road, which leads 32 miles to Horseshoe Canyon and 46 miles to Hans Flat Ranger Station.

When to Go

Brisk spring and balmy fall are ideal for hiking, though prepare for a wide range of weather. In summer, temperatures often hit triple digits; monsoons bring needed rain—and flash flooding. Mild winters are not uncommon, but even a light snow can close down dirt roads.

Visitor Centers

Island in the Sky and Hans Flat/The Maze visitor centers are open all year; Needles closes early Dec. through Feb.

Headquarters

2282 SW Resource Blvd.
Moab, UT 84532
nps.gov/cany
435-719-2100

Camping

There are two campgrounds in the park, the Bates Wilson–designed **Squaw Flat Campground** (26 sites) in The Needles, and **Willow Flat Campground** (11 sites) at Island in the Sky. Both are first come, first served and provide vault toilets, fire grates, and tables. To book one of The Needles three group sites (15 to 50 people) or to obtain a permit camping in the backcountry: *canypermits.nps.gov.*

Lodging

There are no hotels within the park. **Moab** *(discovermoab.com)* is a busy tourist town with numerous campground, lodging, and dining, options. **Monticello** and **Green River,** closer to The Needles and The Maze, offer fewer options.

CANYONLANDS
EST 1964

Canyonlands Excursions

Scott M. Matheson Wetlands Preserves
Moab, Utah

▷ The Nature Conservancy's Scott M. Matheson Wetlands Preserve provides a sharp contrast to the surrounding redrock cliffs and arid desert. It's a bird-watcher paradise, with over 200 species of birds, including spring migrants and summer nesters. Other animals in the area include beavers, muskrats, mule deer, raccoons, and the northern leopard frog. Open year-round, from dawn to dusk. Located east of Canyonlands National Park and south of Arches National Park. *nature.org;* 435-259-4629.

Glen Canyon National Recreation Area
Arizona/Utah

▷ Lake Powell, the desert, and the red-rock canyons offer 1.2 million acres of water-based and backcountry recreation activities, primarily in Utah, from hiking to watersports and boating (rentals available). Guided tours of both the dam (from the Carl Hayden Visitor Center, Page, Arizona) and Lake Powell allow visitors to better understand the area. There are numerous campgrounds (permit required in the Orange Cliffs area). *nps.gov/glca;* 928-608-6200.

Dead Horse Point State Park
Moab, Utah

▷ Dead Horse Point is a rock peninsula located atop a 6,000-foot-high sheer sandstone cliff connected to the mesa solely by a narrow strip of land known as the neck. Stunning vistas of the Colorado River and the surrounding rock strata of canyon country can be seen from the point. Camping (reservation required), hiking, and biking are options. Located next to Canyonlands National Park and 28 miles from Arches National Park. Fee. *stateparks.utah.gov/park/dead-horse -point-state-park;* 435-259-2614.

Manti La Sal National Forest
Central & Southeastern Utah

▷ Spanning 1.2 million acres, the Manti La Sal National Forest includes three mountain blocks in central and southeastern Utah. The National Forest encompasses historic drawings and ruins as well as beautiful mountains and canyons with places to hike, fish, and camp. Take a drive along the scenic byways, or get around by bicycle or horse. Water sports and winter sports round out the outdoors options. The national forest is south of Canyonlands National Park via US 191. *fs.usda.gov/ mantilasal;* 435-637-2817.

Sand Flats Recreation Area
Moab, Utah

▷ Regarded as a public lands treasure, the Sand Flats Recreation Area includes a high plain of slickrock domes, bowls and fins, and in the east it rises in elevation to meet the colorful mesas and nearly 13,000 foot peaks of the La Sal Mountains. Popular among bikers, the area has the popular Slickrock and Porcupine Rim bike trails and three 4x4 trails. Fees apply to day use and camping. Located near Moab, Utah. *sandflats .org;* 435-259-2444.

Westwater Canyon Wilderness Study Area (BLM)
Moab, Utah

▷ Westwater Canyon is characterized by its great scenery and unique geologic features including black pre-Cambrian rock (the oldest exposed rock in Utah), which forms the inner canyon. Considered by many to be the nation's best overnight white-water river trip; most recreation users come primarily to experience rapids, such as Skull and Last Chance. Permits are required for all river trips. Located northeast of Canyonlands and Arches National Parks. The wilderness study area is accessible from the interstate via the Cisco and Westwater exits. 435-259-2100.

Capitol Reef

Utah

Established
December 18, 1971

241,904 acres

"The Reef" is the least known of Utah's five national parks. Its defining geographical feature, the nearly 100-mile-long Waterpocket Fold, is an impenetrable sandstone barricade that kept travelers at bay for centuries. In 1962, the first paved road was built across the Reef, unlocking a monumental wilderness of domes, natural bridges, spires, and slot canyons, and presenting a vanished way of life. Capitol Reef National Park park brings travelers back to a bygone era that reveals America's sturdy pioneer roots.

Capitol Reef's name, according to local lore, derives from early prospectors who'd sailed great waters and were wary of reefs. Speaking of water, the park's geologic layers, thrust on edge by primal geologic forces 35 to 75 million years ago, testify to a story of Permian-era seas, Triassic tidal flats and swamps, Jurassic sand dunes, and late-Cretaceous seas.

The ancient Fremont people left their story on these rocks in the form of petroglyphs. Mormon pioneers arrived in the 1880s, planting thousands of fruit

Along the Scenic Drive

trees at the fertile confluence of the Fremont River and Sulphur Creek. In the 1920s, the area's beauty inspired a local club to envision a state park. Franklin D. Roosevelt responded by creating the Capitol Reef National Monument in 1937. It became a national park 34 years later.

▶ HOW TO VISIT

On a half-day visit, choose either the roadside attractions of Utah 24, including a 1.8-mile hike to **Hickman Bridge,** or opt for the park's **Scenic Drive,** stopping to explore **Grand Wash** or **Capitol Gorge** on foot. (A full day allows you to follow both the Utah 24 and Scenic Drive itineraries.) If you have another day and a high-clearance

four-wheel-drive vehicle, plan an off-road loop through desolate **Cathedral Valley** (64 miles). Or take the southern Notom-Bullfrog Road to the **Burr Trail Road** to explore slot canyons.

Utah 24

Built in 1962, this two-lane highway winds 14 miles through the park's mid-section. It is the only paved road to breech the nearly 100-mile-long **Waterpocket Fold.** Heading east from the town of Torrey, stop at **Chimney Rock,** a spire crowned by golden-hued Shinarump capstone. Enthusiastic hikers can tackle a steep 3.5-mile loop trail for a bird's-eye view of the formation and displays of petrified wood.

A half-mile beyond the trailhead is **Panorama Point turnoff.** Continue to the end of the mile-long dirt spur road, where two trails start at the parking area. One leads 0.1 mile to the **Goosenecks Overlook,** where, 800 feet down, are the entrenched meanders of Sulphur Creek that cut through Kaibab limestone, among the park's oldest exposed rock. (Fossil-rich Kaibab limestone forms the North Rim of the Grand Canyon.) The 0.4-mile **Sunset Point Trail** winds through a garden of weathered piñon pines and leads to a bench that faces one of the park's most photogenic sights. Framed by brick-red towers, the **Fremont River** curves through an escarpment topped by monolithic bone-white Navajo sandstone. Thirty miles away, the highest peak of the Henry Mountains, Mount Ellen (11,615 feet), dimples the horizon.

Continue on Utah 24 past the **visitor center** and Scenic Drive, stopping to peer into the 1896 **Fruita**

A Fruitful Enterprise

The early settlers of Fruita planted nearly 200 acres of orchards. The fruits of their labor helped sustain this Mormon community for most of a century, until the last residents moved away in 1969. Surviving in one of Utah's most remote locations meant relying on a barter economy, which didn't leave much room for luxuries. But who needed a newfangled telephone when you could holler to your neighbor from half a mile away?

Life was very basic but in some ways idyllic. Known as the "Eden of Wayne County," the area even had a forbidden fruit, moonshine, which some residents sold to passing sheepherders and cowboys, away from the disapproving eye of the Mormon church.

The orchards now contain more than 3,000 trees preserved by the National Park Service using the original gravity-fed pipes and ditches. Wander any of the 19 orchards that are unlocked, and, when the harvest begins, you can sample the fruit (handheld fruit pickers and three-legged ladders are available). You can fill a bag, stopping to weigh your harvest at the self-pay station.

Cherries ripen first, around the second week of June; apricots in June and July; pears and peaches in August and September. In September and October, apples are ready to pick. Besides offering many exotic heirloom varieties, these orchards have evolved their own unique strain: the tart Capitol Reef Red apple. You'll find these namesake fruits on the northern edge of the Jackson Orchard. For orchard updates: 435-260-3791.

Schoolhouse, which until 1941 also served as a dance hall and community center. Look for "Fruita Grade School" carved into the rock behind the school, where generations of school kids left their marks.

For ancient examples of rock art, continue 0.3 mile to the **Petroglyph Pullout,** where a boardwalk parallels a wall of Wingate sandstone festooned with bighorn sheep and figures sporting headdresses. The Fremont people left the area around A.D. 1300; petroglyphs weren't all they left behind. The Mormon pioneers reportedly uncovered irrigation ditches in the fields where apple orchards now grow. The Fremont stored their corn and beans in nearby **granaries.** To see a granary, continue 0.75 mile east on Utah 24 to the **Hickman Bridge** parking area and embark on a 1-mile hike that takes in Hickman Bridge, a 133-feet-long arch reaching 125 feet over an arroyo (creek). The last stop on Utah 24 is the 1882 **Benhunin Cabin.** Barely 200 square feet, this sandstone structure housed 13 adults. (The boys bedded in a rock alcove, while the girls slept in a wagon.)

Fruita & the Scenic Drive

Stop at the visitor center to pick up a self-guided brochure of the Scenic Drive, then head to the nearby **Fruita Historic District** for a glimpse of early pioneer life: mule deer grazing the orchards, a classic barn, and the old blacksmith shop containing Fruita's first tractor and a scattering of horse-drawn farming equipment. Farther down the road, stop at the **Gifford Farmhouse,** as much pioneer museum as country bakery (try the apple pie).

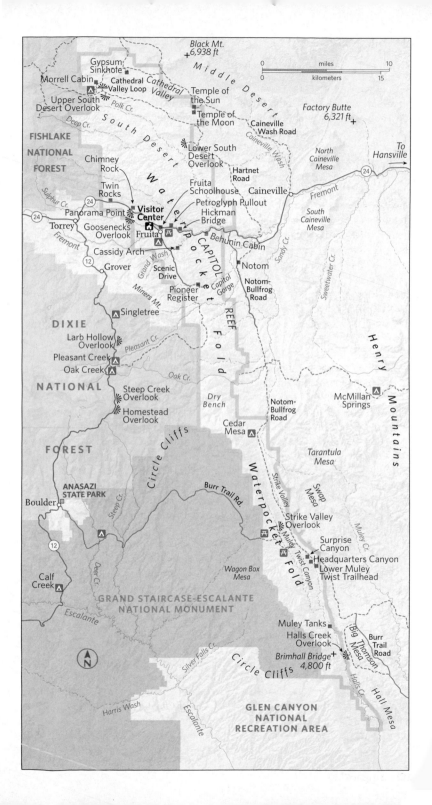

Black Mt.
+ 6,938 ft

Middle Desert

Gypsum
Sinkhole

Morrell Cabin

Cathedral
Valley Loop

Cathedral
Valley

Upper South
Desert Overlook

Temple of
the Sun

Temple of
the Moon

Caineville
Wash Road

Factory Butte
6,321 ft +

Polk Cr.

Deep Cr.

South Desert

FISHLAKE

NATIONAL

FOREST

Lower South
Desert Overlook

Hartnet
Road

Caineville
Wash

North
Caineville
Mesa

To
Hansville

24

Chimney
Rock

Twin
Rocks

Sulphur Cr.

Panorama Point

Torrey

Gooosenecks
Overlook

Fruita

Fruita
Schoolhouse

Petroglyph Pullout

Visitor
Center

Hickman
Bridge

Caineville

Fremont

24

Behunin Cabin

South
Caineville
Mesa

Cassidy Arch

Grover

12

Fremont

Grand Wash

Scenic
Drive

Miners Mt.

Pioneer
Register

Capitol
Gorge

Notom

Notom-
Bullfrog
Road

Sandy Cr.

Sweetwater Cr.

Singletree

DIXIE

Larb Hollow
Overlook

Pleasant Cr.

Pleasant Creek

Oak Creek

Oak Cr.

NATIONAL

Steep Creek
Overlook

Homestead
Overlook

Dry
Bench

Cedar
Mesa

Notom-
Bullfrog
Road

McMillan
Springs

Henry

Mountains

Tarantula
Mesa

FOREST

Circle Cliffs

Waterpocket

Fold

Strike Valley

Swap
Mesa

ANASAZI
STATE PARK

Boulder

Steep Cr.

Burr Trail Rd.

Strike Valley
Overlook

Surprise
Canyon

Headquarters Canyon

Lower Muley
Twist Trailhead

12

Deer Cr.

Wagon Box
Mesa

Muley Twist Canyon

Muley Cr.

Calf
Creek

GRAND STAIRCASE-ESCALANTE
NATIONAL MONUMENT

Escalante

Muley Tanks

Halls Creek
Overlook

Brimhall Bridge +
4,800 ft

Big Thomson Mesa

Burr
Trail
Road

Silver Falls Cr.

Circle Cliffs

Halls Cr.

Hall Mesa

N

Harris Wash

Escalante

GLEN CANYON
NATIONAL
RECREATION AREA

WATERPOCKET

CAPITOL

REEF

FOLD

miles   10

0
kilometers   15

Continue on the Scenic Drive, turning on a graded road to **Grand Wash.** You'll pass the 1901 **Oyler Mine,** whose uranium was used in elixirs back when radioactivity was considered a cure rather than a curse. Farther along, a 1.7-mile-long trail leads to **Cassidy Arch,** named for outlaw Butch Cassidy, who allegedly used Grand Wash to get to Robber's Roost. The Grand Wash road ends where the real fun begins: Hike the narrowing canyon, at one point 600 feet high and 16 feet wide.

Continue on the Scenic Drive to **Capitol Gorge,** another narrow passage. (This was only route between Torrey and Hanksville until Utah 24 opened in 1962.) An easy mile-long walk from the parking area takes you past Fremont petroglyphs (A.D. 600 to 1200) to a **Pioneer Register** etched in stone. A "who's who" of early pioneers, it includes characters such as Cass Hite, a member of Quantrill's Civil War Raiders who struck gold in the park's Glen Canyon and had a town named in his honor (later submerged by Lake Powell). Just beyond lie the **Tanks,** natural water pockets hosting a multitude of aquatic life, including water striders and fairy shrimp.

Cathedral Valley

Tackling the 60-mile unpaved **Cathedral Valley Loop,** which begins 12 miles east of the visitor center on Utah 24, requires a high-clearance vehicle and favorable road and river conditions (for information, 435-425-3791). The drive starts with a fording of the foot-deep Fremont River. The road climbs through the **Bentonite Hills,** a landscape of pastel colors (one of the area's nicknames is Land of the Sleeping Rainbow). After Harnet Mesa, the road loops around **Upper Cathedral Valley,** with fine views of 500-foot-high **monoliths** and the fluted **Walls of Jericho.** A 10-minute hike leads to weather-beaten **Morrell Cabin.** In Lower Cathedral Valley, a short spur road runs to the **Temple of the Sun** and **Temple of the Moon** monoliths. The road continues 15 miles before rejoining Utah 24 at Caineville.

Elsewhere in the Park

Paralleling the eastern escarpment of the Waterpocket Fold from its junction with Utah 24, the **Notom-Bullfrog Road** offers access to remote slot canyons. Continue on to **Surprise** and **Headquarters** Canyons, which provide a good introduction to canyoneering. Both are 2-mile round-trips. **Upper** and **Lower Muley Twist canyons** offer remote backpacking adventures, though it may be adventure enough just to drive up the precipitous **Burr Trail.** This 1880s sheep trail was graded into a road during the uranium boom in 1953, courtesy of the Atomic Energy Commission. Stop at the top of the road to admire the switchbacks you've just navigated, and take in the immense views of Swap Mesa and the Henry Mountains, the last places to be mapped in the Lower 48.

The Burr Trail returns to pavement at the park's western boundary, where you can continue to Boulder, 32 miles away, and loop back to Capitol Reef. But before you do, if you have a four-wheel-drive vehicle, consider taking the spur road, following **Upper Muley Twist Canyon** for 3 miles to the **Strike Valley Overlook,** with the park's best view of the curving Waterpocket Fold.

Spooky Gulch, a narrow slot canyon

Information

How to Get There

From Green River (95 miles east) take I-70 west to Utah 24, which leads to the park's east entrance. From Bryce Canyon National Park (123 miles southwest of Capitol Reef), a more scenic route on Utah 12 loops over Boulder Mountain to Utah 24 and the park's western entrance.

When to Go

Orchard blossoms kick off spring, when ideal hiking temps (60–70°F) are punctuated by spells of frost. Summer mercury hovers in the low 90s, but evenings cool nicely. From mid-July through Sept., afternoon rain can unleash flash floods. Oct. ushers in gold cottonwoods and cooler temps. Intermittent snow cover makes for a winter wonderland.

Visitor Centers

At the junction of Scenic Drive and Utah 24, the year-round visitor center (435-425-3791) has exhibits, a bookstore, and orientation movie.

Headquarters

Capitol Reef National Park
HC 70 Box 15
Torrey, UT 84775
nps.gov/care
435-425-3791

CAPITOL REEF
EST 1971

Camping

Campsites *(fee)* are first come, first served. The **Fruita** campground (71 sites) has restrooms but no hookups. Campgrounds with pit toilets and fire grates are found in **Upper Cathedral Valley** (6 sites) and on the Notom-Bullfrog Road at **Cedar Mesa** (5 sites).

Lodging

There is no lodging in the park. Ten miles east of the visitor center, **Torrey** *(torrey utah.org)* and nearby **Teasdale** *(capitolreef .org/teasdale)* provide lodgings, from motels to the **Lodge at Red River** *(red riverranch.com)*. Lodging and camping facilities can be found in and near Cainville and Hanksville, also to the east.

Grand Canyon

Arizona

Established
February 26, 1919

1.2 million acres

Like the Statue of Liberty, the Grand Canyon is an American icon. (It's almost as if the majesty of the American West has been poured into a limestone riverbed.) Theodore Roosevelt considered it his civic duty to urge every American to see it. And around five million people come to Grand Canyon National Park every year, from all over the globe. Indeed, the canyon is considered one of the seven wonders of the natural world.

People come not because this is the deepest, narrowest, or even longest canyon in the world. It's not. But the sum of these features make it the grandest by far. The park runs for 277 river miles, preserving 1,904 square miles of wilderness. From 258-million-year-old limestone capping the rim to 1.8 billion-year-old Vishnu schist a mile below, from stately ponderosa pine forests to prickly desert scrub, bighorn sheep to Kaibab squirrels, Mother Nature is on full display here.

You can shake the crowds by hitting the trails or visiting the remote North Rim. Seen 10 miles across

View from Desert View Drive, on the South Rim

▶ HOW TO VISIT

On a one-day visit to the **South Rim,** head straight to Mather Point, behind the **visitor center,** and make your way along the rim to **Grand Canyon Village.** Then decide whether to take the shuttle to **Hermits Rest** (the shuttle doesn't run in winter) or drive your own vehicle to **Desert View.** Wherever you end up, stay to watch the sunset. On a second day, explore what you missed the day before on the South Rim, then make the four-hour-plus drive to the **North Rim.** Arrive in time for a late-afternoon hike to watch the sunset from **Cape Royal.** An overnight trip requires advance reservations, usually months in advance. In the case of a mule or river trip, it could be a year.

Grand Canyon Village

If short on time, park at the **visitor center,** but skip the orientation video in favor of the real thing at **Mather Point,** just a 100-yard walk away. The rail-grabbing view extends 10 miles across the chasm, where the forested North Rim descends in monumental ridges, steep canyons, hogbacks, and buttes to the **Colorado River,** one mile below. You'll find the chiaroscuro of sunlight and clouds across the chasm more engaging than any video.

Take in the view on a stroll along the **Rim Trail** to Yavapai Point (0.75 mile). Below you, the **Tonto Platform** flattens out to the edge of the inner gorge. Beyond, **Bright Angel Canyon** rises to meet the North Rim, a cross-canyon gorge created by the massive Bright Angel Fault. A grove of Fremont cottonwoods at the foot of

the chasm from the South Rim, it's 212 miles away. Ninety percent of park visitors stick to the South Rim, where tourism took hold shortly after John Wesley Powell made the first descent of the Colorado River in 1869. The Atchison, Topeka, and Santa Fe Railways reached the South Rim in 1901, paving the way for concessioner Fred Harvey to shape the Grand Canyon experience with mule rides, luxury lodgings, and rustic Western decor, still part of the scene today.

Looking out over the canyon still feels like it did back in 1897, when travel writer Amelia Holleback described the experience: "As if half the world had fallen away before your feet, and after that, you are no longer on the same old Earth."

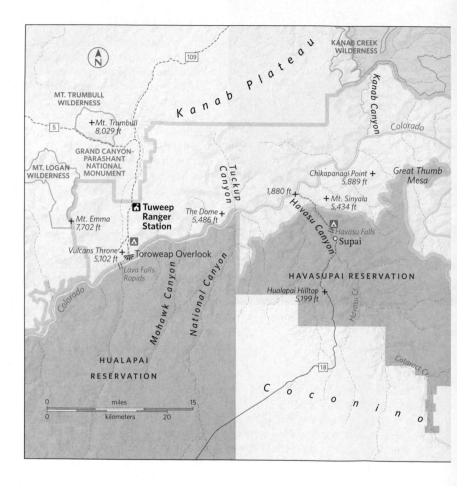

Bright Angel Canyon shades the Mary Colter–designed **Phantom Ranch,** rustic cabins built in 1922 and still reached only by foot, mule, or boat. (Colter designed eight structures in the park.)

The two nearby suspension bridges are the only places that cross the Colorado River for several hundred miles.

At **Yavapai Point,** explore the small museum built in 1928 as an observation station for scientists and visitors.

A topographic model, a geologic column of rock layers, and daily ranger talks provide a crash course on two billion years of Earth history.

You can walk the geologic history of the canyon by going west on the **Trail of Time,** edging the canyon's rim, where each stop is marked by a bronze medallion signifying a time period of a million years. When you reach **Verkamp's Visitor Center** (1.3 miles away), you will have walked

1,840 million years back in time—and straight into the hurly-burly of the **Historic District,** the park's epicenter for eating, drinking, and shopping. The historic complex includes the original 1909 log-built train depot, the 1905 **El Tovar Hotel,** the Mary Colter–designed **Lookout Studio** and **Hopi House,** and the Victorian-rustic **Kolb Studio.** Each interprets the Grand Canyon experience through its unique architecture. And each is worth poking

into for the Native American crafts, landscape photography, curio kitsch, and historical exhibits.

Surprisingly, the busy village is also a great place to spot one of the 74 or so California condors inhabiting the region, especially from mid-April through July. Look for them roosting on the north-facing cliffs or in the Douglas fir trees below the Bright Angel Lodge toward sunset or early in the morning.

Just beyond Kolb Studio, watch backpackers make their way down the **Bright Angel Trail,** a classic 9.5-mile route down to the river. Or try it yourself, at least as far as the first tunnel, 0.2 mile down, where haunting pictographs are a reminder that this once was a prehistoric byway. From the Village, take the blue Village Route shuttle or walk the 2 miles back to the visitor center.

South Rim Along Hermit Road

The only way to explore the area west of the Village and its nine overlooks is via the Hermits Rest shuttle, walking the 7.8-mile Rim Trail that parallels the road, or pedaling a bike. Whatever the method, your first stop is **Trailview Overlook,** a cliffside pull-out where you can watch the mule trains leave each morning down Bright Angel Trail.

From the second pullout, **Maricopa Point,** you can spot ruins of the Orphan uranium mine, which closed in 1969. Owners had planned to build a luxury hotel in its place until Congress passed a law to buy the property and terminate mineral rights, preserving the canyon's integrity. Beyond the site, the road bends back to **Powell Point,** on the South Rim.

The point is named for John Wesley Powell, the indefatigable one-armed visionary who made the first survey of the Grand Canyon in 1869. He started with nine men in four boats. After three months, six emaciated men and two splintered boats emerged from the canyon. Though Powell went on to become director of the U.S. Geological Survey and the first director of the Smithsonian's Bureau of Ethnology,

he is best known for his daring river expeditions.

For river views, however, you'll have to continue on to **Hopi Point.** No need to wait for the shuttle. You can walk the 0.3 mile in 10 minutes. This promontory juts far into the canyon, providing unobstructed views east and west. It's one of the best sunset-watching spots on the South Rim.

The white water churning below is **Granite Rapids,** named by Powell. His place names—Lava Rapids, Marble Canyon, Bright Angel—are descriptive compared to those of his close associate, the geologist Clarence Dutton, who began a more esoteric tradition of labeling landforms with Asian and Egyptian religious names. Thus we have the likes of **Shiva Temple.**

If time's an issue, bypass similar views at **Mohave Point.** Both the road and the trail here skirt the sheer 3,000-foot cliffs at The Abyss and Monument Creek Vista before arriving at **Pima Point,** where an aerial tram once ran supplies 6,000 feet down to an upscale tent camp built in the 1920s by the Santa Fe Railway. Abandoned in 1930, remains can still be glimpsed.

The road ends at **Hermits Rest,** a medieval jumble of stone with a cairn-like chimney, designed in 1914 by Mary Colter. "You can't imagine what it cost to make it look this old," said Colter, who went so far as to have soot rubbed into the stones above the fireplace. The "hermit" who inspired this creation was Louis Boucher, an eccentric prospector, guide, and campsite operator living alone below the rim, known for his white beard and white mule. The alcove fireplace in this snack and curio shop has warmed generations of hikers returning from the

Hermit Trail, a tough 10.8-mile descent to the Colorado River.

Desert View Drive

From the Grand Canyon Visitor Center, Desert View Drive edges the canyon for 23 miles east to Desert View. The only shuttle buses that operate on Desert View Drive provide access to Yaki Point and the South Kaibab trailhead, where cars are prohibited.

To visit **Yaki Point,** board the shuttle at the visitor center, the earlier the better as this is a prime sunrise viewing spot. Another option is to take the 7-mile **South Kaibab Trail** (one shuttle stop before Yaki Point). The trail winds down the spine of Cedar Mesa to the river, but you only have to descend 1.8 miles to **Ooh Aah Point** for a stunning view of Upper Granite Gorge and Zoroaster Temple in the morning light.

Desert View Drive's first major overlook is **Grandview Point.** At 7,400 feet, the towering ponderosa pines have replaced the forest of dwarf juniper and piñon pine. The steep 4.5-mile **Grandview Trail** drops 3,000 feet down to **Horseshoe Mesa,** where early Indians once gathered blue copper ore to use as paint. Miners later worked the ore at Last Chance mine, but it wasn't long before one prospector, John Hance, realized the real gold was in tourism. In the 1880s, he led the

A mule train along the Bright Angel Trail at the South Rim of the Grand Canyon

Main lobby of the El Tovar Hotel

first sightseeing parties into the Grand Canyon, telling tall tales to match the grand landscapes. He claimed to have dug the Grand Canyon himself, and that the river was so muddy that "to get a drink you have to cut a piece of water off and chew it."

The steepest and most hazardous section of the Colorado River, Hance Rapids can be glimpsed from the next overlook, **Moran Point.** This promontory is named after artist Thomas Moran, who joined Powell on his third expedition. This resulted in a 12-foot-long masterpiece, *Chasm of the Colorado,* which was purchased by the U.S. Congress and hung in the U.S. Capitol. Moran's work inspired President Theodore Roosevelt to proclaim the canyon a national monument in 1908.

For a change of pace, stop at the **Tusayan Ruin and Museum,** one of the park's 4,300 archaeological-recorded sites. The short self-guided trail loops

around ancestral Puebloan structures dating to A.D. 1185. Notice the sipapu (hole in the floor) within the circular kiva, the symbolic portal from which ancestors emerged from a previous world. The present-day Hopi believe their ancestors emerged from a similar sipapu at the bottom of the canyon, and still make pilgrimages there.

Upon reaching **Lipan Point,** you can see all the way to the Vermillion Cliffs and the Painted Desert as the river makes a lazy bend around the Unkar Delta and enters the dark inner gorge.

At **Desert View,** Mary Colter's 70-foot **Watchtower** rises along the Rosetta Stone of the Colorado Plateau. Inside, climb the 85 steps of this cryptic modern-day kiva to ponder paintings by Hopi painter Fred Kabotie, petroglyphs, and re-creations of Native American symbology. From the top of the tower—the South Rim's highest point—you can see Navajo Mountain,

Riddles of the Rock

Grand Canyon's stratified formations may look like an open book, but it's written in riddles. Take the Great Unconformity, first noticed by John Wesley Powell on his 1869 expedition. Cambrian rock, 525 million years old, mysteriously rests atop 1.8-billion-year-old Vishnu schist. Missing is 1.2 billion years in the geologic record. The gap is easily seen in the Grand Canyon's inner gorge.

Something happened near the beginning of the Great Unconformity that triggered the Cambrian explosion of life 500 million years ago, when simple, soft-bodied life suddenly diversified into complex organisms with shells and hard skin. The physical evidence of this evolution may be gone—the lack of fossil records tormented Darwin until his death—but theories abound.

The amount of deep geologic time revealed by the Grand Canyon is staggering, but how old is the canyon itself? Powell and others figured on 70 million years, the Colorado River downcutting at the same rate that the Kaibab Plateau was rising—that is, until sediments at the western end of the Canyon conclusively proved the Colorado River couldn't be more than 6 million years old.

Latest studies using thermochronological data suggest that an eastward-flowing paleo-river carved most of the western part of the canyon 70 million years ago, while a different river cut through the eastern section 55 million years ago. The Colorado River then joined the canyons with sections it carved itself, finishing off the job.

Echo Cliffs, and, 5,000 feet below, the sinuous Colorado River.

North Rim

Less crowded and 1,000 feet higher than the South Rim, making it cooler, the remote North Rim also has far fewer facilities, which are clustered at canyon's edge 14 miles south of the entrance station. For an introductory overview, walk right through historic **Grand Canyon Lodge** and onto the 0.25-mile paved trail, which leads to **Bright Angel Point.**

This precipitous rock spine divides Transept Canyon from Roaring Springs Canyon, where gushing springs indeed roar from 3,000 feet below. A self-guiding pamphlet points out, among other things, marine fossils and a 600-year-old juniper tree, while trail's end takes in soul-stirring views of Deva, Brahma, and Zoroaster Temples.

If you want to drop below the rim to the water, take the nearby 14.2-mile **North Kaibab Trail,** which switchbacks steeply down the colorful rock layers. The top portion of the trail provides an invigorating foray through ponderosa pines and white fir. **Coconino Overlook,** 0.75 mile down, or **Supai Tunnel,** 1.7 miles down, are obvious turnaround points.

For the North Rim's most epic views, drive 10 miles northwest through forests of spruce and fir, past meadows bordered by quaking aspen, to **Point Imperial.** At 8,803 feet, this is Grand Canyon's highest overlook, taking in not just the canyon as it widens out of Marble Canyon, but also the Painted Desert and the Navajo Nation lands.

Now backtrack 3 miles to the **Cape Royal Road** and follow it onto the Walhalla Plateau, surrounded on three sides by the canyon. Picnic tables beckon under ponderosa pines at **Vista Encantada.** The second overlook, **Roosevelt Point,** provides a rare glimpse of the confluence of the Colorado and Little Colorado Rivers. And 5.5 miles farther down the road lies the trailhead to 4-mile **Cape Final,** which leads to a spectacular panorama, with distant views of Vishnu and Jupiter Temples. This is your best shot for solitude.

Before reaching road's end at Cape Royal, consider two short side trips. **Walhalla Glade** opposite the Walhalla Overlook reveals the rock outlines of a 900-year-old pueblo. And the half-mile **Cliff Spring Trail** passes an ancestral Puebloan granary before reaching a mossy alcove spring, a natural spa for many of the park's 373 feathered species.

The grand finale at road's end, **Cape Royal** is the southernmost point on the North Rim. The cape's prow is reached via a half-mile paved path edged in sage and fragrant cliff rose. Detour for an exhilarating skywalk atop the flying buttress framing Angel's Window, a Kaibab-limestone arch.

At Cape Royal, settle in to watch the lowering sun lacquer the banded escarpments and towers: Wotan's Throne, Freya Castle, and Vishnu Temple, all in luminous light as shadows deepen across what John Muir called "nature's own capital city."

Into the Canyon

Whether by oar, hoof, or boot, there's no easy way to experience the canyon's inner sanctum. All hikes hereabouts are strenuous. Most hikers stick to the South Rim's 9.5-mile **Bright Angel Trail** for its shade and water. The **South Kaibab Trail** from Yaki Point (6.2 miles) provides a quicker ridgeline descent, but it is a hot, waterless climb back out. (Most hikers return via Bright Angel.) From the North Rim, the only maintained route to the river is the **North Kaibab Trail,** an arduous 14.2-miler. All three trails connect via the **River Trail** at the bottom, where two foot bridges span the river. You can camp at **Bright Angel Campground** *(permit required)* or bunk in the dorm or cabins at historic **Phantom Ranch,** a leafy haven nestled near where **Bright Angel Creek** enters the Colorado River. Lodging reservations should be made a year in advance.

The classic overnight mule trip to Phantom Ranch also can be challenging—to your nerves and knees. (Mules favor the trail's outside edge.) Plan in advance; these trips can fill up a year ahead of time. Mule trips from the North Rim dip below the rim but don't go all the way to Phantom Ranch.

A multi-week raft trip through the arterial heart of the Grand Canyon is for most a life-changing adventure. Along the epic 225-mile float from Lees Ferry to Diamond Creek, the river tumbles through 150 rapids, including infamous **Lava Falls** and **Hance Rapids,** in between more placid stretches. The dam-release water is a hypothermic 46°F, even when mercury hits 110, adding to the extreme nature of this trip. Motorized boat trips and half-canyon trips shorten the time commitment.

Visitors at Mather Point on the South Rim of the Grand Canyon

Information

How to Get There

To reach the South Rim, take Ariz. 64 (US 180 from Flagstaff) from I-40. A slightly longer, less trafficked option via US 89 from Flagstaff skirts the San Francisco Peaks to Ariz. 64 and enters the park at Desert View. The North Rim, 10 miles away as the bird flies, is a four-hour-plus drive from the South Rim.

When to Go

Summer and school vacation times are peak seasons. To avoid crowds, visit from Oct. to April. Spring sees moderate weather, wildflowers, and active wildlife. Turning aspen and mild weather make Oct. an ideal month. The North Rim usually closes mid-Oct. through mid-May. The South Rim stays busy all winter.

Visitor Centers

The South Rim has two visitor centers, the main one near Mather Point and a smaller one at Verkamp, east of the El Tovar Hotel. Both are open year-round. The North Rim Visitor Center is open mid-May to late Oct.

Headquarters

20 South Entrance Rd.
Grand Canyon Village, AZ 86023
nps.gov/grca
928-638-7888

Camping

The park has more than 500 campsites. Reservations *(recreation.gov;* 877-444-6777) can be made at year-round **Mather Campground** on the South Rim and the **North Rim Campground** (mid-May through Oct.). The **Desert View Campground** (May to mid-Oct.) is first come, first served.

Lodging

Plan ahead. Reservations in the park at historic **Hotel El Tovar** and **Bright Angel Lodge,** plus three modern motels (all in Grand Canyon Village), are handled through Xanterra *(grandcanyonlodges .com;* 888-297-2757), as are reservations for **Phantom Ranch,** in the inner canyon. **Yavapai Lodge,** in Grand Canyon Village, is operated by Delaware North *(grand canyon.com;* 877-404-4611.)

Great Basin

Nevada

Established
October 27, 1986

77,180 acres

Carved by glaciers and dominated by Wheeler Peak, more than 13,000 feet high, remote Great Basin National Park protects landscapes of high-altitude desert valleys, salt flats, and rolling ridges. The lakes reflect rocky scenes; the Lehman Caves brim with palaces; and the night skies dazzle with stars.

The park occupies a portion of the South Snake Range that rose up 30 million years ago when plate tectonics stretched the Earth's crust, cracking it into parallel faults. These fractures uplifted into 160 mountain ranges. In between are flat basins where precipitation collects in *playas* (lake beds).

A first impression of the park as just another mountain rising from the desert floor gives way in the face of its wonders, including ancient bristlecone pines and an Ice Age cirque that cradles Nevada's only glacier.

Early trappers called this part of the mountain range "Starvation Country" and steered clear. Ranching and farming brought settlers to the Snake Valley in the mid-1860s. Miners and prospectors followed.

But it wasn't until the discovery of Lehman Caves (actually just one cave)

Stella Lake

in 1885 that visitors began to flock to the South Snake Range. American explorer and mapmaker John Frémont coined the name Great Basin in the mid-1880s.

Declared a national monument in 1922, the Lehman Caves attracted attention from all over the world, as did the harsh beauty of Wheeler Peak. Talk of a national park ensued, spurred on in 1955 with the rediscovery of an active glacier in Great Basin. When bulldozers uprooted bristlecone pines at mining-claim locations on Mount Washington, appeals for a national park gathered strength.

Today, Great Basin National Park incorporates the Lehman Caves National Monument, Wheeler Peak, and bristlecone pine groves. In the

heat of summer, Great Basin provides cool refuge on timberline trails, in forests of limber pine and Engelmann spruce, and deep underground in the intricate marbled cave.

▶ HOW TO VISIT

The park is a 4- to 6-hour drive from Reno, Las Vegas, or Salt Lake City, so consider overnighting in Ely, Baker, or camping in the park. Don't risk missing **Lehman Caves** by showing up without a reservation (775-234-7517). Book the first cave tour of the day, and use the afternoon to drive up **Wheeler Peak** to hike the **Bristlecone Trail.** Check the weather forecast before heading out; thunderstorms are not unusual.

Come sunset, linger at one of the overlooks on the way down. Be sure to look up after dark. You don't want to miss some of the blackest night skies in America. On a moonless night, the Andromeda galaxy can be seen with the naked eye. In summer, park rangers provide night-sky-viewing programs that use high-power telescopes *(fee).*

Lehman Caves

Actually a single multi-chambered cavern turned into a masterpiece of nature when Ice Age water containing carbonic acid from decaying vegetation percolated down fractures in the limestone, depositing calcite crystals to decorate the subterranean cavities. In this "living cave," stalactites continue to grow—about an inch every 100 years.

The human history of Lehman Caves dates back more than 10,000

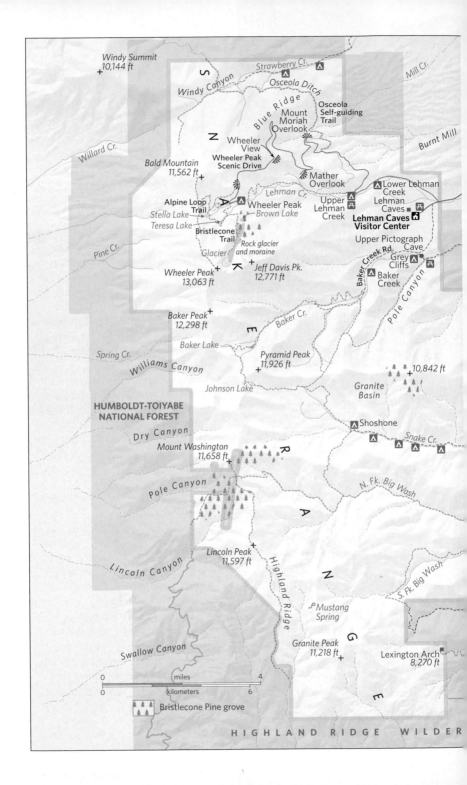

Windy Summit
+10,144 ft

S

Windy Canyon

Strawberry Cr.

Osceola Ditch

Mill Cr.

Blue Ridge

N

Mount Moriah Overlook

Osceola Self-guiding Trail

Burnt Mill

Willard Cr.

Bald Mountain
11,562 ft +

Wheeler View

Wheeler Peak Scenic Drive

Lehman Cr.

Mather Overlook

Lower Lehman Creek

Lehman Caves

Alpine Loop Trail

Wheeler Peak

Upper Lehman Creek

Lehman Caves Visitor Center

Stella Lake

Brown Lake

Teresa Lake

Bristlecone Trail

Pine Cr.

Glacier

Rock glacier and moraine

Upper Pictograph Cave

Baker Creek Rd.

Grey Cliffs

Pole Canyon

Wheeler Peak +
13,063 ft

+ Jeff Davis Pk.
12,771 ft

Baker Creek

Baker Peak +
12,298 ft

E

Baker Cr.

Baker Lake

Pyramid Peak
11,926 ft
+

Spring Cr.

Williams Canyon

Johnson Lake

+ 10,842 ft

Granite Basin

HUMBOLDT-TOIYABE
NATIONAL FOREST

Dry Canyon

Shoshone

Snake Cr.

Mount Washington
11,658 ft

R

N. Fk. Big Wash

Pole Canyon

A

Lincoln Peak
11,597 ft
+

N

Lincoln Canyon

Highland Ridge

Mustang Spring

S. Fk. Big Wash

Swallow Canyon

Granite Peak
11,218 ft
+

G

Lexington Arch
8,270 ft

0   miles   4

0   6
kilometers

Bristlecone Pine grove

E

HIGHLAND   RIDGE   WILDER

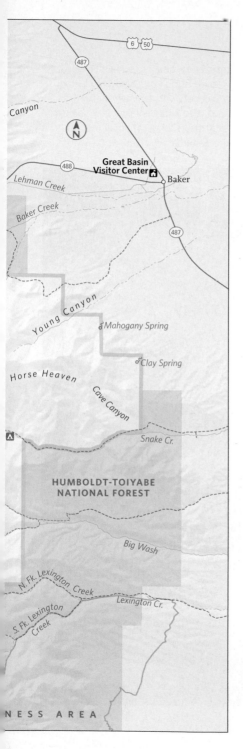

years to paleo-Indians, continuing through the Fremont and Shoshone tribes to the 19th century, when trappers and military expeditions entered the area, followed by ranchers and miners.

In the 1870s, Absalom Lehman established a ranch near what today is called Lehman Creek, where he cultivated food for local miners. He discovered the cave in 1885, but the stalactites were so dense he could not penetrate.

Dynamite and sledgehammers soon opened the way for tourists who marveled at the ornate variety of stalactites, stalagmites, soda straws, flowstone, draperies, popcorn, rimstone pools, and rare cave shields. Helictites branch in all directions, like underwater coral.

While not as vast as Carlsbad Caverns or Mammoth Caves, the more intimate nature of Lehman Caves allows visitors to get close to—but not touch—the delicate formations. Bring a sweater; the temperature is a constant 50°F. Flashlights and cameras are allowed, but no tripods.

The 60-minute **Lodge Room** tour *(fee)* takes in the Gothic Palace, the Music Room and the Lodge Room, while the 90-minute **Grand Palace** tour *(fee)* continues on into the Inscription Room, where early visitors burned their names into the rock with candles. Grand Palace is home to the cavern's most photographed feature, the spectral Parachute Shield.

Tours can be reserved 30 days in advance (775-234-7331 ext. 242). Same-day reservations can be very difficult to secure.

Wheeler Peak Scenic Drive

Rising 4,000 feet in 12 miles, this road travels from sagebrush flats through piñon-juniper forests, past tangled stands of mountain mahogany and manzanita, and into subalpine forests. Numerous pull-offs allow you to focus on scenery between the sharp turns and steep 8 percent grades. (Vehicles and trailers longer than 24 feet are prohibited along the drive.)

Great Basin, dotted with creeks

A trail at the first pull-off leads a quarter mile to the ill-fated 18-mile-long **Osceola Ditch,** built in 1889 by 200 men with hand tools to supply water for gold mining. The ditch failed due to lack of water. Hiking what remains of the wooden flumes is made more interesting by knowing the history.

Continue on to **Mount Moriah Overlook** for far-reaching views of this 12,072-foot peak crowning the North Snake Range. It's also a good place to scan the skies for golden eagles soaring on rising thermals.

A picnic spot at **Mather Overlook,** farther along the scenic drive, takes in views of both Wheeler and Jeff Davis peaks, but **Wheeler View,** farther on, provides a jaw-drop panorama of both Nevada's second highest peak and the rare glacier at the base of a cirque (a deep, steep-walled basin). The Scenic Drive ends at Wheeler Peak Campground and three hiking trails.

The easiest trail is the 0.4-mile wheelchair-accessible **Sky Islands Forest Trail,** an interpretive loop through the Englemann spruce and limber pine trees. But if you are going to hike any trail in the park, it should be the 2.8-mile **Bristlecone Trail,** which climbs above tree line, and if you have time, the 2.7-mile **Alpine Loop Trail.** Combine the two into an exhilarating 5-miler. To do so, bear right on the Alpine Loop Trail, en route to tiny Stella and Teresa Lakes. Filled with snowmelt, these shallow ice-gouged depressions mirror the majestic mountains above. Continue on to join the Bristlecone Trail. Here, a grove of bristlecone pine trees stands, it seems, in stark defiance to the elements, their dense wood burnished by

centuries of wind-driven ice. Along the trail, interpretive exhibits shed light on the ecology of the extraordinary bristlecone pines. Each tree has its

Guardians of Time

Great Basin bristlecone pines are among the oldest living organisms on our planet, dating back to the Bronze Age. Surviving where other trees can't, their contorted limbs have been raked by storms throughout millennia. The timberline conditions—wind-driven ice, freezing temperatures, rocky soil—contribute to their dense insect-resistant wood and slow growth. Their trunks are a visual record of climate history.

As their first investigator, Dr. Edmund Schulman, concluded, when it comes to bristlecones, adversity begets longevity. The trees are treasure chests to dendrochronologists, who study tree-ring growth.

There are three bristlecone groves in the park: on a ridge near Eagle Peak, on Mount Washington, and the only accessible copse, reached via a 1.5-mile trail from the end of the Wheeler Peak Scenic Drive. On this interpretive trail, you'll meet such legendary trees as Adversity (born 100 B.C., died A.D. 1400) and 3,000-year-old Reluctance to Die.

The unmarked trunk of what might be among the oldest trees in the world, nearly 5,000-year-old Prometheus lies farther off the trail. It was unwittingly cut down in 1964 by a graduate student hoping to glean tree-ring data. (A slice of Prometheus is on display in the visitor center.) Outrage over the felling of Prometheus spurred people to action to create a national park.

own personality, and most have names befitting their epic nature and venerable age. Bristlecone seedlings six inches tall are probably older than you are (see p. 229).

If you've got enough daylight, continue another mile through barren scree highlighted by patches of grass, sedge, and perennial herbs to a snowy cirque formed by the sheer rock faces of Wheeler and Jeff Davis Peaks. Here, quartzite rubble covers Nevada's only glacier. Though it measures 300 feet long and 400 feet wide, this alpine glacier is likely to disappear in 20 years due to climate change. On the way back, keep an eye out for the black rosy finches that nest in rocks above the tree line.

Climbing Wheeler Peak

It takes five to eight hours to reach 13,063-foot Wheeler Peak, an 8.6-mile nontechnical round-trip but with an intense 3,000-foot elevation gain. To summit requires strong lungs, determination, and prudent judgment. Start early from the **Summit Trailhead** to avoid getting caught in afternoon thunderstorms, especially in summer.

It's an easy jaunt until you reach the wind-blown saddle, where the trail switchbacks up loose talus to the summit, marked by rock remains of a heliograph station. The effort is more than worth it: Hundred-mile views stretch in all directions.

Elsewhere in the Park

A quarter-mile before the Lehman Caves Visitor Center, take **Baker Creek Road** 2 miles, turning left toward Grey Cliffs campground. Bear left at the fork to **Upper Pictograph Cave.** Colorful pictographs made by the Fremont people sometime between A.D. 1000 and 1300 adorn the cavern's entrance. (Cave entry is prohibited to protect roosting Townsend's big-eared bats.)

Baker Creek Road ends 3 miles farther on, where a popular 6-mile trail continues to Baker Lake. May through July, keep on the lookout for yellow-bellied marmots sunning on rocks near the trailhead. They hibernate the rest of the year.

Also heading out from the edge of Baker Creek Road is a trail that makes a circuit of 11,926-foot Pyramid Peak. Primitive **Baker Lake–Johnson Lake Loop** is a challenging 13-mile day hike or a more relaxed overnight backpacking trip. (A free permit is required for backcountry hiking.)

The route starts at 8,000 feet and follows Baker Creek for a few miles before climbing switchbacks up to a glacier-cut cirque on Baker Peak, where Baker Lake lies. A stunning tableau, the alpine lake is surrounded by beautiful cliffs.

At the east end of Johnson Lake are historic structures from the old Johnson Lake mine. Park rangers warn visitors not to enter mine structures or pits.

The Park Service is reintroducing indigenous Bonneville cutthroat trout into the creeks here. A living legacy from the Ice Age, this subspecies was trapped in these streams when Lake Bonneville drained 15,000 years ago. This ancient lake filled the Great Basin before it burst and flooded the Snake River Basin. The Snake River drains into the Columbia River Basin en route to the Pacific Ocean.

The Gothic Palace in the Lehman Caves

Information

How to Get There

Whether coming from Reno (387 miles west) on I-80, or from Salt Lake City (238 miles northeast) or Las Vegas (296 miles south) via I-15, you'll eventually turn onto US 50, the "Loneliest Road in America." (Check your spare.) Turn south at Nev. 487 and continue 5 miles to the park.

When to Go

The park is open year-round, though the upper reach of **Wheeler Peak Scenic Drive** generally closes Nov. through May depending on weather. Spring wildflowers and fall foliage beckon hikers, but summer brings the highest visitation, when high elevation (6,825 feet at the visitor center) keeps temperatures in the mid-80s. Keep an eye on **Wheeler Peak,** which has its own weather. Violent thunderstorms appear out of nowhere, mostly in July and Aug. Snow can fall at upper elevations any time of the year.

Visitor Centers

The visitor center just north of Baker is open summer only. **Lehman Caves Visitor Center,** inside the park, remains open all year.

Headquarters

100 Great Basin National Park
Baker, NV 89311
nps.gov/grba
775-234-7331

Camping

Of five park campgrounds, **Lower Lehman Creek** (11 sites) and **Strawberry Creek** (8 sites) are open year-round. Others open spring through fall, depending on weather. All are first come, first served, often filling by midday during summer. No hookups—just vault toilets, water, grills, and a seasonal dump station.

Gateway Tourism Contacts

There is no lodging in the park, but the gateway hamlet of **Baker** (pop. 50) offers several quirky motels. You'll find plenty of lodging, including a Prohibition-era hotel (*hotelnevada.com*) in **Ely**, 67 miles away (*elynevada.net*).

Mesa Verde

Colorado

Established
June 29, 1906

52,485 acres

Mesa Verde is the only national park to preserve not only natural wonders but also the spellbinding heritage of an ancient people, the ancestral Puebloans, who found shelter, food, and spiritual inspiration here. The eroded tableland of Mesa Verde National Park takes in more than 5,000 archaeological sites, including cliff dwellings (the park hallmark) that date back more than a millennium. It is the richest archaeological cache in the American Southwest.

Nomadic bands had long crisscrossed the region; the first signs of settlement here date from A.D. 550. People lived in one-room pit houses gouged from the earth and roofed with tree limbs, brush, and dirt.

Over time, the people of the Basket Maker era, so named because of their proficiency in weaving baskets, began building more permanent aboveground structures of sandstone blocks, wood poles, and clay. That style of building continued with the construction of larger and more substantial multi-room structures gathered into villages of 40 to 50 buildings.

Cliff Palace

and perhaps horses here. On a snowy December day in 1888, a couple of local ranchers stumbled onto Cliff Palace—the park's largest and most distinctive cliff dwelling—when looking for lost cows.

News of the extraordinary ruins spread quickly and visitors were soon exploring Mesa Verde and taking artifacts and even human remains by the wagonload. A long and loud outcry against such practices was answered when President Theodore Roosevelt designated Mesa Verde as a national park.

Three weeks later Roosevelt signed into law the Act for the Preservation of American Antiquities that, among other provisions, made illegal the removal of archaeological treasures from federal lands.

► HOW TO VISIT

While it is possible in one day to visit some of Mesa Verde's primary sites and take a ranger-guided tour of one of the three major cliff dwellings, spending a few days allows for time to view and explore much more of what the park offers. There are some 40 pueblo and cliff dwellings visible from park roads and overlooks alone.

Start at the **Visitor Center and Research Center,** where tickets for the tours of **Cliff Palace, Balcony House,** and **Long House** can be purchased. Drive past the **Far View** area to explore the archaeological wonders of **Chapin Mesa.** Devote another day, if you can, to less crowded **Wetherill Mesa.**

The Park Service offers backcountry hikes during the summer, allowing small groups to visit fragile archaeological sites, such as **Mug House** and

Around 1190, the people of Mesa Verde began building sophisticated multi-level cliff dwellings in the rock alcoves of the cliff faces. These alcoves were formed by erosion caused by the freezing and thawing of water as it percolated through permeable sandstone before hitting the more resistant dark shale and then trickling outward. The alcoves offered shelter as well as relatively permanent water seeps. The extra-ordinary cliff-dwelling building phase lasted perhaps 75 years. But by the end of the 13th century, all the people of Mesa Verde were mysteriously gone.

Ute people inhabited the canyon bottoms starting in the 1700s. By the late 1800s, they were running cattle

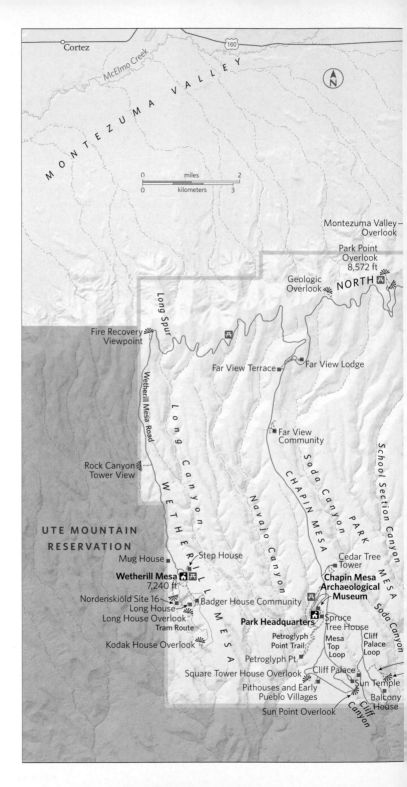

Cortez

160

McElmo Creek

MONTEZUMA VALLEY

N

0   miles   2
0   kilometers   3

Montezuma Valley –
Overlook

Park Point
Overlook
8,572 ft

Geologic
Overlook

NORTH

Long Spur

Fire Recovery
Viewpoint

Far View Terrace   Far View Lodge

Wetherill Mesa Road

Long Canyon

Far View
Community

Soda Canyon

CHAPIN MESA

School Section Canyon

Rock Canyon
Tower View

Navajo Canyon

WETHERILL

UTE MOUNTAIN
RESERVATION

Mug House   Step House

Cedar Tree
Tower

Chapin Mesa
Archaeological
Museum

Wetherill Mesa
7,240 ft

Nordenskiöld Site 16
Long House
Long House Overlook
Tram Route

Badger House Community

Park Headquarters

Spruce
Tree House

MESA

Kodak House Overlook

Petroglyph
Point Trail

Mesa
Top
Loop

Cliff
Palace
Loop

Soda Canyon

Petroglyph Pt.

Square Tower House Overlook

Cliff Palace

Sun Temple

Pithouses and Early
Pueblo Villages

Cliff Canyon

Balcony
House

Sun Point Overlook

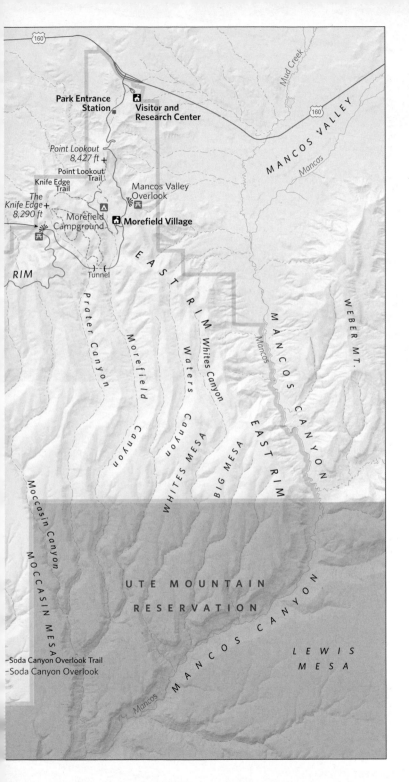

Park Entrance
Station

Visitor and
Research Center

Point Lookout
8,427 ft

Point Lookout
Trail

Knife Edge
Trail

The
Knife Edge
8,290 ft

Morefield
Campground

Mancos Valley
Overlook

Morefield Village

RIM

Tunnel

prater Canyon

Morefield Canyon

Waters Canyon

Whites Canyon

EAST RIM

WHITES MESA

BIG MESA

Mancos

MANCOS CANYON

EAST RIM

WEBER MT.

MANCOS VALLEY

Mancos

160

Mud Creek

160

Moccasin Canyon

MOCCASIN MESA

Soda Canyon Overlook Trail
Soda Canyon Overlook

UTE MOUNTAIN

RESERVATION

MANCOS CANYON

LEWIS
MESA

Mancos

Spruce Tree House

Square Tower House, on a rotating basis *(nps.gov/meve* for information, including tour schedules). Tickets must be purchased in advance *(recreation .gov;* 877-444-6777). Some of these hikes are strenuous, and on unmaintained trails.

Park Entrance to Far View & Chapin Mesa

At the **Visitor Center and Research Center,** just off US 160, purchase tickets for ranger-guided tours of **Cliff Palace, Balcony House,** and **Long House.** Just before the park entrance is a parking area for trailers and other towed vehicles; these are not permitted beyond Morefield Campground because of the park's narrow and winding roads. Following the park road, pull over at the **Mancos**

Valley Overlook for sweeping vistas to the east of a longtime ranching valley with a backdrop of the **La Plata Mountains.**

At **Morefield Campground**—the park's only camping facility—consider taking the 2.2-mile **Point Lookout Trail** for views of much of southwest Colorado. Other vistas await at **Montezuma Valley Overlook, Park Point Overlook,** and the **Geologic Overlook.**

The **Far View** area has the **Far View Lodge** and **Metate Room** restaurant and **Far View Terrace** café (all open late April to late October).

Another 5.5 miles along is park headquarters, at **Chapin Mesa.** The **Archaeological Museum,** with dioramas, chronicles the ancestral Puebloans' life during various periods. There is also an excellent collection of baskets, pottery, weavings, and other items created by Mesa Verde's early people. A 25-minute video gives an overview of Mesa Verde's history and culture. Pick up a self-guiding booklet to **Spruce Tree House** and wind down a short paved trail to visit what is the best-preserved cliff dwelling in the park.

Multi-level Spruce Tree House, protected by an overarching rock alcove, could house as many as 100 people. It features eight kivas (underground ceremonial rooms), one of which is open to visitors, who enter by climbing down a ladder through the rooftop opening.

During spring, summer, and fall, rangers are on duty at Spruce Tree House to answer questions; during winter, rangers conduct free guided tours as weather permits.

The 2.4-mile, self-guided **Petroglyph Point Trail** begins at Spruce Tree House and continues on to a 12-foot-long series of petroglyphs etched on a rock face.

South of park headquarters, Cliff Palace Loop and Mesa Top Loop—two 6-mile loops on Chapin Mesa—wind past some of the prime archaeological treasures of Mesa Verde.

The **Cliff Palace Loop** winds through forests of piñons and junipers to the **Cliff Palace Overlook.** Take a short paved trail for a breathtaking view of Cliff Palace, nestled in a large sandstone alcove above steep-walled Cliff Canyon. Cliff Palace, at 150 rooms on multiple levels, is the largest of the park's cliff dwellings; it could well have housed more than 100 people.

The ranger-guided tours of Cliff Palace (fee) start at the overlook and follow an often steep trail. The

What Happened to the Ancestral Puebloans?

Seemingly at the pinnacle of their culture—architecturally, agriculturally, ceremonially—the ancestral Puebloans disappeared from Mesa Verde over a relatively short period of time. What caused thousands of people to leave their homes and go elsewhere?

Although no one really knows, archaeologists cite several possible reasons. There is evidence of violence in the region, which means that political and social unrest could have contributed. Perhaps as many as 5,000 people lived at Mesa Verde, so the area was likely overpopulated, leading to possible civil strife. Resources such as soil and game—primarily deer and elk—may have become depleted over time. Finally, a 25-year-long drought at the end of the 13th century severely taxed corn, beans, and squash production. Likely a combination of these events contributed to the sudden exodus to the south.

The legends and oral traditions of Pueblo peoples throughout present-day Arizona and New Mexico—Taos, Hopi, Zia, Santa Clara, Acoma, Zuni, and more than a dozen other places—point to the fact that today's Native Americans are descendants of the ancestral Puebloans of Mesa Verde.

experience is magical, inviting you to go back in time 800 or more years and ponder what life was like for the ancestral Puebloans.

Farther along the loop is the parking area for **Balcony House,** another starting point for a ranger-guided tour *(fee)*. Balcony House is a popular destination among adventurous visitors: You must climb 32-foot-tall ladders and scramble through a 12-foot-long tunnel on hands and knees.

Balcony House has 40 rooms and is named for the distinctive balcony jutting out above one of the levels—an unusual architectural feature. For a good view of Balcony House, hike the nearby 1.2-mile **Soda Canyon Overlook Trail.**

Completing the Cliff Palace Loop, turn left on the Mesa Top Loop. Pull into the **Square Tower House Overlook** and hike the short trail to a view below: a four-story remnant of what was once an extensive cliff dwelling. Look across deeply eroded **Navajo Canyon** and scan the opposite canyon wall; you'll see several small cliff dwellings and food-storage rooms tucked into cracks and alcoves in the rock walls.

A short distance farther is the parking area for a fascinating walk through excavated early Mesa Verde dwelling sites—**pit houses** and a **pueblo village.** The small sunken pit houses, which are the earliest permanent dwellings at Mesa Verde, are considered to be the forerunners of the ceremonial kivas. The remnants of three aboveground pueblo sites demonstrate the evolution from pit houses to more sophisticated buildings.

At **Sun Point Overlook,** a dozen cliff dwellings fill the view. **Sun Temple,** an architecturally sophisticated structure, is a puzzle to archaeologists. It apparently was never inhabited; it may have served as a ceremonial center. From the overlook there is a commanding view of Cliff Palace.

Wetherill Mesa

The winding 12-mile road along **Wetherill Mesa** begins at **Far View;** it is open from late May to early September. Vehicles longer than 24 feet are not permitted. Bicycles also are prohibited. At the Wetherill Mesa kiosk, park your car and explore **Step House.** A one-mile, self-guided tour takes visitors to the multi-story pueblo as well as pit houses.

Back at the kiosk, board the tram that takes visitors to the trailhead for **Long House** as well as to other sites in the area. Long House is the second largest cliff dwelling in Mesa Verde, with about 150 rooms and 21 kivas. Long House was excavated between 1959 and 1961 as part of the Wetherill Mesa Archaeological Project, which was jointly funded by the National Park Service and the National Geographic Society; overall this project excavated 15 sites.

The first scientific investigation of Long House and other Mesa Verde dwellings was done in 1891 by a 22-year-old Swedish scientist named Gustaf Nordenskiöld, who excavated ruins, drew site maps, made meticulous notes, and took photographs of the sites, photographs that still capture the mystery of Mesa Verde. A seldom-hiked one-mile trail leads visitors to the overlook of **Nordenskiöld Site 16,** one of the cliff dwellings excavated by the Swedish scientist.

The tram that takes visitors to Long House passes the **Badger House Community,** with sites dating from about A.D. 600.

Spotted bat in the hands of a researcher

Information

How to Get There

The park entrance is on US 160, 10 miles east of Cortez, 8 miles west of Mancos, and 36 miles west of Durango.

When to Go

Mesa Verde is open year-round. Many roads, including the Cliff Palace Loop, and many archaeological sites are closed in winter. The road to Wetherill Mesa is open from late May to early Sept.

Visitor Center & Museum

The **Visitor Center and Research Center** at the park entrance features exhibits, a bookstore, and rangers to help you plan your visit. The center also houses a research facility and storage for more than 3 million artifacts and other objects. The **Chapin Mesa Archaeological Museum,** built in 1924 and open year-round, offers dioramas, artifacts, and Native American arts and crafts, as well as a movie about Mesa Verde.

Headquarters

Mesa Verde National Park
P.O. Box 8
Mesa Verde National Park,
CO 81330
nps.gov/meve
970-529-4465

MESA VERDE EST 1906

Camping

There are 267 camping sites at **Morefield Campground,** the park's only camping facility, and they are available on a first-come, first-served basis. The campground is open mid-May to mid-Oct. and has a grocery store, firewood, showers, laundry facilities, and an RV dump station.

Lodging

Far View Lodge (*visitmesaverde.com;* 970-564-4300 or 800-449-2288), with 150 rooms, is the only lodging in the park; it is open late April–late Oct. The nearby towns of **Cortez, Mancos,** and **Durango** all have lodging (*mesaverdecountry.com*).

Petrified Forest

Arizona

Established
December 9, 1962

138,788 acres

Colors—both bold and subtle—abound at Petrified Forest National Park. The petrified logs themselves are a kaleidoscope of hues ranging from crimson to sapphire, mustard to charcoal, coral to pistachio—and every shade in between. The Painted Desert section of the park—a stretch of rolling badlands—is a palette of pinks, grays, rusts, ochers, whites, and browns that shifts with changes in sunlight and shadow.

Although every one of America's 50 states has deposits of petrified wood, Petrified Forest National Park has one of the greatest concentrations of petrified logs on Earth. The display is spectacular. Several easy hiking trails in the park lead to jumbled masses of downed trees that slowly, cell by cell, turned from wood to stone from 205 to 225 million years ago.

Petrified wood fractures easily, so there's a wide range of sizes to dazzle visitors—from tiny chips and shards to chunks of rock to entire logs stretching from trunk base to treetop on the desert floor. Colors glisten in the sun.

The park's petrified wood is made up primarily of quartz.

report by a paleobotanist prompted further protection.

President Theodore Roosevelt created the Petrified Forest National Monument in 1906 to protect the unique environment. In 1932 the monument was expanded to include more than 93,000 acres. Eight years after the national park was signed into law, some 50,000 acres of the park were designated Wilderness. Federal law prohibits the collection and removal of petrified wood—even the tiniest chips.

But Petrified Forest is much more than scenic beauty and iconic geology. Fossilized here are some of the earliest dinosaurs (including the soaring, leathery-winged pterosaurs) and more than 80 species of animals and plants. The area's human history reaches back 13,000 years, and among the riches of the park are ruins and petroglyph sites that date back some 1,000 years.

The park's recent history hinges on transportation. In 1853, the federal government sent a party of soldiers to explore the 35th parallel as a possible transcontinental route. Between 1857 and 1860, a wagon road was built (a portion of which would become part of Route 66). The railroad came through in the early 1880s. Road and rail access brought settlers and tourists to the region.

In 1895, the Territory of Arizona stepped in to protect the area, which had been exploited by individuals set on taking petrified wood. The colorful stone was hauled off by the wagonload to be used for tabletops, lamps, and mantels; it was dynamited to reveal, it was hoped, amethyst and other quartz crystals. A 1900

▶ HOW TO VISIT

Of all the national parks, Petrified Forest ranks among the most susceptible to the drive-through visit. It is easy for the visitor to cruise along, stopping to gaze over the Painted Desert, and walk a short trail among the giant logs before returning to the freeway. To do this, however, is to miss the secrets awaiting in the 346-square-mile park.

A 28-mile paved road bisects the park from north to south. Casual visitors who come for even a couple of hours can drive the road, stop at the excellent **museum** and **visitor center,** walk into the **petrified groves,** and be on their way.

By spending a full day, visitors can spend more time at the museum and

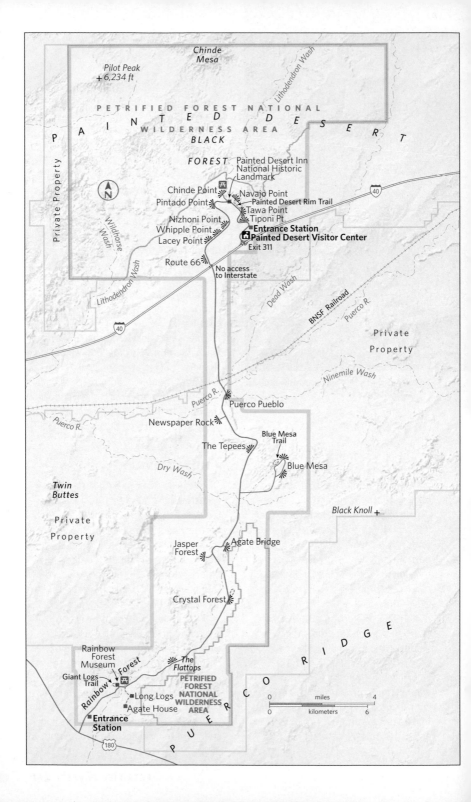

visitor center, stop leisurely at the many informational scenic overlooks, and take their time hiking a half dozen short, mostly easy, trails.

The north entrance to the park is an exit off I-40, about 25 miles east of Holbrook, Arizona; the south entrance is about 19 miles east of Holbrook on US 180. The park can be explored from either direction. Here we will start in the north; simply reverse this tour if you are starting in the south.

The Park Road

The **Painted Desert Visitor Center** welcomes visitors just off I-40, before they enter the park. An excellent movie entitled *Timeless Impressions* explains the park's historic, geologic, and cultural heritages. On hand at the visitor center are rangers who provide information and answer questions. There is also a restaurant and a gift shop, where pieces of petrified wood can be purchased. (These specimens were collected outside the park.)

The park road winds north and then turns south, offering panoramic views of the **Painted Desert,** a colorful swath of badlands that stretches for 150 miles from east of Petrified Forest National Park almost to the Grand Canyon.

Several overlooks, including **Tawa Point, Kachina Point, Chinde Point,** and **Pintado Point,** provide sweeping vistas of the many-colored Painted Desert, including views of **Pilot Peak,** which, at 6,234 feet, is the highest point in the park.

The 1-mile round-trip **Painted Desert Rim Trail** runs from Tawa Point to Kachina Point through vegetation

From Wood to Stone— an Extraordinary Transformation

During the Triassic period, some 217 million years ago, the scene was one of murky forests, swamps, slow-moving rivers, towering conifers, and an array of fish, lumbering amphibians, early dinosaurs, and ferocious 25-foot-long crocodile-like reptiles with rows of saber-sharp teeth. Periodic floods felled the giant trees and stranded them in channels, where they settled into a slurry of mud, sand, and volcanic ash.

Various chemicals, primarily silica, were released from this slurry, and these chemicals began reacting with the wood. Tiny silica crystals began to form and grow; slowly, cell by cell, these crystals encased the wood of the logs, turning it into stone.

The myriad colors result from the various chemicals present in the slurry. The greens come from pure reduced iron mixed with chlorophyll. White is produced from pure silica, black from organic carbon. The blues and purples come from manganese dioxide that originated in volcanic rock. The reds and pinks come from hematite, a form of oxidized iron. Finally, the yellows, browns, and oranges come from goethite, a hydrated iron oxide.

More centuries of mud and silt covered the logs, protecting them from decay.

Powerful geologic forces of plate tectonics and uplifting slowly moved the logs of the Petrified Forest to their current location, and water and wind erosion exposed them to the display we see today.

representative of the region, including Mormon tea, yuccas, prickly pear cactus, and saltbush.

At Kachina Point you'll find the old **Painted Desert Inn,** a southwestern adobe-style lodge built in the 1920s and now a national historic landmark. Exhibits, memorabilia, and public rooms evoke the Route 66 era.

Three additional overlooks, **Nizhoni Point, Whipple Point,** and **Lacey Point,** offer more views of the Painted Desert, with slopes tinted in the earthy shades of a Navajo rug. The colors are especially vivid when the sun shines on sediment still wet from a thunderstorm. A sharp-eyed—and lucky—visitor might spot a small herd of pronghorn antelope in this area.

The park road crosses the paths of Historic Route 66, I-40, and the Burlington Northern Santa Fe Railway before arriving at **Puerco Pueblo,** an ancestral Puebloan village site that dates back 800 years. One of more than 1,000 archaeological sites in the park, Puerco Pueblo, built of sandstone blocks, housed perhaps 200 people in 100 to 125 rooms built around a central plaza.

A 0.3-mile trail allows visitors to explore the partially reconstructed pueblo ruins. Highlights of the trail are views of several petroglyphs etched into rocks; these include a spiral that archaeologists believe worked as a solar calendar. On the day of the summer solstice, a dagger of sunlight stabs between jumbled rocks and pierces the center of the spiral.

Farther south along the road is the spellbinding **Newspaper Rock,** two enormous boulders covered with more than 600 petroglyphs; viewing scopes magnify the etchings into sharp focus.

Winding through **The Tepees** (cone-shaped formations of gray, lavender, and blue rock), the park road comes to the turnoff to **Blue Mesa,** where the paved 1-mile **Blue Mesa Trail** drops into and loops through badlands dotted with petrified logs. Heading south again on the main road, visitors can see the **Agate Bridge,** a single long petrified log spanning a dry wash, and **Jasper Forest,** an eroded bluff from which hundreds of petrified logs have been eroded over time and now litter the valley floor below. Consider this, though: How many more logs lie in the bluff, subject to nature's forces? How many petrified logs still remain uncovered?

At **Crystal Forest,** an easy 0.8-mile trail meanders among hundreds of petrified logs of all sizes and shapes. Here, the colors of the petrified wood can be seen up close. At the southern end of the park is the **Rainbow Forest Museum,** with excellent dioramas and other exhibits, the *Timeless Impressions* film, and fossils from the Late Triassic period. Behind the museum is the **Giant Logs Trail,** a 0.4-mile loop through an impressive forest of petrified logs that includes **Old Faithful,** the park's most massive.

Across the park road bridge from the museum is the trailhead for the **Long Logs** and **Agate House Trails,** which can be combined for a round-trip of 2.6 miles. The Long Logs Trail wanders among the largest concentration of petrified logs in the park. The Agate House Trail leads to a partially reconstructed eight-room ruin inhabited beginning about 1050 B.C. It is constructed of chunks of petrified wood and mud mortar.

Petrified logs show their colors in the sunlight.

Information

How to Get There

The park is 110 miles east of Flagstaff. From Holbrook, AZ, follow I-40 east for about 25 miles to the north park entrance or US 180 east about 19 miles to the south park entrance.

When to Go

Petrified Forest National Park is open year-round. Summer is the most popular season. It can be quite hot, and sudden thunderstorms can mean lightning and high winds. The more temperate fall is a good time to visit as is winter, when occasional light snows dust the petrified logs. Spring brings pleasant temperatures and blooming wildflowers.

Visitor Centers, Museum & National Historic Landmark

The **Painted Desert Visitor Center,** just outside the north entrance, has exhibits, rangers on duty, and the *Timeless Impressions* film, which captures the geology and history of the park. The **Painted Desert Inn National Historic Landmark,** a former lodge, has Route 66 memorabilia

and other historic displays. The **Rainbow Forest Museum,** inside the park's south entrance, offers dioramas, fossils, and the film.

Headquarters

Petrified Forest National Park
1 Park Rd.
Petrified Forest, AZ 86028
nps.gov/pefo
928-524-6228

Camping

There are no designated camping sites in the park. Overnight backcountry permits are free and available at the visitor center.

Lodging

Though no lodging is available in the park, there's a restaurant and a gas station at the Painted Desert Visitor Center. **Holbrook** *(holbrookchamberof commerce.com)* has a wide range of motels and restaurants.

Saguaro

Arizona

Established
October 14, 1994

91,442 acres

The saguaro cactus long ago went from being a mere plant to an iconic symbol depicted all over, from comic strips to magazine advertising. Namesake of Saguaro National Park, its grand, distinctive arm-raised form sends a loud-and-clear message: This the American West.

A nd yet the saguaro (*Carnegiea gigantea)* occupies a very limited range, growing only in a portion of the Sonoran Desert ecoregion of the United States and Mexico. In the United States, the cactus is found in southern Arizona and Baja, Mexico.

In recognition of the saguaro's uniqueness, in 1933 a tract of cactus forest east of Tucson, in what is now the Rincon Mountain District of

the park, was protected as a national monument. Additional land, now the Tucson Mountain District, was added in 1961; 33 years later, the two districts were elevated in status and joined as Saguaro National Park.

The two park districts, 30 miles apart—one east and one west of the Tucson—offer convenient hiking opportunities. Other park options include horseback riding, bicycling,

Saguaro cactus

and mountain biking. The Sonoran Desert habitat remains the park's main attraction—not just the extensive stands of saguaro but a broad range of other plants as well as animals.

The Tucson Mountain District boasts the densest saguaro forests. The larger eastern district—the Rincon Mountain District—extends into the mountains, where woodlands of ponderosa pine and Douglas fir create a striking contrast to the desert below.

Given the diversity of habitats, a hiker can travel from desert scrub (home to roadrunners and peccaries) to conifer forest on 8,666-foot Mica Mountain, where white-tailed deer and black bear roam. Such a journey traverses five major life zones:

desert, grassland, oak scrub, pine forest, and riparian.

▶ HOW TO VISIT

The park can be experienced in one day—or more if you want to do some serious hiking. If you're primarily interested in seeing saguaros, head to the **Tucson Mountain District.** Walk the short **Desert Discovery Nature Trail** and drive the 5-mile scenic **Bajada Loop Drive.** Consider hiking the 0.5-mile **Signal Hill Trail** to see Native American petroglyphs. Ask at the **Red Hills Visitor Center** about longer hikes, such as the 3.5-mile **King Canyon Trail.**

In the **Rincon Mountain District,** the 8-mile **Cactus Forest Scenic Loop Drive** offers a wealth of fine views and saguaros, as well as possibilities for short hikes. For a strenuous hike into the Rincon Mountain foothills, do an out-and-back trek along the **Tanque Verde Ridge Trail** as far as time and energy allow. The trail heads uphill for some 8 miles, with little shade.

Tucson Mountain District

Curvy and steep, Gates Pass Road is the most scenic conduit to this section of the national park, but it's not suitable for very large vehicles, which should instead take Ariz. 86 (Ajo Way) to Kinney Road.

Stop first at the **Red Hills Visitor Center** for up-to-date information and to watch the introductory audiovisual show. Both the **Cactus Garden Trail** and the **Desert Discovery Nature Trail** offer signs that name many of the cacti and other plants in the park.

The striking Red Hills of this part of the park are composed of mudstone

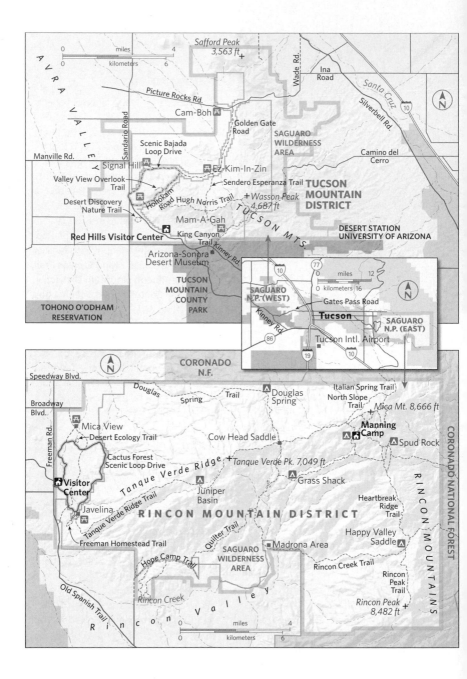

Safford Peak
3,563 ft

Ina Road

Picture Rocks Rd.

Wade Rd.

Santa Cruz

Silverbell Rd.

10

Cam-Boh

AVRA VALLEY

Sandario Road

Golden Gate Road

SAGUARO WILDERNESS AREA

Scenic Bajada Loop Drive

Manville Rd.

Signal Hill

Camino del Cerro

Valley View Overlook Trail

Ez-Kim-In-Zin

Sendero Esperanza Trail

TUCSON MOUNTAIN DISTRICT

Hohokam Road

Hugh Norris Trail

Wasson Peak 4,687 ft

TUCSON MTS.

Desert Discovery Nature Trail

Red Hills Visitor Center

Mam-A-Gah

King Canyon Trail

Kinney Rd.

DESERT STATION UNIVERSITY OF ARIZONA

Arizona-Sonora Desert Museum

TUCSON MOUNTAIN COUNTY PARK

TOHONO O'ODHAM RESERVATION

10

77

SAGUARO N.P. (WEST)

Gates Pass Road

Tucson

Kinney Rd.

SAGUARO N.P. (EAST)

86

Tucson Intl. Airport

19

10

CORONADO N.F.

Speedway Blvd.

Douglas Spring Trail

Douglas Spring

Italian Spring Trail

North Slope Trail

Mica Mt. 8,666 ft

Broadway Blvd.

Mica View

Desert Ecology Trail

Cow Head Saddle

Manning Camp

Spud Rock

Freeman Rd.

Cactus Forest Scenic Loop Drive

Tanque Verde Ridge

Tanque Verde Pk. 7,049 ft

Grass Shack

RINCON MOUNTAINS

Visitor Center

Tanque Verde Ridge Trail

Juniper Basin

Heartbreak Ridge Trail

CORONADO NATIONAL FOREST

Javelina

RINCON MOUNTAIN DISTRICT

Happy Valley Saddle

Freeman Homestead Trail

Quilter Trail

SAGUARO WILDERNESS AREA

Madrona Area

Rincon Creek Trail

Rincon Peak Trail

Hope Camp Trail

Rincon Creek

Rincon Valley

Rincon Peak 8,482 ft

Old Spanish Trail

from an ancient lake bed; the distinctive color of the landscape is the result of iron oxide.

The 5-mile **Scenic Bajada Loop Drive** brims with saguaros. (A *bajada* is a foothill slope with the alluvial soil saguaros prefer.) While you're admiring the forests of saguaro, look for woodpecker-excavated holes that are sometimes used by birds such as kestrels (small falcons) and cactus wrens. Also found in this area of the park is the colorful Harris's hawk (black, chestnut, and white), which builds its nest among saguaro arms.

The loop drive provides access to several trailheads; consider walking the 0.5-mile **Signal Hill Trail,** which passes dozens of petroglyphs. Dating back some 800 years, the evocative markings were made by people of the Hohokam culture.

The 4.9-mile **Hugh Norris Trail** is one of several ways to reach 4,687-foot **Wasson Peak,** the highest point in the national park's western district. It's a strenuous hike, one that rewards with many fine vistas and fascinating rock formations. A shorter way up Wasson Peak is the 3.5-mile **King Canyon Trail,** a portion of which makes a good short hike. Follow the trail 0.9 mile to the Mam-A-Gah picnic area and then return by way of the dry riverbed. Look for petroglyphs along this route, too.

Though it's not part of Saguaro National Park, the **Arizona-Sonora Desert Museum** (*desertmuseum .org;* 520-883-2702), on the park's southern border, is a must for those interested in the natural history of the region. The focus is on the flora and fauna of the Sonoran Desert, with its 1,200 plant species and 230 animal species, from hummingbirds to wolves.

The Arizona-Sonora Desert Museum comprises 98 acres, 21 of which are outside. There's a zoo, an aquarium, a botanical garden, and interpretive hiking trails that meander through desert habitats.

Rincon Mountain District

More than twice as big as the park's western district, the Rincon Mountain District gets more rain, especially in the upper elevations of the Rincon Mountains. If you happen to be in the park after a rainy winter, you may be treated to a splendid display of

Hedgehog cactus in bloom

The Mighty Saguaro

In its lifetime a saguaro cactus may produce 40 million seeds, yet in nature's math it simply needs to replace itself with one mature plant to maintain its population. Think of those odds when you admire a hillside covered with these giants.

Once a saguaro starts growing, it can take a decade to reach 2 inches tall. Young plants are easily uprooted by javelinas or careless hikers, though the major threat comes from desert wildfires.

The largest cactus in the United States, the saguaro can grow more than 50 feet tall and weigh up to eight tons. Plants don't begin to grow their "arms" until they're 50 to 70 years old, and it's believed that some saguaros may live 200 years.

The saguaro's ribs and pleated surface allow it to greatly expand its bulk when rare rains soak the desert. When rain is plentiful and the saguaro is fully hydrated, it can weigh more than 4,500 pounds.

The saguaro's white bloom is the state flower of Arizona. Its fruits have long been important to the Tohono O'odham people, who continue to harvest them each June. The flowers are boiled down to a syrup.

colorful spring wildflowers, from the gold of Mexican poppy to shocking pink penstemon to orange globemallow. Several shrubs and cacti also provide color, including ocotillo, chollas, prickly pear, and hedgehog cactus.

Go slowly and watch for cyclists on the winding 8-mile **Cactus Forest Scenic Loop Drive.** Take advantage of the many scenic overlooks to enjoy the rolling desert landscape and views of the Rincon Mountains. The flat, easy 0.25-mile **Desert Ecology Trail** reflects the ways that plants and animals have adapted to the climate. Only a bit more strenuous, the 1-mile **Freeman Homestead Trail** leads to the remains of an adobe house built in 1933, while interpretive signs along the way tell of early human history.

There's a maze of trails, short and long, in the northwestern part of the Rincon Mountain District, reached by turning north onto Mica View Road, off the scenic loop.

With a permit *(fee),* backcountry camping is allowed at six designated sites within the 57,930-acre Saguaro Wilderness Area. One of the sites, **Manning Camp,** is located in coniferous forest at an elevation of 8,000 feet, providing quite a contrast to the Sonoran Desert below.

For a rewarding, strenuous day hike, consider the **Tanque Verde Ridge Trail,** whose trailhead is close to the Javelina picnic area, along the scenic loop. It's 9 miles to 7,049-foot Tanque Verde Peak, but you don't have to go that far on your hike. You'll experience fine views of Tucson to the west and Rincon Peak to the southeast as you ascend the ridge. Unless you have a camping permit, be sure to turn around in time to return to your vehicle and leave the park by sunset.

Horseback riding is a popular and relaxing way to see the desert landscape with minimal effort (except on the part of the horse, of course). Horses are allowed on many park trails, and local outfitters can arrange guided rides.

Antelope jackrabbit

Information

How to Get There

From Tucson, AZ, 13 miles southeast of the park, take Speedway Blvd. west to Gates Pass Rd. and go north on Kinney Rd. to reach the Tucson Mountain District. Take Speedway Blvd. east and go south on Freeman Rd. and Old Spanish Trail to reach the Rincon Mountain District.

When to Go

Temperatures are most pleasant Oct. through April. Summer is very hot, with temperatures often exceeding 100°F. From July through Sept., afternoon thunderstorms can cause flash floods.

Visitor Centers

Both park districts—**Tucson Mountain** and **Rincon Mountain**—have visitor centers, open year-round.

Headquarters

3693 S. Old Spanish Trail
Tucson, AZ 85730
nps.gov/sagu
Rincon Mountain District
520-733-5153
Tucson Mountain District
520-733-5158

Camping

There are no campgrounds in the park. Backcountry camping *(fee)* in the Rincon Mountain District is allowed with a permit.

Lodging

Lodging is plentiful in **Tucson:** Metro Tucson Convention and Visitor Bureau, *visittucson.org;* 800-638-8350.

Zion

Utah

Established
November 18, 1919

148,732 acres

Within the cloistered walls of Zion National Park, where a dramatic 16-mile river canyon has been sculpted of multi-hued sandstone, it is easy to feel profoundly connected to nature. Cliffs soar 2,000 feet, forming monolithic temples of pure stone that evoke a different kind of awe, one that led an early settler of the canyon, Isaac Behunin, to exclaim: "A man can worship God among these great cathedrals as well as in any man-made church—this is Zion!"

The name stuck. Originally, the area was called Mukuntuweap National Monument when it opened in 1909. It was John Wesley Powell who came up with the Paiute name during his exploration here in 1872), Park bureaucrats switched names when the monument was declared a national park. They believed an unpronounceable Indian name might deter visitors. Now Utah's oldest and busiest national park, Zion attracts more than three million people per year.

Most travelers confine their visits to Zion Canyon, where a shuttle system has reversed the impact of car traffic;

Court of the Patriarchs

wildlife has been drawn back to the park. It's not unusual to see bighorn sheep, wild turkey, and mule deer.

Diversity is Zion's trump card. The rich intermingling of Colorado Plateau, Great Basin, and Mojave Desert eco-systems provides key habitat for rare California condors, endemic Zion snails, and the largest breeding population of Mexican spotted owls in the state. White pine and Douglas fir crown 8,000-foot-high plateaus, while desert cholla and yucca bloom a mile below.

Zion's dominant feature, however, is rock. Most geologists agree that back in Jurassic times this was the planet's largest dune field, blown here from the Appalachian Mountains. The 2,000-foot depth of this sandpile—the Navajo sandstone of today—lies exposed, the result of the downward cutting of the Virgin River and its tributaries. These sandstone palisades are the world's tallest. Ironically, the same forces that created these formations pose their greatest threat. Flash flooding is the principal danger here.

Popularity aside, Zion remains a wilderness. Backcountry visitors have 90 miles of trails to explore within the park's 232 square miles of rugged gorges, terraces, and slot canyons. Front-country visitors need not stray from the 15 miles of paved trails to experience Zion's indelible majesty.

▶ HOW TO VISIT

On a one-day visit, cruise the **Zion–Mt. Carmel Highway** and the **Zion Canyon Scenic Drive** for the best overview of the park. If you have more time, consider heading to the park's scenic heart and exploring hiking trails that are accessed at park shuttle stops. (Frequent free shuttles are the only transportation option in Zion Canyon from mid-March through October—high season.)

Finding parking at Zion can be a challenge. If entering the park after 10 a.m. during high season, leave your car in Springdale, just outside the park, and take the Springdale shuttle, transferring to the Zion Canyon shuttle at the Zion Canyon Visitor Center. Or rent a bike in Springdale for a superb way to visit Zion Canyon. (Shuttles are equipped with bicycle racks.)

Zion Canyon

Board the shuttle at the **Zion Canyon Visitor Center** for the 6.6-mile **Zion Canyon scenic drive.** Though there are nine stops, it makes good sense to ride to road's end at Temple of Sinawava. This way you can beat the crowds and zoom in on the park's most popular attractions: Angels Landing, Riverside Walk, and The Narrows.

On your way to the Temple of Sinawava, absorb the scale of the **Court of the Patriarchs** and the **Great White Throne** monoliths. Notice the shimmering river meandering across the wide, flat-bottom valley, an unusual sight given that canyon rivers usually cut a V-shape deep into bedrock. The valley's thick bed of sediment was laid down by an ancient 350-foot-deep lake created when one of the massive sandstone monoliths avalanched into the river some 4,000 years ago.

At **Temple of Sinawava** (a Paiute name for their coyote god), canyon walls narrow as the river slices through the Navajo sandstone. Take the **Riverside Walk,** a mile-long wheelchair-accessible paved path following the canyon's contours and fringed in sedge and rush. Hanging gardens carpet the cliffs as the river riffles through rock. Listen for the sheeplike bleating of canyon tree frogs, and look closely on water-gleamed rocks for endemic Zion snails. These are the smallest snails in the world, the size of a grain of rice, and they live only in Zion Canyon.

The path ends at the kickoff point for **The Narrows,** Zion's hallmark 2.5-mile hike to Big Spring, along the Virgin River. You'll need a walking stick and water-friendly shoes (not toe-stubbing sandals) to navigate the algae-covered bottom. Breathe in the clean mineral scent of water on rock, and plunge into the calf-deep water.

Life-threatening flash floods are a real danger here. At some spots along

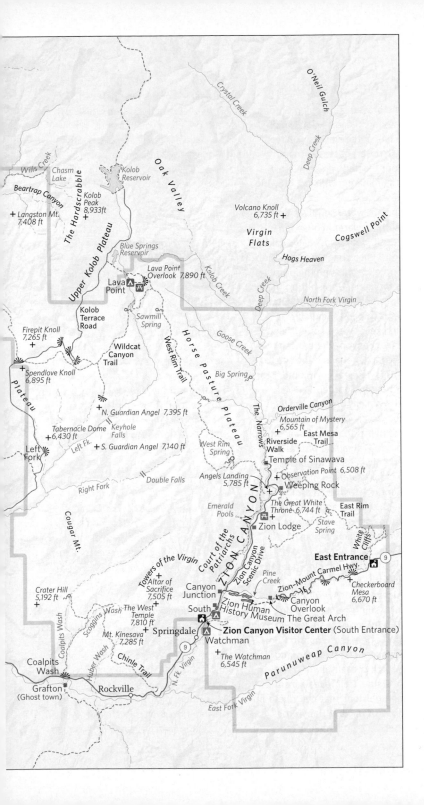

Wills Creek

Chasm Lake

Beartrap Canyon

+ Langston Mt. 7,408 ft

Kolob Reservoir

Kolob Peak 8,933ft

Oak Valley

Crystal Creek

O'Neil Gulch

Deep Creek

Volcano Knoll 6,735 ft +

Virgin Flats

Cogswell Point

Hogs Heaven

Blue Springs Reservoir

Lava Point Overlook 7,890 ft

Kolob Creek

Deep Creek

North Fork Virgin

The Hardscrabble

Upper Kolob Plateau

Lava Point

Kolob Terrace Road

Sawmill Spring

West Rim Trail

Horse Pasture Plateau

Goose Creek

Big Spring

Firepit Knoll 7,265 ft +

Spendlove Knoll 6,895 ft

Plateau

Wildcat Canyon Trail

N. Guardian Angel 7,395 ft

Orderville Canyon

Mountain of Mystery 6,565 ft

East Mesa Trail

Tabernacle Dome +6,430 ft

Keyhole Falls

Left Fk.

S. Guardian Angel 7,140 ft

West Rim Spring

Riverside Walk

Temple of Sinawava

Left Fork

Right Fork

Double Falls

Angels Landing 5,785 ft

Observation Point 6,508 ft

Weeping Rock

The Narrows

Emerald Pools

The Great White Throne 6,744 ft

East Rim Trail

Cougar Mt.

Zion Lodge

Stave Spring

ZION CANYON

White Cliffs

East Entrance 9

Crater Hill 5,192 ft +

Court of the Patriarchs

Towers of the Virgin

Altar of Sacrifice 7,505 ft

Zion Canyon Scenic Drive

Pine Creek

Canyon Junction

Zion-Mount Carmel Hwy.

Checkerboard Mesa 6,670 ft

Scoggins Wash

The West Temple 7,810 ft

South

Zion Human History Museum

Canyon Overlook

The Great Arch

Coalpits Wash

Mt. Kinesava 7,285 ft

Springdale

Watchman

Zion Canyon Visitor Center (South Entrance)

Chinle Trail

9

The Watchman 6,545 ft

Parunuweap Canyon

Coalpits Wash

Grafton (Ghost town)

Rockville

N. Fk. Virgin

East Fork Virgin

Zion's Hanging Gardens

Like the proverbial Hanging Gardens of Babylon, those of Zion National Park are one of the world's wonders. These lush desert oases are found throughout the park, green micro-habitats shimmering with life, growing on bare rock.

A constant water supply is the secret, and the water in question is at least 1,000 years old, having taken that long to fall as rainwater and then slowly percolate through the porous Navajo sandstone. Upon hitting the more impermeable Kayenta siltstone, the water is forced to find an exit, emerging in seeps and springs along the wall of a canyon where these two layers, the sandstone and the siltstone, meet. This is an ideal environment for complex hanging gardens.

It's a rare plant that can grow in such poor soil conditions. Of the 40 species of plants that grow only on the Colorado Plateau, 10 of these are found only in hanging gardens. Delicate black-stemmed maidenhair ferns, shooting stars, scarlet monkey flowers, orchids, and columbines thrive in the cool mossy environment. Dragonflies and hummingbirds add to the scene.

One of the best hanging gardens can be found at Weeping Rock, a classic alcove garden with hypnotizing "rain" issuing from a dripping seep 100 feet above. Across the street from Zion Lodge, the Emerald Pools also compose a complex hanging garden worth contemplating. A walk along Riverside Trail reveals a series of hanging gardens that can't help but recall those of ancient Babylon.

the way, the sheer 1,000-foot walls on either side of the river narrow to just 20 feet across the water. Check with a ranger before you head out.

All in all, The Narrows stretches 16 miles to Chamberlain Ranch. (The one- to two-day hike from the top down requires a Wilderness permit, which can be reserved up to three months in advance.)

Once you've experienced The Narrows, return to the shuttle and make your way to **Big Bend,** where you'll find some of the park's most famous geologic scenery, including the Great White Throne and Cable Mountain. The shuttle also stops at **Weeping Rock,** where a 0.2-mile interpretive trail climbs to a hanging-garden alcove. There are longer, more strenuous trails that leave from Weeping Rock to **Hidden Canyon** (1.2 miles) and **Observation Point** (4 miles).

Before leaving Weeping Rock, scan the top of **Cable Mountain** looming overhead for the ruins of the cable works, which, from 1901 to 1927, carried timber down from the plateau on a 2,000-foot-long aerial tramway. It was constructed by David Flanigan to fulfill an 1863 prophecy by Mormon leader Brigham Young, who said lumber would one day come down from these plateaus "like a hawk flying."

Continue to the shuttle's next stop, **The Grotto,** a shaded picnic area and departure point for those attempting the legendary **Angels Landing Trail,** a minimum four-hour commitment. You can also opt for the mile-long **Kayenta Trail** to the Middle Emerald Pool. After crossing the footbridge, the trail skates above the meandering river, past thorny stands of yucca and prickly pear cactus. Notice the mature cottonwood trees along the river bottom—and the absence of younger trees. Cottonwood saplings are a delicacy for mule deer, which no longer fear feeding in the open now that mountain lions have shied away from busy Zion Canyon. Once you reach the **Emerald Pools,** take some time to explore the three levels of water-filled basins (no wading allowed) and waterfalls streaming off alcoves. (The upper pool is largest and hardest to reach.)

Rather than returning to The Grotto, continue on the paved path for half a mile to **Zion Lodge** (the next stop on the shuttle), where you can savor the champagne light of late afternoon as you stretch out on a two-acre lawn under the shade of a century-old cottonwood. Or replenish lost calories at the lodge's Castle Dome Cafe. The shuttle continues back to the Visitor Center, stopping at **Court of the Patriarchs, Canyon Junction,** and the **Zion Human History Museum.**

Zion–Mt. Carmel Highway

This road (Utah 9) was finished in 1930 to complete the National Park Loop linking Zion with Bryce Canyon and the North Rim of Grand Canyon. This engineering feat entailed boring a 1.1-mile tunnel through solid rock. As you drive east from Canyon Junction (no shuttle), pause midway up the steep switchbacks to view **The Great Arch,** a 600-foot

The north fork of the Virgin River

blind arch recessed into the Navajo sandstone.

Use caution when approaching the Zion–Mount Carmel Tunnel as it frequently converts to one-way traffic when an oversize vehicle passes through. Any vehicle wider than 7' 10" or longer than 11' 4" requires a tunnel permit *(fee),* available at park entrances. After you emerge from the tunnel, park at **Canyon Overlook** for the half-mile walk to the cliff's edge—directly above the Great Arch. Built by the Civilian Conversation Corps in 1933, the path's initial steep steps belie a fairly easy 163-foot elevation gain. The easily gained panorama of white-domed monoliths rimming the canyons is comparable to views available to those who hike the more demanding trails in Zion Canyon.

For the next 5 miles there are pull-outs where you can explore the slick-rock area on foot. As you do, notice the lines in the white Navajo sandstone. Like geologic weather vanes, they indicate the direction of winds that created the dunes almost 200 million years ago. Just before the park's east exit, stop at **Checkerboard Mesa,** where the lines are bisected by vertical joint cracks, creating a unique checkered appearance.

Kolob Canyons Road

The spectacular though infrequently visited Kolob Canyons huddle behind the gray limestone Hurricane Cliffs, which mark the western edge of the Colorado Plateau. From the **Kolob Canyons Visitor Center,** 40 miles north of Zion Canyon, you'll find Kolob Canyons Road. This 5-mile ribbon of red asphalt winds 1,100 feet up into a designated Wilderness. Stop along the way for views of box canyons with deeply incised headwalls cutting into the red bedrock of the Kolob Plateau. To fully experience the Finger Canyons, hike the 2.5-mile **Taylor Creek Trail,** or shoulder a backpack 7 miles on **La Verkin Creek Trail** to **Kolob Arch,** one of the world's largest natural arches. Or take in the big picture at road's end by hiking the half-mile **Timber Creek Overlook Trail** to a small peak with views of Timber Top Mountain rising 3,000 feet from the canyon floor. The Pine Valley Mountains buttress the western horizon, with Mount Trumbull to the south.

Elsewhere in the Park

Zion's epic hike is the 2.7-mile trail to **Angels Landing.** Depart from the Grotto picnic area via Refrigerator Canyon, home to rare Mexican spotted owls (at night, their distinctive "bark" reverberates off canyon walls). The trail corkscrews up the 21 switchbacks called Walter's Wiggles to **Scout Lookout.** The last half mile heads precariously up a narrow sandstone-stepped ridge with 1,500-foot drop-offs. (There's a safety chain to grasp.) Such daring is rewarded with views of Zion Canyon and the Great White Throne—and bragging rights.

The paved **Pa'rus Trail** is far more leisurely, following the Virgin River 1.8 miles from the visitor center to Canyon Junction. Along this bike-friendly trail, birders can cross off their life list any number of warblers, kingfishers, flycatchers, and vireos without breaking a sweat. Early morning or late evening, keep an eye out for deer, coyotes, and foxes coming to water.

Mexican spotted owl

Information

How to Get There

Zion National Park's South Entrance is 46 miles northeast of St. George via Utah 9, and 60 miles south of Cedar City via Utah 17 to Utah 9. Coming from Bryce Canyon National Park or the North Rim of the Grand Canyon, take Utah 9 west from Mount Carmel Junction to the park's east entrance. Kolob Canyons lie just off I-15, 35 miles north of St. George. The nearest international airport is in Las Vegas, 158 miles west.

When to Go

The park is crowded early March through Oct. Spring and especially fall are most rewarding, with mild weather and active wildlife. Summer days can reach above 100°F. Flash flooding poses a real danger mid-July into Sept. In winter, snow occasionally dusts the canyons.

Visitor Centers & Museum

The **Zion Canyon Visitor Center,** at the south entrance, is open year-round; park here for the shuttle. **Kolob Canyons Visitor Center** is also open year-round. The **Zion Human History Museum,** a half mile north of the south entrance, is closed Dec.–March.

Headquarters

Zion National Park
UT 84767
nps.gov/zion
435-772-3256

Camping

South campground (127 sites) is first come, first served. Reservations *(recreation.gov;* 877-444-6777) can be made for **Watchman campground** (176 sites), March to early Nov. Both provide flush toilets, firepits, and water. Six primitive campsites are available at **Lava Point Campground's** six primitive campsites. Backcountry camping requires a permit.

Lodging

The only hotel in the park, **Zion Lodge** is a 1990 re-creation of the original 1925 lodge with 50 rooms, 40 cabins, and restaurant *(zionlodge.com;* 435-772-7700).

Rocky
Mountains

On the Taggart Lake Trail, Grand Teton National Park

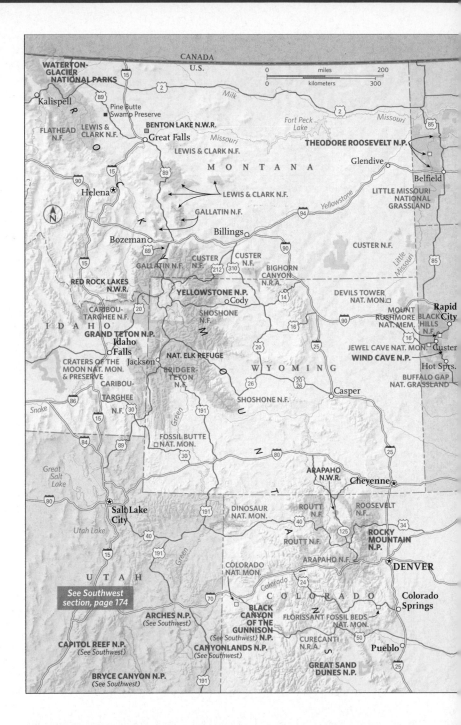

CANADA
U.S.

WATERTON-
GLACIER
NATIONAL PARKS

Kalispell

Pine Butte
Swamp Preserve

BENTON LAKE N.W.R.

FLATHEAD
N.F.

LEWIS &
CLARK N.F.

Great Falls

Milk

Fort Peck
Lake

Missouri

THEODORE ROOSEVELT N.P.

Glendive

Belfield

LEWIS & CLARK N.F.

M O N T A N A

Helena

LEWIS & CLARK N.F.

GALLATIN N.F.

Yellowstone

LITTLE MISSOURI
NATIONAL
GRASSLAND

Bozeman

Billings

GALLATIN N.F.

CUSTER
N.F.

CUSTER
N.F.

BIGHORN
CANYON
N.R.A.

CUSTER N.F.

Little Missouri

RED ROCK LAKES
N.W.R.

YELLOWSTONE N.P.

Cody

SHOSHONE
N.F.

DEVILS TOWER
NAT. MON.

MOUNT
RUSHMORE
NAT. MEM.

BLACK
HILLS
N.F.

Rapid
City

CARIBOU-
TARGHEE N.F.

GRAND TETON N.P.

Idaho
Falls

I D A H O

JEWEL CAVE NAT. MON.

WIND CAVE N.P.

Custer

Hot Sprs.

CRATERS OF THE
MOON NAT. MON.
& PRESERVE

Jackson

NAT. ELK REFUGE

BRIDGER-
TETON
N.F.

W Y O M I N G

BUFFALO GAP
NAT. GRASSLAND

CARIBOU-
TARGHEE
N.F.

Snake

SHOSHONE N.F.

Casper

Great
Salt
Lake

Green

FOSSIL BUTTE
NAT. MON.

ARAPAHO
N.W.R.

Cheyenne

Salt Lake
City

Utah Lake

DINOSAUR
NAT. MON.

ROUTT
N.F.

ROOSEVELT
N.F.

ROCKY
MOUNTAIN
N.P.

ROUTT N.F.

ARAPAHO N.F.

DENVER

U T A H

Green

COLORADO
NAT. MON.

Colorado

C O L O R A D O

Colorado
Springs

See Southwest
section, page 174

ARCHES N.P.
(See Southwest)

BLACK
CANYON
OF THE
GUNNISON
(See Southwest) N.P.

FLORISSANT FOSSIL BEDS
NAT. MON.

CAPITOL REEF N.P.
(See Southwest)

CANYONLANDS N.P.
(See Southwest)

CURECANTI
N.R.A.

Pueblo

BRYCE CANYON N.P.
(See Southwest)

GREAT SAND
DUNES N.P.

miles   200
kilometers   300

Craggy peaks capped by glimmering glaciers, fields run riot with wildflowers, lakes as smooth and blue as a summer sky—these images from the four Rocky Mountains parks epitomize for many just what a national park should look like.

High alpine landscapes are the common denominator. These five parks—Great Sand Dunes included—soar.

Rocky Mountain National Park's riches are best viewed along Colorado's Trail Ridge Road, a 48-mile passage that snakes through the park, ascending among subalpine forests before reaching the alpine tundra, where shrubs and rock-hugging lichen endure the extreme wind and cold.

Yet this region offers more than mountains. The forces that created the peaks further contoured neighboring landscapes. As wind eroded the mountain peaks, dust settled in the San Luis Valley and formed the dunes—some up to 750 feet tall—in southern Colorado's **Great Sand Dunes** National Park (where Tijeras Peak tops out at 13,604 feet).

The Rocky Mountain national parks preserve the spirit of America's frontier, its history, rugged landscapes, and abundance of wildlife. Wyoming's **Yellowstone, Grand Teton,** and Montana's **Glacier/Waterton**—together with surrounding public lands—remain strongholds for the grizzly bear. In some parks visitors can watch elk, bighorn sheep, mule deer, and remnants of the great bison herds that once thundered across the plains.

These parks provide case studies in how wilderness manages itself. In Yellowstone, for instance, the visitor can get a real sense of natural recovery in the wake of historic forest fires. Less encouraging are the real estate developments and plans for industry on the fringes of some parks. Such activities can shrink the habitats of wide-roaming animals, though in some instances parks are adjusting. The formerly threatened elk around Grand Teton and Yellowstone, for example, now congregate in winter to feed in the nearby National Elk Refuge.

Glacier/Waterton

Montana & Alberta, Canada

Established
May 11, 1910

1.1 million acres

Ice Age glaciers carved the foundation of a wonderland of soaring cliffs, misty valleys, long lakes, wildflower meadows, and deep forest. Melted snow and ice pour from the heights; cascades and waterfalls appear at nearly every turn. It feels like a landscape freshly minted. And so it is. The glaciers melted scarcely 12,000 years ago. Note: Glacier/Waterton National Park is actually two parks in two countries, joined in 1932 as a symbol of peace and friendship.

Sprawled across the Continental Divide, Glacier has two sides. The west reflects a Pacific Northwest maritime climate, with abundant moisture, big narrow lakes, and lush forest. On the drier east side, where mountains stand like fortress walls above the great plains, the landscape is more open; lodgepole pine, grassy meadows, and aspen trees are common. The Going-to-the-Sun Road cuts a spectacular transect over Logan Pass, going from one side of Glacier to the other.

When the Rockies lifted up about 75 million years ago, a giant

St. Mary Lake

▶ HOW TO VISIT

Allow plenty of time, a full day if you can, for the 50-mile **Going-to-the-Sun Road,** considered by many to be one of the world's most spectacular highways. Ride the free shuttle to avoid fighting traffic and searching for a place to park. Get off at one stop, hike a distance, then get back on at another.

On a second day, travel the **Chief Mountain International Highway** north to **Waterton Lakes** to enjoy the contrast of peak and prairie.

With more time, sample one or both sides of Glacier/Waterton. West-side highlights include **Lake McDonald,** water-sculpted **McDonald Creek,** and ancient forests of hemlock and red cedar. On the east side, don't miss **Many Glacier,** with stunning scenery and the park's best trails. To the north, **Waterton Lakes,** in Canada, offers more mountain majesty with fewer visitors.

Want off the beaten path? Go north from Apgar to remote **Kintla** and **Bowman Lakes,** or south from St. Mary to **Cutbank** and **Two Medicine Lake.**

You can take a wilderness trip on horseback or foot. Sign up for guided horseback rides at the **Many Glacier, Lake McDonald,** or **Apgar visitor centers.**

Going-to-the-Sun Road

Starting on the west side of the park, get oriented at the **Apgar Visitor Center.** Note restrictions on vehicle size and bicycle use on higher sections of the road. During peak season (June through September), when traffic is heavy and space at turnouts is limited, the free shuttle is a good option.

The road skirts **Lake McDonald,**

slab broke loose and slid toward the east—an event called the Lewis Overthrust. That grand block is the mountainous core of the park.

There are glaciers to be seen, but possibly not for long. Models predict that the glaciers might be gone by 2030 (see p. 269). Yet Glacier was named not so much for living ice as for the tracks of it, the work of Ice Age glaciers over the last two million years. Moraines, hanging valleys, arêtes, cirques, eskers, drumlins, and kames—this is a perfect place to see these glacial landforms.

And the creatures that call this place home? Bighorn sheep, mountain goats, elk, grizzly bears, wolves, and eagles flourish here.

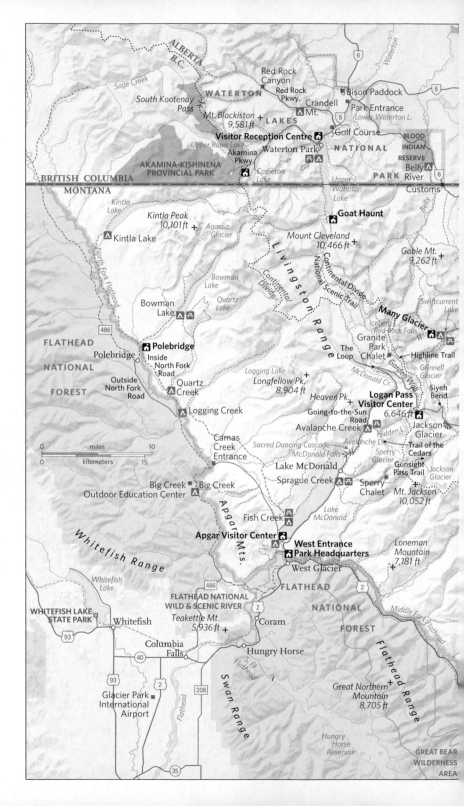

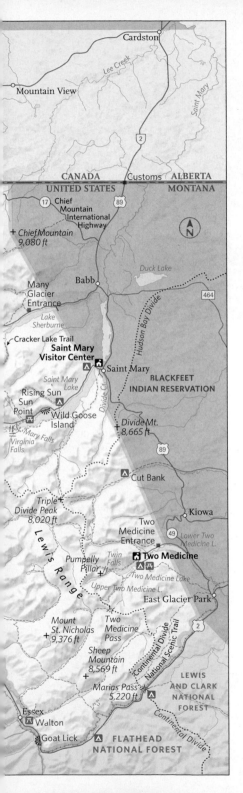

the biggest lake in the park. Its long, narrow bed was gouged out by the bulldozing action of a glacier. Stop at a turnout to admire the view and, lakeside, test your skills with some of the world's best skipping stones.

Although snowy peaks beckon, linger a while along **McDonald Creek.** From a turnout just beyond the lake, cross a footbridge and turn upstream to **Sacred Dancing Cascade,** a quarter mile of tumbling water and polished rock. Several miles farther, stop at Avalanche Creek. Follow **Trail of the Cedars** (0.7 mile), a boardwalk suitable for wheelchairs that winds through an old forest of towering hemlocks, black cottonwoods, and red cedars, some of them more than 500 years old.

Even during busy times, these extensive, cool, fern-filled spaces convey a sense of timeless peace. Trail of the Cedars leads to **Avalanche Gorge,** an exquisite natural creation of red rock, turquoise water, and the intoxicating smell of cold mountain mist. The water comes from Avalanche Lake, perched in a cirque 500 feet above.

Soon the road begins to climb and great peaks heave into view. Pause at **The Loop,** a tight switchback, for views of Heaven Peak and to learn about the Trapper Fire, one of six major fires that burned 135,000 acres in 2003.

A 4-mile trail leads stiffly uphill from here, gaining 2,200 vertical feet before reaching **Granite Park Chalet** (graniteparkchalet.com; 888-345-2649), one of two backcountry lodges remaining from a network built by the Great Northern Railway a century ago.

Another way to get to this part of the park is via the **Highline Trail** from Logan Pass, which starts high and

Refurbished vintage White Motor Company park touring bus

stays high, leading through meadows that range below a long glacier-sharpened ridge called the Garden Wall. It's 7.6 miles to Granite Park; from there it's a short downhill walk back to The Loop.

For the next few miles, the road seems nailed to the cliffs. It bores through tunnels, edges fearlessly around promontories, and passes beneath wispy waterfalls. One of the most famous is across the valley. **Bird Woman Falls** drops in a long ribbon from a classic hanging valley.

Logan Pass is a place to revel in alpine splendor. Snowcapped peaks rise on all sides. Summer wildflowers are abundant. Mountain goats are usually visible, sometimes at close range. (Keep your distance, as with all wildlife.) Pick up a self-guiding pamphlet at the **Logan Pass Visitor Center** and follow the 1.5-mile trail to **Hidden Lake Overlook,** where the ground drops away suddenly to a gorgeous gem of a lake. Or go the other way, along

the **Highline Trail.** Going for even a short walk is rewarding, but note that it involves walking a narrow, exposed ledge that can be disconcerting.

Descending eastward, the road cuts though dark gray rock containing the cabbage-shaped whorls of fossilized algae called stromatolites, The algae lived as slimy colonies along an ocean coast almost a billion years ago. Pull in at **Siyeh Bend,** a sharp turn close to timberline, to scan the meadows for wildlife.

Grizzly sightings are possible here, beneath sharp-spired Going-to-the-Sun Mountain. Legends attributed to the Blackfeet people describe the mountain as a spirit pathway to the sun; others say the name came from the flowery imagination of an early tourist.

Stop at the **Gunsight Pass Trailhead** for a fine view of Jackson Glacier. Among the park's larger glaciers, it's also one of the few visible from a road. Farther along, waterfall lovers should consider walking to

Vanishing Act

In 1850 there were about 150 glaciers in the park. Today there are 26. In a few decades there might be none, and the impact of their loss would run deep. The park is an ecosystem attuned to annual cycles of freezing and melting. Glaciers are a storehouse of winter snow. Released gradually as the glacier melts throughout summer, the water keeps streams flowing, lakes filled, and meadows green. Outside the park, it sustains farm crops and city water systems. Practically every living thing, from alpine wildflowers to fish, rodents to grazing animals, depends to some degree on water pouring from the heights.

The Earth is warming. Winters are shorter and summers hotter. The park gets three times the number of days above 90°F as it did a century ago. Snowfields that once lasted through the summer now disappear in August. Glaciers might not be far behind.

Notable is Grinnell Glacier, high on Mount Gould. A fraction of its former self, it represents the general state of ice and snow in the Rockies. The U.S. Geological Survey has compiled comparative photos of Grinnell and other park glaciers over more than a century. Available for viewing at *nrmsc.usgs.gov/repeatphoto,* these photographs tell a dramatic story of climate change.

St. Mary and Virginia Falls, near the head of St. Mary Lake, and everyone should stop at Sun Point, for the panoramic vista and a stroll along the self-guided nature trail. Farther down the lake, just west of Rising Sun, pull in at Wild Goose Island Overlook for an iconic view, perhaps the most recognized place in all of Glacier.

The road continues 6 miles along the lakeshore, ending at the St. Mary Visitor Center and entrance. The road climbs gently into what many feel is the heart of the park. A cluster of turquoise lakes lies at the meeting place of three valleys beneath towering peaks. As you arrive at Swiftcurrent Lake, the grandeur can stop you in your tracks. When you're ready to move on, check out the rustically gracious Many Glacier Hotel, built in 1915 (glaciernationalparklodges.com; 855-733-4622).

More than anything, Many Glacier is a place for hiking. Warm up on the easy 2.5-mile nature trail around the lake, or go beyond it, past Lake Josephine, onto a nearly level trail to Grinnell Lake, gleaming turquoise at the base of massive Mount Gould. Waterfalls pouring off these formidable cliffs are fed by Grinnell Glacier. Strong hikers can join a ranger for an all-day hike to the glacier overlook.

Other places in the hiker's Many Glacier treasure kit include Iceberg Lake, dotted with floes, high against the Garden Wall (a 4-mile hike, 1,200 feet up); for a nearly level valley-bottom walk, consider Red Rock Falls (3.6 miles, 100 feet up).

Chief Mountain Highway & Beyond

From the town of Babb, the 29-mile Chief Mountain International Highway climbs over rolling hills toward Chief Mountain (9,080 feet), a distinctive monolith marking the easternmost push of the Lewis Overthrust. Shoved into position on top of younger strata, the mountain is older than the rocks beneath it. Chief Mountain has long been sacred to the Blackfeet people.

U.S. and Canada customs stations flank the international border. *(All travelers must present passports or other documents compliant with the Western Hemisphere Travel Initiative.)* A few miles north, sweeping views of the **Waterton Valley** open up. Prominent is Mount Crandell, embraced by the park's two major valleys, Blakiston and Cameron. Ahead and eastward, the open plains stretch seemingly forever. The scenic climax, **Upper Waterton Lake,** waits in the wings, stage left.

It's a good idea to stop at the **Waterton Lakes National Park Visitor Centre** for maps and park information. From here, a short steep hike climbs **Bear's Hump** for a grand overview of Waterton Lake.

There's an easier-to-access viewing area just across the road at the imposing **Prince of Wales Hotel** *(glacierparkinc.com; 406-892-2525).* Perched boldly on a treeless knob at the end of the lake, the hotel is famous for strong winds, period design, afternoon tea Victorian style, and jaw-dropping scenery.

To see more of the lake, take a boat ride to **Goat Haunt,** a **ranger station** on the American side of the border *(glacierparkinc.com; 406-892-2525).* Otherwise, drive the **Red Rock Parkway** through Blakiston Valley. Stop at the first oil well in western Canada, where drillers struck oil in 1902. Fortunately for the future national park, the oil soon played out and the area returned to its wild state. The road ends at a narrow redrock gorge that has been beautifully sculpted by mountain water.

The **Akamina Parkway** begins at Waterton Townsite and follows a glacial valley through woods and meadow for 10 miles to Cameron Lake, cupped high among snowcapped peaks near timberline. Rent a canoe, walk the lakeshore trail, or mosey through the forest to moose-frequented **Akamina Lake.** Robust hikers have numerous options. The trail to Summit Lake climbs 1,000 feet in 4 miles. Make a full day in the high country by continuing all the way back to **Waterton Townsite** via Carthew and Alderson Lakes, a total distance of 12 miles.

Other Sights & Trails

The quiet northwest corner of Glacier features several lakes that rival Lake McDonald for splendor. The bonus is that they receive very few visitors. Follow the North Fork Flathead River through forest and meadow. The river occupies a rift torn open when the mountains slid eastward on the Lewis Overthrust. At **Polebridge,** drop in at the Mercantile, a century-old general store outside the park. Continue to **Bowman Lake** or **Kintla Lake,** fine places to pitch a tent. Indeed, this is a place to linger, especially if you have a canoe or kayak.

The opposite corner of the park, the southeast, is also less traveled. Follow US 89 from St. Mary, then Mont. 49 to Two Medicine. A boat shuttle crosses **Two Medicine Lake,** another long glacial trough. From the far end, a 2.2-mile trail skirts a distinctive spire called Pumpelly Pillar and ends at **Upper Two Medicine Lake** surrounded by colorful cliffs.

Paddling Lake McDonald

Information

How to Get There

US 89 connects to east-side Many Glacier and St. Mary. US 2 cuts around the south end of the park and is the main approach from the west. In Canada, Alberta 6 and 5 approach from the north and east.

When to Go

June through September is best. Access to the park is reduced in early spring and late fall due to weather. Main roads are open year-round. Logan Pass is usually not clear until mid-June. Chief Mountain Highway is open early May–Sept.

Visitor Centers

Glacier's three visitor centers (at **Apgar, St. Mary,** and **Logan Pass**) have varying schedules but are generally open May to mid-Sept. On the Canada side the **Waterton Lakes Visitor Centre** is open mid-May–mid.-Oct.

Headquarters

Glacier National Park
P.O. Box 128

West Glacier, MT 59936
nps.gov/glac
406-888-7800

Waterton Lakes National Park
Box 200
Waterton Park, AB T0K 2M0
waterton.ca
403-859-5133.

Camping

Most of Glacier's 13 campgrounds open late May or early June. Reservations available for limited sites at **St. Mary** and **Fish Creek** *(recreation.gov)*. Waterton Lakes has three campgrounds *(pccamping.ca)*.

Lodging

Xanterra *(glaciernationalparklodges.com;* 855-733-4522) runs five hotels, including **Many Glacier** and **Lake McDonald;** lodging is also available from Glacier Park Inc. *(glacierparkinc.com,* 406-892-2525). For backcountry lodges contact Belton Chalets *(graniteparkchalet.com,* 888-345-2649). Waterton Townsite offers a variety of options *(mywaterton.ca/stay,* 403-859-2224).

Grand Teton

Wyoming

Established
February 26, 1929

310,000 acres

If we imagine what mountains should look like, these are the ones. Snowcapped crags sharpened by glaciers rise abruptly above the sage-covered plain of Grand Teton National Park. A chain of alpine lakes filled with trout sparkles at their feet, while the Snake River winds smooth and fast through tree-lined channels. A gentler range stands to the east; together with the Tetons it encloses the valley called Jackson Hole.

Grand Teton National Park is named for a single mountain, the Grand Teton, 13,770 feet high and the central summit of the Teton Range. It forms, with its immediate neighbors to the south, a sort of alpine triumvirate, the Three Tetons. These mountains and others in the range were called Pilot Knobs by fur trappers some 200 years ago because they could be seen from miles away, in all directions. Other notable peaks include Teewinot, an elegantly descriptive Shoshone term that means "many pinnacles."

Beyond spectacular scenery, the Tetons possess everything a mountain landscape should have. Abundant wildlife includes moose, elk, bison,

Snake River and the Teton Range

viewpoints. Make a loop of it by continuing to **Jackson Lake** and returning to Moose via Moran Junction.

On a second day, hike to one of the **morainal lakes—**Bradley, Taggart, Leigh, or Phelps. For longer hikes, consider the **canyons—**Cascade, Death, Granite, and others. Float the **Snake River,** or rent a canoe at Colter Bay and explore the islands in Jackson Lake.

Teton Park Road & Jenny Lake

Driving north from the town of Jackson, turn off US 89/191/26 at Moose Junction. Drive slowly across the Snake River Bridge, checking the riverside willow thicket for moose. Stop at the visitor center at **Moose** for general information, a bookstore, a theater, and exhibits on park history and nature. The entrance station is just ahead; from there, the Teton Park Road climbs up from the river bottom to emerge on a wide, sage-covered expanse. Suddenly the whole range rockets into view, seeming impossibly steep and high. The mountains will stay close for the rest of the drive, with each mile bringing a new and perhaps even more spectacular perspective.

At **Taggart Lake Trailhead,** a popular 3-mile trail leads to **Taggart Lake** and, beyond it, **Bradley Lake.** The route passes over a glacial moraine. This is typical of lakes at the base of the Tetons. Glaciers, pushing down from the mountains, gouged out the lake basins and left piles of debris that held back the waters. This moraine, visible from the road, burned in a 1985 wildfire. You can see how long it takes

deer, antelope, bighorn sheep, grizzly and black bears, beavers, otters, eagles, and osprey. Vegetation varies with altitude. Sagebrush and cottonwoods thrive on the valley floor. Spruce, pine, and aspen trees climb the mountain slopes. Alpine meadows strewn with wildflowers like spilled treasure occupy the heights. Waterfalls, glacial lakes, a dozen glaciers, and numerous mountain creeks complete the scene.

▶ HOW TO VISIT

If you have one day, drive the **Teton Park Road.** Start with the **visitor center** at Moose, then drive north to the **Jenny Lake area,** stopping for short walks and to pause at scenic

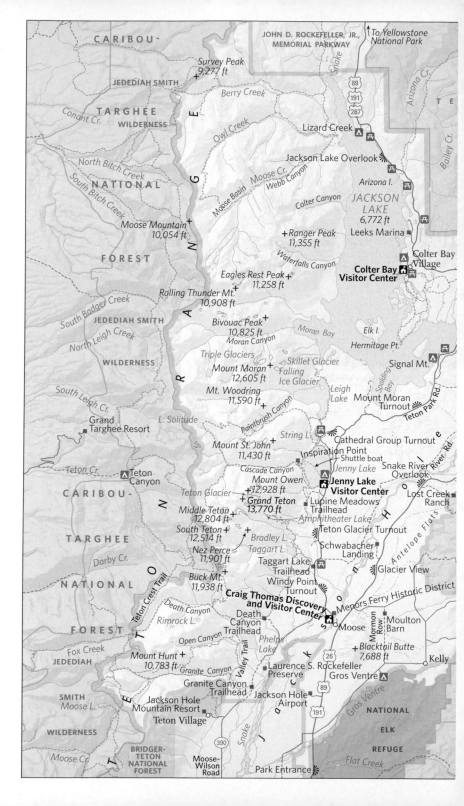

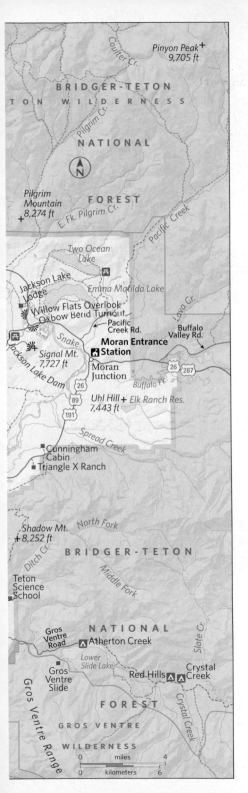

for a forest to recover in this slow-growing mountain setting.

Pause at **Teton Glacier Turnout** for a neck-craning view of the central peaks. The **Grand Teton** (13,770 feet) is the highest in the range and second highest in Wyoming (behind Gannett Peak in the Wind River Range). Shouldering against it on the left (south) is the Middle Teton. The South Teton, third of what French trappers called *Les Trois Tétons,* can't be seen from this angle. A foreground peak, Nez Perce, blocks it from view.

To the right of the Grand [Teton] are sharp-pointed **Mount Owen** and **Teewinot Mountain.** Of the many climbing routes up the Grand, not one is easy; the main route follows the left-hand skyline. Before noon, hikers might be visible on the summit, which is more than 7,000 vertical feet above.

Glacier Gulch is a smooth stone trench plowed by large tongues of ice that spilled from the mountains during glacial periods, when ice covered the mountains and parts of the valley to depths of several thousand feet. (The most recent glaciation ended some 14,000 years ago.)

The small **Teton Glacier** shelters in the cold shade of the Grand Teton's formidable east face. How can you tell glaciers from the numerous snowfields scattered over the Tetons? Snowfields are generally whiter. Glaciers might be covered by fresh snowpack from last winter's snowfall, but the ice can be centuries old. The ice shows its age; it is gray, like elephant hide, broken by crevasses as the snowpack melts under the summer sun.

Across the road to the east stands **Timbered Island,** a moraine that

Jackson Lake and the Teton Range

demonstrates why plants grow in some areas here and not others. Moraines form at the feet of glaciers and contain a jumbled mix of silt, gravel, and rock. The silt holds moisture, which in turn supports dense forest. In contrast, much of the valley floor is an outwash plain: gravel and rock deposited by glacial meltwater, with not as much silt. Water sinks beneath the plain, and trees don't survive in this arid environment. Instead, deeply rooted sagebrush covers the ground.

Driving north, look for pronghorn on the sage slats east and north of Timbered Island. Resembling African antelope but actually a separate family, pronghorn are North America's fastest land animals. Elk, deer, and coyote sightings also are possible.

Just south of Jenny Lake, a road cuts off to **Lupine Meadows** and a popular trailhead. Climbers headed for the standard routes up the Grand start here. Hikers branch off to **Amphitheater Lake,** a stiff climb of 3,000 feet, and just about the closest you can get to the Grand without climbing it. Put that on the day-hike list, and for now continue past South Jenny Lake for 3 miles to **North Jenny Lake Junction.**

The **Cathedral Group Turnout** might slow you down with its view of crags piled upon crags. From here, Teewinot seems a more fitting name than Teton (French for breast or nipple).

If you are inclined to do some easy walking, you can't beat the trail along narrow **String Lake,** with its beaches, shady rest stops, water sometimes warm enough for swimming, and stupendous views.

The nearly level trail continues to **Leigh Lake.** Deep blue, under the soaring walls of Mount Moran, it was named for "Beaver Dick" Leigh, a British fur trapper who arrived in the area with his Shoshone wife, Jenny, in the 1860s. He lost her and their children to smallpox in 1876. She is remembered by the lake that bears her name.

Continue south on the one-way road along the shore of Jenny Lake. The **South Jenny Lake area** (visitor center, store, and ranger station) is the place to park for shuttle boats that provide transport to the half-mile, often crowded trail to **Hidden Falls.** That trail continues to **Inspiration**

Point, offering a fine view of the lake before entering the delightful gorge of **Cascade Canyon,** one of the park's premier hiking routes. Add that to the growing day-hike list.

Jackson Lake & North

Start at **North Jenny Lake Junction** on the Teton Park Road. Well-placed turnouts offer splendid views, with Mount Moran becoming more center stage as you head north. Two prominent glaciers cling to its precipitous flanks, **Falling Ice Glacier,** on the left, and **Skillet,** on the right. Skillet's summit looks flat, like a plateau, but it drops off steeply on the back side.

In the right light, you can see a reddish patch of sandstone on the very top of Skillet, a small remnant of the sedimentary layers that once overlay the entire range. The remnant corresponds to a layer of the same stone now some 24,000 feet beneath the valley floor. Those two layers tell the story of the Teton uplift. Two giant blocks of stone shifted along the Teton Fault. The valley block tilted downward as the mountain block rose, for a total displacement of some 30,000 vertical feet, all in 13 million years or less.

If you're not driving an RV or pulling a trailer, take the turn for **Signal Mountain.** A narrow road winds to the summit. Because it stands by itself, the mountain provides unmatched views of the entire Teton Range, the valley, and the gentler Gros Ventre Range, which bounds Jackson Hole on the east. This is a fine place to appreciate the big picture of Grand Teton's dramatic geology.

Elk of Jackson Hole

It was an ancient migration. Long before settlers arrived in the region in the late 1800s, thousands of elk made an annual autumn pilgrimage down from the surrounding mountains to Jackson Hole and farther along. Residents at the time reported seeing upward of 25,000 elk headed south, with some estimates as high as 50,000. One called it the "annual trek of the elk" to windswept plains beyond the mountains, where snow was shallow and winter forage more easily available. In spring they would return to the mountains.

Settlement ended that. Fences, roads, and other developments cut the elk from their wintering grounds, with terrible results. They starved in large numbers, clustered desperately around haystacks, and even roaming among the houses of Jackson.

Appalled by the tragic loss, residents raised funds to feed hay to the elk, and pushed for government help. That came in 1912 with creation of the National Elk Refuge, which would compensate for the loss of lower-elevation winter range as well as migration routes.

Elk still stream down from the mountains in the autumn, but now they gather on the National Elk Refuge and Wyoming state feed grounds. Winter feeding remains controversial owing to concerns about disease transmission given the numbers of elk involved.

Learn more at the historic Miller House, on the refuge; or the Jackson Historical Society & Museum (jacksonholehistory.com; 307-733-2414).

Returning to the Teton Park Road, continue along the shore of **Jackson Lake** and across the **Jackson Lake Dam.** Constructed in 1907, 22 years before the park was established, and rebuilt several times after, the dam raised the natural lake level by 39 feet. The stored water irrigates farm fields in Idaho.

Past the dam, watch for moose that frequent the willow flats. The Teton Park Road ends just ahead, where it meets Wyo. 26/287. Turning left takes you past **Jackson Lake Lodge,** on the road to Yellowstone, but even if you're headed that way, take a short detour to the right.

One mile away is **Oxbow Bend,** a wide meander of the Snake River flowing gently through marshy flats. In the autumn, bright yellow aspens frame this famous view of Mount Moran across calm water often crowded with ducks, geese, and sometimes American white pelicans.

If headed to Yellowstone, go north. For about 15 miles, the road follows the shore of Jackson Lake, which comes in and out of view through forest and across meadows that in summer become lavish spreads of wildflowers. Stop at **Colter Bay** to enjoy the waterfront. Long pebble-covered beaches stretch in both directions, with dramatic views of Mount Moran and the remote peaks of the northern Tetons.

Rolling Thunder Mountain, Eagles Rest Peak, and **Ranger Peak** dominate the wildest section of the park, an area with no roads and no maintained trails, protected on one side by the lake and on the other by miles of wilderness.

Colter Bay is a prime locale for paddling. Along the intricate shoreline, between the marina and Sheffield Island is ideal for exploring in a canoe or small boat.

To close the circle back to Moose, continue east through the Moran Entrance to Moran Junction, then south on Wyo. 89/191/26. A stop at **Cunningham Cabin Historic Site** offers a glimpse of pioneer life in Jackson Hole.

Here, in 1888, John and Margaret Cunningham started the Bar Flying U Ranch, a beautiful but challenging place to live. Long winters, deep snow, and summer drought prompted the Cunninghams, like many of their neighbors, to sell their land. They left in the 1930s.

Don't miss **Snake River Overlook,** where landscape photographer Ansel Adams made perhaps the most famous picture of the Tetons, with the river curving beneath high forested banks toward the central peaks. You might see rafts and small boats on the Snake River, carrying anglers and sightseers. Eagles and osprey are common sights here.

Several more turnouts command attention as you drive south. If there's time for a short stroll, take the side road to **Schwabacher Landing,**

Two Ocean Lake

braided river channels and beaver dams create a wildlife-rich mix of wetlands, reflecting ponds, meadows, and cool cottonwood forest.

Sunset can be lovely here. Sunrise, when first light hits the peaks, often is unforgettable. Four miles south is Moose Junction.

Other Hikes & Activities

Grand Teton is a hiker's park, and not all the trails are steep. Ambitious hikers might set off from Lupine Meadows for **Amphitheater Lake.** It's a 3,000-foot climb through steep wildflower meadows, with views into the cirque that holds **Teton Glacier.** Or consider a hike in one of the canyons that separate the major peaks. **Cascade Canyon** is deservedly popular.

Shorten the hike by riding the shuttle boat across Jenny Lake. **Lake Solitude** (7.4 miles from the shuttle dock), on the back side of the Grand Teton, is the most popular shuttle boat landing.

Death Canyon is far more appealing than its name would suggest. The trail starts off the Moose-Wilson Road. One mile takes you to a fine overlook of Phelps Lake, then down to the lake and up the canyon as far as you wish to go. With overnight gear (backcountry permit required), you can join the **Teton Crest Trail,** a dazzling high traverse on the other side of the range.

For easier walking, consider one of the lakeside trails around **Colter Bay area,** which lead to gravel beaches on Jackson Lake. **Hermitage Point** is about 4.5 miles each way, depending on the route you choose. Or pick a segment of the little-traveled **Valley Trail** that stretches from Teton Village along the base of the mountains to Jenny Lake.

The **Laurance S. Rockefeller Preserve,** located on the Moose-Wilson Road, was recently opened to the public after Laurance S. Rockefeller donated the private retreat to the park. The **visitor center** and trail system were designed to encourage reflective nature appreciation. An easy 3-mile loop follows Lake Creek to a perfect picnic site on **Phelps Lake.** These trails connect with the **Death Canyon Trail.**

Floating the **Snake River** is a relaxing half-day experience. The scenic river, fast-moving but with no white water, offers shifting views of the mountains and a chance to see eagles, osprey, moose, otters, and other wildlife. Guided fishing trips are also popular. Or take to the pedals; a paved multi-use path runs from Jackson to Jenny Lake, along with multiple side-road options throughout the valley.

For a quiet, out-of-the-way driving option, consider the east side of the valley. Drive along the **Gros Ventre River** to the hamlet of Kelly, then loop north and west, watching for bison and moose, to **Mormon Row,** once home to 22 Mormon pioneer families. The graceful old **Moulton Barn,** at sunrise with the mountains in the background, has become a Teton classic for painters and photographers.

Nearby, the Gros Ventre Road climbs rolling foothills eastward to **Slide Lake,** created in 1925 by an enormous landslide that dammed the river. When the impounded water broke the dam two years later, the sudden flood wiped away the town of Kelly, killing six people.

Beaver

Information

How to Get There

From Jackson, drive north on US 89/26/191 to the main visitor center and entrance station at Moose. From Yellowstone, US 89/287 enters the park via John D. Rockefeller, Jr. Memorial Pkwy. Jackson Hole Airport is in the park.

When to Go

July and Aug. see peak visitation. Wildflowers are abundant. Afternoon thunderstorms keep things fresh. Roads are plowed usually by early May, with snow lingering into June. Sept. and Oct. bring lots of sun, frosty nights, and good wildlife viewing. Winter is as beautiful as it is challenging. Snow falls deep and temperatures drop into the sub-zero range. It's the time for cross-country skiing and snowshoeing. Most of Teton Park Road and Moose-Wilson Road close for the season.

Visitor Centers

There are five visitor centers: **Craig Thomas Discovery and Visitor Center,** at Moose, open daily March through Oct.;

GRAND TETON EST. 1929

Jenny Lake, mid-May to late Sept.; **Colter Bay,** mid-May through Sept.; **Laurance Rockefeller Preserve,** June to late Sept.; **Flagg Ranch,** June through Aug.

Headquarters

P.O. Drawer 170
Moose, WY 83012
nps.gov/grte
307-739-3300

Camping

The park has five campgrounds; most open early to mid-May and close early to mid Oct. Backcountry camping is also an option; permits are offered on a first-come, first-served basis.

Lodging

In the park, Grand Teton Lodge Company runs **Jackson Lake Lodge, Jenny Lake Lodge,** and **Colter Bay Cabins** *(gltc.com;* 307-543-2811). Many lodging options exist in and around **Jackson** *(jacksonhole chamber.com;* 307-733-3316).

Grand Teton Excursions

National Elk Refuge
Jackson, Wyoming

▷ The National Elk Refuge preserves, restores, and manages winter
habitat for the Jackson elk herd. It
also protects endangered birds. In
winter, horse-drawn sleighs take
visitors around the refuge. Fishing
Aug. through Oct. (Wyoming fishing
license required). Located northeast
of Jackson, Wyoming, and directly
south of Grand Teton and Yellowstone
National Parks. US highways 26/191
pass through Jackson and 6 miles into
refuge land. *fws.gov/nationalelkrefuge;*
307-733-9212.

Gros Ventre Wilderness
East of Jackson, Wyoming

▷ One of the three wilderness
areas located within the Bridger-
Teton National Forest, Gros Ventre
Wilderness is known for its wildlife—bighorn sheep, elk, deer, black
bears, wolves, grizzly bears, mountain
lions, and bison—as well as its rocky
alpine peaks. It provides excellent
chances for both backpacking and
horseback trips. Located east of
Jackson, Wyoming, and southeast of
Grand Teton National Park. *fs.usda
.gov/recarea/btnf/recreation/ohv/
recarea/?recid=71647&actid=30;* 307-
739-5500.

John D. Rockefeller, Jr.
Memorial Parkway
Between Yellowstone and Grand Teton NPs

▷ Linking two of the nations' greatest national parks, the Parkway runs
the 82 miles between Grand Teton and
Yellowstone. Set aside as a scenic corridor, this route runs through a gently
rolling track of lodgepole pines. Off the
sides of the road are elk, moose, and
deer. The Snake River crossing provides
a chance to both picnic and launch a
canoe, while the Grassy Lake Road provides a scenic drive into Idaho. *nps.gov/
grte/jodr;* 307-739-3300.

Jackson National Fish Hatchery
Northeast of Jackson, Wyoming

▷ On the grounds of the National Elk Refuge, the Jackson National Fish Hatchery has been raising fish to mitigate fish losses since the middle of the last century. The fish reared here are native Snake River cutthroat trout, which are reintroduced into the waters of Wyoming and Idaho. Sleeping Indian Pond is open for fishing to those with their own equipment (Wyoming license required). Located northeast of Jackson, Wyoming, and south of Grand Teton National Park. *fws.gov/jackson;* 307-733-2510.

National Bighorn Sheep Center
Dubois, Wyoming

▷ The National Bighorn Sheep Center zooms in on the biology and habitat needs of the wild sheep. The center features dioramas that re-create the habitat of the large wild sheep, interactive exhibits about wildlife management, and wildlife films. In fall and winter, the center offers guided and self-guided tours of the local Whiskey Mountain herd in their natural habitat. Center closed Sun. in winter. Fee. Located in Dubois, Wyoming, 55 miles southeast of Grand Teton National Park via US 26E/US 287. *bighorn.org;* 307-455-3429.

Fossil Butte National Monument
Kemmer, Wyoming

▷ Fifty-two million years ago, this semi-arid sagebrush country was the site of Fossil Lake, a rich freshwater Eocene deposit that became a place of fossils, exquisitely preserved freshwater fish. More than 300 fossils are on display at the Visitor Center. Summer activities include fossil preparation demonstrations and exhibit tours. Interpretive trails, a scenic drive, winter snowshoeing, and cross-country skiing round things out. Visitor Center open year-round. Located about 180 miles south of Grand Teton National Park off US 30. *nps.gov/fobu;* 307-877-4455.

Great Sand Dunes

Colorado

Established
September 13, 2004

149,137 acres

Undulating sweeps of sand—the tallest sand dunes in North America—rise precipitously and improbably from the rolling grasslands of the San Luis Valley in mountainous south-central Colorado. Craggy spires of the Sangre de Cristo range soar directly behind the dunes, reaching skyward more than 13,000 feet. A coalescence of grass, sand, water, forest, and rock forms the visually striking ecosystem that is Great Sand Dunes National Park and Preserve.

The dunefield of Great Sand Dunes National Park and Preserve sprawls across more than 30 square miles. At its highest point is Star Dune, towering 755 feet above the surrounding grasslands. Today, visitors from around the world come to visit the magical realm of the dunes.

Some 11,000 years ago, the Clovis people, nomadic hunters and gatherers, roamed the region, hunting the herds of mammoths and prehistoric bison that grazed here. Later, the modern Ute and Jicarilla Apache tribes annually migrated through the area, also hunting and gathering. They

Dunes and the Sangre de Cristo Mountains

collected the inner bark from ponderosa pines for food and medicine; more than 100 ponderosa pines in the park today still show evidence of bark-peeling.

Beginning in the 1600s Spanish explorers from settlements in New Mexico penetrated the region. Legend has it that a dying priest, Francisco Torres, mortally wounded by an arrow, uttered his last words as he looked up at the sunset-burnished mountains above the dunes: "Sangre de Cristo . . . Sangre de Cristo," or Blood of Christ, thus giving the name to the mountain range towering above the dunes.

The first American to visit the Great Sand Dunes, it is believed, was Zebulon Pike, who in 1807 crossed the Sangre de Cristo Mountains from the east and was astonished by what he saw; in his journal he wrote of the dunes, "Their appearance was exactly that of a sea in a storm." By the late 1800s, settlers and miners populated the San Luis Valley and western flank of the Sangre de Cristos. In the 1920s, mining firms contemplated but never acted upon the idea of processing the sands of the Great Sand Dunes for gold.

Concerned about the possible destruction of the dunes, local residents petitioned Congress to protect them. In 1932, President Herbert Hoover signed a bill creating the Great Sand Dunes National Monument.

In 2000, 41,686 acres east and northeast of the dunefield were added, creating the national preserve, and the boundary was also expanded to the west to take in an additional 69,240 acres of sand deposits. By 2004, a large portion of these lands had been acquired by the U.S. government.

Winds that can top 40 miles an hour reshaped the crests of the tall dunes, and smaller dunes may "migrate" several feet in a week.

The region's geology and biology make Great Sand Dunes a fascinating place, unique among America's national parks.

▶ HOW TO VISIT

The **Dunefield** is the highlight of any visit to Great Sand Dunes National Park and Preserve. Climbing, sliding, rolling, sandboarding, and sand sledding in the dunes is a unique experience. If your time is very limited, plan on a half-day visit that includes an hour at the

visitor center and a few hours in the dunes themselves.

A full day or two, however, allows for a more fulfilling exploration of the park. You'll have time, for one, to experience **Medano Creek** area, wonderful for children who enjoy playing in wet sand. Broad and shallow, Medano Creek flows along the east side of the dunes.

Several hiking trails climb high into the forests and peaks of the Sangre de Cristos. The 0.5-mile **Montville Nature Trail** and 3.5-mile **Mosca Pass Trail** climb into the Sangre de Cristo Mountains and offer a skyscraping counterpoint to navigating the great dunes below.

If you have a high-clearance, four-wheel-drive vehicle and a strong sense of adventure, consider driving the **Medano Pass Primitive Road.** It heads to the crest of the Sangre de Cristos at **Medano Pass,** an elevation of 9,982 feet. The trailhead for the 3.8-mile **Medano Lake Trail** is along this road.

The Dunefield & Medano Creek

Enter the park and drive a couple of miles to the **visitor center,** which features a 20-minute video on the region's geology and history, interactive exhibits, displays, a bookstore, and rangers to answer questions and provide information. In summer, check the schedule of ranger-led hikes and programs; these offer excellent, in-depth perspectives on various aspects of the park.

The 0.25-mile **Sand Sheet Loop Trail** through the grasslands starts and ends at the visitor center and offers a

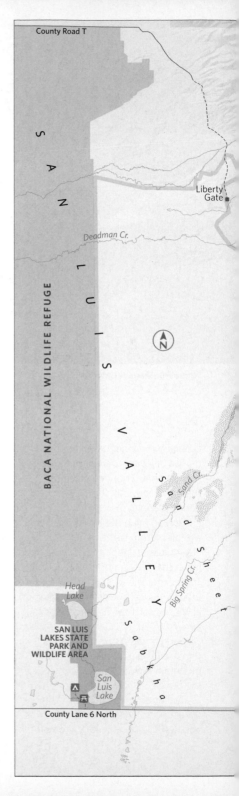

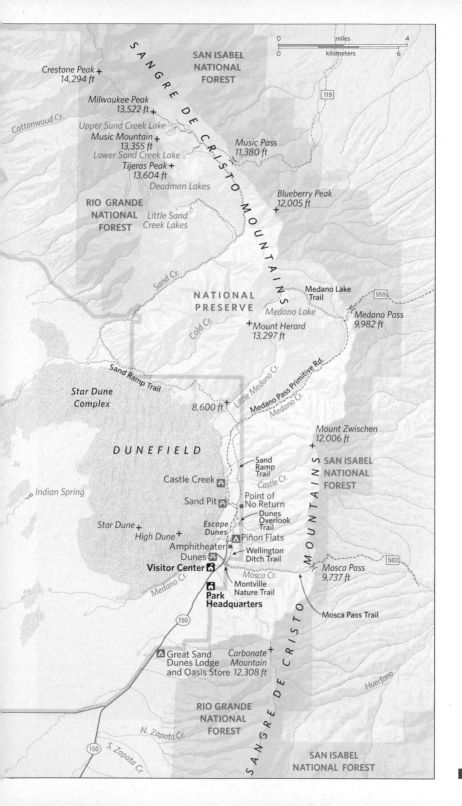

SANGRE DE CRISTO MOUNTAINS

SAN ISABEL NATIONAL FOREST

0   miles   4
0   kilometers   6

Crestone Peak
14,294 ft

Cottonwood Cr.

Milwaukee Peak
13,522 ft

Upper Sand Creek Lake
Music Mountain
13,355 ft
Lower Sand Creek Lake
Tijeras Peak
13,604 ft

Deadman Lakes

Music Pass
11,380 ft

Blueberry Peak
12,005 ft

RIO GRANDE
NATIONAL
FOREST

Little Sand
Creek Lakes

Sand Cr.

NATIONAL
PRESERVE

Medano Lake
Trail

Medano Lake

Medano Pass
9,982 ft

Cold Cr.

Mount Herard
13,297 ft

Sand Ramp Trail

Little Medano Cr.

Medano Pass Primitive Rd.

Medano Cr.

Star Dune
Complex

8,600 ft

Mount Zwischen
12,006 ft

DUNEFIELD

Castle Creek

Sand Pit

Indian Spring

Star Dune

High Dune

Amphitheater
Dunes
Visitor Center

Sand
Ramp
Trail

Castle Cr.

Point of
No Return

Dunes
Overlook
Trail

Escape
Dunes

Piñon Flats

Wellington
Ditch Trail

SAN ISABEL
NATIONAL
FOREST

Medano Cr.

Mosca Cr.

Montville
Nature Trail

Mosca Pass
9,737 ft

**Park
Headquarters**

Mosca Pass Trail

150

Great Sand
Dunes Lodge
and Oasis Store

Carbonate
Mountain
12,308 ft

RIO GRANDE
NATIONAL
FOREST

N. Zapata Cr.

150

S. Zapata Cr.

Huerfano

SANGRE DE CRISTO

SAN ISABEL
NATIONAL FOREST

quick introduction to the park. Note the vegetation, including gooseberry and three-leaf sumac bushes, as well as prickly pear cactus.

A mile north is the **Dunes** parking lot and picnic area, as well as the gateway to hiking and playing in the dunefield. Before reaching the base of the dunes, cross shallow **Medano Creek,** which borders the eastern edge of the

View from the summit of High Dome

dunefield. Children love to frolic in the creek, building sand castles and digging in the wet sand that forms the creek's shifting bottom. Medano Creek, fed by snowmelt from the Sangre de Cristos, reaches its peak flow in late May. Early morning is a particularly good time to look for tracks in the wet sand—mule deer, coyotes, or even a bobcat.

A peculiar characteristic of the creek is the existence of "surge flows," sudden waves of water that sweep downstream. Medano Creek is one of only three or four waterways in the world that have surge flows; some experts believe that Medano Creek offers the best example. Surge flows are created by "antidunes," sand that builds up on the creek bottom, making dune-like formations. In time, the force of the current collapses the antidunes, and the previously impeded water surges downstream in a wave. During high water in the spring, these surges can occur every few minutes.

A short walk on a sandy flat brings visitors to the base of the dunefield. A target of many hikers is **High Dune,** at 650 feet the highest point on the dune front visible from the ground. At 755 feet, **Star Dune,** nearly a mile west of High Dune, is the highest point in the dunefield.

High Dune looks enticingly close, but beware: Hiking in the dunefield is demanding and frustrating. With each upward step, you plunge into the sand a couple of inches and slide backward, so progress can be maddeningly slow. Also, at 8,053 feet, the air is much thinner than many people are used to, so breathing can be difficult. Finally, what looks like a straight uphill climb from the bottom is actually a series

Rocky Mountains Dunes

Most people associate sand dunes with ocean shorelines and sprawling deserts like the Sahara and the Gobi. So just how did the Great Sand Dunes—in the midst of Colorado's Rocky Mountains—come to be? The mountains themselves are part of the answer.

The San Juan Mountains, some 35 miles west of the dunes, were formed by extensive volcanic eruptions some 15 to 35 million years ago. The Sangre de Cristo Mountains, just east of the dunes, began forming some 17 million years ago, the result of tectonic activity—a massive uplift of rock. The Sangre de Cristos is the youngest mountain range in Colorado.

Millennia of erosion washed sediments from both mountain ranges into the broad valley between them, which was filled at times with extensive lakes or systems of lakes. (The modern dunes are related to more recent lakes.)

The strong prevailing winds from the southwest gave flight to the sand, pushing it slowly, gradually against the western flank of the Sangre de Cristos and creating the towering dunes we see today. Storm winds from the northeast compete with the prevailing southwest winds and anchor the Great Sand Dunes in place. While the top few inches of sand are constantly in motion, the dunes themselves do not move. All told, Great Sand Dunes represents only 11 percent of the 330-square-mile deposit of sand in the region. A mesmerizing aspect of the Great Sand Dunes is the ever changing play of light and shadow.

of dunes; you labor up a steep slope of sand, and suddenly it drops precipitously back to almost the level at which you started the climb. But despite these challenges, a climb into the dunefield offers a unique physical experience, and the sweeping views from High Dune and Star Dune are spectacular.

Of course many people simply want to play in the sand: jumping off a dune, rolling to the bottom, and climbing back to do it all again. Sandboarding (the equivalent of snowboarding on sand) and sand sledding down dune slopes are also popular activities. Sandboards and sand sleds can be rented from the Oasis Store (719-378-2222), a mile south, at the park boundary on Colo. 150.

Early mornings and evenings are ideal times to be on the dunes. The temperature is pleasant, the slanting sunlight creates a pageant of ever-changing shadows, and you might see a Great Sand Dunes tiger beetle—or at least its skittery tracks. This beetle is one of seven insects found only in Great Sand Dunes.

Park officials warn that the summer sun can heat the dune sand to 140°F, too hot for bare or sandaled feet (the park recommends wearing ankle boots).

East of the Dunes

Just north of the visitor center you'll find the trailhead for three trails that climb into the foothills and heights of the Sangre de Cristo Mountains. Here you'll hike through forests of Douglas fir, juniper, and piñon pine, and possibly see mule deer among the trees and goshawks drifting above on thermals.

The half-mile Montville Nature Trail winds along burbling Mosca Creek and introduces some interesting human history. A few hundred yards up the trail is the site of Montville, a small town with a post office that dates back to the 1880s.

An early settler named Frank Hastigs built a toll road over Mosca Pass, a low point in the Sangre de Cristos that had served as a passageway through the mountains for centuries. A flash flood in 1911 wiped out the town of Montville.

The 3.5-mile Mosca Pass Trail follows Mosca Creek to the top of Mosca Pass, at an elevation of 9,737 feet. The 1-mile Wellington Ditch Trail heads north along an old ditch dug by early settlers to channel water north from Mosca Creek; this trail ends at the Piñon Flats Campground.

From the campground, a rutted one-lane dirt road leads to the Point of No Return, the beginning of the 11-mile Medano Pass Primitive Road. This route requires a high-clearance, four-wheel-drive vehicle—and some determination. It winds along the edge of the dunefield, crossing stretches of sand that may require deflating tires to 15 psi, then re-inflating them to ford streams and wind uphill on a rocky roadbed to the top of 9,982-foot-high Medano Pass.

Just short of the pass is the trailhead for the Medano Lake Trail that climbs 1,900 feet in 4 miles and ends at sparkling Medano Lake, which lies just below Mount Herard, at 13,297 feet the second highest point in the park. Tijeras Point, 13,604 feet, just north of Medano Lake, is the highest.

Green-eyed honeybee

Information

How to Get There

US 160 runs east–west through southern Colorado. From Walsenburg (at the junction with I-25) follow US 160 west for 59 miles to Colo. 150. Head north on Colo. 150 for 16 miles to the park entrance. From Alamosa, follow US 160 east for 14 miles and turn north on Colo. 150.

When to Go

The park is open year-round. Spring weather ranges from mild and sunny to snowy and windy. The flow in Medano Creek peaks in late May. Summer has warm days and cool nights. Late summer can bring afternoon thunderstorms. Fall colors peak in late Sept. or early Oct. Winter days are chilly and often sunny. Snow decks the Sangre de Cristo Mountains and sometime blankets the dunes, creating a stunning landscape.

Visitor Center

The Great Sand Dunes National Park and Preserve Visitor Center is just a couple of miles inside the park boundary.

Headquarters

11500 Highway 150
Mosca, CO 81146
nps.gov/grsa
719-378-6300

Camping

The park has three campgrounds (176 sites total). In addition there are 18 roadside camping sites along the Medano Creek Primitive Road accessible only by high-clearance, four-wheel-drive vehicles. Backcountry camping is permitted; information and permits can be obtained at the visitor center.

Lodging

There are no lodging options in the park. The **Great Sand Dunes Lodge** (*gsdlodge .com;* 719-378-2900) is a mile south of the park entrance on CO 150. The nearest town is **Alamosa** (*alamosa.org*), about 30 miles southwest of the park on Colo. 160.

GREAT SAND DUNES 2004

Rocky Mountain

Colorado

Established
January 26, 1915

265,795 acres

For as long as Earth has been home to people and mountains, we've looked up with wonder at the grandeur of distant summits. The peaks of Rocky Mountain National Park offer fine examples of this sort of inspiration, with this exception: Here, wonder is replaced by immersion. Few places make it so easy to traverse a true alpine environment.

The park's renowned Trail Ridge Road reaches an elevation of 12,183 feet, crossing the Continental Divide on its 48-mile route across the park. The road climbs from woodlands and meadows to wind for miles through a stark terrain of rock and tundra. Overlooks provide panoramas of some of Colorado's most spectacular landscapes, with rugged peaks rising above glacier-carved valleys and forested foothills. The park encompasses more than 77 mountains above 12,000 feet, including the park's highest point, 14,259-foot Longs Peak.

Though some rock formations in the park date back some 1.8 billion years, the current Rocky Mountains began to take shape about 75 million years ago. Movement of tectonic

Hallet Peak

The scenery of the Colorado high country alone—its lakes, waterfalls, and wildflower-spangled meadows—could explain why Rocky Mountain ranks among the most visited national parks, but it's also one of the finest wildlife-watching areas. Elk, bighorn sheep, moose, and mule deer are easily spotted; mountain lions and black bears are seen by only a lucky few. Nearly 300 species of birds have been spotted within the park.

Every season has its appeal here, but fall is a favorite time for many visitors. On a crisp September day, when the aspens are turning golden and the first snow dusts the highest peaks, it's hard to imagine a more appealing and rewarding place.

plates pushed up a broad plateau, later eroded by rivers and weathering. Around two million years ago, periods of glaciation carved mountainsides; moving ice created U-shaped valleys and pushed up piles of rock debris. When the ice melted, the rock piles were left behind as long ridges called moraines, which can be seen throughout lower areas of the park.

The first humans entered the area about 11,000 years ago. Later, Ute Indians hunted and camped here, moving with the seasons and blazing trails over the Continental Divide.

By the beginning of the 20th century, as the conservation ethic gained force in the United States, many local residents called for a park designation to protect the Colorado Rockies.

► HOW TO VISIT

A one- or two-day visit should include the 48-mile drive across the park on **Trail Ridge Road,** stopping at scenic overlooks and the **Alpine Visitor Center. Bear Lake Road** is another must-travel route; in summer, avoid traffic and parking issues by taking the free shuttle bus. The road provides access to easy strolls around **Bear Lake** and **Sprague Lake** and the short hike to **Alberta Falls.**

A ranger can help you choose a hike along one of dozens of trails, with destinations ranging from waterfalls to mountain peaks. **Dream Lake, Mills Lake,** and **The Loch** pack grand scenery into moderately strenuous hikes; the walk to **Cub Lake** is great for wildlife and wildflowers. In summer, visit **Sheep Lakes** to see bighorn sheep; elk are usually easier to see in fall.

Horseback riding has long been a popular way to enjoy Rocky Mountain

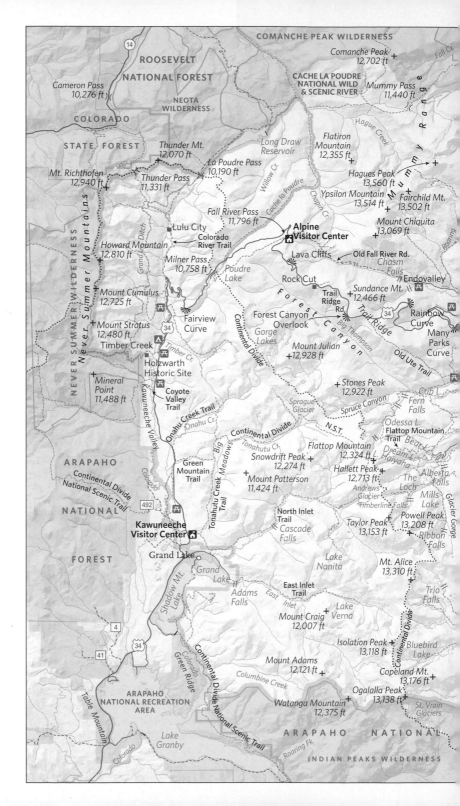

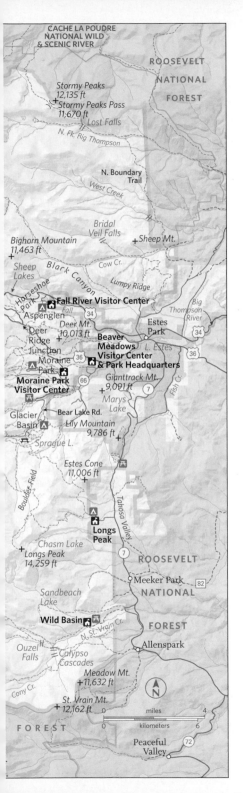

National Park; around 260 miles of trails are open to horses. Two stables are located in the park *(sombrero .com)*, and several outfitters outside the park offer trail rides.

Trail Ridge Road— East Side

With many popular lakes and trails located near the tourist town of Estes Park, the central section of the park east of the Continental Divide gets the great majority of visitation. Because Rocky Mountain is one of our most popular parks, it's important in the peak summer season to get out early.

From Estes Park, US 36 and US 34 access the park and later meet; US 34 becomes Trail Ridge Road. Stop at a visitor center—**Beaver Meadows** (US 36) or **Fall River** (US 34)—as you enter the park. The US 36 route passes the turn for Bear Lake Road, which leads to campgrounds, waterfalls, lakes, and trails.The US 34 route passes through **Horseshoe Park,** which sometimes offers a chance in summer to watch the bighorn sheep that congregate at a natural mineral lick. Rangers and volunteers are present seasonally at **Sheep Lakes** to assist the crowds that arrive to see the animals. In fall, Horseshoe Park is one of several places in the park where elk (and elk-watchers) congregate at dusk.

Nearby is **Old Fall River Road,** a winding, unpaved, 9.4-mile route with many switchbacks and fabulous vistas. The road was seriously damaged by flooding in 2013 but has since been rebuilt. This is a one-way route, so once you start you're committed to reaching the top. Old Fall River Road

Crossing the Rockies

To early European settlers, the peaks of what is today Rocky Mountain National Park must have seemed well-nigh impossible to surmount. Yet by the time Europeans arrived, native people such as the Utes and Arapahos had been crossing the mountains for thousands of years via routes including Flattop Mountain and the Old Ute Trail. Hikers today can follow some of those same ancient paths across the Continental Divide.

Beginning in 1920, visitors to the national park had the option of driving Fall River Road, which climbs 9.4 miles to 11,796-foot Fall River Pass. Winding and narrow, the road had barely been completed before planning began for a better highway through the park.

Construction of Trail Ridge Road began in 1926 and took six years to complete: Work was confined to four snow-free months each summer. Crossing open terrain, with expansive views, the route was planned for maximum scenic impact.

"It is hard to describe what a sensation this new road is going to make," Horace Albright, director of the National Park Service, said in 1931. "You will have the whole sweep of the Rockies before you in all directions."

Since the 1932 opening of Trail Ridge Road, countless travelers have experienced the sensation Albright anticipated. The highest continuous paved road in the United States, this 48-mile highway remains one of the national park's most popular attractions, with spectacular vistas every mile of the way.

has a speed limit of 15 mph, and vehicles over 25 feet and trailers are not permitted.

US 34 and US 36 meet at Deer Ridge Junction, with US 34 continuing as Trail Ridge Road. Note: The route reaches a challenging elevation of 12,183 feet, and lightning can be a real danger when thunderstorms form on summer afternoons.

As you ascend through forests of ponderosa pine into Engelmann spruce and subalpine fir, overlooks such as **Many Parks Curve** and **Rainbow Curve** provide spectacular panoramas of mountains and valleys. Past Rainbow Curve, the road climbs into the alpine world above tree line. At **Forest Canyon Overlook** you'll see the way glaciers cut a U-shaped valley as they advanced. Stop at the **Rock Cut** parking area to walk a short trail that shows how flora survive this harsh environment, covered by snow for eight months of the year.

At the **Alpine Visitor Center** you'll learn about the ecology of the tundra, home to animals such as yellow-bellied marmots, pocket gophers, and white-tailed ptarmigans. Past the visitor center, Trail Ridge Road descends beyond the Continental Divide to reach destinations on the park's west side. (see p. 298).

Bear Lake Road

Bear Lake Road winds 12.5 miles south and west from US 36, just beyond the park entrance station. This dead-end route reaches a wonderful array of destinations, and, as a result, it's extremely popular and sometimes dismayingly crowded. A free park shuttle bus provides a convenient way to reach trailheads along the route. There's even a bus that picks up passengers in Estes Park and delivers them to bus stops in the national park.

Moraine Park is home to the park's most popular campground, as well as trailheads for several excellent hikes. The south side of the valley is a good example of a moraine, a long ridge of rock piled up by a moving glacier. This area is great for wildlife-watching, especially at the shallow ponds along the 2.3-mile route to Cub Lake. Learn more about local geology at the Moraine Park Visitor Center.

Farther along Bear Lake Road, Sprague Lake makes a fine picnic spot, but its best feature is a flat, handicapped-accessible, half-mile trail around the lake. This site is especially enjoyable for families with small children and people who might not be able to walk other park trails.

Another 3 miles up Bear Lake Road is Glacier Gorge Trailhead, with some of the national park's best-loved hikes. It's only 0.8 mile to thundering Alberta Falls, one of the most impressive cascades in the park. In another 0.4 miles you reach a junction where you can choose to continue to Mills Lake (5.6 miles round-trip from Glacier Gorge Trailhead) or The Loch (6 miles round-trip). Both are among the park's most spectacular destinations: alpine lakes surrounded by craggy Rocky Mountain summits. If you choose The Loch, consider continuing another 1.4 miles to Timberline Falls, where Icy Brook cascades over a cliff.

Bear Lake Road ends, naturally enough, at Bear Lake, with a large parking area that often fills up by 9 a.m. in season. The peaks of the Continental Divide loom above Bear Lake, and trails lead to fine destinations such as Dream Lake, Lake Haiyaha, and, for the adventurous, those distant mountain summits. If you want to say you've climbed a peak on the Continental Divide, the 4.4-mile hike up Flattop Mountain is one of the moderate choices in the park—though still a strenuous undertaking, rising 2,849 feet along the trail.

The Southeastern Corner

Colo. 7 south from Estes Park leads to several rewarding destinations, including the very strenuous 8-mile climb to the top of Longs Peak. Lots of people

North American elk

want to say they've reached the 14,259-foot summit, the park's highest point, and lots of people make it. But don't underestimate the difficulty of this trek. Fatalities do occur here; dangers include steep trails, bad weather, and lightning. It is a good idea to talk with a park ranger before attempting the climb. An alternative, though still a challenging, option, is the 8.4-mile round-trip hike to **Chasm Lake,** which sits at the base of Longs Peak's awesome east face, a sheer cliff towering far, far above.

Farther south, the **Wild Basin** area has some excellent trails, including the 1.8-mile route to the lengthy series of falls called **Calypso Cascades.** The waterfalls here are named for the rare calypso orchid, also known as fairy slipper.

It's another 0.9 miles to **Ouzel Falls,** one of the park's most impressive waterfalls. Ouzel Falls is named for the bird called water ouzel or, more accurately, dipper. This small brown bird frequents rocky streams and actually swims underwater to catch prey.

One of the best longer hikes in the Wild Basin area is the strenuous 6-mile (2,478 foot elevation gain) trek to **Bluebird Lake.** With mountain peaks rising above the water, the alpine scene here embodies the essence of the national park.

Trail Ridge Road— West Side

Driving west on Trail Ridge Road past the Alpine Visitor Center, you soon cross the Continental Divide at 10,758-foot **Milner Pass.** It's not a particularly scenic spot, but it marks the place where water flows to the Colorado River instead of the Mississippi. Visitation is lighter on this side of the park, and rainfall is somewhat heavier, giving the forests a lusher look. You're more likely to see moose in the willows along the river than elsewhere in the park.

As you head south through the Kawuneeche Valley, take time to stop at the **Holzwarth Historic Site.** Here a German immigrant began a homestead in 1917, eventually expanding it into a small resort catering to trout anglers, horseback riders, and other vacationers. The historic buildings are well preserved, and park rangers offer tours in summer.

Trailheads along US 34 offer access to routes leading east to mountain summits and alpine lakes. For a less-strenuous introduction to the east-side environment, you can make a loop trail by combining parts of the Onahu Creek, Tonahutu Creek, and Green Mountain Trails. This route of around 7 miles passes through woodlands of lodgepole pine and other conifers and along part of Big Meadows, an expansive open area along Tonahutu Creek. Watch for moose on the first part of this loop.

The most popular hike on the park's west side is the easy 0.3-mile walk to **Adams Falls,** where a cascade thunders through a gorge in a rocky cliff. Most people turn around here, but by continuing another 1.5 miles you'll pass through meadows with splendid summer wildflowers and fine views of Rocky Mountain summits to the east. Reach this trailhead by following West Portal Road through Grand Lake, the community that serves as the western gateway to the national park.

Bierstadt Lake

Information

How to Get There

From Denver, CO (70 miles southeast), take US 36 north to Estes Park.

When to Go

Summer and early fall are the most popular seasons. Although **Trail Ridge Road** is closed from about mid-Oct. to Memorial Day and snow covers hiking trails, many visitors enjoy snowshoeing, cross-country skiing, and wildlife-watching in winter.

Visitor Centers

Beaver Meadows and **Kawuneeche Visitor Centers** are open year-round. **Alpine Visitor Center** and **Moraine Park Visitor Center** are open in summer and early fall.

Headquarters

1000 Highway 36
Estes Park, CO 80517
nps.gov/romo
970-586-1206

Camping

Five campgrounds—**Moraine Park, Glacier Basin, Aspenglen, Longs Peak,** and **Timber Creek**—provide more than 500 sites; recreational vehicles of various lengths are allowed at all locales except for Longs Peak. Check restrictions at *nps.gov/romo/planyourvisit/camping .htm.* Moraine Park Campground remains partially open all winter, while others are open from about late May through Sept. For reservations, *recreation.gov;* 877-444-6777. The park has a great variety of backcountry campsites; a permit (fee in peak season) is required. Check *nps.gov/ romo/plan yourvisit/backcountry.htm* or call the backcountry office, 970-586-1242.

Lodging

There are no facilities within the park. Lodging is plentiful in **Estes Park, Grand Lake,** and other nearby towns. For information, check *visitestespark.com* or *grandlakechamber.com.*

Yellowstone

Wyoming, Idaho, & Montana

Established
March 1, 1872

2.2 million acres

The world's first national park, Yellowstone was established before the states that now surround it became part of the Union. Unknown then to all but Native Americans, Yellowstone soon became a national icon. A great volcano broods beneath the world's largest concentration of geysers and hot springs. Snowcapped mountains water a landscape of lakes, rivers, canyons, and forest, teeming with the full complement of northern Rockies wildlife.

Yellowstone is a rough rectangle measuring 50 by 60 miles draped across the Continental Divide. Seen from space, the park is a high plateau ringed by mountains. At its center lies the caldera, or collapsed crater, of a single supervolcano (see p. 305). The Yellowstone River flows through from the south, filling the great expanse of Yellowstone Lake before plunging into colorful canyons. Geysers, hot springs, and mud pots, found throughout the park, are concentrated most densely along a small river, the Firehole. The park's northern section is distinct from the rest. Lower and more open, with

Morning Glory Pool

▶ HOW TO VISIT
Yellowstone's road system forms a figure 8. Called the **Grand Loop,** it measures 142 miles, with spurs leading in from five entrances. At least three days are needed to sample the park. First, visit the geyser basins between **Old Faithful** and **Mammoth Hot Springs** for a day focused on thermal activity. On the second day, take a drive through the park to see such highlights as **Yellowstone Lake, Hayden Valley,** and the **Grand Canyon of the Yellowstone** for mountains and wildlife. With more time, explore the northern range, where wolves are most likely to be seen.

Join a ranger-led guided walk for a deeper understanding; these are offered throughout the park.

Note that bicycles are permitted on some trails and can be rented in the park (nps.gov/yell/planyourvisit/bicyling).

Old Faithful to Mammoth Hot Springs

Old Faithful Geyser stands at the head of the **Upper Geyser Basin,** a dish-shaped valley about 2 miles long. The **Firehole River** runs down the middle, past hot springs and geysers. Check at the **Old Faithful Visitor Center** for predicted eruption times of the major geysers and to pick up a trail map.

Old Faithful erupts on average every 90 minutes. But it isn't clockwork. Rangers need to see one eruption to predict the interval for the next. If you have time, you can walk the easy half-mile trail around the geyser site. You'll see Firehole River, several hot springs, and, from most points along the way, Old Faithful when it erupts.

milder winters, it is important for wildlife, particularly bison and elk.

In winter, extreme cold, deep snow, and wildlife combine with geyser steam to produce a fantasy landscape of frost crystals and shifting mist. It's beautiful, but challenging to living creatures. Spring brings renewal, as meadows turn green and newborn animals appear. Summer is the time for growth and the fleeting bloom of wildflowers, while autumn is the season of preparation for the coming cold. In Yellowstone, winter is never far off.

The best tip for seeing wildlife and avoiding crowds is to start early in the day. Because most visitors stay close to their vehicles, you can find solitude by walking even a short distance on almost any trail.

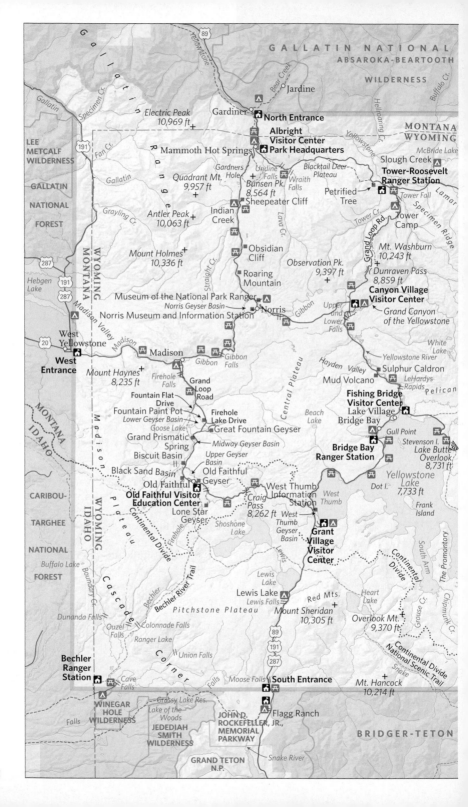

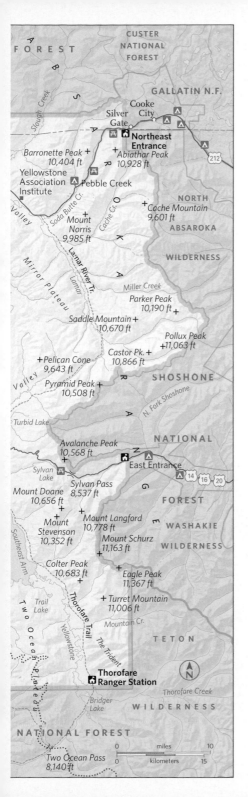

After the eruption, cross the river on the footbridge and head for **Geyser Hill,** where practically every square foot is steaming, erupting, bubbling, or flowing with hot water. You're likely to see at least one geyser erupting, and perhaps a large one. Almost surely, little **Anemone** will perform; it erupts every few minutes.

At **Lion Geyser,** you can choose to finish the loop and return to your car, or continue down-basin, all the way to deep, funnel-shaped **Morning Glory Pool,** named for its startling blue color, reminiscent of its namesake flower.

Back in the car, head north. A quick stop at **Black Sand Basin** is worthwhile. Here, **Cliff Geyser** erupts frequently from an unusual creekside pool, and **Opalescent Pool** has water to match its name. For the next few miles, watch for bison; they like the meadows along the Firehole River. Mature bulls, weighing upward of 2,000 pounds, tend to stay by themselves or with a few comrades. Larger groups consist of cows, calves, and young males.

At **Midway Geyser Basin,** a boardwalk loop leads past two enormous contrasting hot springs. **Excelsior** was a huge geyser during the early years of the park. Now it's a 300-foot-diameter crater filled with steam and vigorously boiling water that sends 4,000 scalding gallons a minute into the river. Beside it, the equally large but placid **Grand Prismatic Spring** flows gently over tiny stone terraces, supporting brightly colored tendrils of algae and bacteria.

Two miles farther, turn right on Firehole Lake Drive. **Great Fountain Geyser** erupts spectacularly but only about twice a day, visible from a platform of concentric reflecting pools. Check the prediction board beside the geyser to see estimated eruption times. You have a much better chance of seeing **White Dome Geyser** erupt, just ahead; its frequent eruptions are wispy sprays, but the cone, which apparently dates from a time when eruptions had greater power, is impressive.

Rejoin the main road at **Fountain Paint Pot,** best known for its pool of bubbling mud. Children love the mud pots and even adults giggle as blobs splurt into the air.

Nearby, **Clepsydra Geyser** has erupted virtually nonstop since the 1959 Hebgen Lake earthquake, magnitude 7.3, kicked it into action.

The scene changes as you head north. Many miles of meadow, forest, and winding rivers lie ahead—favored haunts of bison, waterfowl, coyotes, and occasional elk. As you drive across **Fountain Flats,** look ahead. The flat-topped ridge in the distance is the rim of the caldera from Yellowstone's last great eruption, some 640,000 years ago. This is one of the few places where it's visible; in general, erosion and small subsequent lava flows have obscured what must have been a distinct crater when it was young. So huge and yet so hidden, it's no wonder

Hiking the Mount Washburn Trail

geologists needed years and help from satellite photos to recognize the true scale of the Yellowstone supervolcano.

Just shy of Madison Junction, the river dives into the narrow **Firehole River Canyon,** a series of cascades and a good waterfall. Take the one-way loop drive (2 miles) to view it. There might be river otters in the canyon. Bald eagles perch on dead snags eyeing the water for trout.

At Madison, the Firehole joins the Gibbon River to form the Madison River. Turning left takes you downstream, 14 miles to the west entrance. Instead, continue toward Norris. The cliffs on your left, rising 1,500 feet, are the volcano's caldera rim.

One can only imagine how it might have been to stand on that rim just a few years after the eruption, gazing into a vast smoking crater, a 30-by-50-mile scene of pure devastation. Today, the peaceful meadows along the Gibbon are as gentle as the past was violent.

Turning north, the road climbs past graceful **Gibbon Falls** (84 feet high), leaves the caldera behind, cuts through two large meadows favored by elk and bison, and arrives at Norris.

Take half an hour or so to visit the small **Norris Geyser Basin Museum,** perched above the basin. Located where major faults intersect the fractured perimeter of the caldera, Norris claims the hottest ground in the park. In places, its surface can approach 200°F.

Things change fast here. Porkchop Geyser blew itself up in 1989 while people watched. No one was hurt but temperatures and activity have increased since then, requiring re-routing of nearby trails. **Steamboat**

Big Bang

It's by far the biggest story in Yellowstone. The park is not just a volcanic landscape. It is one volcano, a supervolcano that has been erupting for about 16 million years. The first eruption took place in what is now southeast Oregon. From there, volcanic action appears to have crossed southern Idaho to Yellowstone.

In fact, it wasn't the volcano that moved. Rather, the entire continent had drifted over a "hot spot," a stationary plume of magma that erupts periodically, blowing away everything in its path.

The hot spot has exploded beneath what is now Yellowstone National Park three times. The most recent, 640,000 years ago, left a collapsed crater, or caldera, measuring 30 by 50 miles. The first eruption, 2.1 million years ago, was even bigger. That giant ejected about 600 cubic miles of ash and debris. The destruction is beyond imagination.

What if there were an eruption today? Using weather data to predict ash distribution, a recent study projects that an eruption of 80 cubic miles would drop more than three feet of ash across the northern Rockies and lesser amounts in almost every other part of the United States. That relatively small eruption would be the most devastating natural catastrophe in human history.

The chances of a big eruption in the next century, or even 1,000 years from now, is impossible to predict, but scientists at the Yellowstone Volcano Observatory are watching closely. Follow along at *volcanoes.usgs.gov /observatories/yvo.*

Lower Falls of the Yellowstone

Geyser, largest in the park, erupts rarely but with great power, soaring more than 300 feet in the air.

Near the entrance to the Norris Campground, step back in time at the **Museum of the National Park Ranger.** Here, park visitors can learn about the rich history of rangers in the National Park Service. Exhibits depict the evolution of the profession, from its 19th-century military roots.

Thermal activity continues along the road north. **Roaring Mountain** is a steaming, hissing pile of white rock. **Obsidian Cliff** stands where molten lava cooled quickly, forming black volcanic glass. Native people quarried large amounts of it for stone tools, trading it as far away as Ohio and proving, incidentally, that they knew Yellowstone well. Old reports that they feared and avoided the park have no basis in fact.

The drive ends at **Mammoth Hot Springs,** an ever-changing landscape of travertine terraces, pools, and hot rivulets. Mineral deposits here can grow a foot and more a year. Springs appear, only to dry up and resurface somewhere else. Take the 1-mile loop road to see them, or follow the boardwalks.

Historic Fort Yellowstone, built by the U.S. Army when it ran Yellowstone from 1886 to 1916, now serves as park headquarters.

Canyon to West Thumb

The **Canyon Village Visitor Center** has some of the best interpretive displays in the park, with an emphasis on geology and the volcano. Begin there, then head for the canyon rims where numerous viewpoints and cliff-edge trails provide stunning views into this brightly colored gorge.

The canyon is an ancient geyser basin. Over millennia, hot water and chemical action weakened the rhyolite bedrock, changing it from its original dark gray to a palette of yellows, reds, and oranges. At the canyon's heart thunders 308-foot **Lower Falls of the Yellowstone,** wonderful to see from any angle.

From North Rim Drive you can access **Lookout Point,** with its classic view of the Lower Falls. Below Lookout Point and visible from it, a trail to **Red Rock Point** leads below the canyon rim for a closer view, looking up at the falls. Or consider the strenuous

400-foot descent to the **Brink of the Lower Falls** platform, one of the most thrilling places to stand in the park. Where the green river turns to white froth and plunges into mists far below, you can almost feel the rocks shake. At 308 feet, Lower Falls is the tallest waterfall in the park.

Two miles upstream, the 109-foot **Upper Falls** puts on a show nearly as powerful. The trail to its dizzying brink is short and easy.

A little farther south, turn left and cross the river to the south rim. **Artist Falls** is named for Thomas Moran, whose paintings of Yellowstone helped convince Congress to make it a park and to buy his famous 1872 painting of the canyon. You can see a reproduction in the visitor center for comparison with the real thing.

Above the canyon, the river flows peacefully through wildlife-rich **Hayden Valley.** Plan to stop several times to scan the water for trumpeter swans, white pelicans, Canada geese, and river otters. Watch the rolling grass-covered hills for bison, coyotes, and perhaps bears. Grizzlies prefer open areas like this. In spring, they are drawn to the remains of winter-killed bison and elk; in summer, they dig for rodents and tubers.

You might have no choice but to stop. Traffic moves slowly if animals are near the road. Park regulations require you to keep your distance—at least 100 yards from bears and wolves and 25 yards from other large animals.

Mud Volcano is the dark side of thermal areas. You'll find no jets of clear water here. Rather, this is a primal, sulfur-smelling collection of churning mud pools. **Sulfur Caldron** has a pH similar to the acid in a car battery. **Dragon's Mouth Spring** belches loudly from a hillside cavern. It's an easy place to imagine a real-life dragon emerging through a shadowy curtain of steam.

Continue upriver through forest and meadow to **Fishing Bridge,** at the outlet of Yellowstone Lake. Fishing, once popular here, is no longer permitted. Here, native cutthroat trout feed among clumps of river vegetation. There are far fewer trout in recent years. Predatory lake trout, illegally introduced to the lake in the 1990s, have decimated the native fish population, with far-ranging impact on the lake-based ecosystem.

At the nearby marina, you can book a boat on Yellowstone Lake (nps.gov/yell/planyourvisit/boating.htm).

Driving east a few miles takes you to **Pelican Valley,** open and lush; look for moose along the winding creek. Stretch your legs on the **Pelican Creek Nature Trail,** an easy 1-mile loop through forest to a fine pebble beach.

Consider driving farther along the lakeshore past Steamboat Point and Sedge Bay to **Lake Butte Overlook.** The panoramic view from here is the best in the area. On a clear day, the Teton Range, more than 60 miles away, is plainly visible.

Back on the road, drive 21 miles along the forested shore of **Yellowstone Lake,** North America's biggest alpine lake—136 square miles of surface area with 110 miles of shoreline. The waters are icy despite the numerous hot springs, thermal formations, and even some erupting geysers that scientists have located on the lake bottom.

On the far side of the lake, the Absaroka Mountains stand snowcapped, marking the east boundary of the park.

West Thumb Geyser Basin is unusual for being on the shore of the lake. Some of its thermal features, like Fishing Cone, are actually in the lake. It's worth walking the short boardwalk loop just to see **Black Pool.** Hypnotically blue, it is one of the park's most beautiful hot springs.

Northern Range

The Northern Range gets its name for a simple reason. This is good grazing range in the northern section of the park. In contrast to the higher central and southern sections, the land here is open, with fewer trees, more grass, and less snow in winter. Conditions are good for many animals, especially the big herbivores—bison, elk, mule deer, and pronghorn—all of which are commonly seen here. Behind them come predators, notably gray wolves that, since their reintroduction in 1995, have become a major attraction for wildlife watchers. This is the most likely place to see them.

Begin at **Mammoth Hot Springs** and drive east. After crossing a high bridge over the Gardiner River, the road climbs across forested slopes. Black bears prefer this sort of country, a mix of woods and meadows. Grizzlies are more comfortable in open spaces. If you see a bear, don't judge by color. Only about half the park's black bears are black. The rest are blond, brown, or cinnamon.

Soon the road enters the wide-open spaces of **Blacktail Deer Plateau.** A line of mountains on the southern horizon shows the effects of the great 1988 fires, when an unusually dry early

Bison in the Lamar Valley

summer led to tinderbox conditions. Despite what was then the largest wildfire-fighting effort in U.S. history—25,000 in personnel and $120 million spent—more than a third of the park was affected. Wildfire is a natural force in Yellowstone, which it proved in spectacular fashion that summer. The blaze that burned this area was called the North Fork Fire. It began outside the west boundary of the park and ran nearly 60 miles before autumn snow, not fire crews, finally put it out.

At Tower Junction, go straight to 132-foot **Tower Fall,** then beyond, up a long climb over Dunraven Pass to **Canyon Village.** Turn left across the Yellowstone River. The next few miles are good for bison and boulders. The bison are there for the grazing. The boulders are glacial erratics, carried here by glaciers that flowed from mountains to the northeast. Scattered by the thousand in this area, many of them are paired with mature Douglas fir trees, as if each rock has adopted a tree. In fact, the rocks provided an extra bit of shelter and moisture when the trees were seedlings, helping them grow. Children like to say the trees have pet rocks.

Head back to the main road. Where it meets the Lamar River, it pushes upstream through a narrow canyon into **Lamar Valley,** made famous in recent years as a place to see wolves. Park policy in early years called for removal of predators, including coyotes, mountain lions, wolves, even raptors. Of those, wolves were the only ones exterminated. In 1995, after some 70 years without them, gray wolves were brought back. They have thrived, and their impact runs deep. A healthy ecosystem needs all its players. Yellowstone's cast of characters is once again complete. The best way to spot wolves is to watch for groups of people with long scopes on tripods.

The cluster of log buildings called **Buffalo Ranch** is the site of another conservation success. In 1907, 28 bison were brought here and ranched like cattle. That effort lasted into the 1950s when the herd was judged large enough to successfully roam free. Today the park supports 4,000 or more of the large mammals. Ahead, mountains close in as the road climbs toward the northeast entrance, the town of **Cooke City,** and (open in summer only) the jaw-dropping high route over **Beartooth Pass.**

Other Hikes & Activities

The park's highest road runs from Canyon Village to Tower over **Dunraven Pass.** About 3 miles north of Canyon, stop at **Washburn Hot Springs Overlook** for sweeping views to the south. From here you can truly grasp the scale of the caldera, as explained by an interpretive sign. To get even higher, consider the 2.7-mile hike to the summit of **Mount Washburn** on the old Chittenden Road. The views are unmatched, summer wildflowers are lush, and bighorn sheep are commonly seen.

A few side roads are open to bicycles but not cars. **Bunsen Peak Road** (6 miles) curves around a large open meadow and down a steep canyon, ending at Mammoth Hot Springs. Near Old Faithful, **Lone Star Geyser** is an easy 3-mile trail along the Firehole River. In the Lower Geyser Basin, **Fountain Freight Road** (5.5 miles) passes **Goose Lake,** a fine picnic spot. Park your bicycle and hike to Fairy Falls and Imperial Geyser.

Take a guided boat trip on Yellowstone Lake or explore by canoe or kayak. Experienced paddlers might consider the lake's remote southern section for wilderness trips; only hand-powered craft are allowed there and on **Shoshone Lake.** Permits are required for private boats. Backcountry camping also requires a permit.

To deepen your understanding of Yellowstone, join a ranger-led interpretive program. Offered throughout the park from Memorial Day to Labor Day, program subjects cover the full spectrum of geology, biology, astronomy, history, wildlife management, and more. Activities include guided walks through the geyser basins, along canyon rims and lakeshores, and on backcountry trails. Some take in places unknown and unseen by most visitors. Others are short talks at points of interest. Quite a few are geared toward families and children.

Evening programs, some illustrated with visuals, continue the time-honored tradition of national park campfire talks. All of them are worth doing, and except for the boat cruise on Yellowstone Lake, there is never a charge; it's just a matter of choosing which aspects of Yellowstone you'd like to learn more about. For a schedule, check the park newspaper, free at all entrance stations and visitor centers. The information is also posted on the park website.

The Old Faithful Inn

Information

How to Get There

Yellowstone has five entrances. US 20 and US 191/287 lead to the west entrance. For the north entrance, follow US 89 to Mammoth Hot Springs. The south entrance is reached on US 89/191/287 through Grand Teton National Park. From the east, US 14/16/20 follows the North Fork Shoshone River. The most spectacular route is open summer only. US 212 climbs over 10,947-foot Beartooth Pass, to the northeast entrance.

When to Go

Mid-June to Labor Day is peak season. Spring comes in gradually, with few visitors. Autumn can be spectacular, with cool nights and warm days. In mid-Dec., the park opens for winter; over-snow vehicles only. The northern road from Gardiner to Cooke City stays open all year. Most roads open around mid-April and close at the end of Oct.

Visitor Centers

Of Yellowstone's six visitor centers, only **Old Faithful** and **Mammoth** are open year-round.

Headquarters

P.O. Box 168
Yellowstone National
Park, WY 82190
nps.gov/yell
307-344-7381

Camping

The Park Service operates seven relatively small campgrounds (first come, first served) and five large reservation campgrounds. More than 1,700 sites; check *nps .gov/yell/planyourvisit/campgrounds.htm.*

Lodging

Lodging is available within the park at **Canyon Lodge & Cabins, Grant Village, Lake Lodge Cabins, Lake Yellowstone Hotel & Cabins, Mammoth Hot Springs Hotel & Cabins, Old Faithful Inn, Old Faithful Lodge Cabins, Old Faithful Snow Lodge & Cabins,** and **Roosevelt Lodge Cabins** (*yellowstonenationalparklodges .com;* 307-344-7311). All are seasonal; winter lodging is limited to Mammoth and Old Faithful. Lodgings can fill up a year in advance.

Pacific
Southwest

Dunefield at Stovepipe Wells, Death Valley National Park

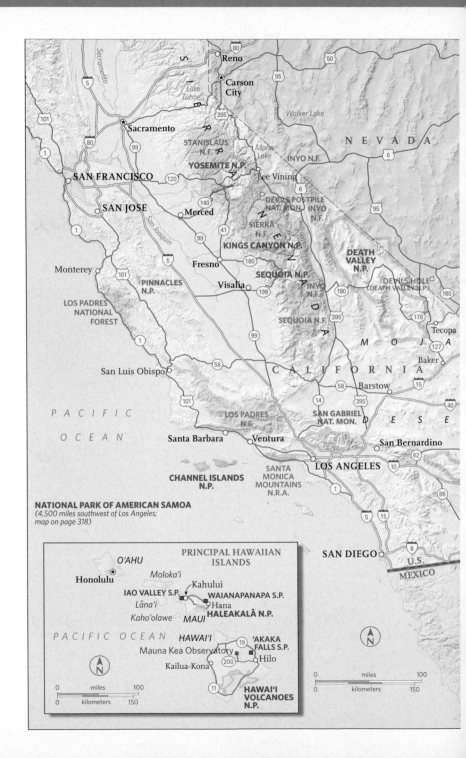

Reno

80

50

Lake Tahoe

Carson City

95

Sacramento

5

Walker Lake

STANISLAUS N.F.

NEVADA

6

Mono Lake

INYO N.F.

YOSEMITE N.P.

Lee Vining

SAN FRANCISCO

120

6

101

80

DEVILS POSTPILE NAT. MON.

INYO N.F.

95

SAN JOSE

140

Merced

1

99

41

San Joaquin

SIERRA N.F.

KINGS CANYON N.P.

Monterey

5

Fresno

180

DEATH VALLEY N.P.

101

PINNACLES N.P.

Visalia

198

SEQUOIA N.P.

DEVILS HOLE
(DEATH VALLEY N.P.)

190

160

LOS PADRES NATIONAL FOREST

INYO N.F.

SEQUOIA N.F.

395

178

1

Tecopa

127

MOJA

Baker

San Luis Obispo

58

99

CALIFORNIA

58

Barstow

15

PACIFIC

101

14

395

40

OCEAN

LOS PADRES N.F.

SAN GABRIEL NAT. MON.

DESE

SE

Santa Barbara

Ventura

San Bernardino

CHANNEL ISLANDS N.P.

SANTA MONICA MOUNTAINS N.R.A.

LOS ANGELES

62

10

86

NATIONAL PARK OF AMERICAN SAMOA
(4,500 miles southwest of Los Angeles; map on page 318)

SAN DIEGO

8

5

15

U.S.

MEXICO

PRINCIPAL HAWAIIAN ISLANDS

O'AHU

Honolulu

Moloka'i

Kahului

IAO VALLEY S.P.

WAIANAPANAPA S.P.

Lāna'i

Hana

Kaho'olawe

MAUI

HALEAKALĀ N.P.

PACIFIC OCEAN

HAWAI'I

'AKAKA FALLS S.P.

19

Mauna Kea Observatory

200

Hilo

Kailua-Kona

11

HAWAI'I VOLCANOES N.P.

0   miles   100
0   kilometers   150

0   miles   100
0   kilometers   150

See Southwest
section, page 174

isitors to the nine national parks of the Pacific Southwest can bask on a tropical isle or climb a snow-clad peak. They can witness the vegetation going from tropical to subalpine in a single scenic drive, observe plants and animals that make their home in only one place in the world, and actually see the Earth build itself.

The island parks, all of them located on volcanoes except for Channel Islands, are microcosms of evolution and laboratories of the effects of humans on the land. At **Hawai'i Volcanoes** and **Haleakalā,** preservation efforts seek to stem the damage done over centuries to the native plants, about 90 percent of which are found nowhere else. Some 2,600 miles southwest of Hawai'i, the **National Park of American Samoa** shelters fragments of tropical rain forest and coral reef as well as an endangered 3,000-year-old human culture. Off the coast of California, the **Channel Islands** safeguard threatened seals, sea lions, and seabirds. They also harbor some 70 different species of endemic plants.

On the mainland, California's **Sequoia & Kings Canyon** and **Yosemite** provide haven for a multitude of plant and animal communities in what John Muir called "the range of light"—the Sierra Nevada. Chaparral and wild oats robe the foothills; cathedral-like groves of conifers embellish slopes; wildflowers overrun alpine meadows. Marmots and pikas scurry on the glacier-carved heights. Thanks to a comprehensive recovery program, California condors once again soar the skies and scavenge the rugged terrain of the newest national park in the United States, **Pinnacles.**

To the south, **Joshua Tree** National Park preserves the unique high Mojave Desert habitat of the giant branching yucca. The 140-mile-long, erosion-sculptured basin that is **Death Valley** National Park—the continent's hottest spot (134°F)—shelters more than 900 plant varieties, as well as bobcats and desert bighorn sheep.

American Samoa

American Samoa

Established
October 31, 1988

13,500 acres—
9,500 land,
4,000 marine

The only national park entirely south of the Equator and one that the U.S. government leases rather than owns, the National Park of American Samoa is a South Pacific Polynesian paradise. The small archipelago boasts deep blue waters, coral reefs (teeming with fish), secluded beaches, and what just might be the most pristine air in the world.

This park is a place that seems to occupy its own world. The islands of Tutuila, Ta'u, Ofu, and Olosega are some 2,600 miles southwest of Hawai'i. Because the national park is leased, local villages have a large stake in the success and management of the park. Villagers who'd had plantations before the park was established continue to work them. No construction is permitted without an agreement between park management and village chiefs.

▶ **HOW TO VISIT**

American Samoa is reached by air. Except for a few villages and the scenic drive that skirts the Pago Pago Harbor and the southern coastline there is little level ground on the park's main island of

Ofu island

Tutuila. For a bird's-eye view, climb the 3.7-mile trail that leads to the 1,610-foot volcanic summit of **Mount Alava.** Along the way, possible bird sightings include white-collared kingfishers, cardinal honey-eaters, and purple-capped fruit doves.

The smaller islands of **Ofu** and **Olosega** have excellent coral reefs and the best snorkeling and scuba diving in the area. Ofu also has what many consider to be the prettiest beach in American Samoa.

Tutuila

The portion of Tutuila that falls within park boundaries is home to the capital, Pago Pago (pronounced "PAHNG-oh, PAHNG-oh," though the locals opt for a single PAHNG-oh).

American Samoa at War

Pago Pago Harbor is the deepest in the Pacific, with a narrow entrance that's easy to protect and a huge bay under Rainmaker Mountain with room for dozens of ships. This made it an important base during World War II. Indeed, for a while during the war soldiers outnumbered locals.

Downtown Pago Pago's beautiful colonial-style Maugaoalii High Court served as the U.S. Navy Headquarters during the war.

For a good harbor view, walk the 0.6-mile trail up to Blunts Point, on the south side of the harbor. The trail falls outside the park's boundaries though it is maintained by the park.

Before you set out on the trail, check the water around the parking area; it's a popular sea turtle hangout.

A drive along the main road will include sightings of pillboxes, small, low concrete emplacements for machine guns and antitank weapons. What makes these pillboxes especially important—and interesting—is that they were under charge of the Fitafita, the Samoan brigade of Samoan Marines who were incorporated into the Marine Corps Reserve.

For a sense of timeless majesty, look north from the beach edging the village of **Vatia.** The beach is tiny, but the views of sweeping mountains and crashing waves are enormous—and unspoiled. (Outside the park, at the east end of the island, the National Oceanic and Atmospheric Administration maintains an air quality station; indeed, the local air serves as the world's baseline for air purity.)

From Vatia, hike the 1.1-mile **Tua-fauna Trail,** which leads through one of the park's three rain forest environments. The flora along the trail is a mix of trees, bushes, and ferns. Unlike many islands in Polynesia, Tutuila is not overrun with invasive, non-native plants.

Above fly fruit bats (flying foxes), which can have wingspans of three feet. The protection of these animals falls under the park's charter. At the trail peak along the ridge, look out over the ocean. From the ridge, it's a short drop to a small, protected beach.

Ta'u and Ofu

The second unit of the park is on the island of Ta'u, about 60 miles due east of Tutuila. Ta'u, where most residents of American Samoa live, is famous for two things: first, it's where Margaret Mead did her Samoan-culture fieldwork; second, according to Samoan tradition, it's where the first humans were created, by Tagaloa.

At the eastern edge of Ta'u, the park protects lowland and montane rain forest, which makes it a birder's paradise. The 5.7-mile **Si'u Point trail** follows an old road through coastal forest. Fine coastline views are part of the experience.

The most remote area of the park is the island of Ofu. Just getting there is an adventure: fly to Ta'u, hitchhike (you'll probably be offered a ride at the airport) to the harbor, and take a small boat out into the open waters to Ofu. (Ofu is actually two islands, Ofu and **Olosega,** connected by a short bridge.) Get the overview on the **Oge Beach Trail,** 2.7 miles along the ridge of Tumutumu, the mountain that runs the length of the island. The trail ends at **Oge,** a coral beach.

In winter, from the island's south side there's a chance of spotting humpback whales. But the real glory of the park is **Ofu Beach,** a marvel of powdery sand and turquoise water.

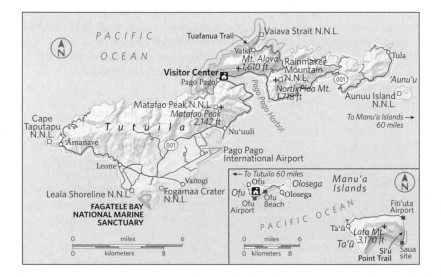

Anemonefish (*Amphiprion melanopus*)

Information

How to Get There

The park is accessed through Pago Pago International Airport. Here you can rent a car as well as arrange for charter flights or boat trips to other islands. Taxis serve Pago Pago, as do buses. (Note: It's okay to sit on someone's lap if the seats are all taken.) Hitchhiking is a way of life on the islands.

When to Go

American Samoa lies around 14 degrees south of the Equator. The islands are pretty much always hot and humid. The hot/wet season runs Oct. through May; the slightly cooler season, from June through Sept.

Visitor Centers

The **visitor center** and **park headquarters** are in Pago Pago, open year-round. This is the best resource for finding routes to the more remote park areas.

Headquarters

National Park of
American Samoa
Pago Pago, AS 96799 USA
nps.gov/npsa
684-633-7082

Camping

Camping is allowed with prior permission from the park superintendent. However, there are no designated camping areas in the park.

Lodging

American Samoa has everything from classic colonial hotels to chain hotel–style lodging *(americansamoa.travel)*. On **Ta'u**, you'll need a homestay; **Ofu** has one lodging, **Vaoto Lodge** *(vaotolodge.com)*. Ask for a room that is catching the wind; the ones that don't can be very hot.

Channel Islands

California

Established
March 5, 1980

249,500 acres

A throwback to bygone California, the Channel Islands lie off the coast between Santa Barbara and Los Angeles. These are secluded gathering places for both wildlife and humans who cherish invigorating escapes from big-city life. Their hacienda days long gone, the five isles have devolved back into nature. Here, paddlers share waters with humpback whales, and campers fall asleep to the sound of crashing waves.

Well into the 20th century the Channel Islands were a real-life version of a John Steinbeck novel, the domain of hearty ranchers, crusty abalone collectors, and eccentric scientists who came to study its natural wonders in splendid isolation. But after the archipelago became a national park, other sorts of people began flocking to the islands: nature lovers and outdoor sports enthusiasts bent on discovering a slice of Southern California that hasn't been paved over or subdivided.

Often called the American Galápagos, the islands and the marine sanctuaries that surround them are an oasis of West Coast flora and fauna. Humpback, gray, blue, and killer

Western Anacapa Island from Inspiration Point

Thousands of Chumash Indians called the islands home when the Spanish arrived; the last native inhabitants were forcibly relocated to mainland missions in the 1820s.

Hacienda life flourished after that, and the tradition lasted until the cusp of the 21st century (see p. 323). Paddlers and photographers, backpackers and scuba divers are today's denizens, although never in numbers that overwhelm this wild side of southern California.

▶ HOW TO VISIT

One of the few offshore national parks in the U.S., the Channel Islands are reached by water or air. The water crossing from Ventura, 60 miles north of Los Angeles, is an adventure all its own, with the morning sun breaking up the fog banks that often shroud the islands, and passengers on the lookout for migrating whales and dolphin pods. Most people visit the islands on day trips, with hiking, kayaking, scuba diving, and snorkeling the main activities. Some visitors overnight at one of 60 campsites; others make the long trek to backcountry camps.

Slender **Anacapa** (one hour by boat), with its historic lighthouse, attracts many visitors, while giant **Santa Cruz** (one hour by boat), with its spectacular sea caves, surf breaks, and secluded beaches, is the main water-sports hub. **Santa Rosa** (3 hours by boat; 30 minutes by air) is the most handsome, a wilderness of rare trees, white-sand strands, and rocky canyons. Far-off **San Miguel** (four hours by boat) is renowned for its copious wildlife, while tiny **Santa Barbara** (three hours by boat) packs a

whales share the offshore waters with great white sharks and 26 species of marine mammals. Elephant seals and sea lions gather in numbers that reach into the tens of thousands. Nearly 400 avian species have been recorded on the islands, which provide a nesting place for millions of shorebirds. There are endemic species of fox, skunk, mouse, snake, salamander, and lizard. The discovery of mammoth bones in 1994 revealed that island terrestrial life was even more diverse (and much larger) in ancient times.

But the Channel Islands also have their human side. Archaeological evidence proves the islands were occupied as early as 13,500 years ago—the oldest human remains found anywhere in North America were found here.

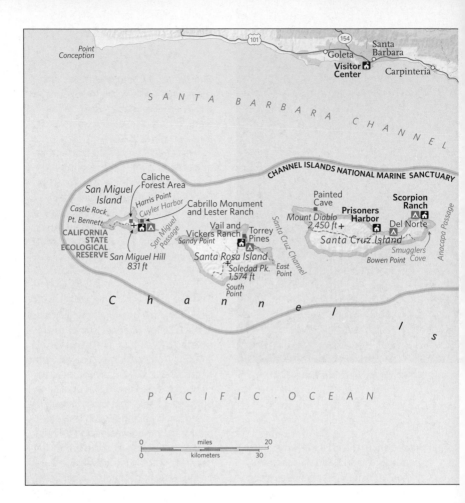

The map depicts the Channel Islands region including Santa Barbara Channel, San Miguel Island, Santa Rosa Island, and Santa Cruz Island.

Map labels:
- Point Conception
- 101
- 154
- Goleta
- Santa Barbara
- Visitor Center
- Carpinteria
- SANTA BARBARA CHANNEL
- CHANNEL ISLANDS NATIONAL MARINE SANCTUARY
- Caliche Forest Area
- San Miguel Island
- Harris Point
- Cuyler Harbor
- Castle Rock
- Pt. Bennett
- CALIFORNIA STATE ECOLOGICAL RESERVE
- San Miguel Passage
- San Miguel Hill 831 ft
- Cabrillo Monument and Lester Ranch
- Vail and Vickers Ranch
- Sandy Point
- Torrey Pines
- Santa Rosa Island
- Soledad Pk. 1,574 ft
- South Point
- East Point
- Painted Cave
- Mount Diablo 2,450 ft
- Prisoners Harbor
- Santa Cruz Channel
- Santa Cruz Island
- Scorpion Ranch
- Del Norte
- Smugglers Cove
- Bowen Point
- Anacapa Passage
- C h a n n e l I s
- PACIFIC OCEAN
- miles 20 / kilometers 30

remarkable amount of nature into just 1 square mile.

Anacapa Island

Long, thin Anacapa is actually three islands separated by narrow channels. **East Anacapa** is the primary destination open to the public; the draw for **Middle Anacapa** is wildlife; while the entire **West Anacapa** is a wildlife reserve that protects the largest breeding colony of the California brown pelican. Despite its diminutive size (it is 5 miles long and a quarter-mile wide), Anacapa is rich in both flora and fauna, home to 265 plant species, the endemic Anacapa deer mouse, and colonies of harbor seals and California sea lions.

After landing at the cove on East Anacapa, visitors quickly ascend 150 stairs to the summit of the mesa-like island and its short hiking routes. A 0.5-mile trail ends at the **Anacapa Light Station** (built in 1932) and its half dozen outbuildings.

A slightly more challenging hiking hike (1.5 miles) heads in the other direction, to **Inspiration Point** and its

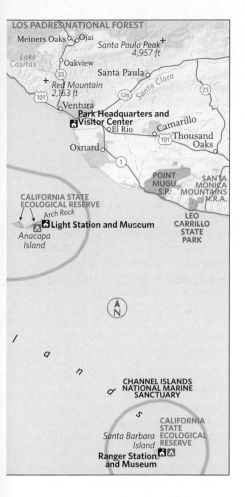

Island Cowboys

A bona-fide part of the Wild West, the Channel Islands have attracted ranchers since the early 1800s. Their rustic way of life lasted well into the 20th century thanks to the archipelago's isolation from mainstream California. A hacienda was established on Santa Rosa in 1844, followed by American ranches on the other islands. Sheep were favored in the early days, with herds as large as 100,000 animals slowly eating their way across the native landscape. Rancho del Medio on Santa Cruz was the most diverse, an islandwide operation that produced beef and wool, as well as olive oil, wine, and nuts for export to the mainland.

By the turn of the 20th century, sheep largely had been replaced by more environmentally friendly cattle. Founded in 1910, Vail & Vickers (V&V) Ranch on Santa Rosa was one of the largest cattle spreads, with thousands of steers ranging free until the spring roundup, when *vaqueros* on horseback herded them to the pier at Bechers Bay for shipment off island. Some ranches endured long after the island was purchased by the National Park Service. Sheep continued to graze Scorpion Ranch on Santa Cruz until 1984, while V&V staged its last cattle roundup in 1998. Several books explore the archipelago's Western heritage, including *Island of the Cowboys* by Kerry Blankenship Allen.

fine vistas of the other islands. With its crystal-clear water, kelp beds, and three sunken shipwrecks, Anacapa is an especially important popular diving destination.

Santa Cruz Island

As the largest island in both the park and the state of California, Santa Cruz sprawls across an area about the size of New York's Staten Island. Although the isle falls entirely within the national park, the Nature Conservancy owns and manages the western and central portions (76 percent of the land area), while the Park Service oversees the eastern end. Towering sea cliffs frame much of Santa Cruz; those on the north shore are punctured by some of the world's largest sea caves. The island's rugged interior is dominated by parallel mountain ranges separated by a deep central valley that actually is an earthquake fault.

Most of the concessioner boats from the mainland call on **Scorpion Anchorage,** jumping-off point for hiking, kayaking, and the island's largest campground. A strenuous 7-mile trail leads over the mountains to **Smugglers Cove,** where there is an old adobe ranch house, an olive grove, and a lovely beach. Hiking is not allowed in the Nature Conservancy zone without a permit. Boaters can visit sunken caverns along the north coast, in particular **Painted Cave,** more than 100 feet wide and a quarter-mile deep.

Santa Rosa Island

With many of its major attractions a relative short walk from the pier, Santa Rosa is user-friendly, with a blend of natural and human history and some of the park's most scenic trails. Beyond the pier is **Vail & Vickers Ranch** (see p. 323), which includes a bunkhouse and barn, corrals, a tiny schoolhouse, and an attractive 19th-century ranch house that is shaded by large cypress trees and can be visited with a guide.

Past the airstrip, the coastal road curves around the edge of Bechers Bay to marshy **Water Canyon,** with a stream that spills down onto a white-sand beach backed by ocher cliffs. Continuing along the road, you soon reach a grove of Torrey pines. Found in only two places (here and San Diego), the tree is one of the rarest native pines

in the United States and the last remnant of a Pleistocene forest that may have once blanketed the entire island.

A nearby spur trail leads to **Black Rock,** an ancient lava flow poised above the sea. Half a mile past the pines, another spur shoots off to a beach where the *Jane L. Sanford* ran aground in 1929, one of more than 140 recorded ships that wrecked in the islands.

The narrow shoreline trail continues east to the rolling sand dunes of **Skunk Point** and its snowy plover nesting area. Energetic hikers can tackle **Black Mountain,** a strenuous 8-mile round-trip from the pier that is well worth the effort for the summit's cloud forest of dwarf trees and stunning views east toward Santa Cruz Island.

Other Islands

Farthest west and least visited are two islands. **San Miguel** is a paradise for pinnipeds (seals and sea lions). As many as 30,000 animals from five different species gather at beaches on the island's westernmost extreme to breed, give birth, and generally lay about. Explorer Juan Rodriguez Cabrillo may have died on San Miguel in 1542, during his milestone cruise up the California coast. His grave has never been found, but the Cabrillo Monument overlooking Cuyler Harbor honors the memory of the skipper who led the first European voyage into these waters.

A mesa formed by underwater volcanic activity, **Santa Barbara Island,** with 5 miles of hiking trails harbors several rare, endemic species, such as the night lizard and live-forever plant.

Western gulls on Anacapa Island

Information

How to Get There

The only way to reach the islands is via concessioner boat, private boat, or small aircraft. From Los Angeles, CA (about 70 miles away), take US 101 north to the Victoria Ave. exit in Ventura, then follow the signs to Channel Islands National Park. Island Packers *(islandpackers.com;* 805-642-1393) operates boats to five islands from Ventura and Oxnard. Several companies organize guided kayak trips (details available on the park website). Channel Islands Aviation in Camarillo, CA *(flycia.com;* 805-987-1301), offers charter flights to Santa Rosa.

When to Go

The park is open year-round, but boats from Ventura Harbor are run less frequently run between late Nov. and early April. Summer offers ideal camping weather, but spring is best for wildflowers, and fall days can be simply glorious for boating and hiking.

Visitor Centers

Robert J. Lagomarsino, 1901 Spinnaker Dr., Ventura, CA, 4.5 miles from the Victoria Ave. exit on US 101. Open year-round.

Headquarters

1901 Spinnaker Dr.
Ventura, CA 93001
nps.gov/chis
805-658-5730

Camping

Each of the five islands has a campground (72 sites total) that is open year-round. Backcountry camping is allowed on Santa Cruz and Santa Rosa islands. All camping requires advance reservations *(recreation.gov;* 877-444-6777).

Lodging

None of the islands offer overnight lodging. Hotels are plentiful in **Ventura,** *(visitventura.com),* **Oxnard** *(visitoxnard .com),* and **Santa Barbara** *(santabarbara .com).*

Death Valley

California & Nevada

Established
October 31, 1994

3.4 million acres

Hottest, driest, lowest, largest . . . Death Valley dazzles, even intimidates, with superlatives. The largest national park in the Lower 48 has indeed recorded the world's highest temperature (134° F), nets less than two inches of rain a year, and contains the lowest spot in North America. But those extremes can add up to fascination. Death Valley National Park is nothing short of spellbinding.

Death Valley is geology laid bare—a scarred, gashed, dissected place where striated canyons gouge forbidding mountains, and where a vast salt-pan floor shimmers under a fierce sun. Ferocity reigns here. Yet Death Valley's 300-plus miles of paved roads and a smattering of oasis-style facilities make it surprisingly easy to visit, though that doesn't diminish at all the park's overpowering impact.

No one has ever taken Death Valley lightly. The native Timbisha Shoshone people understood its hidden generosity—they knew how to harvest its pine nuts and mesquite beans, to hunt its bighorn sheep and mule deer, and to use arrowweed to craft naturally

Badwater Basin

visitor center, food, and lodging. Although it's possible to simply drive through the park in a day, you'd have little time to stop. With two full days, you can radiate out and back from Furnace Creek and visit attractions such as **Ubehebe Crater, Scotty's Castle,** and **Badwater,** the lowest place in North America. With three days, you can include a day in the high country, and an even longer visit gives you time to explore remote terrain (a high-clearance vehicle is needed).

Badwater Road

If you enter Death Valley from the south, you'll cut through the Black Mountains and make your way north on Badwater Road. This byway traces the sub-sea-level floor of Death Valley, flanked by towering mountain ranges to the east and west. If you choose a different entrance, be sure to allot at least a portion of a day to Badwater Road, which links some of the top geological marvels in the park.

This southern approach cuts through two mountain passes on Calif. 178, from which you can glimpse the shimmering salt-pan floor in the distance. And be ready to marvel at the rugged Black Mountains and the multicolored region geologists call the Amargosa Chaos. Once you're on the valley floor, it's evident that it was once a vast lake—look for water-level marks on **Shoreline Butte,** which you can see from the roadside adobe ruins of **Ashford Mill.**

At **Badwater,** you hit bottom, 282 feet below sea level. It's named for a salty pool of water you can see from a short boardwalk. But be sure also to walk out onto the salt-pan floor of the

ventilated homes. But they also knew that summer was no time to linger on a valley floor that bakes at 120 degrees or more for months at a time. They retreated to the same high country that welcomes visitors today.

Gold seekers, prospectors, and borax miners largely displaced the Timbisha people. Mining ruins are among the park's fascinations, as is the possibility of seeing wildlife (coyotes, roadrunners, and perhaps the nocturnal kit fox).

▶ HOW TO VISIT

Death Valley is huge and has multiple entry points. However you approach, make your way to its core, **Furnace Creek,** where you'll find the main valley and look up into the mountains for a sign, impressively high, that reads "Sea Level."

A few miles farther is a dirt-road side trip that leads 1.3 miles to **Devils Golf Course,** a broad fairway of crusty pinnacles. Five miles farther is **Artists Drive,** a paved road that climbs into

Hot, Hot, and Not

Death Valley has recorded the hottest temperature on Earth: 134°F, and summer days are frequently hotter than 120. In 2001, Death Valley went 154 consecutive days with a maximum temperature over 100 degrees. Even the *low* temperature is sometimes over 100.

Several factors combine to account for the intense heat. Because Death Valley is so dry, it lacks plant cover and clouds to filter solar radiation. The barren landscape soaks up sunshine and radiates it back into the air. Because Death Valley lies so low—and is surrounded by tall mountain ranges— the air becomes trapped. Dry air heats much more quickly than moist air—so air that is hot to begin with gets hotter.

Death Valley isn't hot all the time, though. Winters can actually be chilly; some days are in the 30s at the higher elevations. Telescope Peak, at 11,049 feet, is snow-covered much of the year, and snow occasionally comes down as low as Dantes View and Scotty's Castle. Early spring and late fall may be the most pleasant times to visit Death Valley, but visitation numbers are just as high in the summer, when people come from all over the world to experience the novelty of world-class heat.

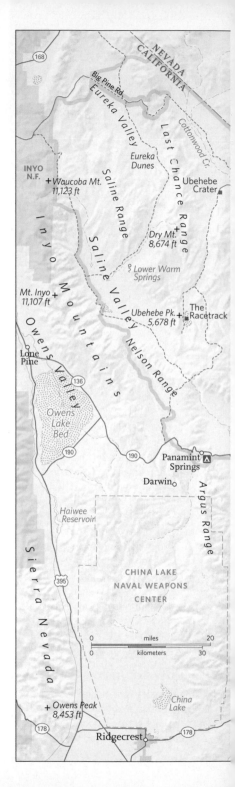

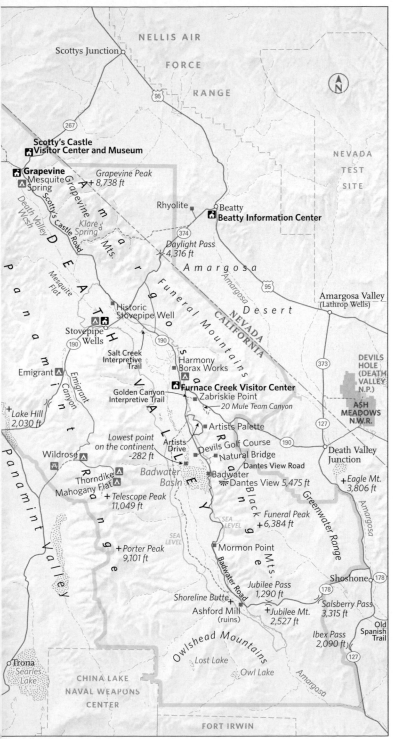

some of the most colorful terrain in the Amargosa Range. Four miles north is **Golden Canyon,** with perhaps the best 1-mile hike in Death Valley.

Furnace Creek & Beyond

Furnace Creek, the park's commercial center, is a natural oasis shaded by date palm trees that has always been the heart of Death Valley—for natives, borax miners, and the earliest park visitors, who began flocking here when Pacific Coast Borax Company developed Furnace Creek Inn in 1927. The modern **Furnace Creek Visitor Center** has fine exhibits and offers ranger programs.

Just outside the park, the **Borax Works** tells the story of mining in Death Valley. Nearby is an 18-hole golf course—at 214 feet below sea level, perhaps the lowest in the world.

Calif. 190 east of Furnace Creek is all about vistas. Just 4.5 miles from Furnace Creek Ranch is **Zabriskie Point,** where an early sun casts a gentle glow on hills of mudstone, clay, and siltstone just below. Steep Dante's View Road, 11 miles from Furnace Creek, leads past mining ruins to the park's most accessible high viewpoint, a breathtaking mile above Badwater and the salt-pan floor of Death Valley.

Allow a full day to make the 54-mile drive north from Furnace Creek to Scotty's Castle and Ubehebe Crater and back, as the road offers worthwhile sights along the way. About 2 miles north of Furnace Creek is the **Harmony Borax Works,** where you can see one of the 20-mule-team wagons that transported borax as far as 165 miles to the town of Mojave.

At **Salt Creek,** a dirt road leads about a mile to the start of a boardwalk alongside a saline creek that harbors an inch-long fish species— the Salt Creek pupfish—that exists nowhere else in the world.

After Calif. 190 veers west toward Stovepipe Wells, Scotty's Castle Road continues north 36 miles to Scotty's Castle—well worth a visit, and reservations are a good idea *(recreation .gov)*. **Scotty's Castle** is the Spanish-Mediterranean mansion built as a retreat by wealthy midwesterner Albert Johnson, and properly called Death Valley Ranch—an impressive, ahead-of-its-time spread that cost more than $2 million in 1920s dollars. **Ubehebe Crater** is just 8 miles from Scotty's Castle. It's worth the side trip to see a landscape that looks like the surface of Mars.

From an intersection 17 miles north of Furnace Creek, Calif. 190 leads west through the outpost of Stovepipe Wells and leads into the often-overlooked **Panamint Mountains.** Traveling west from the intersection, you shortly come to **Mesquite Flats Sand Dunes,** where you can park and explore a vast set of towering dunes.

Past Wildrose Campground, the road turns to dirt and leads to a remarkable sight: a line of 10 stone charcoal kilns that date back to the 1870s. The charcoal fueled silver-mine smelters. From the kilns, a 4.2-mile trail leads to 9,064-foot **Wildrose Peak** and a stunning view of Death Valley.

The only way you can get hiking access to the park's high point, 11,049-foot **Telescope Peak,** farther along the road, is via a high-clearance 4x4 vehicle.

Salt formations with clay deposits on Devils Golf Course

Information

How to Get There

From the south (I-15), follow Calif. 127 north to either Calif. 178 or 190 west into the park. From Las Vegas, take Calif. 160 west to Pahrump, Nevada, then Bell Vista Rd. west to Calif. 127 to Calif. 190. From the Lone Pine on US 395, take Calif. 136 east to Calif. 190. From the southwest, take Calif. 14 north to Inyokern, then Calif. 178 east to Calif. 190.

When to Go

Late spring and late fall are the most pleasant seasons, but visitation is fairly steady year-round.

Visitor Centers

Furnace Creek (park headquarters) on Calif. 190 in the heart of the park, and a small visitor center at **Scotty's Castle** in the north part of the park on Scotty's Castle Road.

Headquarters

P.O. Box 579
Death Valley, CA 92328

nps.gov/deva
760-786-3200

Camping

Park campgrounds, with more than 750 sites, are first come, first served, except for **Furnace Creek** *(recreation .gov;* 877-444-6777). High-country campgrounds are occasionally unreachable in winter. **Stovepipe Wells** offers 14 RV sites *(deathvalleyhotels.com;* 760-786-2387).

Lodging

Concessioner properties include **Furnace Creek Inn** and the **Ranch at Furnace Creek** *(furnacecreekresort.com;* 800-236-7916). For lodging outside the park, visit the park website *(nps.gov/deva/ planyourvisit/lodging.htm).*

Safety

The park service recommends that visitors drink at least a gallon of water per day. Distances between services can be great in the park, so begin your day with all the gas, water, and snacks you'll need.

DEATH VALLEY
EST. 1994

Haleakalā

Island of Maui, Hawai'i

Established
August 1, 1916

33,265 acres

One of the world's most otherworldly landscapes awaits at the summit of the volcano at the core of this spectacular national park on the island of Maui. Named for the volcano (now dormant) that helped shape the land, Haleakalā National Park dominates the island skyline. The park encompasses the basin and portions of the volcano's dramatic flanks. Protected here are some of the most endangered species on Earth.

When first established—in the same year as the National Park Service—only the summit and crater of Haleakalā were protected. They were part of a larger entity called Hawai'i National Park, which also included the summits of Kīlauea and Mauna Loa on Hawai'i Island. In 1961, Kīlauea and Mauna Loa became part of Hawai'i Volcanoes National Park (see p. 342), while Haleakalā was re-designated as Haleakalā National Park.

Visitors reach the lower valley of the Kīpahulu District via the spectacular Hana Highway. The drive is an adventure with a progression of hairpin curves, bridges, and turnouts. It's a byway rich in intensity—azure

Haleakalā crater

sea, black rock, silver waterfalls, and green forest and meadow. The coastal area of Maui was first farmed in early Polynesian times, more than 1,200 years ago.

About two-thirds of the park is federally designated Wilderness. One of the park's main missions is to preserve and protect unique and fragile ecosystems, from sea level to summit, that include rare and endangered plants and forest birds. Much of this flora and fauna are found nowhere else on Earth. In fact, the park provides critical habitat to more endangered species than almost any other in the national park system.

Though commonly referred to as "the crater," the summit of Haleakalā is actually a valley carved by erosion.

Most visitors (more than a million a year) head to the summit, which is easily accessible by car. Others sign up for organized tours, some with hikes to watch the sunrise followed by a downhill bicycle ride outside the park boundary to the town of Kula for breakfast. Though popular at sunrise, the park is beautiful throughout the day, and sunset is just as compelling as daybreak.

▶ HOW TO VISIT

There are no highways or trails connecting the upper and lower areas of the national park. Both districts are truly remote, with medical and emergency assistance at least a 45-minute drive away.

Haleakalā National Park has two access points. The more heavily traveled of the two leads to the Summit District from the tourism-heavy side of the island, between the resort areas of Wailea and Kahului; the other access point is the community of Kīpahulu, on the remote eastern shore, near the town of Hana.

First stop: **Park Headquarters Visitor Center** at 7,000 feet, in the Summit District. Here, get information on trail conditions, permits, interpretive programs, and sightseeing. For all hikes, visitors should be prepared with water, snacks, sunscreen, and proper footwear, and share hiking plans with friends or family outside the park. Due to ever changing conditions, hikers should dress in layers and be prepared for all types of weather.

Several trailheads are located near the Park Headquarters Visitor Center, including **Hosmer Grove** and **Halemau'u Trail,** along with

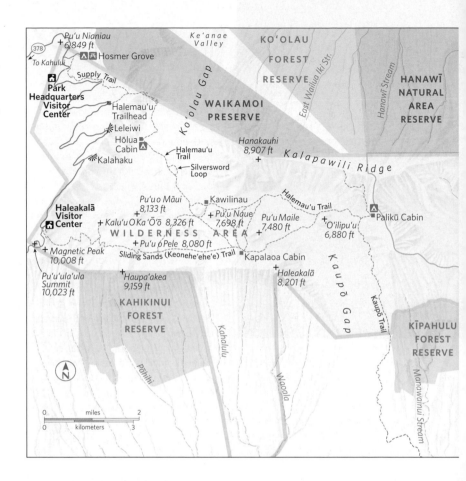

Pu'u Nianiau
+ 6,849 ft
378
To Kahului
△ ⛺ Hosmer Grove
Supply Trail
Park
Headquarters
Visitor
Center
Halemau'u
Trailhead
Leleiwi
Hōlua
Cabin △
Kalahaku
Halemau'u
Trail
Silversword
Loop

Ke'anae
Valley
Ko'olau Gap
WAIKAMOI
PRESERVE

KO'OLAU
FOREST
RESERVE

East Wailua Iki Str.
Hanawī Stream

HANAWĪ
NATURAL
AREA
RESERVE

Hanakauhi
8,907 ft
+
Kalapawili Ridge

Haleakalā
Visitor
Center
Pu'u o Māui
8,133 ft
+
Kalu'u O Ka 'Ō'ō 8,326 ft
WILDERNESS
+ Pu'u o Pele 8,080 ft
+ Magnetic Peak
10,008 ft
+
Pu'u'ula'ula
Summit
10,023 ft

Kawilinau
+ Pu'u Naue
7,698 ft
Pu'u Maile
7,480 ft
AREA
Sliding Sands (Keonehe'ehe'e) Trail

Halemau'u Trail
'O'ilipu'u
6,880 ft
+

Palikū Cabin △

Kapalaoa Cabin

+ Haupa'akea
9,159 ft

+ Haleakalā
8,201 ft

Kaupō Gap
Kaupō Trail

KAHIKINUI
FOREST
RESERVE

Kahalulu
Pāhihi
Waaola
Manawainui Stream

KĪPAHULU
FOREST
RESERVE

N
0 miles 2
0 kilometers 3

two overlook points—**Leleiwi** and **Kalahaku**—that offer spectacular views into the crater. Kalahaku is only accessible from the downhill lane, so it's best to head there on your way back down.

Indeed, a more in-depth exploration of the park can be had by embarking on any of the hiking trails that start at the Hosmer Grove, Halemau'u trailhead, Haleakalā Visitor Center on the crater rim, and the Kīpahulu Visitor Center on the coast, near Hana.

Several miles up the road from the Park Headquarters Visitor Center is the **Haleakalā Visitor Center** (at 9,740 feet) and just beyond that is the **summit** (at 10,023 feet).

From Haleakalā Visitor Center, housed in a historic stone building, you can head out for a day hike or longer. More than 35 miles of trails lead through the crater's Wilderness area, ranging from easy ten-minute walks to trails that require overnight stays.

Keonehe'ehe'e (Sliding Sands) Trailhead, adjacent to Haleakalā Visitor Center, leads down into the crater itself, traversing fascinating, lunar-like terrain. Hawai'i's state bird,

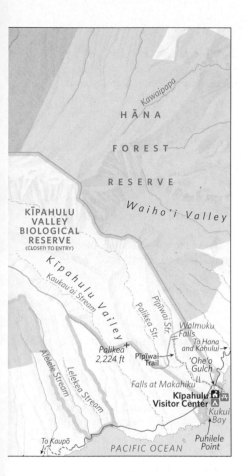

the nēnē, is commonly spotted in this vicinity of the park.

Just outside park boundaries but clearly visible from the summit is Haleakalā Observatory, also known as Science City. Closed to the public, the astrophysical complex is operated by the University of Hawaii, the U.S. Air Force, and others.

Summit District

Hosmer Grove Loop is an easy, rewarding hike that starts 1 mile below the Park Headquarters Visitor Center.

Next to the small campground, a short trail leads through native *'ohi'a lehua* trees and native subalpine shrubland.

In addition to unique flora, Hosmer Grove is a very good area for bird-watching, with native forest birds, including Hawai'i's colorful, endangered honeycreepers, routinely spotted. Come nightfall, Hawaiian hoary bats sometimes make an appearance.

The parking lot at Hosmer Grove is where groups meet for 3.5-hour staff-led hikes through **Waikomoi Preserve,** off-limits except with a guide (inquire at the Park Headquarters Visitor Center for schedule and reservations).

The preserve, located on private land owned by Haleakalā Ranch and managed by the Nature Conservancy of Hawai'i, offers visitors a glimpse into a threatened native Hawaiian rain and cloud forest that a number of endangered birds and insects call home.

Offering both easy and more moderate hiking options is the **Halemau'u Trail,** which begins at 8,000 feet (3.5 miles upslope from the Park Headquarters Visitor Center) and leads 1.1 miles through native shrubland to the rim of **Ko'olau Gap.** Here, the cliffs drop off 1,000 feet, and extraordinary views extend across the upper reaches of the park. This is one of Haleakalā's best short walking experiences.

Pressing forward from the rim, a longer and less traveled trail descends 1,400 feet down a sometimes steep and narrow series of switchbacks to the valley floor. The views along this portion of the trail are remarkable. Across the valley, the landscape is rendered in various shades of muted rust and brown, punctuated by lava flows

Mythology & Mariners

Haleakalā figures prominently in Hawaiian mythology. One of the most widely told stories recalls an achievement of Maui, an ancient Polynesian demigod with many deeds and stories to his name. One of his feats—as it has been told for generations—was to climb to the summit of Haleakalā and lasso the sun's rays in order to slow the sun's passage and prolong the day.

But Maui the demigod was not the only one to ascend to the summit of the dramatic mountain. Thanks to its location on the planet and its elevation, Haleakalā is exceptional for viewing the night sky. Ancient Polynesian mariners studied the sky from this vantage point in order to learn how to navigate to and from South Pacific islands.

The summit of Haleakalā was, and still is, a training ground for navigators studying the stars. But whether studying the stars or teaching students about traditional plant uses, the mountain remains a central feature in modern Hawaiian culture, and the park continues to be a place where the Hawaiian culture is in practice.

and lava cones. In many places, cinder ash covers the the valley floor.

At the 3.7 mile mark of the trail is **Hōlua Cabin** and campground for overnight stays (by permit). Less than a mile beyond the cabin, a short jaunt off the Halemau'u Trail, the 1-mile **Silversword Loop** leads through an area displaying one of the greatest concentrations of 'āhinahina (silversword plants) in the park. A mature

'āhinahina can stand eight feet tall, with misty silver fingers emanating from a spiny center stalk. If you spot one of these unique plants with a large stalk abloom with purple flowers, you will know that plant is getting near to the end of its several-decade life cycle.

The **Halemau'u Trail** is one of the primary hikes in the park. From the trailhead it extends 10.3 miles to the **Palikū Cabin** and the **Kaupō Trail.** The Halemau'u Trail also branches off to **Keonehe'ehe'e (Sliding Sands) Trail.** A hearty, 10-mile route follows Halemau'u Trail out, then loops back to the Haleakalā Visitor Center via Keonehe'ehe'e.

Pu'u'ula'ula Summit

A short drive from the Haleakalā Visitor Center leads to the 10,023-foot summit of the mountain. Exhilarating 360-degree views are had from here; on clear days you can see the peaks of Hawai'i Island.

An enclosed viewing area protects against the wind, and also makes a cozy spot for stargazing at night. Given the clear skies and absence of light pollution, nighttime can be quite amazing at the summit of Haleakalā.

The Keonehe'ehe'e Trail starts at the Haleakalā Visitor Center and descends 2,500 feet through a cinder desert to the crater floor. The trail's Hawaiian name refers to how a he'e—octopus—moves across the reef. In the trail's soft cinders, hikers experience terrain that moves octopuslike underfoot. The footing is safe but challenging, especially for the hike back up the steep trail to the visitor center. (It takes twice as long to hike uphill and out of the crater than it does going down into the crater.)

The first portion of the Keone-he'ehe'e Trail is beautifully desolate, with little shrubbery and no trees or greenery of any sort. The red-hued cinder ash is otherworldly, particularly as you pass the frequent *pu'u* (cinder cones) along the way.

Several offshoots of the main trail lead through the surreal terrain and hook up with the Halemau'u Trail, or loop back to Keonehe'ehe'e. **Kapalaoa Cabin** is 5.6 miles from the trailhead, and **Palikū Cabin** is 10.3 miles from the trailhead. Permits are required at both cabins for overnight stays.

One of the less traveled and most spectacular trails in the upper regions of the national park is **Kaupō Trail,** one of the premier hikes in Hawai'i. The upper trailhead is near Palikū Cabin (9.2 miles from the Visitor Center). The annual average of 30 inches of rain at the summit pales against Kaupō Gap's 420 inches per year. The precipitation is responsible for the lush scenery. Numerous waterfalls can be seen from the trail.

Many hikers find that going up the rugged and steep Kaupō Trail is considerably easier than hiking downhill. The trail traverses the outer wall of the verdant *pali* (cliff), with broad views of Hawai'i Island, and down to the southeastern shore of Maui.

The Kaupō Gap trail actually goes beyond park boundaries, through privately owned lands. Local property

A park ranger helps a visitor craft a hat of coconut leaves.

owners have granted hikers permission to cross their land, with the stipulation that they not stray from the designated trails.

Kīpahulu/Waimoku Falls

To get to the **Kīpahulu District** from Kahului, you'll make one of the all-time great drives in the Hawaiian Islands, the **Hana Highway.** It's a 68-mile road that runs along the scenic east coast of the island. And it's a legendary road, with more than 600 hairpin curves, 59 bridges, and numerous scenic turnouts. Figure on stopping for at least a few photo opportunities along the way. All told, it can easily take more than 2.5 hours to get to **Hana.**

The Kīpahulu District and the coastal area of Haleakalā National Park are far different from the park's upper reaches. At Kīpahulu the terrain is green with tropical rain forest vegetation and silver with waterfalls. Three miles of trails, parts of which are boardwalk, lead through this lush, inviting landscape.

Hana and Kīpahulu were once densely populated and farmed. The Kīpahulu portion of Haleakalā National Park was added not only to preserve the scenery, but also to allow a glimpse into traditional Hawaiian lifestyles, which are documented at the **Kīpahulu Visitor Center.** Nearby, traditional agricultural practices, such as the cultivation of taro, are being carried forth at Kapahu Living Farm.

The Visitor Center is a good first stop for cultural exhibits and hiking advice. Short trails branch out from here to the coast and upslope. Follow the **Pīpīwai Trail** through a bamboo forest to view the **Falls at Makahiku**

(at the 0.5 mile mark) and **Waimoku Falls** (2 miles). The park is closed to visitors beyond the Waimoku Falls viewpoint due to possible rockslides and flash flooding from the waterfalls. In addition, above Waimoku Falls is the **Kīpahulu Valley Biological Reserve,** which is closed to visitors to protect critically endangered species.

Though many sources make reference to the Seven Sacred Pools that are supposedly found in the Kīpahulu section of the park, rangers are quick to clarify that no such place exists within the park. The reference is most likely to the freshwater pools found at **'Ohe'o Gulch,** but in fact there are far more than seven pools at the gulch. Freshwater is considered sacred in Hawai'i as the source of life.

While it is tempting to swim in the freshwater **Pools of 'Ohe'o,** which are accessed via a trail that begins at the Visitor Center, rangers advise against it. Visitors can easily slip on the smooth rocks or can be swept out to sea without a moment's notice by "freshets"—flash floods that come without warning as the result of upcountry rains.

Rockfalls also are common. And there is another danger: In modern Hawai'i, even clear, calm, fresh waters can be home to parasites such as *Giardia leptospirosis.* A spontaneous thirst-quenching moment could result in months of medical care.

Still, with its lush (non-native) bamboo forest, gushing waterfalls, and access to the beautiful and remote coast of southeastern Maui, Kīpahulu is one of the most scenic areas of the park. There is a wealth of idyllic spots for a picnic, relaxation, and solitude.

Hana waterfall

Information

How to Get There

The Summit District's park headquarters and Haleakalā's 10,023-foot summit can be reached from Kahului via Hawaii 37 to 377 to 378. Driving time to the summit from Kahului is approximately 1.5 hours. Visitors should drive very cautiously; the road bisects endangered species habitat. The Kīpahulu District is reached via Hawaii 36 to 360 to 31. Driving time from Kahului is approximately 3.5 hours. Fill your gas tank and bring food with you; neither is available in the park. Both districts are remote.

When to Go

The park is open year-round, 24 hours a day. Temperatures commonly range between 30°F and 65°F. With the wind-chill factor, the summit temperature can drop below freezing.

Visitor Centers

Park Headquarters Visitor Center, at 7,000 feet; Haleakalā Visitor Center, at 9,740 feet; Kīpahulu Visitor Center, at Mile marker 42 on Hana Hwy.

Headquarters

P.O. Box 369
Makawao, HI 96768
nps.gov/hale
808-572-4400

Camping

The Kīpahulu District has a drive-in campground (100 sites), as does the Summit District at Hosmer Grove (50 sites). Both accommodate campers on a first come, first served basis. Hiking access to all Wilderness campgrounds and cabins is via the Sliding Sands and Halemau'u trails or Kaupō Gap. Permits from Park Headquarters Visitor Center are required for backcountry camping. Advance reservations are necessary for backcountry cabins.

Lodging

Kula provides the closest lodging to the Summit area; many visitors stay in hotels in Wailea and Kihei *(gohawaii.com/maui)*. The nearest lodging to Kīpahulu is in Hana *(hanamaui.com)*.

Haleakalā Excursions

Wai'ānapanapa State Park
Hana, Maui

▷ Low volcanic cliffs line the rugged coastline of Wai'ānapanapa State Park and offers a reprieve from the long drive along the Hāna Highway. Features include a native hala forest, legendary cave, heiau (religious temple), natural stone arches, sea stacks, blow holes, and a small black-sand beach. Hike the ancient coastal trail. Camping permit required. Fifteen miles from Haleakalā National Park. *dlnr.hawaii.gov/dsp/parks/maui/ waianapanapastate-park;* 808-984-8109.

Iao Valley State Park
Wailuku, Maui

▷ The peaceful 'Īao Valley, with its emerald peaks and lush valley floor, is home to one of Maui's most recognizable landmarks, the 'Īao Needle, an imposing erosional remnant significant for its role in the 1790 battle. Paths lead through a botanical garden, along 'Īao Stream, and to the ridge-top observation pavilion with views of the needle and surrounding valley. Parking fee. Forty miles northwest of Haleakalā National Park. *dlnr.hawaii .gov/dsp/parks/maui/iao-valley-state -monument;* 808-984-8109.

Kealia Pond NWR
South Central Maui

▷The Keālia Pond National Wildlife Refuge is home to endangered waterbirds, including the Hawaiian black-necked stilt (ae'o) and Hawaiian coot ('alae ke'oke'o). It is an ideal wintering location for migratory birds coming from Alaska, Canada, and occasionally Asia. Activities include bird-watching, educational programs, and volunteer habitat-restoration projects. Thirty-five miles southwest of Haleakalā National Park. *fws.gov/refuge/kealia_pond;* 808-875-1582.

Waikamoi Preserve
Eastern Maui

▷ Part of the Nature Conservancy, Waikamoi Preserve has been set aside to protect hundreds of Hawaii's native species. This high rain forest on the slopes of Haleakalā Volcano shelters 13 bird species, including the rare 'akohekohe, the kiwikiu, the scarlet 'i'iwi, and the green 'amakihi. The preserve also protects more than 41 species of rare plants. Access by guided tours only, offered on Thursday morning; reservations required. *nature.org/ourinitiatives/regions/northamerica/unitedstates/hawaii/placesweprotect/waikamoi;* 808-572-4400.

Polipoli Spring State Park
South Central Maui

▷ Cold, wet, foggy, and somewhat mystical, Polipoli Spring State Recreation Area has a climate similar to that of the Pacific Northwest, plus 10 acres of conifers and towering redwoods. Visitors hike and bike the miles of trails in the park and adjacent forest reserve. Note: There's hunting within the confines of the park. Thirty-three miles southwest of Haleakalā National Park. *dlnr.hawaii.gov/dsp/parks/maui/polipoli-spring-state-recreation-area;* 808-984-8109.

Kanaha Pond Wildlife Sanctuary
Kahului, Maui

▷ The 245-acre Kanaha Pond Wildlife Sanctuary, in downtown Kahului, protects endangered waterbirds, including the pink-legged Hawaiian black-neck stilt. More than 909 species of birds can be found here. Kanaha is one of two twin fish ponds ordered built by the King of Maui in the early 1700s. Birdwatching kiosk. Twenty-five miles from Haleakalā National Park, near Kahului Airport. *dlnr.hawaii.gov/wildlife;* 808-984-8100.

Hawai'i Volcanoes

Island of Hawai'i, the "Big Island"

Established
August 1, 1916

333,086 acres

Stretching from the Pacific shoreline to the 13,677-foot summit of Mauna Loa, on the Big Island, Hawai'i Volcanoes National Park encompasses two major active volcanoes, Kīlauea and Mauna Loa. The park's seven ecosystems showcase aspects of Hawai'i that go far beyond the beach. A visit to Hawai'i Volcanoes is an up close lesson in volcanic geology, Hawaiian culture, rare species of flora and fauna, and Polynesian mythology.

Volcanoes have their own language. Here in the park, visitors discover the difference between *'a'ā* and *pāhoehoe* lava; peer at *pu'u* formations; look and listen for *pueo*, *'amakihi*, and *'apapane* birds; and photograph the amazing sight of a lone *'ōhi'a* bush emerging defiantly from a thin crack in a solid sheet of black lava.

The park's seven major ecological zones range from rain forest to upland forest, sea coast to alpine, and lowland to woodland and subalpine. The two major volcanoes that lie mostly within the park's boundaries, Kīlauea

Kīlauea's Halema'uma'u Crater lights the morning sky.

and Mauna Loa—in fact, the entire island—sit atop the underwater "hot spot" in the 3,600-mile-long Hawaiian Island–Emperor Seamount chain. This hot spot is responsible for the flow of bright red magma that issues from rifts on the sides of Kīlauea (and occasionally Mauna Loa), creating the newest land on Earth.

▶ **HOW TO VISIT**

Visitors can get a good sense of the park—and the 70-million-year-old volcanic dynamism of Hawai'i—in as little as three hours by visiting the Kīlauea Visitor Center and Jaggar Museum, and driving down Chain of Craters Road to the ocean, where signs point out the many lava flows that have

shaped the landscape over the years. Even a half-day visit to the park's busiest areas reveals dramatic destruction, hard-fought renewal, and the creation of new land. But driving through the park or spending a day or more walking some of the park's more than 150 miles of trails, and maybe camping out fosters a much deeper appreciation of the park's many geologic subtleties, its rare wildlife, and the ancient Hawaiian culture that still holds this land sacred.

More than 1.5 million people a year visit Hawai'i Volcanoes National Park. Most want to see the active lava flow. And while the most recent surface lava flows have occurred outside park boundaries, don't be dissuaded. The park is a treasure trove for both casual visitors and avid volcano enthusiasts. To be sure, the erupting summit of Kīlauea is a must-see.

Start at **Kīlauea Visitor Center,** just inside the park's main entrance. Here, rangers answer questions about what to see and do, and informative displays provide a basic history and lay of the land.

About 2 miles from the visitor center on Crater Rim Drive is the **Jaggar Museum** and an overlook that provides a view of Kīlauea Caldera. This is as close as visitors can get to the caldera (a large crater typically formed by a major collapse of the volcano's mouth). An easy hike along **Crater Rim Trail,** which links the visitor center and the Jaggar Museum, leads past several steam vents and provides spectacular views into the crater.

The last summit eruption started on March 18, 2008, when rocks and lava blew from the **Halema'uma'u Crater** and spread across 65 acres, creating a vent and a boiling lava lake. As this

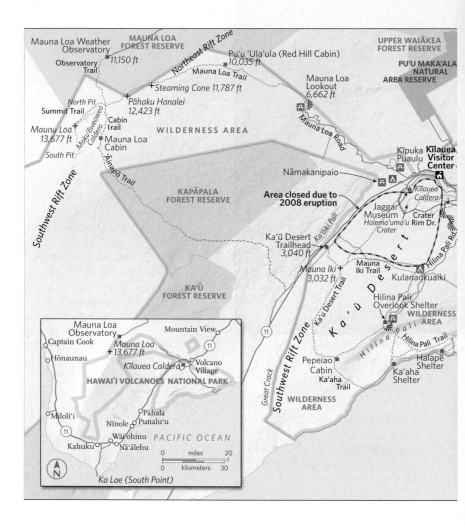

The following labels appear on the map:

Mauna Loa Weather Observatory
MAUNA LOA FOREST RESERVE
Northeast Rift Zone
Pu'u 'Ula'ula (Red Hill Cabin) 10,035 ft
UPPER WAIĀKEA FOREST RESERVE
Observatory Trail 11,150 ft
Mauna Loa Trail
Mauna Loa Lookout 6,662 ft
PU'U MAKA'ALA NATURAL AREA RESERVE
Steaming Cone 11,787 ft
North Pit Summit Trail
Pāhaku Hanalei 12,423 ft
Cabin Trail
WILDERNESS AREA
Mauna Loa Road
Mauna Loa 13,677 ft
Moku'āweoweo Caldera
South Pit
Mauna Loa Cabin
'Āinapō Trail
Kīpuka Puaulu
Kīlauea Visitor Center
Southwest Rift Zone
Nāmakanipaio
Kīlauea Caldera
KAPĀPALA FOREST RESERVE
Area closed due to 2008 eruption
Jaggar Museum
Halema'uma'u Crater
Crater Rim Dr.
Ka'ōiki Pali
Ka'ū Desert Trailhead 3,040 ft
Hilina Pali Rd.
KA'Ū FOREST RESERVE
Mauna Iki 3,032 ft
Mauna Iki Trail
Kulanaokuaiki
Ka'ū Desert Trail
Hilina Pali Overlook Shelter
WILDERNESS AREA
Ka'ū Desert
Hilina Pali
Hilina Pali Trail
Halapē Shelter
11
Southwest Rift Zone
Pepeiao Cabin
Ka'aha Trail
Ka'aha Shelter
Great Crack
WILDERNESS AREA

Inset map:
Mauna Loa Observatory
Mountain View
Captain Cook
Mauna Loa 13,677 ft
11
Hōnaunau
Kīlauea Caldera
Volcano Village
HAWAI'I VOLCANOES NATIONAL PARK
Miloli'i
Pāhala
Nīnole
Punalu'u
11
Wāi'ohinu
PACIFIC OCEAN
Kahuku
Nā'ālehu
0 miles 20
0 kilometers 30
N
Ka Lae (South Point)

book goes to press, that eruption was ongoing, and geologists think it might continue for another century.

Vents in the caldera are continuously issuing steam and volcanic fumes that can be seen any time of day. But it is at night (the park is open 24 hours) that the lava lake inside Halema'uma'u Crater gives off an eerie red glow stretching to the sky, dark and brimming with stars. Come at sunrise (you could have it all to yourself).

Crater Rim Drive & Beyond

An 11-mile loop, Crater Rim Drive encircles the summit caldera, passing through lush rain forest and desert (closed between the Jaggar Museum and Chain of Craters Road). The two most popular day hikes in the park start just off Crater Rim Drive. **Thurston Lava Tube** (Nāhuku) is the shorter of the two (2 miles) and most family friendly. It is named after one

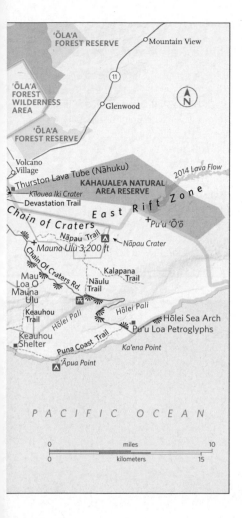

A more strenuous adventure can be found along 4-mile **Kīlauea Iki,** which starts in a rain forest on the crater rim and descends 400 feet to the crater floor. As you pass through the rain forest on your way down the trail, keep an ear to the tree canopy, where the calls of a brilliant crimson 'apapane bird, whose only known habitat is Hawai'i, can often be heard. And keep an eye to the sky, where white-tailed tropicbirds and Hawaiian hawks often soar.

The trail offers ample evidence of the challenges faced by park rangers and volunteers as they attempt to eradicate the non-native plants—particularly Himalayan yellow ginger, a weed with lovely, fragrantly scented yellow blooms—that in many cases are crowding out endemic species.

The crater floor is the site of the last major eruption of Kīlauea Iki (1959). Lava erupted from a vent in the crater wall for five weeks, with one geyser of lava spewing 1,900 feet in the air, setting a record for the highest lava fountain ever measured in Hawai'i.

The black rock that forms the crater floor across which hikers traverse is actually the hardened surface of the 400-foot-deep lava lake that formed when the eruption occurred. The experience is eerie and unforgettable.

Chain of Craters Road

This is the park's main byway, which begins at the park entrance and heads along the East Rift of Kīlauea before continuing down to the coast. The road drops 3,700 feet in 19 miles before reaching the water. Along the way, signs are posted showing where

of the park's greatest advocates, Honolulu businessman Lorrin Thurston, who discovered the tube in 1913. The trail leads to a lush fern forest and through a massive, moist lava tube that once had a river of yellow lava running through it. Thurston Lava Tube is where the tour buses stop; it is one of the busiest spots in the park. If you come before 9 a.m., before the crowds, you might see Hawaiian honeycreepers and hear their sweet songs.

various eruptions issued forth—a history in lava flows: 1969, 1972, 1979—and scenic overlooks where the devastation and the eventual rebirth of the landscape can be viewed.

About halfway down the road, a turn in the road opens onto a vast panoramic view of the Pacific Ocean. From there, Chain of Craters Road descends quickly to sea level, ending at a natural roadblock, where lava covered the coastal part of the road in 1986. Turn around at **Hōlei Sea Arch.** Take the short walk to the cliff's edge to view the sheer drop-off to the crashing waves.

Hilina Pali Road

Turn off Chain of Craters Road onto the 11-mile, one-lane Hilina Pali Road to reach **Hilina Pali Overlook.** The views from this vantage point are expansive—extending over the 2,000-foot cliff and down to the vast Pacific. From here, you can take the Ka'ū Desert Trail. This less-traveled 4.8-mile wilderness trail, in one of the park's most remote areas, skirts the rim of Hilina Pali, offering panoramic ocean views.

The trail is distinctive for the wide, black *pāhoehoe* lava flows through which it crosses. This is a transition

Hiking in Kīlauea Iki Crater

area where water flows in during heavy rains, creating erosion gullies and rivers.

Plants such as Pele's hair and Pele's tears, as well as ash, mineral rock, and lava terrain add up to a remarkable tableau as unforgettable as the panoramic views down to the unusual ash dunes near the coast.

Coastal Trails

There are more than 32 miles of Pacific coastline in Hawai'i Volcanoes National Park, with more than 20 miles of well-marked trails on or near the water. The trails can be accessed from several points, including Hilina Pali Overlook; the **Mau Loa o Mauna Ulu** pullout on the Chain of Craters Road; and the **Pu'u Loa** parking area, also off Chain of Craters Road.

From Hilina Pali Overlook, the 3.6-mile **Hilina Pali Trail** to **Ka'aha** is a favorite among park visitors. The trail leads down the mountainside via a switchback stone walkway built in the 1930s. The terrain flattens out and traverses a region used for bombing practice during World War II.

At Ka'aha, broad coastal views reveal numerous sea arches in what is one of the most pristine areas of the park.

From Ka'aha, you can continue along the Hilina Pali Trail for a 6-mile trek across a magnificent tabletop bluff and then back down to the ocean at **Halapē,** a favored destination of hearty wilderness hikers.

Though the hike to Halapē can be grueling, the payoff is a small sandy beach where a tent can be pitched (permit required) under palm trees next to the ocean, where rare and endangered Hawaiian hawksbill turtles nest.

The **Puna Coast Trail** between the Halapē campsite and the **Pu'u Loa** trailhead is just over 11 miles; it can be hot many months of the year. The hike leads past **'Āpua Point,** where the ocean is accessible (albeit dangerous: rip tides are common and swimming not recommended), and through vast lava fields.

Across Chain of Craters Road from the Puna Coast Trailhead is the more popular 1-mile **Pu'u Loa Petroglyph Trail,** which leads to tens of thousands of ancient Hawaiian rock carvings. It is the largest petroglyph field in Hawai'i.

Another fascinating, moderately strenuous hike accessed from Chain of Craters Road leads into the **Mauna Ulu** eruption (1969–1974) area. The **Nāpau Trail** is a two- to three-hour round-trip.

Be sure to pick up the trail guide that tells the story of one of the most spectacular eruptions in recent memory, described by eyewitness volcanologist Wendell Duffield as "the thrill of a lifetime. The roar of a lava fountain imitates the sound of a full-throttle jet engine in a commercial jetliner. The ground shakes in constant tremor in a primeval form of deep-bass music created by molten rock surging through its tubular eruption pipe on a path to the surface."

Mauna Loa Summit

The higher elevations of the park are far less user-friendly and should only be attempted by experienced hikers in extremely good physical condition. It's more mountaineering than hiking. Conditions can change rapidly near the summit of Mauna Loa, and you have to be ready to bivouac overnight in the wilderness in freezing temperatures and whiteout conditions.

Kīlauea Volcano Drama

Kīlauea Volcano's destructive side became national news in the latter half of 2014. Lava flow from an eruptive vent in Pu'u O'o (outside park boundaries) overran parts of Pāhoa, an old sugar plantation town of about 1,000 residents on the southwest side of the volcano. Homes, businesses, and the town's main highway were threatened. Fearing that access to the rest of the island would be cut off if the lava crossed the highway, authorities set up an emergency evacuation route through Hawai'i Volcanoes National Park utilizing the historic Chain of Craters Road. (Opened in 1965, parts of Chain of Craters Road, including 8.5 miles of the scenic coast, had been covered and blocked by lava for 37 years of its 49-year existence.)

The 2014 flow wasn't the first time lava had affected residential communities near the park. A previous flow (1986–1992) destroyed homes in Kalapana, a community 10 miles from Pāhoa. In 2010–2011, lava returned to Kalapana and took additional homes, some of which had been rebuilt on top of the earlier flow.

"There's nothing like it," said a resident who was building on top of the lava. "It's the newest land on Earth." He continued, "We are all at the mercy of Madame Pele," referring to the volcano's resident fire goddess. "And she clearly has her own way of doing things."

But for those prepared to attain the 13,677-foot-high summit there are rich rewards. The views on a clear day can stretch across the island to sister volcano Mauna Kea (a few feet taller, at 13,803 feet), down to the Kona coast and the Pacific Ocean, and into **Moku'āweoweo Caldera**.

The **Mauna Loa Trail** begins at the Mauna Loa Lookout, a 13.5-mile drive from Hawaii 11 (roughly 15 miles from the Kīlauea Visitor Center), at an elevation of 6,662 feet.

From the lookout, a 7.5-mile trail ascends 3,400 feet through sub-alpine scrubland and above tree line to **Red Hill Cabin,** with eight bunks (permit required), pit toilets, and a water-catchment tank. Plan on carrying in drinking water.

The trek from Red Hill Cabin to the summit is arduous, and fascinating for its tale of recent geologic history. The trail leads past 1880, 1899, 1942, 1975, and 1984 lava flows. The terrain is a series of fissures leading through the rift zone. There are lava cones where ramparts with lava splatters are seen, and a series of false summits before the real one.

Mauna Loa Cabin is located on the crater rim, a rugged 11.6-mile ascent from Red Hill Cabin. Stays are limited to three nights per cabin site (permit required).

A 4.7-mile trail leads from Mauna Loa Cabin around the rim of Moku'āweoweo Caldera, to the true summit, with evidence of Mauna Loa's most recent eruption (three weeks in 1984) clearly visible.

Linger here a while, as it is a memorable accomplishment to arrive at one of the truly grand views in the Pacific.

Kilauea Visitor Center

Information

How to Get There

From Hilo, drive 30 miles southwest on Hawaii 11 (45 minutes). From Kailua-Kona, drive 96 miles south on Hawaii 11 (2- to 2.5-hour drive).

When to Go

The park is open year-round. Summer is typically the busiest season, although some of the lower elevation hikes across lava (Ka'ū Desert Trail, for example) can be hot and dry in summer months. Winter weather can be chilly and wet at mid-level and higher elevations. At the higher elevations of Mauna Loa, blizzards, high winds, and whiteouts are not uncommon any time of year.

Visitor Center & Museum

Kīlauea Visitor Center is just inside the park's main entrance; Jaggar Museum is 3 miles farther along on Crater Rim Drive. Both are open year-round.

Headquarters

1 Crater Rim Drive
Hawai'i Volcanoes
National Park, HI 96718
nps.gov/havo
808-985-6000

Camping

Operated by concessioner Volcano House (*hawaiivolcanohouse.com;* 808-756-9625), Nāmakanipaio is a drive-in campground (12 sites and 10 cabins) with restrooms, water, picnic tables, and barbecue pits; Kulanaokuaiki (8 sites) is a walk-in camping area, available on a first-come, first-served basis.

Lodging

Historic Volcano House (*hawaiivolcano house.com;* 808-756-9625), built in 1846, is across Crater Rim Drive from park headquarters. For places to stay outside the park visit: *gohawaii.com/en/big-island.*

Joshua Tree

California

Established
October 31, 1994

794,000 acres

The signature spiny tree with the upturned branches accounts for the park's name, but the enduring appeal of Joshua Tree National Park derives from its wide-open desert spaces spiced with arid mountain ranges and fantastic boulder formations. The transition from high Mojave Desert to low Colorado desert and echoes of tough old desert prospectors add to the park's fascinations.

Joshua Tree almost immediately dispels the notion that a desert is an austere, monochromatic place. Abundance prevails here, not only in terms of surprisingly dense and varied vegetation, but also in the textures of the landscape. Every view in every direction in the park takes in at least one rugged mountain range or a massive pile of stacked boulders, to the delight of rock climbers from all over the world.

As for vegetation, Joshua trees dominate the higher elevations (between 2,500 and 4,000 feet) of the park's northern half. But desert life is extremely sensitive to elevation change. When you drop in elevation,

Joshua trees etched against the sky at sunset

and low desert. A swing from west to east along **Park Boulevard** serves up an excellent cross-section of the park. Adding time for Pinto Basin Road to the south spotlights the transition from Mojave to Colorado Desert. Note: The park has no gas or food.

Park Boulevard West

First-time visitors should consider approaching via the town of Joshua Tree and the park's West Entrance. Here Park Boulevard threads through a landscape that is classic high Mojave desert, replete with forests of Joshua trees. This approach ensures some time in **Hidden Valley,** where a 1-mile nature trail leaves from a picnic area and winds among towering boulders; watch for rock climbers belaying one another on formations such as Sports Challenge and Hidden Tower. Interpretive signs point out the variety of cactus, shrubs, and trees. All the while, you can imagine this secluded enclave as the hideout of cattle and horse rustlers who used the valley to stash and rebrand their ill-gotten charges.

A half mile down Barker Dam Road from Park Boulevard and Hidden Valley are the entrances to **Keys Ranch** and **Barker Dam.** Both manifest the legacy of Bill Keys, who mastered the art of thriving in the harsh desert environment—from 1907 to 1969. With reservations, you can tour Keys Ranch and see how he managed to tend and water crops and fruit orchards and provide for a family of nine. Even if you miss the tour, you can take the 1.1-mile loop walk to Barker Dam, one of Keys's chief water sources. Following winter or summer rains, a lake backs up behind the dam and provides the

creosote bushes and Mojave yuccas steal the show. Enter or cross a wash and suddenly you're amid smoke trees and palo verde. Native fan palms rise high in desert oases. Whimsical plants like ocotillo and cholla cactus also vie for attention, and wildflowers put on a dazzling show in spring—and occasionally in fall, after summer thunderstorms. Little wonder that early park advocates wanted to call it Desert Plants National Park.

► HOW TO VISIT

It's possible to drive all of Joshua Tree's paved roads in a single, hurried day, but if possible, allow at least a couple of days in the park to appreciate the distinct character of both high

Wild, Wild Life

From bighorn sheep to rattlesnakes to 250 bird species, wildlife thrive in Joshua Tree. Unlike other parks, there's no sure-bet location for spotting creatures in Joshua Tree. The trick is to be alert everywhere, and to be outside early in the morning and toward sunset, when most wildlife are most active.

Desert tortoises have lived in the Mojave for thousands of years, but their numbers have been declining, and they're now considered a threatened species. They spend 95 percent of their lives underground; still you might spot one of these vegetarians snacking on grasses or wildflowers.

Visitors may or may not see a coyote, though those who are in the park toward sunset or camping overnight are likely to hear them vocalizing—an eerie and thrilling part of the desert soundtrack. Their yips and howls are ways of communicating with one another, especially as they hunt.

Bighorn sheep are the size of small deer. Males bear the huge, trademark curving horns; females have much smaller horns. They tend to stick to rocky hills and mountains where they forage on plants. You might spot them near water sources such as Barker Dam, Cottonwood Spring, or 49 Palms Oasis.

Finally, a creature you'll prefer not to see or hear is the rattlesnake. The park has seven species of rattlers, all with triangular heads and rattles on the ends of their tails. They are most likely to be out at night or when the weather is mild. If you happen to see or hear one—there's no mistaking the sizzling sound of the rattle—just back away or give it a very wide berth.

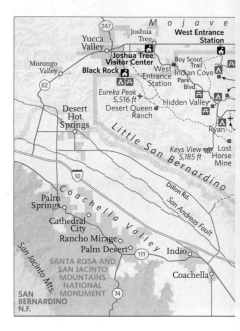

unlikely spectacle of shorebirds wading in the middle of the Mojave. On the same walk is an overhanging boulder decorated with native petroglyphs that are just a bit too vivid—they were shamefully "enhanced" by a Hollywood film crew in the early 1960s. The original work was either Serrano or Chemehuevi; no one is certain. Also from the Barker Dam parking area, a 1.1-mile trail leads to **Wall Street Mill,** a stamp mill built by Keys to process ore from his Desert Queen Mine. Here ghostly ruins can be inspected up close, including old utility trucks slowly decaying in the desert sand.

A couple of miles south of Hidden Valley is the **Ryan** area and the intersection with Keys View Road. A 5-mile side trip leads to **Keys View,** where views stretch to Mount San Jacinto (10,500 feet) rising above the low-desert Coachella Valley. On the way to

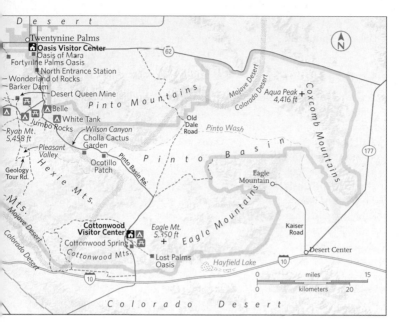

Keys View is **Lost Horse Valley,** probably the densest stand of Joshua trees in the park.

Back on Park Boulevard, adjacent to **Ryan Campground,** take the 0.5-mile walk to the impressive adobe ruins of **Ryan Ranch,** homesteaded by Jep and Tom Ryan in the 1890s. A bit farther along, just after Park Boulevard. swings east, is the 5,461-foot summit that bears their name. A 1.5-mile trail climbs to the top of **Ryan Mountain** and serves up a glorious view of all of Joshua Tree.

Park Boulevard Central

Between Ryan Mountain and Pinto Basin Road, a 9-mile stretch of Park Boulevard connects a string of sights including favorite rock-climbing spots such as **Hall of Horrors** and **Oyster Bar.** About 5 miles from Ryan

Mountain, a side trip down **Geology Tour Road**, an 18-mile round-trip, takes sights, from washes to dry lakes to granite boulders, that represent the full variety of desert geology. High clearance and four-wheel-drive are required to make the full drive. Just across Park Boulevard is a 1-mile side trip to **Desert Queen Mine**. A half-mile walk from the trailhead leads to a lookout above the ruins and mine shafts of Mojave's most productive and longest-running mine.

Back on Park Boulevard, **Jumbo Rocks** is another renowned climbing site, and a favored campground as well, where sites are framed by towering boulders. About 0.5 miles farther along, **Skull Rock** stands just beside the road—shaded indentations in a giant boulder make it look like a giant, sunbaked granite cranium. Less than a mile beyond, Skull Rock forms the intersection of two popular picnic areas—**Live Oak** and **Split Rock.**

Pinto Basin Road

At the intersection of Park Boulevard and Pinto Basin Road, known as Pinto Wye, you can exit the park to the north or venture south to experience the transition from high Mojave Desert to low Colorado Desert. Park Boulevard leads 8 miles north to the **Oasis Visitor Center** and the **Oasis of Mara**, where palm trees signify the site of an old Serrano Indian settlement.

Pinto Basin Road leads south from Pinto Wye, dropping down to the Colorado Desert en route to the Cottonwood Visitor Center. The road passes by two of the park's smaller campgrounds—Belle (18 sites) and White Tank (15 sites). From White Tank, a 0.3-mile loop walk leads to **Arch Rock.** The granite arch spans about 35 feet and rises 15 feet high. From White Tank the road descends about 2,000 feet into the broad **Pinto Basin,** dominated by seemingly endless expanses of creosote.

As you make the transition into the Colorado Desert, framed by the **Pinto Mountains** to the east and the **Hexie Mountains** to the west, it feels even more wild and remote than the more lush high desert. Along the way, two stops showcase some of the park's more unusual plants. In the **Cholla Cactus Garden** (10 miles from Pinto Wye), a trail winds amid a wide expanse of cholla, a cactus that looks more fuzzy than spiny, but it's assuredly a look-but-don't-touch plant. One mile south is **Ocotillo Patch.** The tall, spindly plant is one of the signatures of the Colorado Desert. Its

lanky stems rise some 12 feet high. When moisture is available, ocotillo produce green leaves and sprout orange-red flowers.

Thirty miles south of Pinto Wye is the **Cottonwood Visitor Center,** a campground, and the trailhead for a short walk into **Cottonwood Spring Oasis**. You may or may not see water seeping from the spring, but you'll see evidence of its presence—notably the tall fan-palm and cottonwood trees, which are often filled with songbirds. Like any water source in the desert, these springs attract wildlife, so approach quietly and you might spot a bighorn sheep or a coyote grabbing a drink.

South of Cottonwood, Pinto Basin Road cuts through **Cottonwood Canyon,** an area frequented by bighorn sheep. The road flirts with a broad, sandy wash whose dominant plant is the distinctive smoke tree, a Colorado Desert denizen whose branches look like puffs of smoke. Seven miles south of Cottonwood, the road exits the park and joins I-10.

Black Rock & Indian Cove

Two areas of the park accessed from the north via Calif. 62 are not connected by road with the rest of the park. In the northwest part of Joshua Tree is **Black Rock**, a favorite with hikers for its access to trails in the high, rocky hills above the campground. **Indian Cove** is in the north-central part of Joshua Tree, where campsites are situated on the edge of a vast maze of boulders known as the **Wonderland of Rocks**. The boulder piles stretch several miles south, clear to the Barker Dam area near Hidden Valley.

Key Ranch

Information

How to Get There

To enter Joshua Tree's high-desert north, take Calif. 62 west from Palm Springs to park entrances in Yucca Valley (28 miles), Joshua Tree (35 miles), or Twentynine Palms (48 miles). To enter from the south, take I-10 to Cottonwood Springs Rd., 50 miles from Palm Springs.

When to Go

The park is open year-round. Spring and fall are the most popular times to visit. Spring is particularly nice: Rainy winters bring out showy displays of wildflowers. Winters can be pleasant though chilly. Summers are very hot, and thunderstorms are occasionally fierce.

Visitor Centers & Nature Center

Oasis Visitor Center at headquarters is three blocks south of Calif. 62 on Utah Trail in Twentynine Palms; **Joshua Tree Visitor Center,** just south of Calif. 62 on Park Blvd. in Joshua Tree; **Cottonwood Visitor Center,** 6 miles north of I-10; **Black Rock Nature Center** is adjacent to the campground in Yucca Valley.

Headquarters

74485 National Park Dr.
Twentynine Palms, CA 92277
nps.gov/jotr
760-367-5500

Camping

The park has eight campgrounds (401 sites). Most camping is first come, first served, but sites at **Black Rock** and **Indian Cove** can be reserved Oct.–May *(recreation.gov;* 877-444-6777).

Lodging

There is no lodging inside the park. Motels and inns can be found in the towns of **Yucca Valley** *(yuccavalley.org),* **Joshua Tree** *(joshuatreechamber.org),* and **Twentynine Palms** *(29chamber.org).*

Safety

Temperatures can be extreme—hot summer days and cold winter nights. Beyond visitor centers, water is available only at park campgrounds. Carry at least a gallon of water per person per day.

Pinnacles

California

Established
January 10, 2013

27,214 acres

Pinnacles—America's newest national park—is a geologic playground, a rumpled volcanic landscape of protruding lava spires, massive rocky bastions, and crenellated cliffs interlaced with dense, woody chaparral and woodlands of oak and pine. Located in west-central California, in the Gabilan Range (part of the Coast Range), Pinnacles National Park offers 32 miles of hiking trails and an impressive roster of fauna (there are more than 500 species of moths in the park alone).

According to geologists, the jutting volcanic spires that make Pinnacles so uniquely picturesque originated some 23 million years ago in the Neenach Formation of volcanoes and lava flows near present-day Lancaster, California, 195 miles southeast of the park. Formidable tectonic pressures slowly, over millennia, moved part of the Neenach Formation northwest along the San Andreas Fault to the park's current location. The inexorable forces of water and wind erosion helped sculpt today's awe-inspiring geologic display. The story, however, is far from over. Geologists estimate that

The park's namesakes are the eroded leftovers of an extinct volcano.

plants and animals. Large mammals—mountain lions (elusive and rarely seen), gray foxes, and bobcats—abide along with black-tailed deer, rabbits, songbirds, raptors, and the distinctive California condor. Eight lizard and 13 snake species (including rattlers) also call Pinnacles home. If you stay late, watch and listen for bats: 14 species of bats fly the night sky. The greatest diversity of wildlife, though, is found among smaller species, with 40 species of dragonflies; 70 of butterflies; 400 of bees; and 500+ of moths. Some 80 percent of the park is chaparral—dense, low-growing vegetation that blankets the more arid parts of the park.

Along streambeds and in moister areas, valley oaks, sycamores, cottonwoods, and buckeyes provide welcome shade. And, in spring, plenty of wildflowers splash color across the landscape: goldfields, bush lupine, poppies, paintbrush, and sticky monkeyflower, among others.

Pinnacles is moving northwest along the San Andreas Fault—in the direction of San Francisco—at an average of two inches a year.

The haunting beauty of this region spurred early conservationists—particularly local homesteader Schuyler Hain—to propose protection for the area in the 1890s and early 1900s. President Theodore Roosevelt designated Pinnacles a national monument on January 16, 1908, protecting 2,060 acres of the region's most prominent volcanic formations.

Over the years the monument expanded as new acreage was added. By the time Pinnacles National Park was established, nearly half its acreage was designated Wilderness.

Pinnacles is a wonderland of wild

► HOW TO VISIT

A reality of visiting Pinnacles is that there is an entrance on the east side of the park and one on the west, but the roads do not connect. The drive from one side to the other requires a 90-minute trip outside the park.

Most visitors come primarily to hike or climb. Park officials caution that the rocks are primarily volcanic rhyolite and tuff, which are often soft and crumbly. Check on conditions with a ranger before climbing.

Both the **East Entrance** and the **West Entrance** offer multiple opportunities for easy to strenuous hikes, for exploring talus caves, and for rock

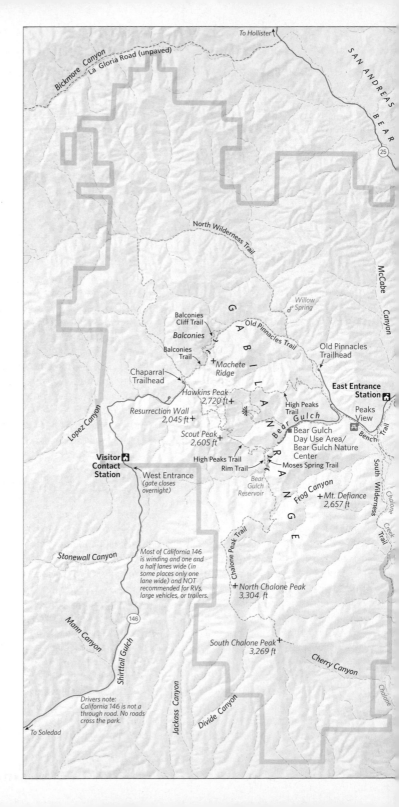

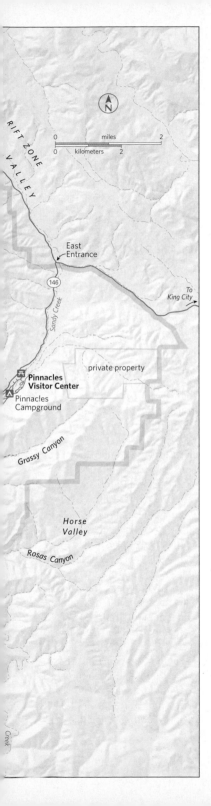

climbing, wildflower spotting, wildlife watching, and night-sky viewing. A note of caution: Pinnacles is in an arid climate and, particularly in summer, can be very hot (over 100°F) and dry. And temperatures can swing more than 50 degrees in a given 24-hour period.

East Entrance

The East Entrance to Pinnacles is one of the two park gateways that offer access to hiking trails. About 2 miles into the park, stop at the **Pinnacles Visitor Center** to view exhibits, find park information, and discuss hikes with a ranger. Limited supplies—including drinking water—are available here. The only campground in the park, Pinnacles Campground, is near the visitor center, and a picnic area is close by.

The moderately easy **Bench Trail** winds from the campground along Chalone and Bear Creeks. **Bench Trail**—dotted with California poppies in spring—provides access to numerous other trails, including the moderate 6.5-mile round-trip **South Wilderness Trail,** which branches off from the Bench Trail. Watch for a trail marker on the right, about a quarter mile from the campground.

Continue driving for a couple of miles and turn left into the **Bear Gulch Day Use Area,** which includes park headquarters, trailheads, and the **Bear Gulch Nature Center.** Open seasonally, the nature center has a topographic relief map and displays about the park's natural features and history. The trailhead for the strenuous 5.3-mile **Condor Gulch-High Peaks Loop Trail** is located here. This trail

California Condors at Pinnacles

California condors—a species of vulture with nine-and-a-half-foot wingspans—today drift on thermals high above the Pinnacles rock formations. An endangered species, the California condor was all but extinct in the wild by the 1980s, when the California Condor Recovery Program was instituted.

In 2003, Pinnacles joined with the Ventana Wildlife Society as part of the program to reintroduce condors into the wild. "Pinnacles is part of the historic range of the California condor," explains Jennie Jones, a biologist with Pinnacles National Park, "so it made sense that we participate in the recovery program."

Today, park biologists monitor the 60 re-introduced condors in central California, tracking their daily activities, including nesting, by radio transmitters. Pinnacles is the only national park to manage a relief site.

"What we're doing here is meaningful," says Jones. "We're making great steps toward re-establishing an important endangered species." And visitors to Pinnacles can almost daily benefit from this program as they watch these magnificent birds soaring above the volcanic peaks.

takes hikers 1,500 feet into the **High Peaks,** the heart of Pinnacles.

About a quarter mile farther is a parking area for several trails. The moderate 2.2-mile **Moses Spring-Rim Trail Loop** winds through woodlands to views of rock formations. Off the Moses Spring Trail is one of the park's "caves," with a trail running through it. The **Bear Gulch Cave** is actually a talus cave, a narrow canyon that has filled in with rockfall; over time, flowing water has eroded a passage that hikers (with large flashlights or headlamps) can pass through. Check with a ranger before hiking here.

At the reservoir at the end of the Moses Spring Trail, the **Chalone Peak Trail** leads 3.3 miles to the top of **North Chalone Peak,** at 3,304 feet the highest point in the park.

West Entrance

The **Visitor Contact Station,** just inside the park boundary, has exhibits, rangers to help with planning, and an excellent brief video on the features and history of Pinnacles.

At the end of Calif. 146 is the **Chaparral Trailhead** parking area, access point for several trails. The moderate 2.4-mile clockwise **Balconies Cliffs–Balconies Cave Loop Trail** winds past a precipitous slab of rock called **Machete Ridge** and into the massive **Balconies Cliffs.** This russet-hued range soars above. The trail drops into a valley where the 0.4-mile **Balconies Cave Trail** meanders through another talus cave.

The strenuous 9.3-mile unmaintained **North Wilderness Trail** climbs among the ridgetops and descends to the **Old Pinnacles Trail,** which links to the **Balconies Trail** and back to the parking area. Finally the strenuous 4.3-mile **Juniper Canyon Trail** loops upward into the High Peaks range. In the springtime, the first half mile of this Juniper Canyon Trail is a riot of resplendent wildflowers, including yellow fiddlenecks.

Indian warrior (*Pedicularis densiflora*)

Information

How to Get There

To reach the East Entrance, follow Calif. 25 south from Hollister, CA, then turn west on Calif. 146. To reach the East Entrance from the south, follow Calif. 25 north and turn west on Calif. 146. For the West Entrance, head east on Calif. 146 from Soledad, CA. Calif. 46 is a steep, winding road that for much of the way is no wider than one and a half lanes. An automatic gate at the West Entrance opens at 7:30 a.m. and closes at 8:00 p.m.

When to Go

The park is open year-round. Mid-Feb.–early June is ideal: wildflowers are blooming, and the heat is not yet intense. Summer through early fall can be very hot and dry. Later fall brings colorful foliage. Weekends can be quite crowded.

Visitor Center & Visitor Contact Station

The **Pinnacles Visitor Center** at the East Entrance, open 9 a.m. to 5 p.m., has exhibits and a small bookstore.

The **West Side Visitor Contact Station** offers a short video on the park. Rangers are available at both the visitor center and contact center to provide information and help plan hikes.

Headquarters

5000 Highway 146
Paicines, CA 95043
nps.gov/pinn
831-389-4485

Camping

The park's only campground (149 sites; showers) is near the Pinnacles Visitor Center at the East Entrance. For reservations: *recreation.gov;* 877-444-6777.

Lodging

There is no lodging in the park. Places to stay can be found in **Soledad** (*ci.soledad .ca.us*) and **Hollister** (*hollister.ca.gov*) or in **Salinas** (*ci.salinas.ca.us*), a larger city with opportunities for visiting both sides of the park.

Sequoia & Kings Canyon

California

Sequoia
Established
September 25, 1890

Kings Canyon
Established
March 4, 1940

865,964 acres
(total)

The largest tree on earth (by volume). The highest mountain in the contiguous United States. One of the deepest canyons in North America. Some of the most remote wilderness in the Lower 48. It's all about grand scale in Sequoia & Kings Canyon National Parks—and yet these adjoining and jointly administered parks also offer a multitude of intimate natural treasures and experiences, in the backcountry as well as closer to the heart of things.

"Going to the woods is going home," wrote 19th-century naturalist and conservationist John Muir, and few woodlands were as important to him as his "giant forest" of sequoias—the epicenter of Sequoia National Park. Muir and many other like-minded thinkers, decried the wholesale logging of sequoias and other trees throughout the Sierra Nevada and fought to preserve them. Their efforts were rewarded when Sequoia was established as the nation's second national park. A week after this announcement, the amount of protected lands tripled with the addition of Grant Grove

Horses work the trail.

sequoia groves in the two parks, including the most visited, Giant Forest in Sequoia National Park and Grant Grove in Kings Canyon. These groves, particularly in the early morning and early evening when the crowds are thinner and the sunlight softer, evoke an aura of solemnity and majesty; people often refer to them as outdoor cathedrals. And the imposing height and girth of the sequoias themselves inspire an enduring sense of awe. Mixed in with the sequoia trees are white fir, sugar pine, yellow pine, and incense cedar.

► **HOW TO VISIT**

Visitors with limited time should certainly drive **Generals Highway,** making several short stops between the **Giant Forest** and **Grant Grove,** with some of the largest trees on Earth. Relatively easy hiking trails meander through these two sequoia groves and yield a sense of the grandeur of the mammoth trees.

Devoting two to four days will allow for a much fuller appreciation of the diversity of what Sequoia & Kings Canyon National Parks have to offer: a tour of sparkling **Crystal Cave;** a **Moro Rock** climb, with breathtaking views; a spellbinding drive along the **Kings Canyon Scenic Byway** into the canyon of the South Fork Kings River; and a steep, narrow, and winding drive up to the scenic **Mineral King** region of Sequoia National Park.

Generals Highway

From Calif. 198 via the **Ash Mountain Entrance,** drive the **Generals Highway** for approximately 50 miles

National Park—now part of Kings Canyon. Over the next century, the two parks expanded and now encompass more than 1,300 square miles. More than 93 percent of the parks are designated wilderness land.

More than 826 miles of hiking trails—including the Pacific Crest National Scenic Trail—penetrate the High Sierra, a wonderland for backpackers. Mount Whitney, at 14,494 feet the highest peak in the United States outside of Alaska, is a beloved destination.

Casual visitors and day hikers have ample opportunities to explore sequoia groves, marble caves, glacier-carved canyons, rampaging rivers, surging waterfalls, and much more. There are more than 30 distinct

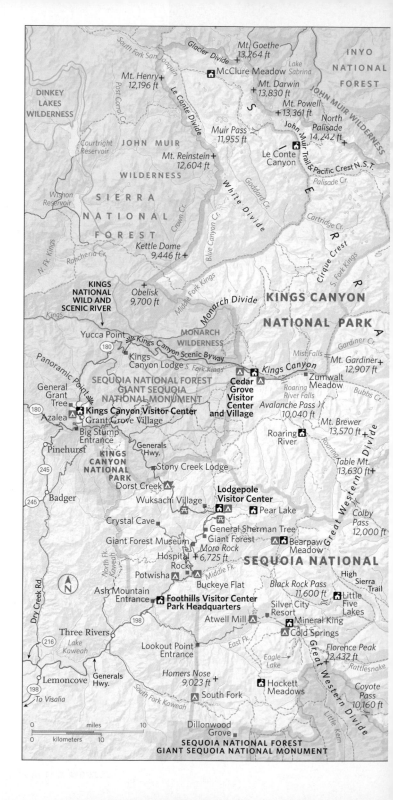

INYO NATIONAL FOREST

Glacier Divide

Mt. Goethe
13,264 ft

Lake Sabrina

McClure Meadow

Mt. Henry
12,196 ft

Mt. Darwin
13,830 ft

Le Conte Divide

Mt. Powell
13,361 ft

North Palisade
14,242 ft

JOHN MUIR WILDERNESS

Muir Pass
11,955 ft

John Muir Trail & Pacific Crest N.S.T.

Le Conte Canyon

Palisade Cr.

DINKEY LAKES WILDERNESS

Courtright Reservoir

Post Corral Cr.

JOHN MUIR

Mt. Reinstein
12,604 ft

White Divide

Goddard Cr.

S I E R R A

Wishon Reservoir

WILDERNESS

N. Fk. Kings

SIERRA

NATIONAL

Crown Cr.

Blue Canyon Cr.

Cartridge Cr.

Cirque Crest

S. Fork Kings

FOREST

Rancheria Cr.

Kettle Dome
9,446 ft

Kings

KINGS NATIONAL WILD AND SCENIC RIVER

Obelisk
9,700 ft

Middle Fork Kings

Monarch Divide

KINGS CANYON

NATIONAL PARK

Panoramic Point

Yucca Point

MONARCH WILDERNESS

180

Kings Canyon Scenic Byway

Kings Canyon Lodge

S. Fork Kings

Kings Canyon

Mist Falls

Gardiner Cr.

Mt. Gardiner
12,907 ft

Zumwalt Meadow

Bubbs Cr.

General Grant Tree

SEQUOIA NATIONAL FOREST GIANT SEQUOIA NATIONAL MONUMENT

Cedar Grove Visitor Center and Village

Roaring River Falls

Roaring River

180

Azalea

Kings Canyon Visitor Center

Grant Grove Village

Avalanche Pass
10,040 ft

Mt. Brewer
13,570 ft

Great Western Divide

Big Stump Entrance

Pinehurst

KINGS CANYON NATIONAL PARK

Generals Hwy.

Roaring River

Mt. Brewer
13,570 ft

Table Mt.
13,630 ft

245

Badger

Stony Creek Lodge

Colby Pass
12,000 ft

Dorst Creek

Wuksachi Village

Lodgepole Visitor Center

245

Pear Lake

Crystal Cave

General Sherman Tree

Giant Forest Museum

Giant Forest

Bearpaw Meadow

Dry Creek Rd.

Moro Rock

Hospital Rock

6,725 ft

SEQUOIA NATIONAL

N

North Fk. Kaweah

Middle Fk.

Potwisha

Buckeye Flat

Black Rock Pass
11,600 ft

High Sierra Trail

Little Five Lakes

Ash Mountain Entrance

Foothills Visitor Center Park Headquarters

Silver City Resort

Mineral King

Three Rivers

198

Atwell Mill

Cold Springs

216

Lake Kaweah

Lookout Point Entrance

East Fk.

Eagle Lake

Florence Peak
12,432 ft

Rattlesnake

Great Western Divide

Lemoncove

198

Generals Hwy.

Homers Nose
9,023 ft

Coyote Pass
10,160 ft

To Visalia

South Fork Kaweah

Hockett Meadows

Little Kern

0 miles 10
0 kilometers 10

Dillonwood Grove

South Fork

SEQUOIA NATIONAL FOREST GIANT SEQUOIA NATIONAL MONUMENT

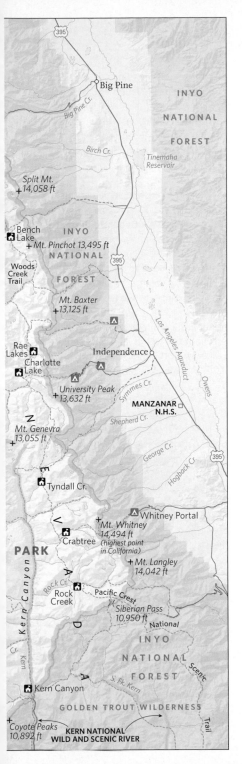

through the heart of the developed area of Sequoia & Kings Canyon National Parks. Just northeast of the entrance is the **Foothills Visitor Center,** with exhibits on the low-lying chaparral ecosystem of this part of the park. The Wilderness Office, where information and permits relating to overnight backpacking and camping can be obtained, is in a separate building nearby.

Six miles on, stop at **Hospital Rock** to see outdoor exhibits about Native Americans. Here, members of the Western Mono people lived from prehistoric times to the late 1800s. Their pictographs and bedrock mortars—hollowed-out depressions in the rock for grinding acorns into flour—can be seen here.

The twisting, switchbacking Generals Highway soon leads to the turnoff to **Crystal Cave,** which is open late May through fall, weather permitting. A tour of the cave must be planned in advance; tickets for the 45-minute tour can be purchased at either the **Foothills** or **Lodgepole Visitor Centers.**

Tour participants meet at the parking area, descend a steep half-mile paved path along a canyon wall, and enter the cave, which stays at a constant 50°F. The cave gets its name from its unique geology—it is formed of glistening marble (not the usual limestone of most caves), and the marble formations glimmer and reflect light in stunning displays.

The Generals Highway soon reaches the **Giant Forest** area. Stop at the excellent **Giant Forest Museum** to gain an overview of the sequoia ecosystem. The 1-mile paved **Big Trees Trail** departs from the museum and loops through a spectacular sequoia grove. For a unique perspective on the Giant Forest, climb **Moro Rock,** the road to which closes with snow.

The Mightiest of Trees

Sequoias grow only in one region in the world—on the west flank of the Sierra Nevada in California between 5,000 and 7,000 feet of elevation. There are 75 distinct groves in this region. Sequoias need gentle terrain and moist, not soggy, soil to flourish.

Though not the tallest of trees (coastal redwoods stake that claim), giant sequoias are the largest by volume and in many ways the most visually impressive. John Muir said that the sequoia "seems to be immortal," and indeed they can live to be more than 3,000 years of age. Their cinnamon-hued bark can be as thick as two and a half feet, a buffer that helps the trees resist fire. Tannin in the bark proves resistant to insects, and the heartwood resists rot.

Natural wildfire is an important aspect of the sequoia ecosystem. Fire clears out the underbrush around the base of the sequoias and allows sunshine in. The heat from wildfires prompts the opening of the green cones on the tree, allowing them to release the seeds; it also prepares the soil for the seeds, which are about the size of rolled oats.

For decades federal officials suppressed wildfires, thinking that by so doing they were protecting the groves. Today, in addition to managed natural wildfires, there are controlled burns to encourage the dispersal of sequoia seeds.

Moro Rock is a towering granite dome that juts to an elevation of 6,725 feet. Some 400 steps carved into the rock (along with occasional rest areas) lead to the top, with exceptional views of the surrounding woodlands and, on clear days, the Coast Range, some 100 miles west.

From the museum, drive to the parking area for the all-star of Sequoia National Park, the **General Sherman Tree,** named by an early rancher for General William Tecumseh Sherman. A short trail leads to this largest tree on Earth, by volume, and it is staggering in its immensity and presence. It soars 274.9 feet, and its circumference is 102.6 feet at its base. It is estimated to weigh 1,385 tons and be between 2,000 and 3,000 years old. After marveling at the General, take the easy 2-mile **Congress Trail** that meanders through the Giant Forest grove of sequoias.

Passing the turnoffs to the **Lodgepole Visitor Center** and **Wuksachi Village,** continue on Generals Highway for 27 miles to the **Grant Grove Village** in Kings Canyon National Park. Along the way, consider climbing **Little Baldy,** another granite dome. A steep 1.7–mile trail gets you to the top.

Just past the exhibit-filled **Kings Canyon Visitors Center,** follow the road on your left to the **General Grant Tree Trail,** an easy 0.33-mile paved loop that leads to the second largest tree, by volume, on Earth. It rises to a height of 268.1 feet and has a circumference of 107.5 feet at its base. Named for Ulysses S. Grant, the General Grant Tree was proclaimed the Nation's Christmas Tree on April 28, 1926, by President Calvin

Coolidge; an annual observation of this event takes place in December.

The **North Grove Loop Trail** weaves for a mile and a half through an impressive grove of sequoias interspersed with sugar pines and white fir. A poignant counterpoint to the majesty of the groves of thriving sequoias in Sequoia and Kings Canyon National Parks can be seen

Camping amid the sequoias on the floor of Kings Canyon

along **The Big Stump Trail,** south of Grant Grove, near the **Big Stump Entrance** on Calif. 180. This easy 1-mile trail takes hikers on a circuit that includes the enormous stumps of dozens of sequoia trees logged more than a century ago, including the massive **Mark Twain Stump,** which can be walked on. This trail is an eloquent reminder of what has been lost—but also what has been saved.

Kings Canyon Scenic Byway

From Grant Grove follow Calif. 180 north and then east for 36 miles into **Sequoia National Forest** and then back into Kings Canyon National Park. The Kings Canyon Scenic Byway, accessible only in summer, is aptly named. The scenic beauty of the canyon of the **South Fork Kings River** is truly breathtaking.

At **Yucca Point,** high above the river, a panorama of steep plunging canyon walls and the rushing South Fork awaits visitors. The byway then begins to wind precipitously down the mile-deep canyon to the river in the **Cedar Grove** area of Kings Canyon National Park. Here the terrain changes from a V-shaped, river-carved canyon to the flatter, gentler U-shape of a glacier-carved canyon.

Grassy meadows and woodlands of sugar pine, white fir, ponderosa pine, black oak, live oak, and incense cedar fill the valley, and the trees offer welcome shade. Past **Cedar Grove Village,** which includes a visitor center, lodge, snack bar, and market, stop at the **Roaring River Falls** for the short hike to view the waterfall. This cascade tumbles though a granite chute on its way to the South Fork Kings River. A short distance ahead, park at the **Zumwalt Meadow** trailhead and enjoy a mile or so stroll across the river on a suspension bridge and around grassy Zumwalt Meadow; massive granite walls that rival those found in Yosemite Valley soar a mile above the meadow.

Mineral King

Open only in summer, the narrow, winding 25-mile road to the Mineral King area of Sequoia National Park is a challenge for cars and pickup trucks; trailers and large RVs are not permitted. The road branches off Calif. 198 3 miles north of the town of Three Rivers, south of the Ash Mountain Entrance. A glacier-carved alpine valley with meadows and forests, Mineral King was added to the park in 1978; its name dates back to the 1870s, when prospectors hoped—incorrectly, it turned out—that there would be a treasure trove of gold and other precious ores in the ground here. Today, hikers and backpackers consider this land solid gold.

Various wilderness trails start from the valley, including some that lead into the High Sierra. Trail information and permits for overnight backpacking can be obtained at the **Mineral King Ranger Station.**

A popular trail for day-hikers is the 6.8-mile, moderately difficult **Eagle Lake Trail,** which begins at the Eagle-Mosquito parking area. It climbs first gently, then steeply to **Eagle Creek,** then on to the **Eagle Sinkholes,** where flowing water disappears into the Earth. Continue on to sparkling **Eagle Lake.**

Evening in Kearsarge Pass, Kings Canyon

Information

How to Get There

From Visalia, CA (about 40 miles south-west), take CA 198 to the Ash Mountain Entrance to Sequoia National Park, where the Generals Highway begins. From Fresno, CA (35 miles west), take CA 180 to the Big Stump Entrance to Kings Canyon National Park.

When to Go

Both parks offer year-round access. However, the Generals HIghway (the road between the parks) may close during the winter. The Kings Canyon Scenic Byway and the roads to Mineral King, Crystal Cave, and Moro Rock are closed in the winter. Summer is the busiest season, especially on weekends.

Visitor Centers and Museum

Sequoia: The **Foothills Visitor Center** near the Ash Mountain entrance is open year-round. The **Mineral King Ranger Station** is open summer and early fall. The **Lodgepole Visitor Center** is open year-round. The excellent **Giant Forest Museum** is open year-round.

Kings Canyon: The Kings Canyon Visitor Center in Grant Grove Village is open year-round. The Cedar Grove Visitor Center is open daily in summer.

Headquarters

47050 Generals Highway
Three Rivers, CA 93271
nps.gov/seki
559-565-3341

Camping

There are 14 campgrounds—with more than 2,000 campsites—in Sequoia & Kings Canyon National Parks. Permits are required for all wilderness trips.

Lodging

Sequoia: The **Wuksachi Lodge,** 2 miles north of the Lodgepole Visitors Center, has 102 rooms. **Kings Canyon:** The **Grant Grove Lodge** (9 cabins plus 40 tent cabins) and **John Muir Lodge** (36 rooms) are located in the Grant Grove area. The **Cedar Grove Lodge,** open summers only, has 18 rooms.

Yosemite

California

Established
October 1, 1890

747,956 acres

Grandeur. Nobility. Majesty. These are the sorts of words that spill from the lips of nearly every visitor to Yosemite National Park, for it truly is a realm of jaw-dropping beauty. Spectacular natural wonders abound. Granite monoliths and domes, towering sequoia groves, sweeping grassy meadows, plunging waterfalls, and rampaging creeks and rivers merge in one of America's most treasured parks.

" It is by far the grandest of all the special temples of Nature I was ever permitted to enter," naturalist and conservationist John Muir wrote of Yosemite. From the remote rocky crags of the High Sierra Nevada at the western perimeter of the park to the sinuous meanders of the placid Merced River in Yosemite Valley, Yosemite is a symphony of contrasts: the percussion of cascading waterfalls, the hum of breezes through cedar and pine, the thrum of a sudden rainfall. The abundant wildlife adds its own pageant of sound—the chattering of a western gray squirrel, the screech of a Steller's jay, the lonely howl of a coyote, the squeak of a tiny pika high in its rocky home.

Hiking up the granite to Half Dome

mountains and get their good tidings," encouraged John Muir.

The protection of Yosemite lands had its beginnings during the Civil War. On June 30, 1864, answering the vigorous campaign of early conservationists, President Abraham Lincoln signed into law a bill protecting Yosemite Valley and the Mariposa Grove of sequoias, granting their oversight to the state of California. Never before had a government set aside wilderness lands to be preserved forever.

In the late 1880s, John Muir and others spoke convincingly to protect more of the Yosemite region by establishing it as a national park—following the example of Yellowstone. In 1890, Congress set aside 1,500 square miles as Yosemite National Park; Yosemite Valley and the Mariposa Grove became part of the national park in 1906.

In addition to sounds, Yosemite is also a contrast of sights and experiences. On a busy summer weekend, as many as 20,000 visitors can throng Yosemite Valley, with resulting crowds, noise, and traffic jams. Just a mile or two along a trail, though, can place a hiker in welcome seclusion, with the opportunity to truly appreciate the park. But no matter how crowded, the park continues to serve up its treasures. Sights and sounds remain thrilling no matter how many people are experiencing them. But no matter what the time of year, you can pretty well depend on having sunrise all to yourself.

An overnight or weeklong backpacking trip into the high country can be transformational. "Climb the

▶ HOW TO VISIT

Yosemite is extensive. A one-day tour of Yosemite Valley reveals exceptional natural beauty and geology but shortchanges visitors when it comes to the diverse nature of the park. An itinerary of three to four days gives you a chance to visit more than just the high points.

In addition to a day's hiking and sightseeing in **Yosemite Valley,** a one-day drive to the inspiring vistas of **Glacier Point,** on the way to the **Wawona** area and **Mariposa Grove** of sequoias, adds dimension to your visit as does a one-day drive along the **Tioga Road** to **Tuolumne Meadows,** high in the Sierra. Drive to **Hetch Hetchy** to see a canyon that once rivaled Yosemite Valley.

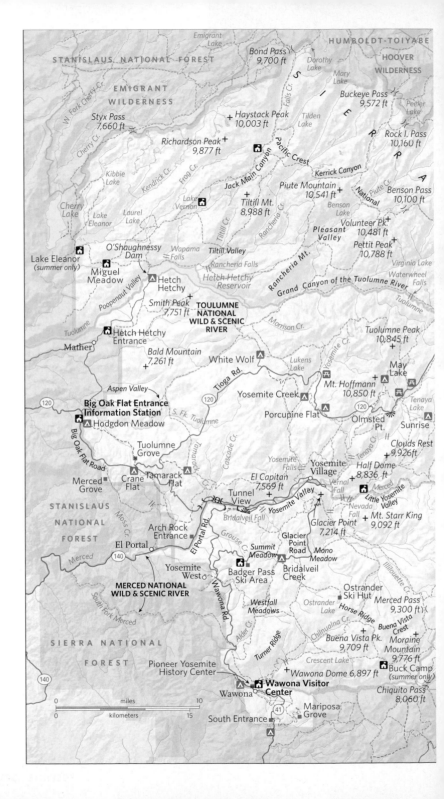

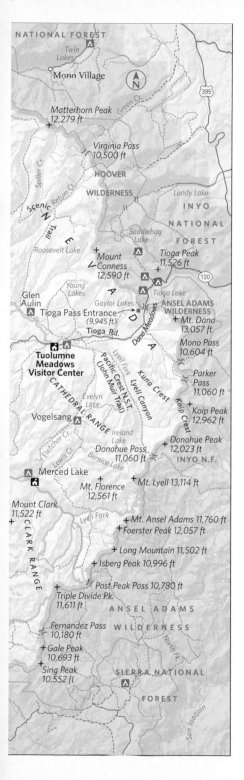

Yosemite Valley

Some four million visitors come to Yosemite each year, and virtually all spend at least a day in Yosemite Valley. It can be extremely crowded, especially in summer. Instead of driving, consider taking the free Yosemite Valley shuttle bus that winds through the eastern part of the Valley and has 19 stops at which visitors can disembark to appreciate various attractions. Another option is to walk or bike—the mostly flat, 13-mile **Valley Loop Trail** snakes through the entire valley and gives hikers the time to appreciate the myriad wonders of Yosemite.

A good starting point is the **Valley Visitor Center** (shuttle stops 5 and 9), which offers exhibits as well as an award-winning film on the history and geology of the park, shown in a widescreen theater.

The visitor center is part of **Yosemite Village,** where you'll find shops as well as the **Yosemite Museum** and the **Indian Cultural Exhibit,** which interprets the cultural history of the Miwok and Paiute peoples of Yosemite region. The **Ansel Adams Gallery** pays tribute to the renowned Yosemite photographer and has prints for sale.

Permits for backcountry wilderness excursions can be obtained during the summer at the nearby **Wilderness Center.**

To escape the bustle of Yosemite Village, take an easy 1-mile hike into quiet **Cook's Meadow,** just south of the visitor center. The loop runs through a lush meadow along the Merced River and offers views of Glacier Point, Half Dome, Sentinel Rock, and Yosemite Falls.

The trailhead to **Lower Yosemite**

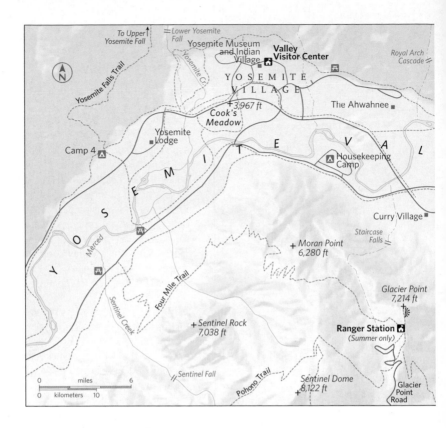

Fall (shuttle stop 6) is about a mile west of the Village. The 0.5-mile trail brings visitors to the misty base of the Lower Fall, which, along with the upper and middle falls, forms **Yosemite Falls,** at 2,425 feet the highest waterfall in North America—and the fifth highest in the world. The strenuous 3.6-mile hike to **Upper Yosemite Fall** (trailhead near shuttle stop 7) offers sweeping views of Yosemite Valley.

Farther west, linger in the meadow near the base of the soaring rock edifice of **El Capitan,** one of the largest granite monoliths in the world. Its vertical wall rises 3,593 feet above the valley floor and is a destination revered by rock climbers. Ascents of "El Cap" may take several days;

climbers sleep in slings. On the southwest side of the valley, the short trail from the parking area to **Bridalveil Fall** rewards hikers with views of this wispy 620-foot waterfall.

Heading east along the gently flowing **Merced River,** vistas of **Half Dome** materialize through the trees. This natural monument, its vertical north wall scraped flat by glaciers, is one of the hallmarks of Yosemite.

The climb up 8,836-foot Half Dome (trailhead at shuttle stop 16) is an extremely strenuous 17-mile undertaking that should only be entertained by serious hikers in excellent condition. The same trail, though, leads first to the top of **Vernal Fall** (a strenuous 3-mile round-trip) and then to the top

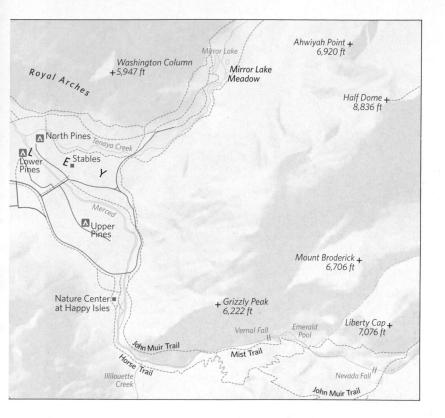

of **Nevada Fall** (a strenuous 7-mile round-trip).

Easier hiking, off to the right of the trailhead, brings visitors to the **Nature Center at Happy Isles** (open in summer), with exhibits and nature trails. Happy Isles is the northern terminus of the 210.4-mile **John Muir Trail,** which begins at the top of Mount Whitney in Sequoia National Park (p. 362) and traverses the most rugged sections of the High Sierra. Construction of the trail was begun in 1915, the year after Muir's death; it wasn't completed until 1938.

An easy 1-mile hike from shuttle stop 17 leads to **Mirror Lake,** which reflects massive Half Dome. Circling back to Yosemite Village on the shuttle, look up on the north wall of the valley to see the **Royal Arches,** glacier-carved granite vaults.

Glacier Point & Mariposa Grove

Leaving Yosemite Valley on the Wawona Road (Calif. 41), stop at the **Tunnel View** turnout for the classic vista of the valley, from El Capitan to Half Dome and beyond—one of the most photographed scenes on Earth. Beyond the tunnel, drive about 7 miles to a left turn onto **Glacier Point Road**.

The 16-mile road twists and turns through deep forests of pine and fir. At the **Sentinel Dome** parking area, a

El Capitan

moderate 1-mile trail leads to the top of Sentinel Dome, which commands a view second only to Half Dome. Along the way are the gnarled remains of a Jeffrey pine. Continue east to the large parking area at **Glacier Point,** one of Yosemite's must-see wonders.

Here are spellbinding views of the High Sierra to the north and east as well as the entire sweep of Yosemite Valley. You can see the granite parapets of El Capitan and Half Dome; Yosemite, Vernal, and Nevada Falls; and sparkling Mirror Lake—all from a bird's-eye vantage point 3,214 feet above the valley.

Back below, continue approximately 12 miles on Calif. 41 to the

Quite a Camping Trip

Perhaps the most significant camping trip in the history of American conservation took place in May 1903. President Theodore Roosevelt, already predisposed to the ideas of preservation, once proclaimed, "We are not building this country of ours for a day. It is to last through the ages." Roosevelt wanted to meet with John Muir to better understand the wilderness needs of the West. He wrote to Muir, "I want to drop politics absolutely for four days, and just be out in the open with you."

Muir showed the President Yosemite Valley, the stunning vistas from Glacier Point, and took him camping under the sequoias in Mariposa Grove. They grilled steaks over an open fire, slept out under the stars, and spoke at length of their experiences exploring nature and the challenges facing the West. "I stuffed him pretty well regarding the timber thieves, and the destructive work of the lumbermen, and other spoilers of the forests," recalled Muir. On the fourth night, a storm dumped four inches of snow on their sleeping bags. "This is bullier yet!" exclaimed Roosevelt, and Muir knew that he had found a President who truly appreciated nature and could grasp the big picture. Indeed, Roosevelt was instrumental in convincing California to cede Yosemite Valley and the Mariposa Grove to Yosemite National Park in 1906. And during his administration, he created 5 national parks, 23 national monuments, 55 wildlife preserves, and 150 national forests. That's quite a legacy for a four-day camping trip.

Wawona area, with its Victorian-style hotel and dining room, a golf course, tennis courts, and pool. Nearby is the **Pioneer Yosemite History Center,** where historic buildings remind visitors of Yosemite's cultural past; in summer, costumed interpreters portray historic characters from more than a century ago.

From Wawona, a 5-mile drive ends at the **Mariposa Grove** of sequoias—the first such grove to be protected from timbering. What you find here are some of the tallest living things on Earth. Parking is minimal, so taking a free shuttle bus from Wawona may be a desirable option.

Approximately 500 mature sequoias thrive in Mariposa Grove, including the largest, the **Grizzly Giant,** which towers 209 feet tall and has a 96.5-foot circumference at its base. The **Fallen Monarch** sequoia most likely was blown down by high winds. The **Wawona Tunnel Tree,** however, was done in by man—its massive trunk was hollowed out in 1881 so wagons, and later automobiles, could drive through and pause for photographs. The tree fell in 1969.

Tioga Road & Tuolumne Meadows

Follow the Big Oak Flat Road out of Yosemite Valley and at **Crane Flat** (gas available) take the **Tioga Road,** Calif. 120, east toward Tuolumne Meadows (possibly closed mid-November to late May, depending on weather).

For nearly 50 miles, the road winds higher and higher through subalpine and alpine terrain. Stop at **Olmsted Point** for a stunning view: the back of Half Dome and a sea of other granite formations. At **Tenaya Lake,** take the flat 2.5-mile loop trail around the lake; surrounding peaks are reflected in this serene high country lake at 8,149 feet of elevation.

In spring, **Tuolumne Meadows** is bedecked with snowbanks, meandering streams formed by snowmelt, and brown sodden grasses. By midsummer, though, it has become a wonderland of green grasses, alpine wildflowers (including marsh marigolds, monkeyflowers, and Indian paintbrush), and jutting granite spires. Backpackers, day hikers, and rock climbers from around the world fill the meadows.

A 2-mile trail to the top of **Lembert Dome** offers sweeping vistas of the meadows. The **John Muir Trail** and the **Pacific Crest National Scenic Trail** (which follows the route of the John Muir Trail, 210 miles from Sequoia National Park) enter Tuolumne Meadows through grassy **Lyell Canyon.** Some visitors enjoy hiking just a few miles of these famous trails. The Pacific Crest Trail continues north toward the Grand Canyon of the Tuolumne River on its way to Canada. A few miles farther east on the Tioga Road is **Tioga Pass,** the east entrance to Yosemite, and at 9,945 feet, the highest automobile pass in California.

Hetch Hetchy

About 40 miles north of Yosemite Valley lies Hetch Hetchy, a valley to rival the beauty of Yosemite. John Muir called it "a grand landscape garden, one of Nature's rarest and most precious mountain temples," and he noted that it is "a wonderfully exact counterpart of the great Yosemite."

As early as 1882, Hetch Hetchy had been looked at as the possible site for a dam and reservoir to supply drinking water and electric power to the San Francisco area.

For decades dam proponents and conservationists, led eloquently by Muir, hotly debated the reservoir, but finally Congress passed the Ryker Act in 1913 authorizing the construction of the dam. The loss demoralized Muir, and some think helped contribute to his demise and death the following year.

To reach Hetch Hetchy, take Calif. 120 from **Crane Flat** to the **Big Oak Flat** park entrance. Just outside the park, take a right on **Evergreen Road,** which winds through miles of charred trees, the result of the devastating August 2013 Rim Fire, which affected 250,000 acres of land in the national park.

Re-entering Yosemite National Park at the Hetch Hetchy Ranger Station (open year-round with varying hours), follow the **Hetch Hetchy Road** to the parking area for **O'Shaughnessy Dam,** which contains the 8-mile-long reservoir. Swimming and boating are not permitted. From atop the dam, visitors can look east to see granite domes, forested slopes, and mighty waterfalls—not unlike those of Yosemite Valley.

Gushing **Wapama Falls,** visible from the dam, is a moderate 2.5-mile hike. The **Laurel Lake/Lake Vernon/Rancheria Falls Loop,** a 29-mile wilderness trail, takes hikers to High Sierra lakes and beautiful views of the Hetch Hetchy region. Overnight backpacking permits for this and other longer wilderness trails are available at the ranger station.

Giant Sequoia, Mariposa Grove

Information

How to Get There

From Oakhurst (about 15 miles south) take Calif. 41 to the South Entrance. From Mariposa (about 25 miles west) take Calif. 140 to the Arch Rock Entrance. From Groveland (about 25 miles northwest) take Calif. 120 to the Big Oak Flat Entrance. From Lee Vining (about 10 miles east) take Calif. 120 to the Tioga Pass Entrance. The Yosemite Area Regional Transportation System (YARTS) offers bus service from Merced, Sonora, and Mammoth Lakes.

When to Go

Yosemite is open year-round, although the Glacier Point Road from Badger Pass Ski Area to Glacier Point and the Tioga Road to Tuolumne Meadows can be closed mid-Nov. to late May, depending on weather. In general, avoid holiday weekends and expect crowded conditions in Yosemite Valley during late spring, summer, and early fall. Winter can bring heavy snows to the high country and light to moderate snows at lower elevations.

Visitor Centers and Museums

The **Valley Visitor Center** is next to the **Yosemite Museum,** which focuses on the cultural history of the Miwok and Paiute peoples. The **Happy Isles Nature Center** and the **Tuolumne Meadows Visitor Center** are open in summer. The **Wawona Visitor Center** is open spring through fall.

Headquarters

9039 Village Drive
Yosemite National Park, CA 95389
nps.gov/yose
209-372-0200

Camping

There are 13 campgrounds in the park (total of 1,445 sites).

Lodging

Delaware North Companies Parks & Resorts manages lodging facilities at Yosemite *(yosemitepark.com)*. For more lodging information, visit *yosemite.com/ where-to-stay.*

Pacific Northwest

Diablo Lake in North Cascades National Park

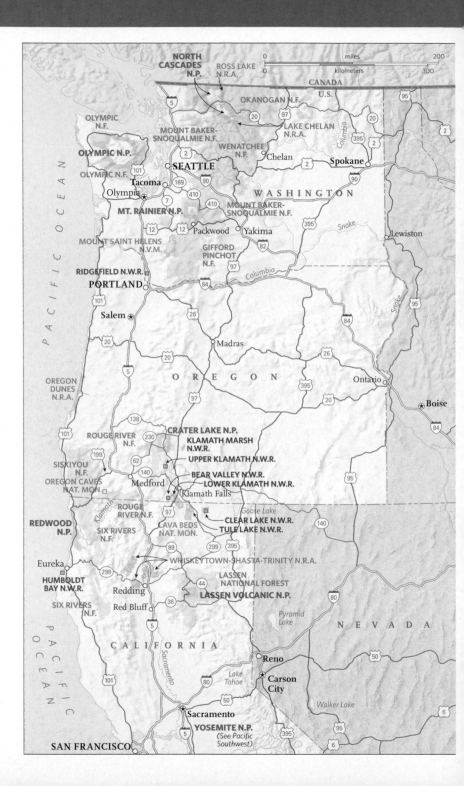

WATERTON-GLACIER
NATIONAL PARKS
(See Rocky Mts.)

CANADA
U.S.

93

89

*Flathead
Lake*

M O N T A N A

90

93

**See Rocky Mountains
section, page 262**

15

93

I D A H O

20

*American Falls
Reservoir*

86

Snake

84

93

*Great
Salt
Lake*

80

93

U T A H

**See Southwest
section, page 174**

Ely

50

**GREAT
BASIN N.P.**
*(See
Southwest)*

93

E ast Coast loggers pushed west in the late 19th and early 20th centuries, downing mile after mile of the continent's primeval forests. Today, almost all of the large ancient forests left in the Lower 48 states grow in the Pacific Northwest, most of them in national forests and the region's six rugged national parks.

Visitors can hike the cathedral-like glades of Douglas fir, western red cedar, and other conifers of **Mount Rainier, Olympic,** and **North Cascades** in Washington. The redwoods in the California park named for them—**Redwood National Park**—include trees in their second millennium, some of the tallest on Earth. In Olympic, temperate rain forests soar near some of the nation's wildest coastline; only there and at Mount Rainier do such forests still exist in the United States.

Washington State's youngest park, North Cascades, is also its youngest mountain range, with the razor-sharp alpine peaks and deep valleys of geological youth to prove it. All of these ancient forests and mountain peaks knit together the lives of hundreds of species of plants, animals, and microbes in a web still being studied. Yet that web is increasingly threatened as trees in private, state, and national forests are cut down.

The Northwest is also known for its volcanoes, many of which, including Mount Rainier and Mount St. Helens, lie in the Pacific Ring of Fire, the great belt of crustal instability responsible for three-quarters of the world's active volcanoes. Visitors to California's **Lassen Volcanic** National Park can see evidence of the planet's violence in broken mountains and boiling mud pots. To the north at Oregon's **Crater Lake,** you can imagine the titanic forces that collapsed a mountaintop, turning it into a lake 6 miles wide and the nation's deepest. And it's easy to marvel at the majesty of cloud-swathed Mount Rainier, which grew on a foundation of lava flows from extinct volcanoes, and now shoulders breathtaking wildflowers and more glaciers than any other U.S. peak south of Alaska.

Crater Lake

Oregon

Established
May 22, 1902

183,224 acres

More than 5 trillion gallons of water fill the crater—what remains of Mount Mazama. With a surface area of 21 square miles and depth of 1,943 feet, Crater Lake is the deepest lake in the United States. In addition the size of Crater Lake National Park, it is the stunning sapphire water that etches itself in memory.

Nearly 8,000 years ago, Mount Mazama in southern Oregon exploded in an eruption 100 times more powerful than the one that decimated Mount St. Helens in 1980. During the ancient cataclysmic eruption, the mountain basically collapsed in on itself to form a vast cliff-lined basin. Over the centuries, precipitation, mostly in the form of snow (524 inches a year on average), flowed in the caldera and, with no outlet to drain the water, Crater Lake was born. Nestled near the western shoreline, Wizard Island represents Mazama's attempt to rebuild itself. It was pushed up by volcanic activity some 2,500 years after the eruption.

While the core of the park is Crater Lake itself, the surrounding mountains and high plateaus offer visitors unique lessons on volcanic terrain.

Snowmelt feeds Crater Lake.

► HOW TO VISIT

Park highlights can be experienced in a day, but a long weekend is best. For single-day visits, plan an early start from **Rim Village** to get the dramatic early-morning light across the lake. Start north on **Rim Drive** to complete the 33-mile loop clockwise for best viewing and lighting throughout the morning. Stop to take the short hike up the **Watchman Trail** for a look east across the blue lake before continuing to the north rim.

The **Cleetwood Trail** leads down to the lakeshore. The hike is easy, but be prepared for the steep 1-mile return (there is no other way to get back to the rim). The final leg of the loop runs through the forests and valleys south of the lake.

Rim Drive

Rim Drive circles the lake, but not always along the rim of the caldera. Rim Village, on the southwestern corner of the crater, offers grand views of the lake from the **Sinnott Memorial Overlook.** From here, the broad expanse of the deep blue lake seems to mock the sky by offering itself as a truer, richer blue.

The lake's mesmerizing color results from its absolute clarity. As light penetrates the lake there are no impurities to reflect it. And since water molecules absorb all light in the spectrum other than blue, only the blue light is reflected back.

Leaving Rim Village, head north along the Rim Drive. Plan to take your time as the road is curvy and narrow—and can be crowded in peak season. *(Note that trailers and oversize vehicles are not recommended on the eastern half of the drive.)* Just over a mile from Rim Village, pause at **Discovery Point.**

It was near here in 1853 that a group of gold seekers found themselves standing on the rim, looking down on what they casually named Deep Blue Lake. This was the first recorded non-native visit to the lake, but with no way to reach the lake itself, the prospectors had no choice but to continue north on their quest for gold.

At Mile 4, stop and stretch your legs. The 0.8-mile **Watchman Trail** affords one of the best hikes in the park, with views directly down onto Wizard Island. Just north stands **Hillman Peak.** The 8,151-foot summit marks the highest point on the actual crater rim. Named after the gold hunter who funded the prospecting

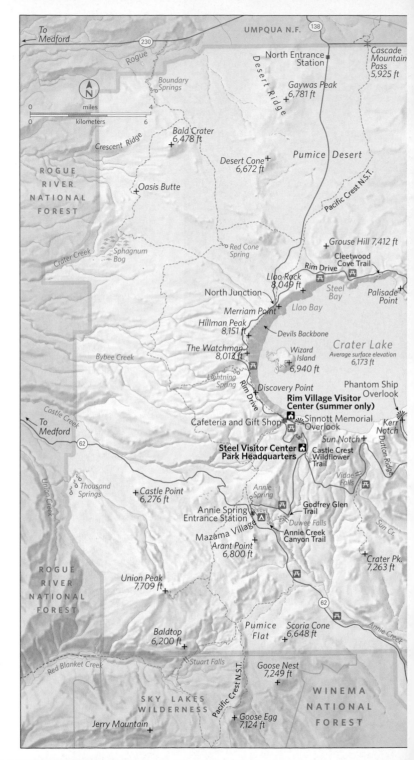

To Medford ←

UMPQUA N.F.

230

Rogue

Boundary Springs

N

miles 0 — 4
kilometers 0 — 6

Crescent Ridge

Bald Crater 6,478 ft

Desert Cone 6,672 ft

Desert Ridge

North Entrance Station

138

Cascade Mountain Pass 5,925 ft

Gaywas Peak 6,781 ft

Pumice Desert

ROGUE RIVER NATIONAL FOREST

Oasis Butte

Crater Creek

Sphagnum Bog

Red Cone Spring

Pacific Crest N.S.T.

Grouse Hill 7,412 ft

Cleetwood Cove Trail

Llao Rock 8,049 ft

North Junction

Rim Drive

Steel Bay

Palisade Point

Merriam Point

Llao Bay

Hillman Peak 8,151 ft

Devils Backbone

Crater Lake
Average surface elevation 6,173 ft

Bybee Creek

The Watchman 8,013 ft

Wizard Island 6,940 ft

Lightning Spring

Rim Drive

Discovery Point

Phantom Ship Overlook

Rim Village Visitor Center (summer only)

Cafeteria and Gift Shop

Sinnott Memorial Overlook

Kerr Notch

Castle Creek

To Medford

62

Steel Visitor Center Park Headquarters

Sun Notch

Castle Crest Wildflower Trail

Dutton Ridge

Vidae Falls

Thousand Springs

Castle Point 6,276 ft

Annie Spring

Godfrey Glen Trail

Union Creek

Annie Spring Entrance Station

Duwee Falls

Mazama Village

Annie Creek Canyon Trail

Sun Cr.

Arant Point 6,800 ft

Crater Pk. 7,263 ft

Union Peak 7,709 ft

ROGUE RIVER NATIONAL FOREST

62

Baldtop 6,200 ft

Pumice Flat

Scoria Cone 6,648 ft

Annie Creek

Stuart Falls

Goose Nest 7,249 ft

Red Blanket Creek

Pacific Crest N.S.T.

WINEMA NATIONAL FOREST

SKY LAKES WILDERNESS

Jerry Mountain

Goose Egg 7,124 ft

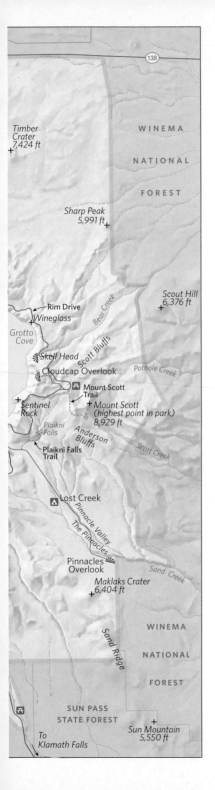

Timber Crater 7,424 ft

WINEMA

NATIONAL

FOREST

Sharp Peak 5,991 ft

Bear Creek

Scout Hill 6,376 ft

Rim Drive
Wineglass

Grotto Cove

Scott Bluffs

Skell Head
Cloudcap Overlook

Pothole Creek

Mount Scott Trail

Sentinel Rock

Mount Scott (highest point in park) 8,929 ft

Plaikni Falls

Anderson Bluffs

Scott Creek

Plaikni Falls Trail

Lost Creek

Pinnacle Valley

The Pinnacles

Pinnacles Overlook

Sand Creek

Maklaks Crater 6,404 ft

Sand Ridge

WINEMA

NATIONAL

FOREST

SUN PASS STATE FOREST

Sun Mountain 5,550 ft

To Klamath Falls

---

expedition that recorded the existence of the lake in 1853, the rocky crag of Hillman Peak is all that remains of what was once a secondary volcano on the flank of Mount Mazama. When Mazama erupted and the summit collapsed, it took most of Hillman with it.

Continuing north, the road forks at 6.1 miles. Stay right to continue on the Rim Drive; it is here that the road becomes too narrow and winding for oversize vehicles. The road angles well away from the crater rim for the next 2 miles before reaching a picnic area high above **Steel Bay.**

The bay's namesake, William Gladstone Steel, first read about the lake in an 1870 Kansas newspaper. His family moved to Portland, Oregon, in 1872; Steel visited the lake in 1885. From that moment on, he worked tirelessly to preserve Crater Lake.

The Pumice Desert

Heading north from the Rim Drive at North Junction, North Entrance Road leads through open meadows and forests of scrub pines. But most impressive are the broad fields of feather-light rocks dotting the Pumice Desert.

This expanse of volcanic debris is the result of a volcanic eruption that took place some 7,700 years ago. It blasted a huge quantity of pumice that dropped across this plain, creating a deposit nearly 200 feet thick. The porous rock—it floats!—and sand lack nutrients to support life, so the desert remains mostly barren, with just a few tough grasses sprouting here and there from the great field of gray stone.

His efforts came to fruition after he made a personal pitch to President Theodore Roosevelt. Roosevelt signed the legislation designating Crater Lake National Park early on in the 20th century, making it our sixth national park (just four years after another northwest park, Mount Rainier, became the fifth national park in the United States).

Just beyond Steel Bay is the trailhead of the **Cleetwood Cove Trail,** which usually opens mid- to late June. The path descends 1.1 miles from the rim to the lakeshore along a modest grade carved into the wooded slopes of the northern edge of the caldera. The trail ends at a boat dock from which a park concessioner operates a motor launch for trips along the lake. In addition, this is the only place where it is safe and legal to be on the lakeshore. Visitors here are welcome to swim in the cold, cold lake.

Near the 15-mile mark of Rim Drive **Skell Head observation point** provides open views west across the lake to Wizard Island and Hillman Peak above it. The 8,929-foot mountain just to the east of Rim Drive boasts an old fire lookout tower, and provides stunning views west across the breadth of the lake.

A mile farther on is the start of the **Mount Scott Trail.** The 2.5-mile trail climbs steeply at times, through piercing fragrant pine forests and brilliant wildflower meadows, before reaching the summit.

At Mile 24, stop at **Phantom Ship Overlook** to peer down at Phantom Ship—the only other island on the lake besides Wizard. The outline of Phantom Ship resembles a pirate's ship and gains its name from the fact that it disappears completely against the crater's walls when viewed from much of the rim. Make your way to Kerr Notch, where the phantom ship is easily viewed.

Past Kerr, Rim Drive veers away from the crater and weaves through the rich forest ecosystem of the mountain's southern flank. The gentle **Castle Crest WIldflower Trail,** near park headquarters, provides fascinating information about the local flora and fauna. The trail meanders through meadows awash with delicate wildflowers during most of the summer.

The Lake

To experience the lake itself, hike down the mile-long **Cleetwood Trail** to the dock on the shore of the lake. From here, concessioner Xanterra (888-774-2728) offers boat tours of the lake.

The standard interpretive boat tour circumnavigates the broad lake in two hours, providing fine lessons on the geology and history of Crater Lake as you take in the vast beauty of the lake and its surroundings. Indeed, the tour comes with great views of Phantom Ship and the cinder-cone peak of Wizard Island. The standard tour runs hourly during peak season, typically July through September.

A thorough exploration of **Wizard Island** is also possible, with optional half-day or all-day drop-offs that allow time to get a sense of this volcanic cinder cone. From the island dock, a mile-long trail weaves upward through a series of switchbacks to the crater at the cinder cone's summit (6,940 feet). The rim of this crater within a crater provides views of the lake that only a tiny fraction of visitors ever get to see.

Crater Lake in winter

Information

How to Get There

Ore. 62 cuts through the southern portion of the park complex, providing access from Medford. US 97 runs just east of the park, offering access to the north end by way of Ore. 138. Nearby airports: Klamath Falls Regional Airport and Roge Valley International Airport, in Medford.

When to Go

Because of the park's position high in the Cascade Mountains, winter comes early and lingers long. Most of the park's roads aren't clear until late June or early July (they start gathering snow in late Oct.). The Rim Drive typically closes for the winter season by Nov. 1. Rim Village remains open year-round for winter recreational activities.

Visitor Centers

The **Rim Village Visitor Center,** located along the rim 7 miles north on Ore. 62, is open late May through late Sept. **Steel Visitor Center** 4 miles north of Ore. 62 operates year-round.

Headquarters

P.O. Box 7
Crater Lake, OR 97604
nps.gov/crla
541-594-3000

Camping

The park complex offers two camp-grounds, **Mazama Campground** has 200 sites, three-quarters of which may be reserved *(craterlakelodges.com)*. The 16 tent sites at **Lost Creek Campground** are first come, first served. A free permit, available from park headquarters, is needed for backcountry camping.

Lodging

Crater Lake Lodge at Rim Village (mid-May through Oct.) and the **Cabins at Mazama Village** (mid-May through mid-Oct.) are both operated by Crater Lake Lodge *(craterlakelodges.com)*. For lodging outside the park check with the Klamath County Chamber of Commerce *(klamath.org/visitors/)* or the Medford/Jackson County Chamber of Commerce *(medfordchamber.org)*.

Crater Lake Excursions

Klamath Marsh Refuge
Chiloquin, Oregon

▷ An important nesting, feeding, and staging habitat for waterfowl and the sandhill crane, the Klamath Marsh Refuge, located along the Williamson River, is a sanctuary designed for the bird-lover. With 40,000 acres of wet meadows and open-water wetlands, the refuge is home to the Oregon spotted frog, a candidate for the endangered species list. Canoeing, kayaking, fishing (after July 1). Located 71 miles east of Crater Lake National Park, off US 97. *fws.gov/refuge/klamath_marsh;* 541-783-3380.

Newberry National Volcanic Monument
Bend, Oregon

▷ At more than 54,000 acres, Newberry National Volcanic Monument offers plenty of opportunities to view the "Lava Lands" of central Oregon from atop an active volcano. The monument includes lava tubes, cinder cones, obsidian flows, and an eerie forest of lava casts. Camping, fishing, biking, and hiking. Some facilities and trails open only seasonally. Located 100 miles north of Crater Lake National Park, via US 97N. *fs.usda.gov/recarea/deschutes/recarea/?recid=6615966159;* 541-593-2421.

Oregon Dunes National Recreation Area
Reedsport, Oregon

▷ Towering dunes—some as high as 400 feet—stretch along the Pacific coast, inviting exploration. Fully 32,000 acres are open to off-road vehicles. The area shelters 426 wildlife species, including black bear, black-tailed deer, and tundra swan. Hiking, camping, boating, fishing, horseback riding, and swimming. Located 200 miles west of Crater Lake National Park, off US 101. *fs.usda.gov/recarea/siuslaw/recarea/?recid=42465;* 541-271-6000.

Oregon Caves National Monument
Cave Junction, Oregon

▷ Found deep in the Siskiyou Mountains are the caves commonly known as the "Marble Halls of Oregon." The caves formed as acidic groundwater from the ancient forest above dissolved the surrounding marble creating the formations. Indeed, this is one of the world's few marble caves. Guided tours offered late March through the end of October. Located 130 miles southwest of Crater Lake National Park, off US 199. *nps.gov/orca;* 541-592-2100.

Prospect State Scenic Viewpoint
Prospect, Oregon

▷ The small, idyllic Prospect State Scenic Viewpoint is tucked away in a secluded forest area with picnic tables and hiking trails that lead to Pearsony Falls, the Rogue River, and Mill Creek Falls. Hiking, picnicking, and wildlife viewing. (No potable water.) Located 22 miles southwest of Crater Lake National Park via Oreg. 62W. *oregon stateparks.org;* 541-560-3334.

Rogue Wild and Scenic River
Grants Pass, Oregon

▷ The 84 miles of the scenic Rogue River, stretching from Grants Pass to Gold Beach, vary from the rush of white water to water smooth as glass. Wildlife to spot: salmon, bald eagles, osprey, and mink. Whitewater rafting, canoeing, swimming, fishing, bird-watching. Also on tap are jet boat tours *(fee)*. Located 80 miles from Crater Lake National Park via I-5. blm.*gov/or/resources/recreation/ rogue;* 541-471-6500.

Lassen Volcanic

California

Established
August 9, 1916

106,000 acres

One of the least discovered parks in the western United States, Lassen Volcanic National Park is a real-world laboratory that shows how landscapes evolve over time following a major volcanic eruption. Boiling springs, mudflows, lava fields, and cinder cones reflect the park's violent geologic legacy. But Lassen is much more than basalt and ash. The park also harbors numerous lakes and meadows, thickly forested areas, and a rich catalog of wildlife.

The origins of this volcanic landscape stretch back more than three million years, when powerful mudflows, or lahars, rushed down the flanks of Mount Yana, covering a 2,000-square-mile area—including what is now Lassen Volcanic National Park. There has been volcanic and hydrothermal activity ever since, culminating in a massive stratovolcano called Brokeoff Mountain (Mount Tehama), which dominated the landscape between 600,000 and 400,000 years ago. When American explorers and pioneers first reached the area in the early 19th century, they most

Volcanic peaks and thick forest

Earth where visitors can view all four volcano types—plug dome, cinder cone, shield, and composite—within a relatively small area. Lassen Peak is the southernmost active volcano in the Cascade Range. Lassen and Mount St. Helens were the only volcanoes to erupt in the Lower 48 states during the 20th century.

All told, more than 75 percent of the park is designated Wilderness—easily accessed, even via day hikes.

▶ HOW TO VISIT

Nearly everyone who visits the park drives the the 30-mile stretch of **Lassen Volcanic National Park Highway** that meanders past volcanic peaks and through hydrothermal areas between the **Kohm Yah-mah-nee Visitor Center** and **Manzanita Lake.**

While the scenic drive reaches many of the tectonic highlights, it offers only a hint of Lassen's pristine backcountry. Less-traveled unpaved roads take visitors to secluded spots like **Cinder Cone** and **Butte Lake** in the park's northeast corner and the hydrothermal splendor of **Warner Valley** in the south, as well as quiet **Juniper Lake** in the southeast.

Lassen Volcanic National Park Highway

The 30-mile drive, part of the Volcanic Legacy Scenic Byway, offers spectacular vistas, trailheads to hydrothermal landmarks, and picnic areas where you can kick back and enjoy the view. Located just beyond the southwest entrance, **Kohm Yah-mah-nee Visitor Center** provides a broad introduction to the park's wonders, with exhibits

likely assumed the volcanoes were dormant. So it would have come as a huge surprise when Lassen Peak rumbled to life in 1914, a three-year episode that included a massive eruption in May 1915 that spewed ash, rock, and lava over much of the park's northwest quadrant.

Even before that last eruption, Lassen was deemed a geological wonder. In 1907, President Theodore Roosevelt designated both Cinder Cone and Lassen Peak as national monuments. A year after the 1915 eruption, they were combined into Lassen Volcanic National Park, one of several units of the nascent national park system.

The park is unique on several levels. It's one of the few places on

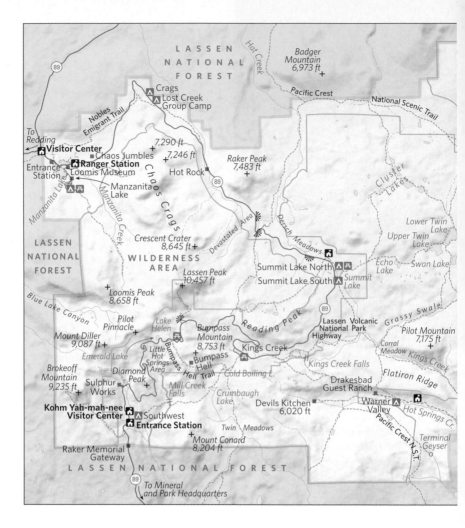

and a short video on local history and nature. From the terrace behind the visitor center, you can gaze upward at Mount Diller, Diamond Peak, Pilot Pinnacle, and the other ragged mounts that once formed the base of Brokeoff Volcano.

Stock up on food, drinks, and reading material at the visitor center stores—no provisions are available between here and Manzanita Lake.

Making your way north on the highway, your first stop should be **Sulphur Works** (Mile 0.8), a mosaic of fumaroles (steam vents) and mudpots that tumbles down the mountain slopes on both sides of the road. The smoldering hillside, easily the most accessible of the park's hydrothermal features, derives its name from the odorous hydrogen sulfide escaping from the vents.

After twisting around Diamond Peak, the highway continues its climb to petite **Emerald Lake** and the Bumpass Hell parking area (Mile 5.8).

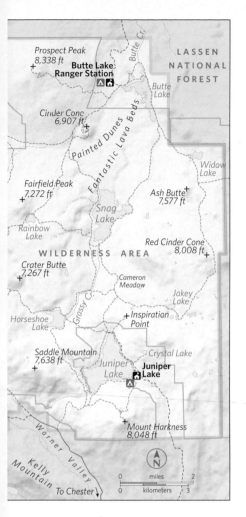

Looking northward, the view takes in mirror-like Lake Helen and towering **Lassen Peak** (10,457 feet), named after Peter Lassen, an early-19th-century Danish blacksmith, rancher, and prospector who pioneered the region. To the south are Little Hot Springs Valley and a seemingly endless spread of mountain ridges. One of the park's most popular hikes leads 3 miles downhill to **Bumpass Hell,** a large and very active hydrothermal basin best viewed from the

John Muir at Lassen

Although he is best known for his travels in Yosemite and Alaska, John Muir also visited the Lassen region before it was designated a national park. During a meandering 1888 expedition that took him to Mount Shasta and other areas of the Pacific Northwest, Muir undertook a short side trip to explore the volcanic wonders around Lassen Peak.

"Miles of its flanks are reeking and bubbling with hot springs, many of them so boisterous and sulphurous they seem ever ready to become spouting geysers like those of the Yellowstone," he later wrote in the book *Mountains of California.* But the great Scottish American naturalist seemed most impressed with what would be named Cinder Cone and the Fantastic Lava Flow, which he described in precise detail.

Muir mentions being fatigued by the task of hiking through the thick ash around the cone. And he relates a story of how the small volcano was formed several hundred years before his visit: "[The Pitt River Indians] tell of a fearful time of darkness, when the sky was black with ashes and smoke that threatened every living thing with death, and that when at length the sun appeared once more it was red like blood."

boardwalk that hovers very close to the bubbling pools.

Those planning to scale Lassen Peak should pull into the parking area at Mile 7.1, which marks the start of a steep 2.5-mile trail to the summit.

After breaching the highest point

along the highway (8,512 feet), the road plunges downward into Kings Creek Meadow. At Mile 13.1 you'll see a turnout for the trail to **Kings Creek Falls,** which tumbles 50 feet over a lava ledge.

Linger along the shore of tranquil **Summit Lake** (Mile 16.5), warm enough in summer for a swim. The highway continues northward to an area ravaged by the 1915 eruptions. Having largely recovered from the volcanic havoc, the **Devastated Area** (Mile 19.8) now seems misnamed. But a short interpretive trail describes the violent pyroclastic flow that decimated this area just a century ago.

Nobles Emigrant Trail—a popular covered-wagon route during the mid-19th century—crosses the highway at several places, including Mile 26.3, where the pioneer path is still visible through the woods, just beyond the historical marker.

The pines soon give way to **Chaos Jumbles** (Mile 27.5), the remains of a rock avalanche that raced across the landscape some 350 years ago at an estimated 110 miles per hour. Unlike the Devastated Area, the Jumbles remains a no-man's-land of volcanic demolition, strewn with giant boulders and dwarf trees. Civilization reappears at **Manzanita Lake** (Mile 29.3), with its cabins, campground, and store.

Loomis Museum, housed in a historic stone building erected in 1927, displays dramatic black-and-white photos of Benjamin Loomis, who risked life and limb to capture the 1915 eruption on film. From Memorial Day through Columbus Day (weather permitting), the Manzanita Lake camp store rents kayaks for forays onto the lake.

Elsewhere in the Park

The pristine **Butte Lake** area is accessed via Calif. 44, along the northern edge of the park. With thick woods on one shore and the **Fantastic Lava Beds** on the other, the lake offers a stark contrast in Lassen landscapes. Starting from the lake parking area, you can follow a section of the old Nobles Emigrant Trail along the jagged edge of the lava beds to **Cinder Cone.** Amazing and menacing, the 6,907-foot mount is composed of volcanic scoria rock discharged from the earth around A.D. 1666. A spur trail leads to the cone's summit and its shallow crater. The view from the top is perhaps the best in the park, a dramatic panorama of the nearby lava beds and Painted Dunes with Lassen Peak (and others) on the western horizon.

Tranquil **Juniper Lake** lies at the end of a 13-mile road from Chester, on the park's southern flank. A ranger station and primitive campground are the only facilities, but you can bring in your own canoe or kayak and paddle the lake. Hiking trails lead to nearby sights like **Snag Lake** (at the southern end of the Fantastic Lava Beds) and the vintage 1930 fire lookout tower atop **Mount Harkness,** an 8,048-foot-high shield volcano.

Chester is also the starting point for the 17-mile drive to **Warner Valley** and its hydrothermal wonders. In addition to swimming in the naturally heated pool at **Drakesbad Guest Ranch,** you can hike or ride horses to local "hot spots" like Terminal Geyser and Devils Kitchen. Warner Valley is also the best place in the park to access the **Pacific Crest Trail,** which cuts a zigzag path right across the middle of Lassen.

Fishing on Manzanita Lake

Information

How to Get There

From Sacramento, CA (about 180 miles south), take I-5 north to Exit 649 in Red Bluff, then Calif. 36 east to Calif. 89 north. The park's southwest entrance and visitor center are about 5 miles from the 36/89 junction. Other routes include Calif. 44 from Redding, CA, to the Manzanita Lake Entrance Station, and a combination of US 99, Calif. 70, and Calif. 89 from Sacramento to the southwest entrance.

When to Go

The park is open year-round, but many park facilities are closed generally between mid-Oct. and late May. The main park highway is closed during the winter season, and the Kohm Yah-mah-nee Visitor Center may close at any time due to weather.

Visitor Center

Kohm Yah-mah-nee, about 5 miles north of the turnoff from Calif. 36, is closed Mon. and Tues. early Dec. through March.

Headquarters

P.O. Box 100
38050 State Highway 36E
Mineral King, CA 96063
nps.org/lavo
530-595-6100

Camping

Eight developed campgrounds (430 sites) take reservations *(recreation.org;* 877-444-6777). Backcountry camping requires a free permit (530-595-4480 for information, or visit the Kohm Yah-mah-nee Visitor Center).

Lodging

Lodging is limited to two park locations open June to mid-Oct. The historic **Drakesbad Guest Ranch** *(drakesbad .com;* 866-999-0914) is 17 miles north of Chester, CA, in Warner Valley, and the **Manzanita Lake Camping Cabins** is in the park's northwest corner *(lassenrecreation .com;* 877-444-6777). For other choices check *nps.gov/lavo/planyourvisit/lodging .htm.*

Mount Rainier

Washington

Established
March 2, 1899

236,381 acres

Towering nearly 8,000 feet above the neighboring Cascade peaks, Mount Rainier forms the roof of Washington State, reaching 14,411 feet into the sky. Mount Rainier National Park, in all its diversity, represents a unifying icon for Washington's grand landscapes. The great mountain can be viewed from hundreds of miles away, from every compass point. It is the most identifiable landmark around.

For centuries, Tahoma—the name given to the mountain by native tribes—represented a mighty source of power. Centuries on, many believe that Mount Rainier National Park owes its status in large part to the citizens of Seattle and Tacoma, who recognized the majesty of the area. Rainier and its surrounding forests were designated Mount Rainier Forest Reserve in 1893; six years later it was designated a national park.

The park boasts an array of terrain, including vast fields of flower parklands. Beyond the meadows are more than 300 lakes, dozens of waterfalls, 25 glaciers, and 50 permanent snowfields.

Mount Rainier

flank, offers some of the best and most accessible snow recreation in the Pacific Northwest. The National Park Service keeps the road from Longmire to Paradise plowed and open year-round, conditions permitting; the road is closed at night. Most other roads open late June or early July and close by early December.

Because the snowpack typically tops 20 feet or more, snowshoers and cross-country skiers are free to ramble anywhere they'd like in Paradise Valley. Check the weather and avalanche conditions prior to heading out.

When snow levels drop mid-winter, snowshoers also find great options in the **Longmire area.** The Trail of the Shadows and the section of the Wonderland Trail from Longmire east along the Nisqually River are two easy snowshoe routes.

► HOW TO VISIT

For a summer visit, travelers can see the best of the park in a day provided they get an early start. Begin at the **White River Entrance** and follow the road to its end, **Sunrise Visitor Center.** From here, on a clear day, the northeastern face of Mount Rainier sparkles in the first light of the day. From Sunrise, continue on to the **Stevens Canyon Entrance** to explore some more. In late afternoon, head to the heavenly meadows of **Paradise.** Linger here into the evening for the chance to catch the peak bathed in the amber light known as alpenglow. With more time, head to the park's northwest corner far off the beaten path.

If planning a winter visit, **Paradise Basin,** on Mount Rainier's southern

East Side: Sunrise & Stevens Canyon

From the **White River Entrance,** the road leads to White River Campground and great hiking opportunities up the **Glacier Basin Trail.** The road climbs away from the river and switchbacks up to a long ridge ending at Sunrise. Look for climbers on the glaciers directly above **Steamboat Prow—a** V-shaped rock a third of the way up the mountain's face.

Several trails leave Sunrise, all with grand views of the towering northeastern face of Mount Rainier. For a short exploration of the ridgetop meadows, venture up the 1.5-mile **Sourdough Ridge Nature Trail,** with fine views and good examples of the local flora and fauna.

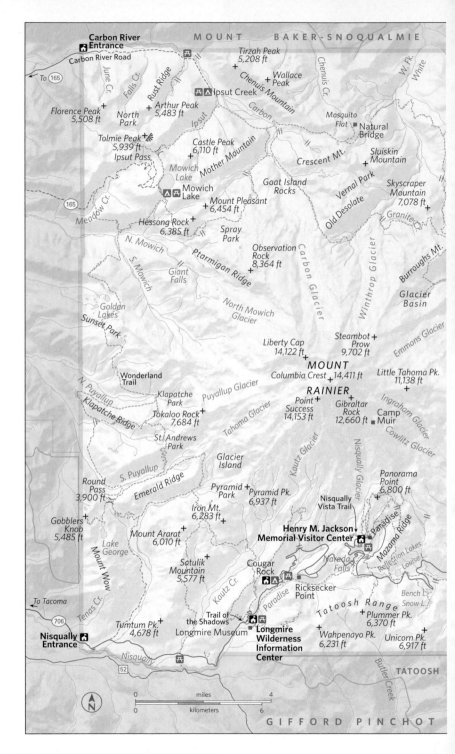

MOUNT BAKER-SNOQUALMIE

Carbon River Entrance
Carbon River Road

To 165

Tirzah Peak
5,208 ft

Wallace Peak

Chenuis Mountain

Chenuis Cr.

W. Fk. White

Ipsut Creek

Carbon

Mosquito Flat

Natural Bridge

Florence Peak
5,508 ft

North Park

Arthur Peak
5,483 ft

Ipsut

Tolmie Peak
5,939 ft
Ipsut Pass

Castle Peak
6,110 ft

Mother Mountain

Crescent Mt.

Sluiskin Mountain

Mowich Lake

Mowich Lake

Goat Island Rocks

Vernal Park

Old Desolate

Skyscraper Mountain
7,078 ft

Granite

165

Meadow Cr.

Mount Pleasant
6,454 ft

Hessong Rock
6,385 ft

Spray Park

Observation Rock
8,364 ft

Carbon Glacier

Winthrop Glacier

Burroughs Mt.

Glacier Basin

N. Mowich

S. Mowich

Giant Falls

Ptarmigan Ridge

North Mowich Glacier

Golden Lakes

Sunset Park

Emmons Glacier

Liberty Cap
14,122 ft

Steambot Prow
9,702 ft

Little Tahoma Pk.
11,138 ft

Wonderland Trail

MOUNT

Columbia Crest + 14,411 ft

RAINIER

N. Puyallup

Klapatche Ridge

Klapatche Park

Puyallup Glacier

Tahoma Glacier

Point Success
14,153 ft

Gibraltar Rock
12,660 ft

Camp Muir

Ingraham Glacier

Cowlitz Glacier

Tokaloo Rock
7,684 ft

St. Andrews Park

Kautz Glacier

Nisqually Glacier

Round Pass
3,900 ft

S. Puyallup

Glacier Island

Emerald Ridge

Pyramid Park

Pyramid Pk.
6,937 ft

Panorama Point
6,800 ft

Nisqually Vista Trail

Gobblers Knob
5,485 ft

Lake George

Iron Mt.
6,283 ft

Mount Ararat
6,010 ft

Henry M. Jackson Memorial Visitor Center

Paradise

Mazama Ridge

Reflection Lakes

Louise L.

To Tacoma

706

Mount Wow

Satulik Mountain
5,577 ft

Kautz Cr.

Cougar Rock

Nakeda Falls

Bench L.

Snow L.

Ricksecker Point

Tatoosh Range

Plummer Pk.
6,370 ft

Tenas Cr.

Tumtum Pk.
4,678 ft

Trail of the Shadows
Longmire Museum

Paradise

Longmire Wilderness Information Center

Wahpenayo Pk.
6,231 ft

Unicorn Pk.
6,917 ft

Nisqually Entrance

Nisqually

52

Butler Creek

TATOOSH

0   miles   4
0   kilometers   6

N

GIFFORD PINCHOT

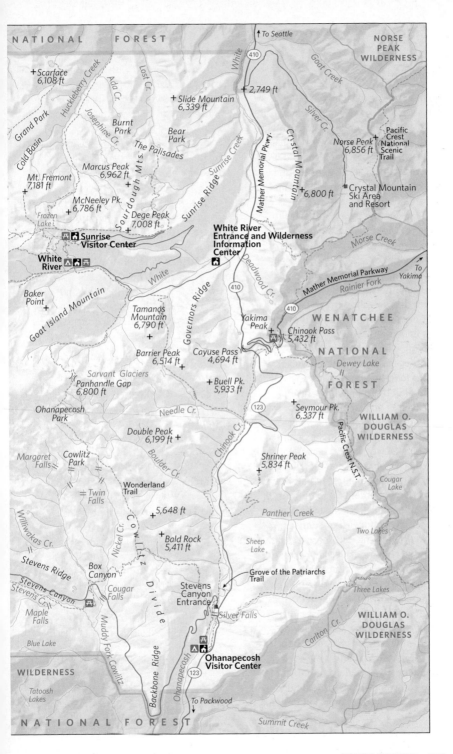

NATIONAL   FOREST

↑ To Seattle

NORSE PEAK WILDERNESS

Scarface 6,108 ft

Grand Park

Cold Basin

Huckleberry Creek

Lost Cr.

Ada Cr.

Josephine Cr.

Slide Mountain 6,339 ft

+ 2,749 ft

Goat Creek

Silver Cr.

Burnt Park

Bear Park

The Palisades

Sunrise Creek

Mather Memorial Pkwy.

Crystal Mountain

Norse Peak 6,856 ft

Pacific Crest National Scenic Trail

Marcus Peak 6,962 ft

Sourdough Mts.

Mt. Fremont 7,181 ft

McNeeley Pk. 6,786 ft

Dege Peak 7,008 ft

Sunrise Ridge

+ 6,800 ft

Crystal Mountain Ski Area and Resort

Frozen Lake

🏕🏠 Sunrise Visitor Center

White River 🔺🏠🏕

White River Entrance and Wilderness Information Center 🏠

Deadwood Cr.

Morse Creek

Baker Point +

Goat Island Mountain

White

Governors Ridge

410

Mather Memorial Parkway

Rainier Fork

To Yakima

Tamanos Mountain 6,790 ft

Yakima Peak

410

WENATCHEE

Barrier Peak 6,514 ft

Cayuse Pass 4,694 ft

Chinook Pass 5,432 ft

NATIONAL

Dewey Lake

Sarvant Glaciers

Panhandle Gap 6,800 ft

+ Buell Pk. 5,933 ft

FOREST

Ohanapecosh Park

Needle Cr.

123

Seymour Pk. 6,337 ft

WILLIAM O. DOUGLAS WILDERNESS

Double Peak 6,199 ft +

Chinook Cr.

Shriner Peak 5,834 ft

Cougar Lake

Margaret Falls

Cowlitz Park

Boulder Cr.

Wonderland Trail

+ 5,648 ft

Panther Creek

Two Lakes

Twin Falls

C
o
w
l
i
t
z

Nickel Cr.

+ Bald Rock 5,411 ft

Sheep Lake

Williwakas Cr.

Stevens Ridge

D
i
v
i
d
e

Box Canyon

Grove of the Patriarchs Trail

Three Lakes

Stevens Canyon
Stevens Cr.

Cougar Falls

Stevens Canyon Entrance

🏕

WILLIAM O. DOUGLAS WILDERNESS

Maple Falls

Silver Falls

Blue Lake

Muddy Fork Cowlitz

Backbone Ridge

Ohanapecosh

🔺🏕🏠 Ohanapecosh Visitor Center

Carlton Cr.

WILDERNESS

123

Tatoosh Lakes

To Packwood

NATIONAL   FOREST

Summit Creek

Pacific Crest N.S.T.

Natural World

The massive hulk of Mount Rainier stands seemingly impervious to time. But the mountain is constantly in flux. Mudflows scour valleys. Glaciers calve-off huge blocks of ice. And great bursts of steam vent out of the summit crater, evidence of the volcanic nature of the big peak.

Plants in the park also deal with change. The rugged plants that survive in harsh winter conditions are actually quite fragile. Because many reside well above the 5,000-foot level, and because the annual snowfall at that elevation can exceed 50 feet per year, vegetation in the meadows enjoys a very short season (July through mid-September). And so any plants damaged by wayward hikers take a long time to recover. To avoid damaging these meadows, hikers should stay on established trails.

Photographers seeking shots of wildflowers from within the meadows themselves should seek fields far off the beaten track and remain on the trail; one step into a meadow will damage vegetation. Good options for off-the-beaten-track meadows can be found north and west of Sunrise.

Animals in the park learn to survive in tough conditions. If they become accustomed to handouts from humans during peak tourist seasons, they are at a disadvantage when it comes to surviving after the tourist crowds leave. Such feeding also poses the risk of disease transmission. So for the safety of the animals, no food should be given out, even to the bold little camp-robber jays that flit and fly around picnic areas and campgrounds.

For a longer hike with a bit more history, push on west along Sourdough Ridge to **Frozen Lake** (1.2 miles from Sunrise) and on up to a stony promontory at the end of Fremont Ridge, just 2.8 miles from Sunrise. Here stands a rustic wooden fire tower. **Fremont Lookout** was in use throughout the first six decades of the 20th century.

A less strenuous hike can be found by angling south along the **Burroughs Mountain Trail** from Frozen Lake. The trail rolls over the nearly flat summit of First Burroughs at 2.5 miles, and then climbs a half mile to Second Burroughs. Both ridge-top summits provide panoramic views of Rainier and its flanking peaks. Other destinations to explore out of Sunrise include Berkeley Park, Grand Park, Skyscraper Peak, and Shadow Lake.

After exploring the Sunrise area you can head south on Wash. 410 and Wash. 123 to the **Stevens Canyon Entrance.** Head up Stevens Canyon Road and stop near the Stevens Canyon Entry Station to walk the 1.5-mile trail into the **Grove of the Patriarchs.** To get into the grove, located on a large island in the Ohanapecosh River, you'll have to cross a scenic, and swaying, suspension bridge. The stand of massive old trees shows the grandeur of Washington's old-growth forests. Some of the grove's 1,000-year-old hemlocks, Douglas firs, and western red cedars tower nearly 300 feet tall and rival California's redwoods in girth.

South Side: Stevens Canyon & Paradise

A drive west from the Stevens Canyon Entrance leads up the long, deep cut of the canyon. Nearly 10 miles west of Wash. 123, stop at **Box Canyon.** A half-mile trail wanders along the Cowlitz River—or rather, along the top of the 100-foot-deep slot canyon carved by the Muddy Fork of that river. Head 1 mile north along the gorge to reach the Nickel Creek backcountry camp.

As the road climbs west, it reaches **Reflection Lakes,** about 16 miles from Wash. 123. Park here for a grand road-side photo op: the looming summit and its reflection in the shallow lake.

Hiking opportunities in this part of the park include a gentle stroll around the small lake; the 1.3-mile trail to **Pinnacle Peak;** and, above the Stevens Canyon Road, a trail (under a mile) through tree-studded meadows that leads to **Bench Lake.** The far side of the lake is bordered by a rim of rock that drops away in a dramatic cliff, making Bench something of a naturally occurring infinity pool. The trail climbs south a half-mile away from Bench to **Snow Lake** in the deep cleft of rock below Unicorn Peak.

Beyond Reflection Lake, the road leads upward to Paradise. This heavenly alpine landscape earned its name in 1885. The daughter-in-law of the original settler in the area, James Longmire, ventured into the meadows for the first time and declared, "Oh, what a Paradise."

In the early part of the 20th century, sprawling campgrounds and a small golf course marred the spectacular meadows; those blemishes have since been removed and revegetation initiated

The meadows today are almost just as they were when Martha Longmire first saw them more than a century ago. Of course, the best way to experience the grandeur of the area is by

A western red cedar

foot. A strenuous 1.7-mile loop up to **Alta Vista** offers meadow views and summit scenery. A 1.2-mile trail leads out along the edge of the **Nisqually Glacier valley** with views south to the Tatoosh Range.

The best route for those up for a strenuous hike is the 4-mile loop up along **Skyline Trail.** Panorama Point, along the way, is the start of the climber's route to **Camp Muir** at the 10,188-foot level and on to the summit.

Leaving Paradise, you'll descend the Paradise River Valley to its junction with the Nisqually River. Just a couple miles from Paradise, stop at **Narada Falls.** A 0.25-mile trail leads to grand views of the 168-foot fantail cascade.

Just over 11 miles from Paradise awaits **Longmire.** Natural springs in these forested meadows prompted James Longmire to construct a hotel and spa in the 1880s. Though not the Longmire original, a hotel—the **National Park Inn**—is an overnight option for today's travelers.

Learn about the park's history at the **Longmire Museum,** and explore the trails that meander through the area. The **Trail of the Shadows,** an interpretive route, loops through the meadows, while day hikers can venture up Eagle Peak, Rampart Ridge, or along the local stretch of the 93-mile **Wonderland Trail** that encircles Mount Rainier.

Northwest Corner: Mowich Lake & Carbon River

While nature lovers and adventurers such as John Muir and James Longmire climbed the mountain and explored the southern portion of what became Mount Rainier National Park, another sort of explorer ventured into the northwest corner.

Throughout the early 20th century, miners dug under the hills of the upper Carbon River basin, searching for everything from coal to gold. The good news is that the rich forest ecosystems quickly healed the scars left by those seeking to take the region's riches, reinstating riches of a more respectful type.

From Wash. 410 in the town of Buckley, turn south on Wash. 165 and follow it into the Carbon River Valley, where the road forks. Wash. 165 climbs away from the river to Mowich Lake, while the Carbon River Road leads to the northwestern corner of the park. There the road is closed to automobile traffic.

Mountain bikes are allowed on the 5 miles of closed road from the park boundary to **Ipsut Creek,** but riders must get off their bikes and hike if they want to discover part of the 8.5-mile **Carbon Glacier Trail.**

Beyond the Carbon River, Wash. 165 becomes a gravel road, making the final 10 miles to **Mowich Lake** a bit dusty and rough. But from the shores of Mowich, visitors can explore a number of trails with spectacular views and scenic wonder. The **Tolmie Peak Lookout Trail** (2.8 miles) wanders around the perimeter of Mowich Lake before climbing to the old fire lookout tower atop the peak.

The 3-mile **Spray Park Trail** weaves in and out of the park, straight up the flank of Mount Rainier itself, climbing above timberline to a sprawling alpine parkland on the edge of the mountain's glacier fields.

Rain-washed flora

Information

How to Get There

From Seattle (95 miles northwest), travel via I-5, Wash. 512, and Wash. 7 to the Road of Paradise. From Packwood (10 miles south), take Wash. 123 and Stevens Canyon Rd. to the Ohanapecosh Entrance. Check the park website for driving details.

When to Go

The Nisqually Entrance to Paradise is open year-round. Most other roads open late June or July and close by early Dec. Wildflowers in the Paradise and Sunrise areas peak in early Aug., as do the crowds. Backcountry trails are snow-clogged until mid-July. Mid-Sept. typically offers good weather and fewer crowds.

Visitor Centers & Museum

Longmire Information Center, open year-round; **Longmire Museum and Ohanapecosh Visitor Center,** open May–Oct.; **Henry M. Jackson Memorial Visitor Center,** open May–late Oct. and weekends the rest of the year; and **Sunrise Visitor Center,** open July–Sept.

Headquarters

55210 238 Ave. E.
Ashford, WA 98304
nps.gov/mora
360-569-22111

Camping

Two of the park's three campgrounds, **Cougar Rock** and **Ohanapecosh,** allow reservations during peak season and generally fill up. **White River Campground** is first come, first served. The Forest Service maintains campgrounds near Mount Rainier at **La Wis Wis, The Dalles,** and **American River.** NPS and USFS sites may be reserved at *recreation.gov* (626 sites). Backpackers need backcountry camping permits. For information, 360-569-4453.

Lodging

The facilities in the park, **National Park Inn** (25 rooms) and **Paradise Inn** (open May through Oct., 121 rooms), are operated by Mount Rainier Guest Services (*mtrainier guestservices.com*). For lodging in neighboring communities: *visitrainier.com.*

North Cascades

Washington

Established
October 2, 1968

504,000 acres

At some 2 million years old, Washington's Cascades are among the youngest mountains on the continent. The peaks are jagged and tall, not yet worn down by the ravages of time. The valleys are deep and sharp-edged because the rivers are still at work on the tough stone. And the flora and fauna are resilient, surviving and thriving in the challenging vertical world of North Cascades National Park.

This is not simply a park—it's a sprawling wilderness complex that encompasses the national park as well as the Ross Lake National Recreation Area and the Lake Chelan National Recreation Area. These three units add up to some of the most rugged and remote wilderness in the United States.

The high peaks and deep valleys cradle more than 300 glaciers.

The early explorers who traveled these mountains quivered at the thought of having to return the same way they came. The peaks bear names that inspire dread: Mount Terror, Mount Despair, Mount Fury, Desolation Peak,

Jagged peaks crown more than 300 glaciers.

Mount Challenger, and Damnation Peak, to name a few.

North Cascades is more than rocks and ice, however. The park complex holds one of the last intact ecosystems in the country. Nearly all the species that lived here when Europeans first reached North America, from grizzly bears to tiny butterflies, can still be found here.

Wild runs of chinook (king) and sockeye salmon fill the rivers during spawning season, which brings out bald eagles and ospreys, as well as otters. Mountain lions and wolves hunt the complex's black-tailed deer and mountain goats, while wolverines stalk anything that comes their way.

Towering Douglas fir and western hemlock dominate the forests of the northern and western portions of the park complex, which receives more than 100 inches of precipitation a year. Across the Cascade Crest, in the Lake Chelan National Recreation Area and the southern part of the park, forests tend more toward drought-hardy ponderosa pine, larch, and red fir. East of the crest, rainfall is 35 inches a year.

The sheer ruggedness of the park complex makes it challenging to experience. Few roads penetrate the region. Wash. 20, the North Cascades Highway, is the only paved road leading into the park complex. It follows an east-west corridor of the Ross Lake National Recreation Area, alongside the Skagit River.

This corridor separates the two district units of the park, the North and South Units. The Lake Chelan National Recreation Area sits at the southern tip of the South Unit. The dusty Cascade River Road provides access to hikers and climbers, while a boat service carries visitors to the north shore of 50-mile-long Lake Chelan.

But while roads are scarce, trails abound. More than 350 miles of hiking and horse trails ramble through the park complex, including the northern end of the 2,600-mile Pacific Crest Trail that runs from Mexico to Canada along the spine of the Sierra Nevada and Cascade Range.

▶ HOW TO VISIT

Visitors with limited time should focus on the **North Cascades Highway.** This route offers the most scenic cross-Cascades drive in Washington. The road enters the **Ross Lake National Recreation Area** just past the small town of Marblemount.

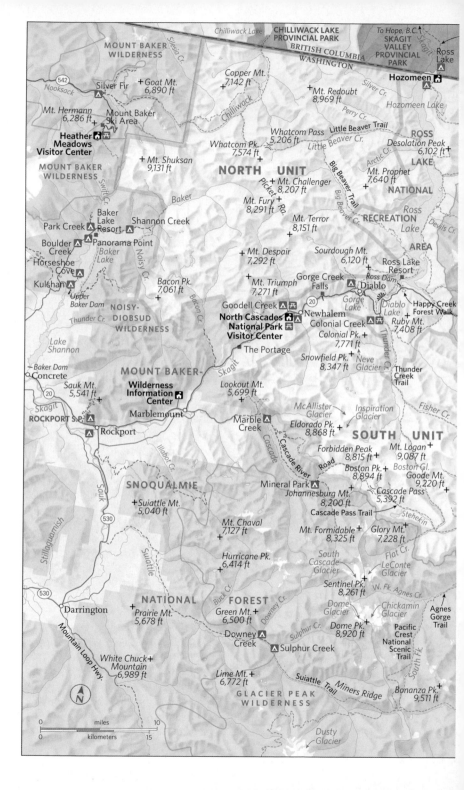

As the road climbs higher, the Skagit River becomes more robust, tumbling through the rocky gorge below Diablo Dam, which generates power for the City of Seattle.

Should you have more time, head to Chelan Lake, just beyond the park boundary. In the town of Chelan you can access the small, historic community of Stehekin via boat or floatplane. (Car isn't an option.)

North Cascades Highway

The valley narrows considerably as you approach the mountains and the park complex. The **North Cascades National Park Wilderness Information Center** sits just outside the tiny community of Marblemount (the last gas stop for 74 miles), and just east of Marblemount the highway enters the **Ross Lake National Recreation Area** and closely follows the Skagit River upstream.

As you near the small town of **Newhalem,** the ragged crests of the Pickets Range stand in relief against the northern skyline. (Newhalem is home to the crews that work on the two dams upriver.)

Near mile marker 120, outside Newhalem, stop at the **North Cascades National Park Visitor Center.** This is the place to pick up brochures and get questions answered; there are no park-entry facilities on the North Cascades Highway.

Just 5 miles east, the highway passes another small company town, **Diablo,** home to park complex employees. Diablo was founded as a rest stop for weary miners seeking relief from the rigors of the North Cascades during the early days of the 20th century.

The town's founding family, the Davises, generated the valley's first electricity, with a small waterwheel-driven turbine. Today, the Skagit River's power generation relies on the giant **Diablo** and **Ross Dams** (plus Gorge Dam, the first dam completed for the Skagit River Hydroelectric project, upriver from Newhalem). Diablo Dam is a few miles east of the town of Diablo.

The waters of Diablo Lake sparkle milky green thanks to the large amount of minerals carried into the lake by glacier-fed rivers. The slowly moving glaciers churn up a fine powdery silt that fills the rivers, creating what's known as "glacier milk." When dumped into deep lakes, this mineral-rich water reflects blues and greens, giving lake water a rich emerald hue.

Diablo Lake is a popular boating venue. Visitors without watercraft of their own can enjoy an hour-long excursion with the Seattle City Light's Excursion Tours *(seattle.gov/light/tours/skagit/boat.asp)*, which runs from Diablo Dam up to Ross Dam and back.

East of Diablo Dam, the highway curves south to follow the lake's shoreline up **Thunder Creek Bay.** Stop at the **Colonial Creek Campground** and day-use area to stretch your legs and explore the 1-mile **Thunder Woods Nature Trail.** This easy loop provides a great interpretive lesson in the local flora and fauna as it rolls through grand old stands of western red cedar and Douglas fir.

Sword ferns and salmonberries line the route, and birds such as the ever-present gray jays (a.k.a. camp robber jays) and towhees flit through the trees and share their songs. For something a little more strenuous, push on up the **Thunder Creek Trail** as far as you'd like—up to 19 miles—before turning back.

Another stop is warranted at Mile 132 and the **Diablo Lake Overlook.** From here, the lake's sparkling emerald waters can be clearly seen in contrast to the stark, dark green of the surrounding forests. The **Happy Creek Forest Walk** provides a nice forest stroll just a bit farther up the highway, near Mile 134. This 0.25-mile loop trail winds through lush forest.

The North Cascades Highway leaves the park complex and enters the Okanogan National Forest 5 miles east of Happy Creek. It follows southeastward along the eastern boundary of the North Cascades National Park South Unit. The road crests **Rainy Pass** and, just beyond, **Washington Pass.** The views here are gloriously panoramic, with the surrounding rocky spires and the jagged peaks of the park's South Unit on full display.

On clear, sunny days, look for climbers scaling the sheer rock of **Liberty Bell** and **Early Winter Spires.** Dropping from Washington Pass, the highway rolls into the Methow Valley, where the town of **Winthrop**—with an Old West feel—offers shops, cafés, and lodges.

During winter, a portion of the North Cascades Highway is closed to vehicles but can be used by skiers and snowshoers.

Lake Chelan & Stehekin

Traveling east from the park complex on Wash. 20 you'll reach the junction with US 97, alongside the Columbia

Volcanoes & Glaciers

The rugged terrain of the North Cascades National Park owes its existence to fire and ice. Volcanic fire thrust the mountains upward, while Ice Age glaciers carved them back down. Ice remains a major factor in the park today, with nearly 42 square miles of glacier ice covering parts of the park and its national recreation areas.

Every year, glacier melt provides billions of gallons of water for the area's lakes and rivers. Communities on both sides of the Cascades depend upon that water for household needs, irrigation, and hydroelectricity.

But the glaciers are shrinking. For the past several decades, the summer melt (ice loss) has far exceeded the winter accumulation (ice gain). In the North Cascades, the glaciers have lost upward of 50 percent of their total mass over the last century. (That enormous loss equals about 400 billion gallons of water to the Skagit River alone, equivalent to a 44-year water supply for Skagit County.)

The National Park Service's long-term monitoring programs measure and track this changing face of the park. Researchers estimate that the glaciers have lost nearly 5 billion gallons of water in a recent seven-year period.

The North Cascades National Park and its recreations areas contain the greatest concentration of glaciers in the United States outside of Alaska. But in the face of dramatic climate change, scientists fear this rich collection of mountain glaciers will be gone in the not too distant future.

River. A few miles south is the city of **Chelan,** at the south end of **Lake Chelan,** which is just outside the park complex. The long, snaking lake fills a deep glacier-carved valley for more than 50 miles. With a depth of 1,486 feet, Chelan is the country's third deepest lake (behind Crater Lake and Lake Tahoe).

Lake Chelan's impressive length and depth have generated a number of myths, including one that has the lake occupied by a Loch Ness Monster–type creature. Dubbed "Shelly" by locals, the great "monster" (seen in blurry old black-and-white photographs) was most likely one of the many massive trees that fall into the water from the steep, timbered slopes of the upper lake.

From the head of the lake, getting back into the park complex requires a long hike up the shoreline trail. There's a quicker option. The *Lady of the Lake* boat service *(ladyofthelake.com)* runs from Chelan to **Stehekin** daily year-round (with two runs daily in the summer). Commercial floatplane service is also available from Chelan through Lake Chelan Sea Planes *(chelanseaplanes.com)*.

The small community of Stehekin, nestles on Lake Chelan's north shore, in the shadow of Purple Mountain, offered welcome respite to gold prospectors and miners who came this way at the end of the 19th century. By the early 20th century, Stehekin had become a favored remote getaway among adventure seekers.

Today, in addition to foot, boat, and plane, the community of 75 permanent year-round residents can be reached by horseback. The Stehekin Valley itself sports 22 miles of roads—and community shuttle bus service May through October.

Stehekin offers a rich historical experience, with the **Buckner Homestead Historical District** at its heart. This farm was settled in 1889 by Bill Buzzard, who grew crops, from potatoes to apples, that were shipped downlake to Chelan.

In 1910, Buzzard sold the homestead for $5,000 to William Buckner, a Californian in search of a new life. The Buckner family moved in the following year. William's son, Harry, ran the farm after his parents moved back south to escape the frigid Northwest winters. The property was sold to the National Park Service in 1970 to become part of the Lake Chelan National Recreation Area, but the sale terms allowed Harry Buckner to live out his days there. He died in 1976.

Today, the Buckner home provides lodging for National Park Service employees, and the entire farmstead is maintained as a historic interpretive center open to visitors.

After touring Stehekin's historic district, head out to explore the majestic natural history of this portion of the park complex. Indeed, the easy 2.5-mile **Agnes Gorge Trail** provides some of the area's most scenic hiking. Be prepared for dramatic gorge views, and, in summer, wildflowers dotting the way. Take the community shuttle up the Stehekin River Valley to the High Bridge Guard Station, cross the bridge, and make your way to the trail, which heads south.

Agnes Gorge Trail winds up the Agnes Creek Valley through fragrant pine forests before coming out onto the rim of Agnes Gorge—a 210-foot chasm carved into the mountainside.

(The trail once crossed the river at the head of the gorge, but the suspension bridge that provided passage came down long ago.)

Dozens of additional trails radiate from the Stehekin Valley, some climbing for just a few miles, while others lead out for multiday adventures

The **Pacific Crest Trail,** which crosses the Stehekin Valley at High Bridge, is a good choice. One of two National Scenic Trails that pass through the park complex (the Pacific Northwest Trail is the other), the Pacific Crest Trail covers about 18 miles in the park complex. Overnight camping here requires a backcountry permit.

Cascade River Road

The Cascade River Road runs from Wash. 20 in Marblemount southeast along the Cascade River into the South Unit of the park. The 23-mile road is mostly gravel, and the upper end receives only periodic maintenance, so it can be rough and sometimes impassible. Also, portions of the road are wide enough for only one car. Check with the rangers at the Wilderness Information Center in Marblemount for up-to-the-minute road conditions as well as travel restrictions.

The road ends at a trailhead parking area that provides access to **Cascade Pass** (about 4 miles) and points beyond. Backpackers cross Cascade Pass to descend into Stehekin. Climbers also use the trail as the jumping-off point for summit attempts on nearby peaks, including Forbidden Peak (8,815 feet), Boston Peak (8,894 feet), and Sahale Mountain (8,680 feet).

Columbia black-tailed deer

Information

How to Get There

From Seattle (116 miles southwest), travel via I-5, and US 20—the North Cascades Highway. To access the park's South Unit from Marblemount, drive east on the Cascade River Road; get to the North Unit via Wash. 542—the Mount Baker Highway—out of Bellingham. Ferries and chartered floatplanes leave the town of Chelan for Stehekin, in the park.

When to Go

Park roads close sometime in October. The *Lady of the Lake* ferry runs year-round to Stehekin, which offers snowshoe and cross-country skiing opportunities. Backcountry trails start to clear in May around the lower valley and lakes, but snow lingers into July along the higher elevations.

Visitor Centers

North Cascades information centers are generally open May through Oct.: **North Cascades Visitor Center,** Newhalem; **Wilderness Information Center,** Marblemount; **Golden West Visitor Center,** Stehekin, and the **Visitor Information Center,** Sedro Woolley.

Headquarters

810 State Route 20
Sedro Woolley, WA 98284
nps.gov/noca
360-854-7200

Camping

Ross Lake NRA has three campgrounds, open May–Sept. *(recreation.gov;* 877-444-6777). **Lake Chelan NRA's** primitive campgrounds are hike-in (permit needed; 509-699-2080, ext. 14) or boat-in (federal dock permit required). 353 sites total.

Lodging

Ross Lake Resorts (accessible by boat or foot; *rosslakeresort.com);* **North Cascades Lodge** *(stehekinlanding.com);* **Silver Bay Resort** *(silverbayinn.com);* and **Stehekin Valley Ranch** *(stehekinvalleyranch.com).* For lodging outside the park, check *nps .gov/noca/planyourvisit/local-chambers -of-commerce.htm.*

Olympic

Washington

Established
June 29, 1938

922,651 acres

Olympic National Park earned widespread recognition (and international biosphere reserve status) because of its grand temperate rain forests—vast valleys of moss-laden forests filled with giant ancient trees and tumbling, crystal-clear rivers. Above the majestic emerald valleys stand glacier-covered peaks and jagged rocky ridges. West of the forested valleys runs a seemingly endless undeveloped stretch of wilderness beach.

To experience the richest variety of life, you need to visit a rain forest. And when it comes to rain forest, North America trumps every other continent in the world. The planet's greatest density of biomass (the total mass of organisms in a given area) is found in the temperate rain forests of Olympic National Park. The trees of the forest represent a large percentage of the equation. Indeed, the park's huge conifers are some of the biggest living things on the planet. The cathedral forests of Sitka spruce, western hemlock, bigleaf maples, and western red cedar fill the river valleys on the

Olympic wilderness coast

century, when the United Nations recognized the unique nature of the park and designated it a World Heritage site in 1981.

For all its natural beauty, majestic forests, and rugged terrain, the park area was initially protected because of its elk. Theodore Roosevelt awarded the region its national monument status most of all because he wanted to ensure the protection of a species of elk found primarily in the rain forest valleys on the west side of the park.

By 1912, the elk population on the Olympic Peninsula had dwindled to fewer than 150 animals. The protections covered by the national monument and, later, national park designations, kept hunters from taking those last few animals.

Today, the elk thrive and rightfully bear the name of their protector. Roosevelt elk are the largest species of elk in North America. In Olympic National Park, they have ready access to rich and plentiful food sources.

▶ HOW TO VISIT

This is a big park, and all the access roads are winding two-lane highways that can slow down travel times. Plan two days for a basic visit and at least a week for a more thorough exploration of Olympic.

For a basic park experience, head to Port Angeles and drive up to **Hurricane Ridge.** The 17-mile park road climbs steeply as it heads from near sea level to more than 5,000 feet in elevation.

Explore the verdant meadows and enjoy the stunning views—grand panoramas to the north encompass Canada's Vancouver Island across the

west side of the main body of Olympic National Park, providing habitat for Roosevelt elk and black-tailed deer. The richness of these valleys boggles the imagination.

Moss coats just about every surface, and lichen drapes from nearly every limb. Trees grow to more than 250 feet tall and upward of 200 feet in circumference. These are trees that rival their famous California cousins, the redwoods and sequoias, in size and grandeur.

President Theodore Roosevelt protected the area as a national monument in 1909, and his distant cousin Franklin D. Roosevelt designated it as a national park 29 years later. The park gained an added level of protection and distinction late in the 20th

Strait of Juan de Fuca east to Mount Baker and the peaks of the North Cascades. To the south, the Olympic Mountains stretch across the horizon, highlighted by Mount Olympus and its gleaming glaciers. After a morning spent exploring the mountains, drive west on US 101 to **Lake Crescent.** Spend the afternoon hiking one of the many trails of the area.

On day two continue south on US 101 through Forks to the Hoh River Valley. Drive up the river road to explore the world-famous **Hoh Rain Forest** before continuing south to the coastal strand of beach. The park's **Kalaloch Lodge** (a good option for an overnight) is close to the highway, with grand views of the wild Pacific Northwest coast. From Quinault,

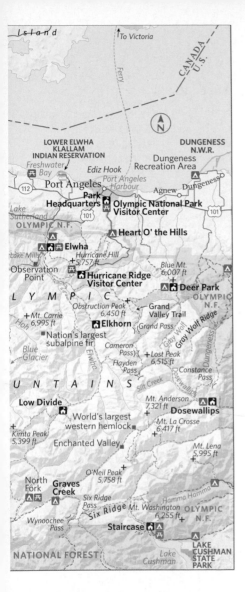

de Fuca. Thanks to the wonderfully scenic **Hurricane Ridge Road,** visitors can easily experience the panoramic views afforded by the open ridge. Looking south from the Hurricane Ridge summit, visitors see the park's central wilderness and the glacier-covered summit of **Mount Olympus.** A short trail to the north provides views across the strait to Victoria, British Columbia, and the interior peaks of Canada's Vancouver Island. To the northeast lie Mount Baker and the craggy peaks of North Cascades National Park, and to the southeast stands the sentinels of the eastern Olympics—Mount Deception, Mount Mystery, Mount Constance, and The Brothers, among others.

A mile and a half past the **Hurricane Ridge Visitor Center,** the road comes to an end at the base of **Hurricane Hill.** A gentle trail leads up the small grade, climbing through brilliant subalpine flower meadows. Going higher, the scenery becomes increasingly dramatic, with magnificent views of the interior Olympics and the valley carved by the mighty Elwha River coming into clearer view with each footstep.

The views from the summit, site of an old lookout, are grand, with wildflowers at your feet and the Olympic Range, dominated by Mount Olympus, just beyond reach, or so it would seem.

Explore the sprawling majesty of the ridge-top meadows before returning to Port Angeles and continuing west. Six miles from the park visitor center in Port Angeles, turn west onto Wash. 112 to access the **Elwha River** and the former site of the Elwha Dam. This is one of two dams removed by Olympic National Park in 2011 to restore the ecosystem of the Elwha River. By 2013, native salmon

US 101 leads to Aberdeen. Turn east on US 12 to Elma, then northeast on Wash. 8 back to US 101 near Olympia. Take I-5 back to Seattle.

Hurricane Ridge & the North Side

Towering over Port Angeles, **Hurricane Ridge** runs parallel to the Strait of Juan

had already returned to the river, and for the first time in nearly a century, salmon spawned in the park's section of the Elwha.

Back on US 101, drive west to **Lake Crescent.** The **Marymere Falls Trail** provides a leisurely 1.8-mile hike through forest to a slender ribbon of liquid beauty—the 90-foot Marymere Falls. About 10 miles past the Lake Crescent Lodge, leave US 101 by turning south on to Sol Duc River Road. The **Sol Duc Falls Trail** pierces a magnificent old-growth forest alongside the Sol Duc River.

The trail leads to one of the most scenic waterfalls—Sol Duc Falls—in the Olympic Mountains. This low, thundering cascade drops into a narrow gorge alongside the trail. The falls serve as a fine reward for the 2-mile hike.

East Side

US 101 runs north between Hood Canal and the park, providing access to the valleys that radiate out from the center of the park. The eastern half of the park receives less than a quarter of the rain totals on the west side of the park, or around 25 to 30 inches annually. As a result, you'll find fewer ferns, less moss, and far more rhododendrons growing here.

Indeed, it's not unusual to see enormous rhododendron bushes in this section of the park. These are bushes that can tower some 30 feet above the forest floor. Come spring, the forests turn vibrant pink as the rhododendrons explode into bloom.

Starting in Hoodsport, turn west off US 101 onto Wash. 119 to reach **Lake**

Hiking along Hurricane Ridge

Cushman and the **Staircase Ranger Station** at the end of the road. This scenic valley offers one of the best short hikes on the east side of the park, so take the time to amble along the 2.5-mile **Staircase Rapids Loop** for a gentle immersion into the rhododendron and fir forests of the area.

The route follows the south bank of stunningly clear **North Fork Skokomish River** before crossing a sturdy bridge at the head of the tumbling whitewater rapids. Often spotted overhead here are kingfishers, bald eagles, and ospreys watching the river for prey.

The return portion of Staircase Rapids Loop goes through lush forest adjacent to the river and even delves into an old burn to provide a lesson in forest-fire renewal.

Back at Hoodsport, make your way north on US 101, past rivers that run through and out of the park. In this area are two of the primary valleys with park access, the Dosewallips and the Quilcene.

As US 101 approaches the northern edge of the Olympic Peninsula, it curves westward to Sequim and on to Port Angeles, where you'll find the **Olympic National Park Visitor Center,** which is the headquarters for the park.

The Wet Side—Rain Forest & Beaches

The temperate rain forests of North America produce the largest accumulation of organic matter on Earth. In the park, the magnificent old-growth hemlocks, Sitka spruces, and red cedars contribute to that distinction. But the endless layers of moss, lichen, ferns, and other evergreen materials

Wild Peninsula

The heart of what would become Olympic National Park proved nearly impenetrable for the early white settlers who arrived in the mid-1800s and began to farm here. Until that point, it was local native tribes that ventured up the narrow, steep river valleys. Indeed, no recorded crossings of the Olympic Mountains existed until well into the 1880s. In 1885, a party led by U.S. Army Lieutenant Joseph P. O'Neil left Port Angeles to attempt a north-to-south crossing of the range. It took them a month to reach the crest of Hurricane Ridge (reached today in under an hour along a 17-mile road). They briefly explored the surrounding area before a courier arrived with instructions for O'Neil to report for duty at Fort Leavenworth, Kansas.

It took four years before another major expedition was launched to attempt the crossing. In 1889, the *Seattle Press* newspaper funded an exploratory expedition into the region's interior. The group—the Press Expedition—planned to follow the Elwha River into the mountains, but the winter of 1889–1890 was unusually harsh.

On May 20, 1890, the exhausted members of the Press Expedition staggered out of the Quinault forest toward the Pacific coast. The group succeeded in making the 50-mile cross-country trip, but it took them six months. Today, well-maintained hiking trails make the core of their route—from the Elwha River over the Low Divide to the Quinault Valley—an enjoyable backpacking trek for a long weekend.

that blanket every surface, usually several feet deep, also make up a portion of the biomass total. All that greenery sprouts from rich soils fed by up to 150 inches of rainfall annually.

The most iconic temperate rain forest in the world is found south of the town of Forks, off US 101. The **Hoh River Road** leads up through the Hoh Rain Forest. For more than a drive can provide, hike the 17-mile **Hoh River Trail** at road's end. The trail can be enjoyed whether you walk just a few hundred yards or hike up to the very shoulders of Mount Olympus. Regardless of the length of the adventure, the Hoh River Trail provides an unforgettable experience in a valley that plays host to massive old-growth western red cedar, Douglas fir, bigleaf maple, and Sitka spruce, all of which are draped with long, flowing beards of green.

Traveling south from the Hoh River, US 101 angles westward to brush against the edge of North America. At this corner of the park, the coastal strand stretches over 70 miles. It's a wilderness landscape that starts at the mouth of the Queets River and runs north to the Makah Indian Reservation. US 101 follows 10 miles of this coastal access from **Ruby Beach** south to **Kalaloch.**

The word "beach" can be misleading. The beaches of the park's coastal strand have nothing to do with white sand and turquoise water. Here, the Pacific Ocean pounds into the rocky edge of the continent, leaving cobblestone beaches and jagged headlands in its wake.

Just offshore rise an array of sea stacks—rocky remnants of the former coastline before the tides carved it. The rocky knobs rising from the surf tend to be popular hangouts for seabirds such as tufted puffins, as well as for marine mammals; seals and sea lions are commonly seen. Occasionally black bears venture down out of the coastal forests.

Though some of the park's more remote sections provide the best wilderness experiences, they naturally can be hard to reach. To get a great taste of the park's wild beaches and the powerful Pacific that grinds them down, make your way to **Kalaloch beach,** next to **Kalaloch Lodge.** The waterfront lodge provides overnight accommodations in the main building as well as a number of small cabins that dot the bluffs above the beach.

Northern Coast

Explorers with plenty of time may consider venturing west to **Ozette.** This remote park outpost offers grand adventures on the wild and scenic coast. The experiential highlight of this area is the 9-mile triangular **Ozette Loop,** which starts at the drive-in campground (one of 16 in the park).

The northern leg of the Ozette Loop angles west-northwest from the lakeshore, and for most of its 3-mile length, it is rustic boardwalk. (Be aware that these boardwalk planks can be slippery when wet—trekking poles and hiking shoes are highly recommended.)

At 3 miles, the trail gives way to the Pacific beach at **Cape Alava,** just south of the Ozette River. From the cobblestone strand it is 3 miles to **Sand Point.** Boardwalks cover much of the trail heading northeast, back to Lake Ozette.

Sea star at low tide

Information

How to Get There

Few roads penetrate far into the massive park, but scenic highways encircle the park, providing good access for most of it. US 101 wraps around three sides of the park, with US 12 passing the park's southern boundary. Visitors approach via the Bainbridge Island Ferry from downtown Seattle, or across the Tacoma Narrows Bridge from Tacoma.

When to Go

The park offers great activities year-round. Hurricane Ridge sports multiple hiking trails and during the winter, scenic snowshoe routes and even a small rope-tow ski area. In the west-side rain forests, it can rain at any time.

Visitor Centers

The main **Olympic National Park Visitor Center** is in Port Angeles.

Headquarters

600 E. Park Ave.
Port Angeles, WA 98362

nps.gov/olym
360-565-3130

OLYMPIC
EST 1938

Camping

Olympic National Park operates 16 drive-in campgrounds, first come, first served, except **Kalaloch Campground** and the group site at **Sol Duc.** To reserve, 360-962-2271. Backcountry permits are available from visitor and information centers, ranger stations, and online.

Lodging

Within the Park lodging is available at: **Kalaloch Lodge** *(thekalalochlodge.com;* 360-962-2271), **Lake Crescent Lodge** *(olympicnationalparks.com;* 360-928-3211), **Sol Duc Hot Springs Resort** *(olympic nationalparks.com;* 360-327-3583), **Log Cabin Resort** *(olympicnationalparks .com;* 360-928-3325), and **Lake Quinault Lodge** *(olympicnationalparks.com;* 360-288-2900). For a list of neighboring communites with accomodations check: *nps.gov/olym/planyourvisit/lodging.htm.*

Redwood

California

Established
October 2, 1968

131,983 acres;
includes state parks

The world's tallest known trees stand in the redwood forests of the northern California coast. Redwoods National Park blends federal and state lands into a harmonious ode to grandeur. While giant trees get top billing, Redwood is much more than supersize flora. The park also protects 37 miles of pristine Pacific coast, wild rivers and streams, rich wildlife populations, and relics of pioneer days.

Few national park areas have stirred such controversy as Redwood. The park was born of a long and sometimes violent struggle to save big trees from industrial logging—and the region as a whole from environmental devastation. The battle began shortly after World War I, when members of such organizations as the Save-the-Redwoods League realized that some of the world's tallest living things were quickly disappearing. Combining private donations and state funds, the league purchased tracts of redwood forest that during the 1920s became Prairie Creek State Park, Del Norte Coast State Park, and Jedediah Smith State Park.

Foothill Trail, Prairie Creek in the Redwood National Park

The number of people visiting the cathedral-like groves has expanded from fewer than 40,000 a year when Redwoods was first created to more than 800,000 today. They come to gawk at trees that, at more than 350 feet in height, would tower over the Statue of Liberty.

► HOW TO VISIT

Although US 101 runs through the heart of the park, the highway provides nothing more than a fleeting glimpse of the forest giants. Closer inspection requires leisurely drives down side roads or discovering forest trails on foot. Just outside the town of Orick, the park's **Redwood Creek** section is accessible via Bald Hills Road. Although their exact location is a well-guarded secret, some of the world's tallest known trees thrive in this drainage area. **Prairie Creek** lies at the heart of the park, a large meadow surrounded by trails through redwood forest or down Fern Canyon to gorgeous Gold Bluffs Beach. The park continues on the north side of the Klamath River in the form of **Del Norte Coast Redwoods** and **Jedediah Smith Redwoods State Parks.**

Nearly flat roads lend themselves to casual biking, and there are eight backcountry cycling routes. One can also explore the groves on horseback, or paddle Smith River and the lagoons via kayak or canoe.

Conflict started up again in the 1960s when clear-cut logging in the region reached fever pitch. Discovery of the world's tallest known tree in the threatened Tall Trees Grove by a National Geographic Society team expedited the call for federal protection. With powerful allies such as the Sierra Club and Lady Bird Johnson, the campaign finally resulted in the creation of Redwood National Park.

Land was added a decade later— including the groves with the tallest trees. In 1994, the National Park Service and the California Department of Parks and Recreation signed an agreement to manage the three redwood state parks and the national park cooperatively.

Redwood Creek

Sixteen miles north of Trinidad, past Patrick's Point, the coast highway meanders around the Humboldt Lagoons and into the national and

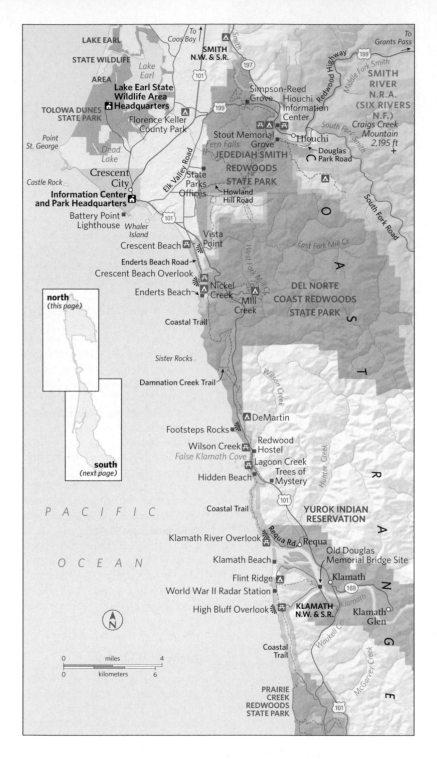

LAKE EARL
STATE WILDLIFE
AREA

Lake Earl

To
Coos Bay

SMITH
N.W. & S.R.

197

Simpson-Reed
Grove

Hiouchi
Information
Center

To
Grants Pass

199

SMITH
RIVER
N.R.A.
(SIX RIVERS
N.F.)

Craigs Creek
Mountain
2,195 ft

Redwood Highway

Middle Fork Smith

South Fork Smith

Lake Earl State
Wildlife Area
Headquarters

TOLOWA DUNES
STATE PARK

101

Florence Keller
County Park

Point
St. George

*Dead
Lake*

Stout Memorial
Grove

Hiouchi

Fern Falls

JEDEDIAH SMITH
REDWOODS
STATE PARK

Douglas
Park Road

199

Castle Rock

Crescent
City

Information Center
and Park Headquarters

Battery Point
Lighthouse

*Whaler
Island*

State
Parks
Offices

Elk Valley Road

Howland
Hill Road

O

A

S

T

South Fork Road

101

Crescent Beach

Vista
Point

Enderts Beach Road

Crescent Beach Overlook

Enderts Beach

Nickel
Creek

Mill
Creek

West Fork Mill Cr.

East Fork Mill Cr.

DEL NORTE
COAST REDWOODS
STATE PARK

Coastal Trail

north
(this page)

Sister Rocks

Damnation Creek Trail

south
(next page)

DeMartin

Footsteps Rocks

Wilson Creek

False Klamath Cove

Redwood
Hostel

Lagoon Creek
Trees of
Mystery

Wilson Creek

Hunter Creek

T

Hidden Beach

P A C I F I C

Coastal Trail

101

YUROK INDIAN
RESERVATION

R

Klamath River Overlook

Requa Rd.

Requa

Old Douglas
Memorial Bridge Site

O C E A N

Klamath Beach

Flint Ridge

World War II Radar Station

High Bluff Overlook

KLAMATH
N.W. & S.R.

Klamath

169

Klamath

Klamath
Glen

A

N

G

N

miles

0   4

kilometers

0   6

Coastal
Trail

Waukell Cr.

McGarvey Creek

E

PRAIRIE
CREEK
REDWOODS
STATE PARK

101

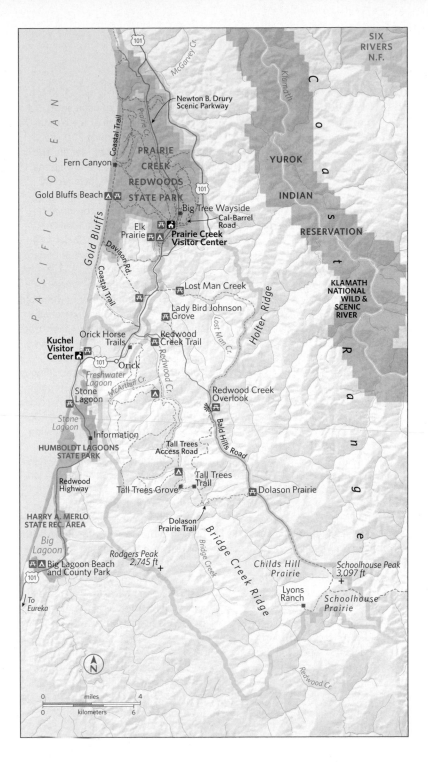

PACIFIC OCEAN

SIX RIVERS N.F.

101

McGarvey Cr.

Newton B. Drury
Scenic Parkway

Klamath

Coast

PRAIRIE
CREEK
REDWOODS
STATE PARK

YUROK

INDIAN

Prairie Cr.

Coastal Trail

Fern Canyon

Gold Bluffs Beach

Big Tree Wayside

101

Cal-Barrel
Road

Elk
Prairie

Prairie Creek
Visitor Center

RESERVATION

Gold Bluffs

Davison Rd.

Coastal Trail

Lost Man Creek

Holter Ridge

KLAMATH
NATIONAL
WILD &
SCENIC
RIVER

Lady Bird Johnson
Grove

Lost Man Cr.

Orick Horse
Trails

Redwood
Creek Trail

Kuchel
Visitor
Center

Redwood Cr.

101

Orick

Freshwater
Lagoon

McArthur Cr.

Stone
Lagoon

Redwood Creek
Overlook

Bald Hills Road

Stone
Lagoon

Information

Ra

Tall Trees
Access Road

HUMBOLDT LAGOONS
STATE PARK

Tall Trees
Trail

n

Redwood
Highway

Tall Trees Grove

Dolason Prairie

HARRY A. MERLO
STATE REC. AREA

Dolason
Prairie Trail

g

Big
Lagoon

Rodgers Peak
2,745 ft

Childs Hill
Prairie

Schoolhouse Peak
3,097 ft

e

Big Lagoon Beach
and County Park

Bridge Creek

Lyons
Ranch

Schoolhouse
Prairie

101

Bridge Creek Ridge

To
Eureka

Redwood Cr.

N

0   miles   4
0   kilometers   6

state parks just before the turnoff to **Thomas H. Kuchel Visitor Center.** Kuchel is a great place to get maps, brochures, and the scoop on daily ranger-led activities.

Many of the guides and outfitters for the park's southern region are based in **Orick** (2 miles away), an old logging town with a frontier feel. A jumping-off point for horseback trips into the park, Orick hosts a rodeo in July.

The wooded valleys and ridges east of Orick, along Redwood Creek, harbor the world's tallest known living things, including a record-holding 380-foot-tall (and growing) beauty whose exact location is known only to a handful of people (see "Big Tree Hunters," right). Scattered along Redwood Creek is the old-growth forest included in the original national park boundaries. Around this core are areas that were clear-cut prior to their addition to the park in 1978. An ambitious restoration program has revitalized this once devastated landscape.

Bald Hills Road, which starts 1 mile north of Orick, meanders through both the old-growth and restored parts of the Redwood Creek watershed. The road climbs to **Lady Bird Johnson Grove,** where the First Lady dedicated the national park in 1968. Continuing on, you'll reach the **Redwood Creek Overlook,** with views to the Pacific.

Just beyond the overlook is the turnoff for **Tall Trees Access Road,** which leads to a fabled redwood grove of the same name. Access to this road is by permit only (you need a combination for the locked gate), available for free at the Kuchel Visitor Center and the Crescent City and Hiouchi information centers. Only 50 permits

Big Tree Hunters

Humans have long been awed by the sheer size of the coastal redwoods. Over the past 200 years, people have labored to identify and save the world's tallest known trees. Conservationists have included UC Berkeley paleontologist John C. Merriam, controversial conservationist Madison Grant, Dr. Paul Zahl of the National Geographic Society, and renowned amateur naturalists Chris Atkins and Michael Taylor.

Doyen of the modern "tree huggers" is Dr. Stephen Sillett of Humboldt State University, who has personally climbed and measured the tallest trees in Redwood National and State Parks, and elsewhere along the northern California coast. Sillett started climbing big trees while a student at Oregon's Reed College in the 1980s and decided to dedicate his career to researching and preserving the biggest living things on the planet. "I've come to think of them as individuals," he says of the towering giants. "Each one is such a character."

Working in concert with the National Park Service, Sillett no longer publishes the names or locations of the world-record trees to save them from souvenir hunters and illegal climbing that could damage them.

"They don't have any defense but anonymity," Sillett says. "They're big trees—they can't run away."

are issued each day, on a first-come, first-served basis. If you can secure a pass, drive the twisting dirt road all the way down to the parking area for the **Tall Trees Trail** and set off on foot.

You'll see plants that sprouted around the time that Rome's Colosseum was under construction. It was in this grove in 1963 that National Geographic Society naturalist Dr. Paul Zahl discovered a *Sequoia sempervirens* measuring 367.8 feet in height—a world record at the time and one of the sparks for national park status.

Continuing up Bald Hills Road you'll see the landscape go from redwood forest to a mosaic of Oregon white oak woodlands and broad meadows (prairies) spangled with wildflowers in the spring. At the southernmost reach of the park, you can hike a 2-mile trail to the historic **Lyons Ranch,** with pioneer-era barns, a bunkhouse, and a cemetery—remains of a 19th-century sheep farm. Old roads wind to the top of nearby **Schoolhouse Peak,** highest point in the park (3,097 feet) and an excellent perch from which to gaze down the valley to the Pacific Ocean.

Prairie Creek

Six miles north of Orick is the turnoff from US 101 to the **Newton B. Drury Scenic Parkway,** which leads into **Prairie Creek Redwoods State Park.** The "prairie" is the vast meadow amid the redwoods where Roosevelt elk often graze. A small state park visitor center is located on the north side of the grassland. Nearby, the 0.3-mile **Revelation Trail** provides a powerful example of a redwood forest. Some of Prairie Creek's largest and most majestic trees are found along the 2.2-mile **Foothill Trail,** between the visitor center and Cal–Barrel Road.

A 4.5-mile trail winds down to lush **Fern Canyon,** a deeply eroded gorge flanked by a "hanging wall" of ferns

and slender waterfalls. The canyon's antediluvian feel made it a movie star. Steven Spielberg filmed parts of *The Lost World: Jurassic Park* in the gorge, which also appeared in the BBC series *Walking with Dinosaurs.* You can follow the canyon's meandering stream down to **Gold Bluffs Beach.** Heavy surf and cold temperatures make swimming iffy, but the beach is a great place to picnic and listen to seabirds.

Heading north from the prairie, **Newton B. Drury Scenic Parkway** runs 8 miles past old-growth redwoods

Walking a redwoods trail

before intersecting with US 101. Along the way are legendary giants like Big Tree (23.7 feet in diameter). Numerous trailheads start from the parkway, including the 1.8-mile **Ossagon Trail,** which leads to a secluded beach, where the huge rocks can be used for bouldering. Past its confluence with the parkway, US 101 descends into the **Klamath River Valley,** homeland of the Yurok people, California's largest Native American tribe. Their reservation, 1 mile on either side of the river, stretches 43 miles inland. Just before the bridge is a turnoff for the **Coastal Drive Loop,** a largely unpaved route to **Klamath Beach** and its World War II radar station, disguised as a farmhouse and barn.

North of the Klamath

After crossing the river and skirting around Klamath town, turn left onto Requa Road and follow the signs 2 miles to the **Klamath River Overlook.** Perched at more than 600 feet, the bluff affords a dramatic view of the estuary and ocean, with the possibility of spotting migrating whales and sea lions far below. Three miles up US 101 from Requa junction is **Trees of Mystery,** a historic roadside attraction founded in 1931. The privately owned park is renowned for its Sky Trail cable-car ride through the redwood canopy and giant chainsaw sculptures, relics of redwood tourism of yore. Continuing to the coast, the highway passes a series of scenic stops including Lagoon Creek, where the short **Yurok Loop Trail** affords vistas of sea stacks and coastal bird colonies. Beyond False Klamath Cove, the highway enters **Del Norte Coast**

Redwoods. Look for a pullout at Mile 16, start of the spectacular **Damnation Creek Trail,** which descends 1,100 feet to a secluded rocky beach. Eight miles farther north is a turnoff to the lovely beaches and tidepools along **Enderts Beach Road.**

Most visitors take US 101 through Crescent City to reach **Jedediah Smith Redwoods State Park,** named for explorer and trapper Jedediah Smith, who in 1828 became the first non-native to walk amid the giants. Those who prefer the road less traveled can cruise **Howland Hill Road,** a rugged route that runs through an old-growth forest called the **National Tribute Grove,** dedicated to Americans who fought in World War II. Several trails start here. One trail loops through **Stout Memorial Grove**. In 1929, soaring Stout Grove became one of the first stands of coastal redwoods set aside for protection when a 44-acre parcel was donated to the California state park system by the widow of lumber baron Frank D. Stout. Its riverside location and the way late-afternoon sun filters through make the grove a favorite.

The **Smith River** flows through the state park, warm enough between June and August to entice rafters, paddlers, and swimmers. There are plenty of spots for fishing, too—cutthroat trout in the summer and salmon or steelhead during the fall and winter. A footbridge over the river links Stout Grove with the Jed Smith campground. Tucked among the campsites, the **Jedediah Smith Visitor Center** offers information, exhibits, and interpretive programs. US 199 leads back to the coast through another redwood-rich area that includes the Simpson Reed Grove and other big tree stands.

Female elk

Information

How to Get There

From San Francisco, CA (about 310 miles south), take US 101 north via Santa Rosa and Eureka. Or take Calif. 299 from Redding, CA; US 199 from Grants Pass, OR; and US 101 from Coos Bay, OR.

When to Go

Redwood is open year-round, but has crowded trails and bumper-to-bumper roadways during summer season. Spring is great for wildflowers, autumn for chromatic leaves, while winter is cool and rainy but redwood groves are less crowded.

Visitor Centers

Thomas H. Kuchel Visitor Center, off US 101, south of Orick, CA; open year-round. Both **Prairie Creek Visitor Center,** off US 101 north of Orick, and **Jedediah Smith Visitor Center,** off US 199, northeast of Crescent City, CA, open summer only.

Headquarters

1111 Second St.
Crescent City, CA 95531
nps.gov/redw
707-465-7335

REDWOOD
EST 1968

Camping

Three national park campgrounds—
Jedediah Smith (86 sites), **Mill Creek** (145 sites), and **Elk Prairie** (75 sites)—accept reservations (*reserveamerica.com;* 800-444-7275). **Gold Bluffs Beach** (26 sites) is first come, first served. Backcountry camping requires a free permit, available from the Thomas H. Kuchel Visitor Center.

Lodging

No overnight lodging inside the park, but there are plenty of choices in nearby communities. Check out *nps.gov/redw/planyourvisit/lodging.htm.*

Alaska

Wrangell Mountains, Wrangell–St. Elias National Park

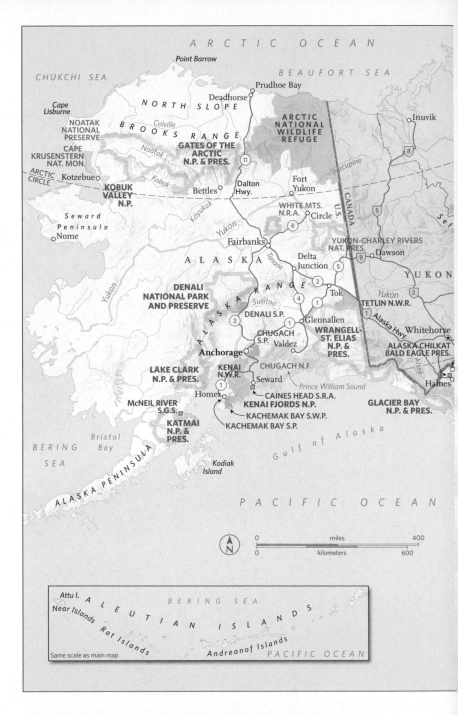

ARCTIC OCEAN

CHUKCHI SEA

Point Barrow

BEAUFORT SEA

Prudhoe Bay

Deadhorse

NORTH SLOPE

Cape Lisburne

NOATAK NATIONAL PRESERVE

BROOKS RANGE

Colville

Noatak

CAPE KRUSENSTERN NAT. MON.

GATES OF THE ARCTIC N.P. & PRES.

ARCTIC NATIONAL WILDLIFE REFUGE

Inuvik

Porcupine

ARCTIC CIRCLE

Kotzebue

Kobuk

KOBUK VALLEY N.P.

Dalton Hwy.

Bettles

Fort Yukon

WHITE MTS. N.R.A.

Circle

Koyukuk

Seward Peninsula

Nome

Yukon

Fairbanks

Tanana

CANADA

U.S.

Sel

Dawson

YUKON-CHARLEY RIVERS NAT. PRES.

ALASKA

ALASKA

RANGE

DENALI NATIONAL PARK AND PRESERVE

Susitna

DENALI S.P.

Delta Junction

Tok

YUKON

TETLIN N.W.R.

Yukon

Alaska Hwy.

Whitehorse

Yukon

CHUGACH S.P.

Glennallen

WRANGELL-ST. ELIAS N.P. & PRES.

ALASKA CHILKAT BALD EAGLE PRES.

Anchorage

Valdez

LAKE CLARK N.P. & PRES.

KENAI N.W.R.

CHUGACH N.F.

Seward

Prince William Sound

Alsek

Haines

McNEIL RIVER S.G.S.

Homer

CAINES HEAD S.R.A.

KENAI FJORDS N.P.

KACHEMAK BAY S.W.P.

KACHEMAK BAY S.P.

GLACIER BAY N.P. & PRES.

KATMAI N.P. & PRES.

Bristol Bay

BERING SEA

ALASKA PENINSULA

Kodiak Island

Gulf of Alaska

PACIFIC OCEAN

0   miles   400
0   kilometers   600

N

BERING SEA

Attu I.

Near Islands

ALEUTIAN

Rat Islands

ISLANDS

Andreanof Islands

PACIFIC OCEAN

Same scale as main map

In 1867 Secretary of State William Seward bought Alaska from Russia for two cents an acre—and the public labeled the vast empty land Seward's Folly. Today, more than 17 billion barrels of oil have gushed through the Prudhoe Bay pipeline, while Alaska's protected wilderness and wildlife attract visitors by the thousands.

Picture Alaska in your mind, and a number of scenes materialize: huge brown bears fishing for salmon; rugged coastline where glaciers calve icebergs into the sea; Denali, the highest peak in North America; herds of caribou migrating across tundra; broad rivers where rafters float for days, far from signs of civilization; and even a field of sand dunes north of the Arctic Circle.

Eight national parks protect more than 41 million acres of these natural treasures. **Katmai** and **Lake Clark** lie along the Pacific Ring of Fire—a region of active volcanoes, earthquakes, giant brown bears, and salmon. Whales, sea lions, and flocks of seabirds seek out the cold, food-laden waters of **Glacier Bay** and **Kenai Fjords. Wrangell–St. Elias** is a jumble of mountains and glaciers so rugged that many remain untrodden by humans. Above the Arctic Circle, **Gates of the Arctic** and **Kobuk Valley** protect the tundra and migrant herds of caribou. By comparison, **Denali** seems "civilized," with its nearby railroad and hotels; yet here the wildlife is so abundant and so visible that the park is referred to as a "subarctic Serengeti."

Alaska parks include national preserves that allow hunting, vast wilderness areas that prohibit buildings and roads, and native-owned lands still used for subsistence in a tradition thousands of years old.

While parks work to protect what's wild, man's hand doesn't always help matters. The *Exxon Valdez* accident in 1989 underscores the potential for long-term consequences for the habitat.

Denali

Alaska

Established
February 26, 1917

6,075,029 acres

There's no best way to take on Denali National Park. It's miles and miles of possibilities. Of all of Alaska's parks, Denali offers the widest range of experiences—from simple nature walks and guided bus tours deep into the park to backpacking trips across the tundra, and, for winter travelers, multiday backcountry dog-mushing trips. And for the most adventurous? An expedition on "The High One."

It often surprises people to find that Denali—originally called Mount McKinley National Park—wasn't created in honor of the park's namesake mountain. Actually, it all started with the Dall sheep. Hunter-naturalist Charles Sheldon visited the land during the summer of 1906 and became extraordinarily interested in the animals, writing that he was "determined to return and devote a year to their study." On that return visit, just a year later, he became ever more entranced with the wildlife and the landscapes. His experiences in the park and his conversations with a guide, Harry Karstens, gave way to ideas about preservation.

Denali (20,310 feet)

First-time visitors shouldn't shortchange themselves: Denali is not the kind of place that you can "do" in a day. Or a month, really. Give yourself at least two days (camping out if you can), so you have enough time to travel by both bus and foot, and take in a ranger-led program or two. No matter how you take on Denali, book as much of your adventure ahead of time as possible. Lodging in and around the park can fill up quickly for the peak season of July and August.

Denali Park Road: Bus Options

The Denali Park Road's 92 miles wend through splendid landscapes– past rivers, through mountain passes painted with wildflowers, and—fingers crossed—by Dall sheep and grizzlies. If you don't win a spot in the annual road lottery, you can't make the drive on your own unless you have a camping reservation at the **Teklanika River Campground** at Mile 29.

Limiting vehicle traffic helps preserve wildlife-viewing opportunities near the road. Park visitors have to take a tour bus or shuttle bus if they want to go beyond the **Savage River Check Station**. The Park Road drive can be a nail-biter, so leaving it to the professionals isn't a bad idea.

The park offers three narrated tour bus trips, running from 4.5 to 12 hours, with bus drivers constantly on the lookout for wildlife. For those short on time, the Denali Natural History Tour is an easy choice. Traveling just 17 miles along the road to **Primrose Ridge,** the tour focuses on people who have used this land stretching back thousands of years.

Denali offers surprises at every turn. The sun may catch Polychrome Pass just so, exploding the colors of the volcanic rock and plants that grow low on the tundra. A golden eagle may take flight from a ridgeline, or one of the park's blond Toklat grizzlies may amble through a valley. Or you might hear the whistling of a hoary marmot as it warns family members of a predator in the area.

▶ HOW TO VISIT

The park grabs the attention of some 500,000 people a year. Its only thoroughfare is the 92-mile **Denali Park Road.** With private vehicles restricted to the first 15 miles of the road, the way farther in is by bus, foot, bicycle (bring your own), snowshoe, or dog sled.

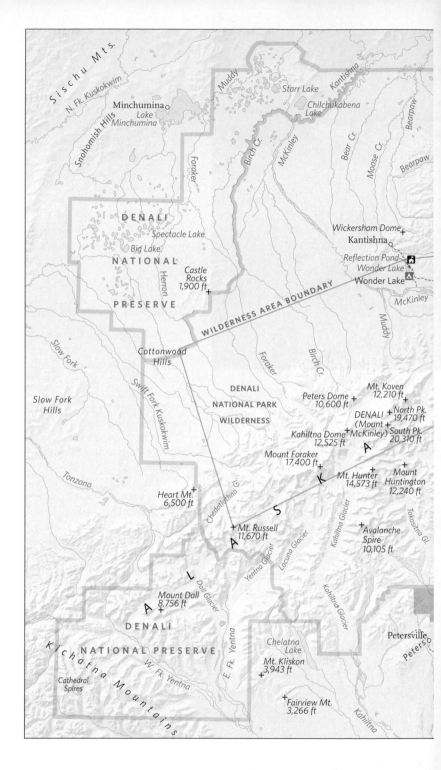

Sischu Mts.

N. Fk. Kuskokwim

Snohomish Hills

Minchumina
Lake
Minchumina

Starr Lake

Chilchukabena
Lake

Muddy

Birch Cr.

McKinley

Bear Cr.

Moose Cr.

Bearpaw

Bearpaw

Kantishna

DENALI

Spectacle Lake

Big Lake

NATIONAL

Castle
Rocks
1,900 ft

Foraker

Herron

PRESERVE

Wickersham Dome
Kantishna

Reflection Pond
Wonder Lake
Wonder Lake

McKinley

Muddy

WILDERNESS AREA BOUNDARY

Slow Fork

Slow Fork
Hills

Swift Fork Kuskokwim

Cottonwood
Hills

Foraker

Birch Cr.

DENALI

NATIONAL PARK

WILDERNESS

Peters Dome
10,600 ft

Mt. Koven
12,210 ft

Kahiltna Dome
12,525 ft

DENALI
(Mount
McKinley)

North Pk.
19,470 ft

South Pk.
20,310 ft

Tonzona

Heart Mt.
6,500 ft

Chedotlothna Gl.

Mount Foraker
17,400 ft

Mt. Hunter
14,573 ft

Mount
Huntington
12,240 ft

A

K

S

Mt. Russell
11,670 ft

A

Yentna Glacier

Lacuna Glacier

Kahiltna Glacier

Tokositna Gl.

Avalanche
Spire
10,105 ft

L

Dall Glacier

Mount Dall
8,756 ft

A

Kahiltna Glacier

DENALI

NATIONAL PRESERVE

Kichatna Mountains

Cathedral
Spires

W. Fk. Yentna

E. Fk. Yentna

Chelatna
Lake

Mt. Kliskon
3,943 ft

Fairview Mt.
3,266 ft

Petersville

Peterso

Kahiltna

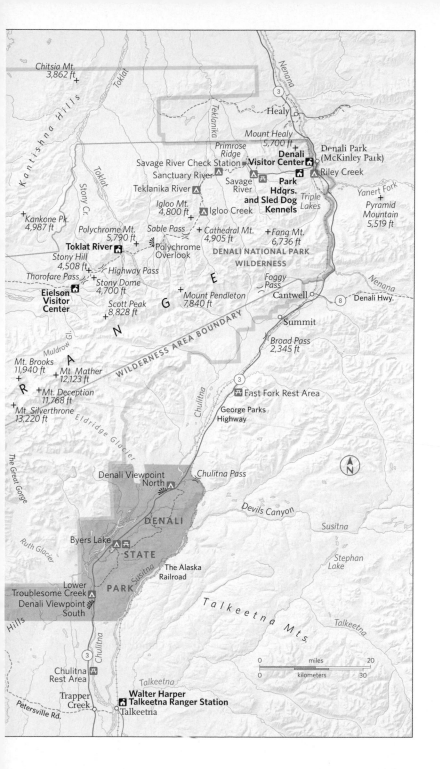

Chitsia Mt.
3,862 ft

Kantishna Hills

Toklat

Teklanika

Nenana

3

Healy

Mount Healy
5,700 ft

Primrose
Ridge

Denali
Visitor Center

Denali Park
(McKinley Park)

Savage River Check Station

Sanctuary River

Teklanika River

Savage
River

Park
Hdqrs.
and Sled Dog
Kennels

Riley Creek

Triple
Lakes

Yanert Fork

Pyramid
Mountain
5,519 ft

Stony Cr.

Toklat

Igloo Mt.
4,800 ft

Igloo Creek

Kankone Pk.
4,987 ft

Polychrome Mt.
5,790 ft

Sable Pass

Cathedral Mt.
4,905 ft

Fang Mt.
6,736 ft

Toklat River

Polychrome
Overlook

DENALI NATIONAL PARK

WILDERNESS

Stony Hill
4,508 ft

Highway Pass

Foggy
Pass

Thorofare Pass

Stony Dome
4,700 ft

Eielson
Visitor
Center

Scott Peak
8,828 ft

Mount Pendleton
7,840 ft

Cantwell

Nenana

8

Denali Hwy.

Summit

Muldrow Gl.

Broad Pass
2,345 ft

Mt. Brooks
11,940 ft

Mt. Mather
12,123 ft

WILDERNESS AREA BOUNDARY

Mt. Deception
11,768 ft

Eldridge Glacier

Chulitna

3

East Fork Rest Area

Mt. Silverthrone
13,220 ft

George Parks
Highway

The Great Gorge

Denali Viewpoint
North

Chulitna Pass

Devils Canyon

Susitna

Ruth Glacier

DENALI

Byers Lake

STATE

Stephan
Lake

Susitna

The Alaska
Railroad

Lower
Troublesome Creek

PARK

Denali Viewpoint
South

Hills

Talkeetna Mts.

Talkeetna

Chulitna

3

Chulitna
Rest Area

Talkeetna

Trapper
Creek

Petersville Rd.

Walter Harper
Talkeetna Ranger Station

Talkeetna

N

0   miles   20
0   kilometers   30

Photography buffs—and others who want to focus on the animals and plants of Denali—should take the seven- to eight-hour Tundra Wilderness Tour. The bus turns around at **Toklat River** (Mile 53) and **Stony Overlook** (Mile 62), both known for spectacular mountain views.

Go Deep

Immerse yourself in the worlds of Denali's wolves, birds, geology, and much more through an Alaska Geographic field course. Each two- to five-day class puts you in the field with naturalists, photographers, and other experts for a focused deep immersion into the subject at hand. Several classes even place students in the role of citizen scientists, giving them the opportunity to measure glaciers or conduct archaeological testing. The glaciology course gives you the chance to experience backcountry camping.

Most of the classes use the Murie Science and Learning Center Field Camp as a base. With shared tent cabins and group meals in the yurt, students feel like they're at a science camp for adults.

The field courses often require a little leg muscle for hikes that traverse spongy tundra, go up narrow ridgelines, and across talus. Read the course descriptions carefully. It makes sense to contact Alaska Geographic to see if your fitness level is a good match for the class that interests you. (Bonus for teachers: Many of the courses offer professional development credits through the University of Alaska.) For more information, *alaska geographic.com;* 907-683-6432.

Though it makes for a long day (it's not unusual to see people napping on the way back), the best way to get an overview of the park is through the 11- to 12-hour Kantishna Experience. The tour runs the full length of the road out to the historic mining community of **Kantishna.** Given that there's usually snow at the end of the road into late May, this tour isn't offered until early June.

If hiking or backcountry camping is in your plans, skip the tour bus in favor of one of the park shuttle buses or a camper bus. There's no narration on these buses, though most of the drivers are happy to answer questions (try to hold off as they're making some of the more head-spinning turns along the road). And of course, the drivers stop for wildlife.

The shuttle buses offer a good deal of flexibility. You can hop off at any time to embark on a hike or simply take a stroll. When you're ready to continue along or head back, just flag down a bus. On busy days you may have to wait a while before a bus with an empty seat shows up. Camper buses, which run June to September, have room for gear and bikes.

Scenic Stops Along the Way

The **Savage River Bridge** (Mile 14.8) marks the farthest advance of a glacier that flowed north out of the Alaska Range and across the valley thousands of years ago. A short way on, the road winds below **Primrose Ridge** before dropping into a marshy flat with spruce trees leaning every which way—the result of permafrost thaws that cause the land to slump.

Before crossing the **Teklanika River Bridge,** get your camera so you can photograph the river below. For an even better vantage, continue on to the Tek Rest Area, about a mile east of the bridge at Mile 30. At Mile 34, you'll pass **Igloo Mountain** and **Cathedral Mountain**—favorite hangouts of Dall sheep. One of the best spots to watch for grizzly bears is **Sable Pass** (Mile 39). This is the only portion of the park closed to foot traffic. Sable Pass is richly endowed with the various roots and berries that grizzlies favor.

After the pass, the road climbs to what should be a mandatory stop: **Plains of Murie,** which overlooks **Polychrome Pass.** From this vantage point, Denali can appear as though it was painted onto the sky. The colors can be so vivid that it all looks unreal.

It was in the area of Mile 53 that Charles Sheldon wintered in 1907 and fell in love with the land and the animals. He would spend the next nine years lobbying for the creation of a national park.

Shortly beyond, bicyclists should remember to keep breathing as the road climbs to its highest point, **Highway Pass** (3,980 feet). The next climb, to **Stony Hill Overlook,** may, weather permitting, bring on oohs and aahs as Denali—just under 40 miles away—comes into view. This high ground is favored by the park's caribou herd.

At Mile 66, take a break to explore the **Eielson Visitor Center,** where (once again, weather permitting) the

Biking the park road with the Alaska Range in the background

viewing areas put Denali in the spotlight. For another take on the landscape around Eielson (and one that rivals Polychrome for color), step inside to see artist Ree Nancarrow's "Seasons of Denali" quilt.

Some of the best photography spots beyond Eielson include **Wonder Lake** and along the moderate 1.5-mile trail from the **Wonder Lake Campground Reflection Pond** (Mile 85).

Hiking & Biking the Park Road

One of the best times to bike the Denali Park Road is late spring, just before the buses begin running. Secure a spot at **Riley Creek Campground**—no reservations are necessary before the peak season begins—and pedal or drive your bike to the **Teklanika River.** Bring plenty of food and water; there's none available along the way.

If exploring the park in winter appeals to you, you're in luck. During the winter months, snowshoers and cross-country skiers pretty much have the road to themselves.

No matter how you travel the road, on clear days you can get a glimpse of Denali, the mountain once known as Mount McKinley, starting at Mile 9. But even if the mountain is hiding in the clouds during your visit, the road offers a near-endless supply of delights.

Off Road

Few spots in Denali are off-limits to hikers. Unless you have experience with backcountry hiking, however, ask the rangers at the visitor center to help you match a hike with

your skill set. Be sure to bring maps, water, food, and extra clothing with you. The park has a small number of maintained trails, ranging from simple nature walks (many of these close to the visitor center) to the challenging **Mount Healy Overlook Trail,** a 9-mile out-and-back hike that climbs some 1,700 feet in less than 4.5 miles.

Whether on trail or off, pack out everything you bring in. And, when off-trail, make sure you and your fellow hikers spread out. This helps ensure that your touch on the land is light.

Another worthwhile hike takes you to **Primrose Ridge,** which gets its name from a purple flower that grows only in the park. **Primrose Ridge Trail** is favored by birders. Start your hike from the west side of **Savage River Canyon** or one of the ridges west of **Savage River** (Mile 17 to 20). The new 4-mile **Savage Alpine Trail** is a good alternative to Primrose Ridge that gets you above tree line.

Sled Dog Kennels

For dependable animal sighting, there's no better stop than the sled dog kennels. The dogs are used to patrolling the wilderness core of the park, which is closed to snowmobiles. During summer months, three times a day, rangers share information on the importance of dog teams in the national park—and demonstrate the power and speed of the resident huskies. (Buses leave the Denali Visitor Center for the kennel programs.) The kennels are also open to visitors during the winter months, though there's no guarantee the dogs will be home—that's their working season.

Sled dog and ranger

Information

How to Get There

From the Anchorage area, proceed north on the George Parks Hwy. From Fairbanks, drive south on the George Parks Hwy. The Alaska Railroad offers daily service from Anchorage and Fairbanks from mid-May to mid-Sept.; in winter, weekends only.

When to Go

Summer solstice (June 20 or 21) brings 21 hours of sunlight to Denali. July usually offers the best weather. Open year-round, the park offers the most services from late May to mid-Sept. The park explodes with fall color late Aug. or early Sept.

Visitor Centers

Denali Visitor Center, Mile 1.5 on the Park Road; **Wilderness Access Center** (for park buses and campground reservations), Mile 1; **Eielson Visitor Center,** Mile 66 (accessible by park bus); **Murie Science and Learning Center,** Mile 1.4, serves as the winter visitor center. Climbers must stop at the **Walter Harper Talkeetna Ranger Station,** 100 miles south of the entrance, for permits.

Headquarters

Mile 3 on the Park Road
Denali Park, AK 99755
nps.gov/dena
907-683-9532

Camping

The park's six campgrounds offer a total of 274 campsites; for details, *reserve denali.com.* For backcountry camping, permits are available at the **Backcountry Information Center** (Mile 1 on the Park Road), open mid-May to mid-Sept.

Lodging

Lodging within the park is found at four private lodges (on private land): **Camp Denali & North Face Lodge** *(campde nali.com);* **Denali Backcountry Lodge** *(alaskadenalitravel.com);* **Kantishna Roadhouse** *(kantishnaroadhouse.com);* and *(katair.com/skyline.html).* Outside the park, there are many lodging options in the towns of Cantwell and Healy *(denalichamber.com).*

Gates of the Arctic

Alaska

Established
December 2, 1980

8,400,000 acres

The northernmost national park in the United States, entirely north of the Arctic Circle, Gates of the Arctic National Park and Preserve is a wilderness landscape of plains between mountains that rise in jagged majesty. It is a rich land populated by Porcupine caribou, musk ox, Dall sheep, grizzlies, black bears, moose, wolves, and waterfowl. Gates of the Arctic is a dramatic reminder of an ancient world.

This is archetypal Alaska, with its towering mountains and wealth of wildlife—to see and hear. Night after night, the haunted howl of wolves fill the air. Gates of the Arctic National Park (and Preserve; see p. 446) occupies the heart of Alaska. The park is primarily boreal forest, which consists of spruce, birch, willow, and aspen,

all stunted by permafrost. Millions of ponds dot the valleys, home to a world of waterfowl.

The park includes the Endicott Mountains to the east and the Schwatka Mountains in the southwest, both sub-ranges of the grand Brooks Range, which stretches more than 700 miles across Alaska and Canada.

Hikers in Thunder Valley

▶ HOW TO VISIT

Gates of the Arctic is truly remote. The only way to access the park is to fly or hike in, unless you're really good with sled dogs and extreme winter weather. But charter planes make the entire park accessible to visitors.

The park has no trails; visitors can hike anywhere, though it is important to know that river crossings are cold and dangerous, and that tussocks (clumps of sedge grasses growing in mounds from ground that's often boggy) can really slow you down.

No matter where you choose to hike, prepare to be challenged. That said, there are few feelings as satisfying as hiking into an arctic valley, looking at a landscape very few ever get to see, and knowing you got there

under your own power. Guide services out of Bettles and, to a lesser extent, Coldfoot offer a range of exploration options. Commercial operators offer trips on the **Noatak** and **Alatna Rivers.**

Bettles & Flight-Seeing

For most people coming to the park, Bettles is the hub. At first glance, the town looks like little more than a runway and a bar. A few people live here, but a lot more work hereabouts, guiding fishermen out for sheefish, arctic char, and trout; taking hunters to areas outside the park; and guiding campers to the best corners of the park. A stop at **park headquarters** here is highly recommended for general orientation and for the lecture on bears and safety.

Flight-seeing Gates of the Arctic out of Bettles puts visitors in a position to grasp the park's diverse landscapes. There are rivers that squeeze through tiny passes between mountains, tundra that looks like a finger-painted garden, and mountains that stretch on seemingly forever.

The **Arrigetch Peaks,** granite spires topping out at 4,000 feet, rise from the **Endicott Mountains.** The peaks' name means "fingers of the outstretched hand" in the Inupiat dialect, but these are more like claws, sharp and jagged.

Anaktuvuk Pass

Several operators in Fairbanks offer day trips to Anaktuvuk Pass, a village surrounded by jagged mountains. The population of the village hovers around 300, and people here live in much as their ancestors did. The villagers remains dependent upon

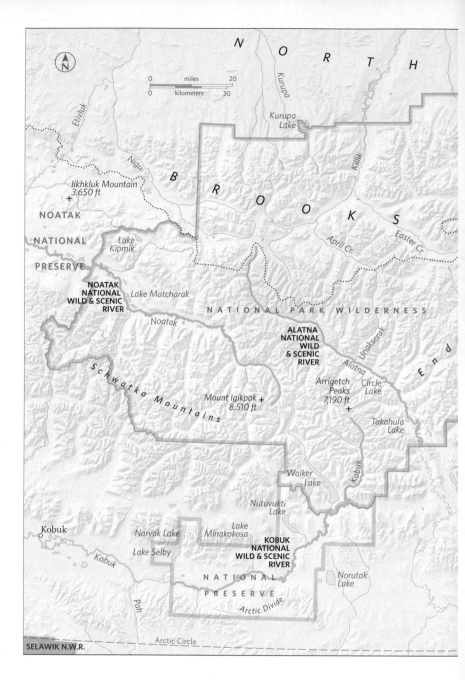

understanding the land: knowing when the caribou are coming; reading weather in the colors of the mountains. Villagers meet flights that are coming in from Fairbanks if they are expecting freight deliveries. At the airport, the villagers sell handsome hand-crafted masks and other traditional objects.

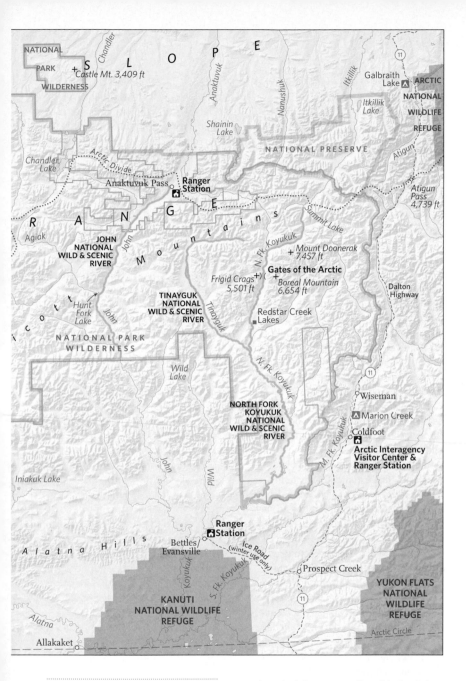

By Water

Quite a few rivers in the park make for good canoeing and river-floating (most visitors use collapsible boats). A week on the **Alatna River** gives visitors a chance to see the diversity of the park, from tundra to forest.

Put in at **Walker Lake** for the **Kobuk River,** which can be paddled from Gates of the Arctic all the way down

Arctic National Wildlife Refuge

Gates of the Arctic National Park and Preserve covers a small portion of Alaska north of the Arctic Circle and west of the Dalton Highway. East of the highway, the Arctic National Wildlife Refuge preserves some 19,640,000 acres, making it more than twice as large as Gates of the Arctic National Park. Inside the refuge's borders are a coastal plain, calving grounds for the Porcupine caribou herd, a river of animals that can exceed 198,000 individuals during migration.

The landscape varies from the flat tundra of the coastal plain to the Brooks Range. Many Arctic rivers, such as the Wind and the Hulahula, flow through the Brooks Range to the north and south.

The Arctic Preserve was long used by Alaska Native hunters. They didn't leave a lot of traces behind, not much more than some campfire rings and caribou fences that have rotted back into the tundra.

The future of the Arctic Refuge is a matter of great controversy: There is oil under the territory where the caribou calve. The issue is an international one because the Porcupine caribou herd migrates between Alaska and Canada.

Travel to the refuge can be arranged out of Fairbanks: Charter flights take hikers and campers from Alaska's version of the big city into one of the world's deepest wildernesses. Go prepared, and go prepared to be amazed.

to Kobuk Valley National Park. But the glory waterway is the **Noatak River,** which offers the best way to see the park on a multi-day trip. The Noatak, only a portion of which is in the park, flows east-west, cutting through the park amid rolling mountains and the occasional glacier erratic. On the hills above the river, caribou and musk ox browse the tundra, while grizzly bears seek out caribou and musk ox.

On its journey to the coast from the Brooks Range, the Noatak River travels nearly 400 miles through the largest intact river basin ringed by mountains. Deep wilderness, **Noatak Basin** is one of the least disturbed natural ecosystems in the world. It was designated a UNESCO Biosphere Reserve in 1976.

The views from the water are spectacular. The **Schwatka Mountains** form a wall to the south; to the north, lower hills sweep into passes favored by caribou. Beaches are covered in moose tracks. Wolves yip in the middle of the night (which, in summer, is never fully dark).

Jackdaws fly out of willows that hug the river, seeking water to grow. Every now and then the river runs past a pingo (a mound of earth covered by ice). Pingos can be 200 feet high, and when the sun hits them just right, it seems as if they're glowing.

The river itself is an easy paddle, rarely more than Class I. Paddling experience, though, is recommended for trips in spring, when runoff increases the speed of the water. A number of outfitters run multi-day float trips on the Noatak, usually taking out at **Lake Matcharak,** which is large enough to accommodate floatplanes.

The Alanta River, looping through a pass in the Brooks Range

Information

How to Get There

Air taxis connect the park with Bettles; it's easy (although expensive) to get to Bettles or Anaktuvuk Pass from Fairbanks. More remote destinations require additional advance planning. You can drive to Coldfoot, on the Dalton Highway, 280 miles north of Fairbanks, and hike into the park—or charter a plane. In winter, an ice road, built primarily of snow, connects Bettles and Dalton, crossing rivers with no bridges.

When to Go

The park is open year-round. A winter visit is a challenging and potentially dangerous proposition. July and Aug. are nearly perfect. After the summer, the tundra is washed with autumn color.

Visitor Center

The park's visitor center (907-692-5494), in **Bettles,** is open year-round, daily in summer and weekday afternoons in winter.

Headquarters

Bettles Visitor Center
P.O. Box 26030
Bettles, AK 99726
nps.gov/gaar
907-692-5494

Camping

You can camp anywhere in the park; no permit is needed. It is wise, however, to register your itinerary with park officials. Observe all bear precautions, including using bear-resistant food canisters. Take enough extra food and water to allow for being weathered in for a few days—a not uncommon occurrence.

Lodging

Operated by concessioners, **Iniakuk Lake Wilderness Lodge** *(gofarnorth .com;* 877-479-6354) and **Peace of Selby Wilderness Lodge** *(alaskawilderness .net;* 907-672-3206) offer cabins in the park. There is one lodging option in Bettles, the concessioner-run **Bettles Lodge** *(bettleslodge.com;* 907-692-5111).

Glacier Bay

Alaska

Established
December 2, 1980

3,280,198 acres

When John Muir came into Glacier Bay for the first time, in 1890, "sunshine streamed through the luminous fringes of the clouds and fell on the green waters of the fiord, the glittering bergs, the crystal bluffs of the vast glacier, the intensely white, far-spreading fields of ice ... making a picture of icy wildness unspeakably pure and sublime." Glacier Bay National Park retains that magic, offering everything you want to see in Alaska, viewable in a single day.

George Vancouver, a British naval officer, sailed this way in 1794 to map the region. There was no bay then, just a 5-mile inlet; all around were mountains and glaciers.

Before Vancouver's explorations, local Tlingit people, who had called the area home for centuries, were forced to flee 20 miles south when the glaciers suddenly advanced.

Since Vancouver's time, the ice has retreated some 60 miles, leaving a deep glacial fjord now populated by plants and animals. Today, of all the tidewater glaciers in the park, 13 reach to the Gulf of Alaska.

Steller sea lions on South Marble Island

► HOW TO VISIT

Most people see Glacier Bay from the deck of a ship. Many cruise companies have itineraries that include the bay, and a park concessioner runs a day boat. Some craft go all the way up to the **West Arm.**

The eastern arm, **Muir Inlet,** is the domain of small private boats and kayaks. The only developed hiking trail starts at **Bartlett Cove,** near headquarters. But you can hike just about anywhere you'd like in the park. The only limits: ice and impassable thickets of alder.

Main Channel

What attracts most visitors is the wildlife, including sea otters, humpback whales, harbor porpoises, and Steller sea lions. A popular spot for the sea lions, which can grow to more than 1,000 pounds, is **Marble Islands.** It's not uncommon here to see well more than a hundred sea lions barking and pushing at each other, trying to get the best spots on the sun-warmed rocks.

South Marble Island and other nearby islands are a wonderland for bird-watching—not just southeast Alaska's usual suspects, bald eagles and ravens, but also cormorants, pigeon guillemots, murres—and the birds that cause everybody to stop and notice: tufted and horned puffins, with their brightly colored beaks. More than 274 species of bird have been spotted in the park.

Past the Marble Islands, the channel divides at **Tlingit Point.** During the glacial retreat, the ice split around this point, carving out the two arms of Glacier Bay. What was once a single huge river of ice became the **Grand Pacific Glacier** to the west, **Muir Glacier** to the east. The point remains a favorite camping spot for kayakers.

West Arm

Ships continue up the West Arm, following the path of the **Grand Pacific Glacier** and offering misty glimpses of the highest range of coastal mountains in North America, topping out at over 15,300 feet on Mount Fairweather.

From here up to the end of the bay, the water becomes less the usual silver of southeast Alaska and more aquamarine, the result of glacial silt from melt and runoff. Harbor seals

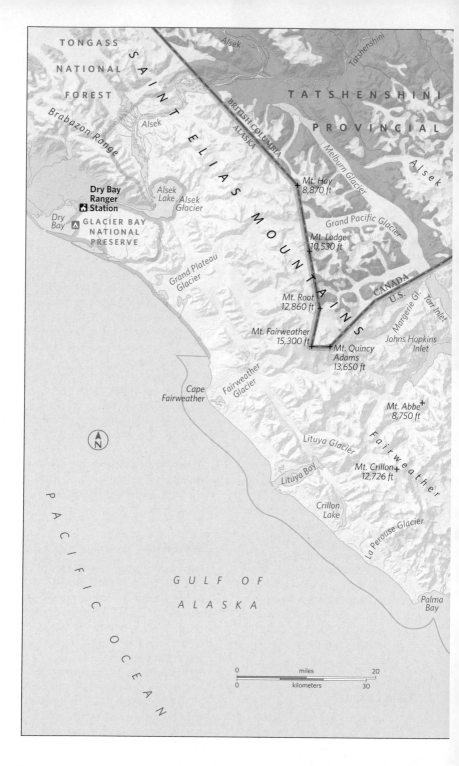

TONGASS

NATIONAL

FOREST

Brabazon Range

SAINT

Alsek

BRITISH COLUMBIA
ALASKA

TATSHENSHINI

Tatshenshini

PROVINCIAL

Melburn Glacier

Alsek

Mt. Hay
8,870 ft

Alsek
Lake   Alsek
        Glacier

Dry Bay
Ranger
Station

Dry
Bay

GLACIER BAY
NATIONAL
PRESERVE

Grand Plateau
Glacier

ELIAS

Grand Pacific Glacier

Mt. Lodge
10,530 ft

MOUNTAINS

CANADA
U.S.

Mt. Root
12,860 ft +

Margerie Gl.

Tarr Inlet

Mt. Fairweather
15,300 ft +
         +Mt. Quincy
          Adams
          13,650 ft

Johns Hopkins
Inlet

Cape
Fairweather

Fairweather
Glacier

Mt. Abbe +
8,750 ft

N

Lituya Glacier

Fairweather

Lituya Bay

Mt. Crillon +
12,726 ft

Crillon
Lake

La Perouse Glacier

PACIFIC

GULF   OF

ALASKA

Palma
Bay

OCEAN

0   miles   20
0   kilometers   30

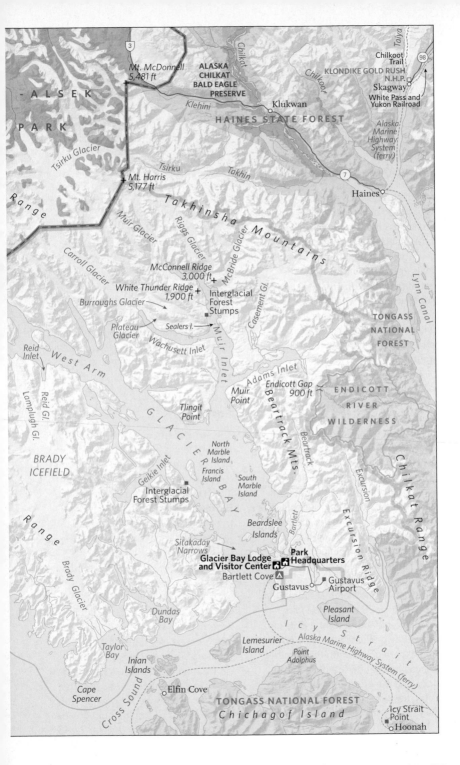

gravitate to silt areas, coming here to have pups. In the mountains around the channel there's still a good chance you could spot mountain goats and maybe even bears.

Whale-Watching Icy Strait

Glacier Bay empties into Icy Strait, a broad channel that runs east-west across the top of the Alexander Archipelago. Almost directly across the water from the mouth of Glacier Bay is Point Adolphus, one of the best places in Southeast Alaska to watch humpback whales. Dozens of these giants—up to 60 feet long and weighing 40 tons—take to the rich upwellings of the point, superb feeding grounds.

Whales around the point tend to be a lot more active than they are at many other spots, affording a better chance to see breaching. When the entire whale comes out of the water, it can seem like a slow-motion effort.

Excursions to Point Adolphus can be booked in Gustavus or at Icy Strait Point, in the village of Hoonah, originally settled by the Tlingit people. The best way to see the whales, though, is from a kayak, which puts you on their level. There's nothing quite like being close enough to a whale to hear it exhale, but visitors must comply with strict Marine Mammal Protection and the Glacier Bay National Park distance regulations. Rent a kayak in Glacier Bay or Gustavus. Some paddling experience is definitely required because navigating the strait can be tricky. But the effort put out is worth it. Any day you see a whale slowly rolling in the sea is a very good day.

Mile-wide **Margerie Glacier** is about 55 miles from Bartlett Cove. Only a mile from the Canadian border, Margerie calves regularly: Huge chunks of ice break off the face of the glacier and crash into the sea. And not only do glacier chunks break off above the waterline, they can do so underneath as well.

A few hundred yards away is **Grand Pacific Glacier.** Maybe it's not as grand as it was when it covered the entire bay, but it still stretches back more than 25 miles. Not long before Muir was here, scientists say, Grand Pacific retreated some 10 miles in a ten-year span. It is not retreating now, but it is thinning. Between Grand Pacific and Margerie glaciers, it seems almost as if the world ends here in a wall of sapphire blue ice.

East Arm

The eastern arm of Glacier Bay, **Muir Inlet,** is a lot quieter and less trafficked than the West Arm. From Tlingit Point, the inlet passes the **Plateau Glacier.** Most kayakers head to **McBride** and **Burroughs glaciers.** Others stick to the main channel, out of Rowless Point, for views of **Burroughs** and **Casement** glaciers (west and east, respectively) dramatically framed by jagged crevasses.

The inlet dead-ends at **Muir Glacier,** about 30 feet tall, 0.5 mile wide, and 12.5 miles long, Muir is retreating quickly: Since 1941, the glacier has moved back more than 7 miles, and has thinned by more than 2,000 feet at its thickest points. The odds are you'll have the bay just about to yourself here, nothing but you and the masssive, waning glaciers.

Columbine (*Aquilegia*) in the temperate rain forest near Bartlett Cove

Information

How to Get There

In summer, Alaska Airlines (*alaskaair.com*) offers daily flights between Juneau and Gustavus, the closest airport to the park (9 miles away); a number of small carriers fly floatplanes and single-engine craft, including Wings of Alaska (*wingsofalaska .com*) and Alaska Seaplanes (*alaskasea planes.com*). The Alaska Marine Highway (*dot.state.ak.us/amhs*), the state's ferry system, runs boats between Juneau and Gustavus twice a week in summer. Private boat and charter planes are the only way to access the park off-season.

When to Go

Open year-round, the park is most visited between mid-May and mid-Sept. Most services close down the rest of the year.

Visitor Centers

Glacier Bay Visitor Center and **Headquarters** are located in Bartlett Cove. For private boat and camping permits, contact the **Visitor Information Center** (open May through Sept.; 907-697-2627), across from the dock.

Headquarters

P.O. Box 140
Gustavus, AK 99826
nps.gov/glba
907-697-2230

GLACIER BAY
EST 1980

Camping

The only campground (33 sites) in the national park is in **Bartlett Cove,** about a quarter mile from headquarters. For backcountry camping, widely available throughout the park, a free permit is required May through Sept., as is attendance at an orientation session, which includes information on dealing with tides and bears. Bear-proof food containers are required. The entire park is bear country (remember, bears can swim).

Lodging

Concessioner-operated **Glacier Bay Lodge** (*visitglacierbay.com;* 888-229-8687), open late May to early Sept., is in Bartlett Cove, along with park headquarters. Nine miles from the park, the town of **Gustavus** (*gustavusak.com*) has a wide variety of accommodations.

Glacier Bay Excursions

Misty Fiords National Monument
Ketchikan, Alaska, area

▷ A natural collage of 3,000-foot sea granite cliffs, steep fjords, and thick rain forests accessible only by boat or small plane. Ketchikan, 22 miles away, serves as the gateway to the Misty Fiords. Visitors can either rent kayaks or arrange to be dropped off and picked up by tour boat to take advantage of the few designated trails for trout and salmon fishing. Guides can be hired. Cabins available. Located 300 miles southeast of Glacier Bay National Park. *fs.usda.gov/attmain /tongass/specialplaces;* 907-225-2148.

Admiralty Island National Monument
Juneau, Alaska, area

▷ This one-million-acre monument is home to one of the highest concentration of brown bears in the world. Pack Creek, preserved as the Stan Price State Wildlife Sanctuary, offers the best viewing points. Advance reservations required July to late August. Located 15 miles from Juneau, the monument can be accessed by boat or floatplane from Juneau. Located south of Glacier Bay National Park. *fs.usda .gov/detail/tongass/recreation/nature viewing/?cid=stelprdb5401890;* 907-586-8790.

Mendenhall Glacier
Near Juneau, Alaska

▷ Thirteen miles long, the Mendenhall Glacier covers the space between the Juneau Icefield and Mendenhall Lake. One of the best views of the expanse comes from the Mendenhall Visitor Center (closed April). From here, several trails branch off and allow visitors alternative views of the glacier, as well as black bears, coyotes, porcupines, snowshoe hares, and mountain goats. Located 14 miles northwest of Glacier Bay National Park via plane or boat. *www.fs.usda.gov/detail/tongass/about -forest/offices/?cid=stelprdb5400800;* 907-789-0097.

Alaska Chilkat Bald Eagle Preserve
Haines, Alaska

▷ Home to the world's largest concentration of bald eagles, the preserve offers visitors the opportunity to view these majestic birds in their natural environment. The best area from which to view them is from the Haines Highway pullouts between Miles 18 and 22, around the Chilkat River salmon runs. Spotting scopes, interpretive displays, and viewing platforms can be found at the pullouts. Peak eagle-spotting season is October to February. Located 110 miles northeast of Glacier Bay National Park. *nr.alaska.gov/parks/ units/eagleprv*; 907-465-4563.

Chilkat State Park
Haines, Alaska

▷ Visitors can observe bears, moose, whales, seals, sea lions, eagles, blue herons, and a wide variety of shore-birds. Many of these animals as well as the Rainbow and Davidson glaciers can be seen from the log cabin visitor center in the park. Activities include hiking, camping, fishing, and boating. Open mid-May to mid-September. Located 7 miles south of Haines and 100 miles northwest of Glacier Bay National Park. *dnr.alaska.gov/parks /aspunits/southeast/chilkatsp*; 907-766-2234.

Russell Fjord Wilderness
Near Yakutat, Alaska

▷ Russell Fjord Wilderness is home to wolves, mountain goats, brown bears, and black bears including the rare black bears of "blue" coloring that live only near glaciers. The park's most dramatic geologic features are the Hubbard Glacier and the Russell and Nunatak fjords. The rugged interior can be accessed only via floatplane or boat from Yakutat (12 miles west) or by float-plane from Juneau (200 miles southeast). Located northwest of Glacier Bay National Park. *wilderness.net/NWPS/ wildView?WID=506*; 907-784-3359.

Katmai

Alaska

Established
December 2, 1980

4,093,077 acres

Remote yet easily accessed by floatplane, Katmai National Park hooks visitors from the very start—whether on a day trip to the bear-viewing stations at Brooks Camp, on a float trip down the Alagnak River, or camping in the Valley of Ten Thousand Smokes. The park's 4 million acres provide a lifetime's worth of return trips, each one a chance to explore this wild world on a deeper level.

With no roads into the park, every trip to Katmai starts with an adventure of travel by boat or floatplane, over sparkling lakes and powerful rivers, with bear on the shores.

The park got its start in 1918, when President Woodrow Wilson established Katmai National Monument to protect the Valley of Ten Thousand Smokes, a landscape formed in 1912 when Novarupta Volcano was birthed. The stunning eruption—which went on for 60 hours—was so powerful that more than 100 miles away, skies were darkened with ash.

The bears and the valley are the obvious lures. Opportunities abound for fishing, hiking, kayaking, canoeing,

A bear and its quarry

welcome, it's best to spend some time at Brooks by booking a cabin—though they're pricey—or, better, a spot at the campground. Overnighters can hike during the day and wait for the day-trippers to fly back out before heading to the bear-viewing platforms.

There's a good reason for the mandatory 20-minute ranger and video introduction. The bears are everywhere. But for guaranteed sightings, walk 1 mile from Brooks Camp to one of the three viewing platforms, including the most coveted spot at **Brooks Falls.** There visitors watch brown bears fish for salmon, hang out under the falls, and, most dramatic of all, go head to head to determine dominance.

If planning to stay at Brooks for more than a day, reserve a spot on the **Valley of Ten Thousand Smokes** tour. After a somewhat slow 23-mile drive—which includes three very bumpy (but fun) stream crossings and stops for a first look into the valley and, of course, for wildlife along the way—the bus arrives at the Robert F. Griggs Visitor Center. Those comfortable hiking in bear country on their own should opt to bring their own lunch and imme-diately set off down the 1.5-mile trail. Otherwise, sign on for lunch and a hike *(fee)* in the company of a park ranger. Once in the valley, it's ash and pumice as far as the eye can see.

For a stunning view of **Naknek Lake,** hike up **Dumpling Mountain.** The 8-mile out-and-back trail climbs 800 feet in the first 1.5 miles. The last 2.5 miles to the summit weave through a variety of land-scapes, including boreal forest and alpine tundra. Be ready to spot every-thing from bears to wildflowers,

and photography. It's all just a float-plane ride away.

► HOW TO VISIT

From day trips to weeks-long back-country adventures, Katmai is a land of outstanding options. If time is short, take a bear-viewing trip on a float-plane out of Kodiak or Homer. For a longer trip that offers a good variety of outdoor experiences—and a great fireplace where you can swap tales with other travelers—head to **Brooks Camp.**

Brooks Camp & Valley of Ten Thousand Smokes

Brooks is an experience that shouldn't be missed. Though day-trippers are

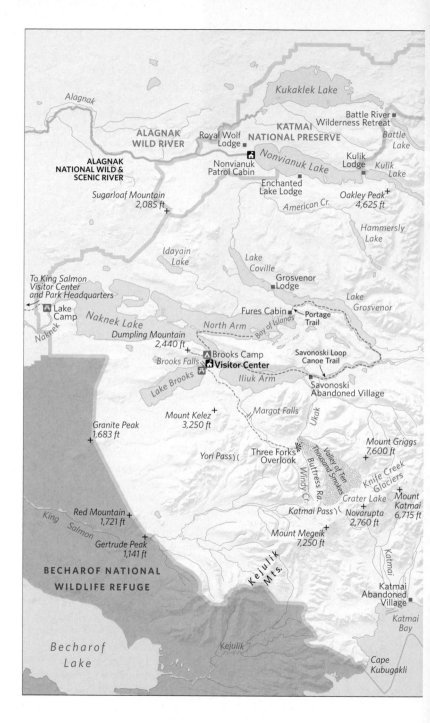

Alagnak

ALAGNAK
WILD RIVER

ALAGNAK
NATIONAL WILD &
SCENIC RIVER

Sugarloaf Mountain
2,085 ft

Kukaklek Lake

Royal Wolf
Lodge

Nonvianuk Lake

KATMAI
NATIONAL PRESERVE

Battle River
Wilderness Retreat

Battle
Lake

Nonvianuk
Patrol Cabin

Enchanted
Lake Lodge

American Cr.

Kulik
Lodge

Kulik
Lake

Oakley Peak
4,625 ft

Hammersly
Lake

Idayain
Lake

Lake
Coville

Grosvenor
Lodge

Lake
Grosvenor

To King Salmon
Visitor Center
and Park Headquarters

Lake
Camp

Naknek

Naknek Lake

Dumpling Mountain
2,440 ft

North Arm

Bay of Islands

Fures Cabin

Portage
Trail

Brooks Camp
Visitor Center

Savonoski Loop
Canoe Trail

Brooks Falls

Lake Brooks

Iliuk Arm

Savonoski
Abandoned Village

Mount Kelez
3,250 ft

Margot Falls

Ukak

Granite Peak
1,683 ft

Yori Pass

Three Forks
Overlook

Windy Cr.

Buttress Ra.

Valley of Ten
Thousand Smokes

Mount Griggs
7,600 ft

Knife Creek
Glaciers

King

Salmon

Red Mountain
1,721 ft

Crater Lake

Katmai Pass

Novarupta
2,760 ft

Mount
Katmai
6,715 ft

Gertrude Peak
1,141 ft

Mount Megeik
7,250 ft

BECHAROF NATIONAL
WILDLIFE REFUGE

Kejulik
Mts.

Kejulik

Katmai

Katmai
Abandoned
Village

Becharof
Lake

Katmai
Bay

Cape
Kubugakli

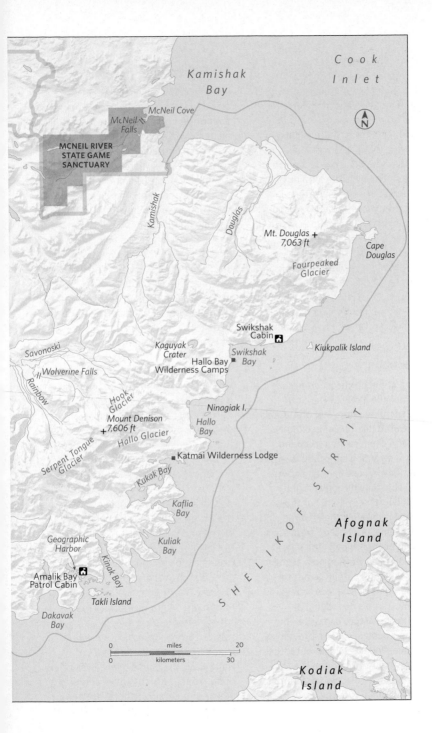

Cook
Inlet

Kamishak
Bay

McNeil Cove

McNeil
Falls

MCNEIL RIVER
STATE GAME
SANCTUARY

Kamishak

Douglas

Mt. Douglas +
7,063 ft

Cape
Douglas

Fourpeaked
Glacier

Swikshak
Cabin

Kiukpalik Island

Kaguyak
Crater

Swikshak
Bay

Savonoski

Hallo Bay
Wilderness Camps

Wolverine Falls

Hook
Glacier

Ninagiak I.

Mount Denison
+ 7,606 ft

Rainbow

Hallo Glacier

Hallo
Bay

Serpent Tongue
Glacier

Katmai Wilderness Lodge

Kukak Bay

SHELIKOF STRAIT

Kaflia
Bay

Afognak
Island

Geographic
Harbor

Kuliak
Bay

Kinak Bay

Amalik Bay
Patrol Cabin

Takli Island

Dakavak
Bay

| 0 | miles | 20 |
| 0 | kilometers | 30 |

Kodiak
Island

including chocolate lilies, lupine, and wild irises, and foliage that colors the landscape with purples, yellows, reds, and more greens than you ever thought existed.

The much shorter **Cultural Site Trail,** just 0.1 miles, is a walk back in time, with a quick introduction to the area's human history, ending at a reconstructed semi-subterranean dwelling (pit house) based on archae-ological findings about homes that may have been built here as early as A.D. 1200.

Get a bear's-eye view of **Brooks River** by hiring a fishing guide for a few hours. Even inexperienced anglers will get a thrill learning to fly-fish in the company of brown bears.

The Neighbor

Sitting at the northeast corner of Katmai, the McNeil River State Game Sanctuary offers one of Alaska's most coveted bear-viewing experi-ences, with chum salmon grabbing the bears' attention early July to mid-August. Viewing and camping spots are available only through a tightly controlled lottery system. For those who make it through, the rewards are great. One lucky group witnessed 74 brown bears fishing in the river at one time. The viewing area at the falls sits 2 miles from the campsite; be prepared to walk across a creek or lagoon. There's no lodging at McNeil, just a 14-spot campsite—but the campground is staffed, provides a cook cabin, and has two pit outhouses and a washhouse. The camp is acces-sible by air taxi. To apply for a permit to McNeil, *adfg.alaska.gov.*

Water & Air Trips

Experienced paddlers find plenty of challenge and delight on the 80-mile **Savonoski Loop.** Highlights include an overnight stop at **Fures Cabin.** A one-room house built of spruce logs by trapper and miner Roy Fure in 1916, it's now available as a public-use cabin (for reservations, *recreation.gov*). Or you can take a trip down the braided **Savonoski River.** Prepare for por-tages, plenty of bugs, and lots of wind along the way. The full trip, which starts and ends at Brooks Camp, takes between four and ten days.

For a shorter boating trip good for less experienced paddlers, hire a guide to take you to the picturesque **Bay of Islands** on the North Arm Naknek Lake, 22 miles from Brooks Camp.

But for those who are set on bear-viewing, there might be no greater thrill in Katmai than a day trip in a floatplane to view the animals from on high. Bear guides lead trips from Homer, Kodiak, and many other com-munities. The pilots know which areas are most likely to have bears at differ-ent points in the summer.

Once the animals are spotted from the air, the pilots touch down on the water, and guides lead small groups to view bears from a close—but safe—distance, no viewing platform neces-sary. Watch as the massive males try to show one another up in the battle for a mate or, at times, take a long snooze after getting their fill of salmon. Some top spots for viewing include **Geographic Harbor** and **Hallo Bay.** The flights themselves offer quite a thrill, with the water and land below offering up incredible patterns and colors.

Katmai caldera

Information

How to Get There

To get to Brooks Camp, take a regularly scheduled flight from Anchorage on to King Salmon. From there, book an air taxi or powerboat ride for the last hop to Brooks. Plan ahead. For day trips or flights to other areas of the park, including the Pacific coast of the park, charters on a floatplane can be booked from places such as Kodiak, Homer, and Anchorage. Check *nps.gov/akso/management/ commercial_services directory.cfm* for information on flight/guide services.

When to Go

The park is open year-round. For hiking, fishing, and boating, the best time to visit is June to mid-Sept. July, Sept., and Oct. are peak bear-viewing months. Summer brings changeable weather, with temperatures that can dip into the 30s.

Visitor Centers

King Salmon Visitor Center, next to the King Salmon Airport. Open year-round. **Brooks Camp Visitor Center,** reachable by charter plane. Open June to mid-Sept.

Headquarters

1000 Silver St.
Building 603
King Salmon, AK 99613
nps.gov/katm
907-246-3305

Camping

The park's only organized campground is at **Brooks Camp.** Reservations are required and can be made at *recreation. gov.* For backcountry camping, there's no limit to available space in the park.

Lodging

Lodging within the park is managed by concessioners. Katmailand runs **Brooks Lodge** and **Grosvenor Lodge** *(info@ katmailand;* 800-544-0551). Several fishing lodges on privately owned land pepper the park. Check with *visitbristol bay.org/* for additional information.

Kenai Fjords

Alaska

Established
December 2, 1980

669,983 acres

Sandwiched between the Kenai Mountains and the Gulf of Alaska, Kenai Fjords National Park, the smallest of Alaska's national parks, brings to life what people who have only dreamed of visiting the state might imagine. Here, for both day-trippers and intrepid adventurers to explore, is a vast swath of ice and snow, glaciers, rocky coastline, bands of forest, and, soaring above it all, bald eagles on the hunt for their next meal.

The ice is the main draw—but it's just the start. (Add to the mix bears, birds, and, on the glaciers, ice worms.) The Harding Icefield and the more than 30 glaciers it feeds extend over 700 square miles. A remnant of the Pleistocene era, Harding Icefield was once part of a massive ice sheet that blanketed most of what is now Alaska. At thousands of feet thick, ice remains an important part of the landscape, covering some 51 percent of the park. The crown, literally, of Kenai Flords, Harding Icefield is the largest icefield situated completely within the United States.

Aialik Bay with Harris Peninsula in the background

► HOW TO VISIT

The best bet for those who want a good overview is to take a day cruise or a flight-seeing trip to see the fjords and the glaciers, and then spend a day hiking to the icefield (or, at least, part of a day to get part of the way—the trail can be quite a challenge). But there also are easy hikes that get you great glacier views. Another way to experience the park is by floatplane or helicopter. The bird's-eye view underscores the enormity of the park's icy landscapes. For the unabashedly adventurous? Go deep: Sign up for a multi-day paddling trip.

No matter how you decide to enter the park, for safety's sake keep an eye out for creatures from the start of your adventure.

Kenai is a birder's delight, with seabirds nesting along the coastline. Watch for puffins speeding by over the water. Up high, train your eye for peregrine falcons or, walking the treeless slopes, mountain goats. And while you are cruising the water, harbor seals could float by on an ice floe, or an orca might, with no warning, leap high into the air, with shouts of "Did you see that?" coming from your fellow passengers on deck.

Exit Glacier & Harding Icefield

The only section of the park accessible by road, the **Exit Glacier** area provides several hiking trails to appeal to a wide range of comfort levels. No matter which trail you choose to wander down (or, in some cases, up), bring water, layers of clothing, and, to avoid surprising bears and other wildlife, make noise as you hike.

If you're after a quick-and-easy chance to look at the glacier, turn left at the **Exit Glacier Nature Center** and head down the 1-mile wheelchair-accessible trail to **Glacier View.** For a more challenging option that takes you close enough to the glacier to see its electric robin egg's blue color, continue on to the 1.2-mile trail to **Edge of the Glacier.**

If a good workout and a goes-on-forever view of the **Harding Icefield** sounds like a fine day out, consider the 8.2-mile out-and-back **Harding Icefield Trail.** The trail climbs about 1,000 feet for each mile on the way up. Good spots to stop along the way include **Marmot Meadows** at Mile 1.4 and **Top of the Cliffs Overlook** at Mile 2.4. Keep in mind that there's usually

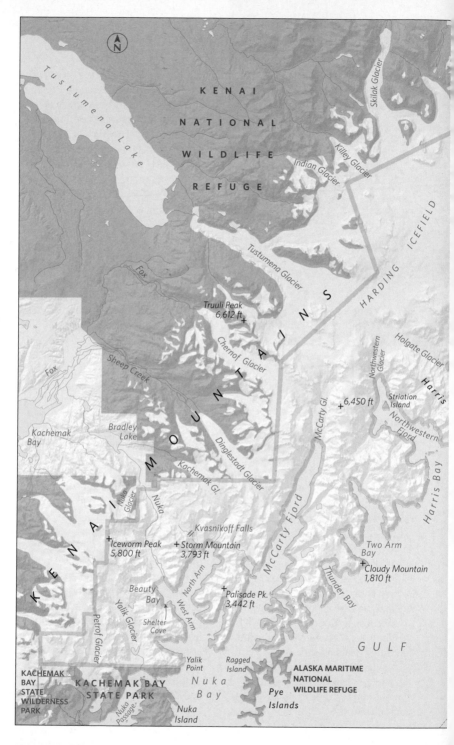

N

K E N A I

N A T I O N A L

W I L D L I F E

R E F U G E

Tustumena Lake

Fox

Skilak Glacier

Killey Glacier

Indian Glacier

Tustumena Glacier

HARDING ICEFIELD

Truuli Peak
6,612 ft

Chernof Glacier

M O U N T A I N S

Fox

Sheep Creek

Bradley Lake

Kachemak Bay

Holgate Glacier

Northwestern Glacier

+6,450 ft

Striation Island

Harris

Northwestern Fiord

McCarty Gl.

Harris Bay

Dinglestadt Glacier

Kachemak Gl.

Nuka Glacier

Nuka

Kvasnikoff Falls

+Iceworm Peak
5,800 ft

+Storm Mountain
3,793 ft

K E N A I

Beauty Bay

North Arm

West Arm

Yalik Glacier

Shelter Cove

Petrof Glacier

McCarty Fjord

Two Arm Bay

+Cloudy Mountain
1,810 ft

Thunder Bay

+Palisade Pk.
3,442 ft

G U L F

KACHEMAK BAY STATE WILDERNESS PARK

KACHEMAK BAY STATE PARK

Yalik Point

Nuka Passage

Nuka Bay

Ragged Island

Nuka Island

Pye Islands

ALASKA MARITIME NATIONAL WILDLIFE REFUGE

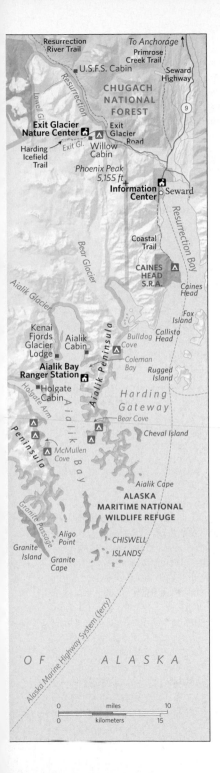

snow at the top of the trail well into the summer (or, some years, all summer long).

Be prepared to hike on mud and snow or to cut the hike short—you'll still get in plenty of views of the glacier and icefield. The trail is also open throughout the winter but may be extremely challenging because of ice and deep snow.

On the Water

No matter how many times you hear it, it never gets old. Listening to the crack of a calving glacier—and the splash that follows as the ice bombs into the water—is an unforgettable experience. The best chance to hear that crack is via a full-day boat tour, which covers a good 100 miles.

Tours leave from Seward's small boat harbor and head into **Resurrection Bay.** You'll see fjords, wildlife, and tidewater glaciers (sheets of ice that extend to meet the sea).

The boats go by **Caines Head**— site of a World War II fort—and **Callisto Head,** before going around **Aialik Cape** into far calmer **Aialik Bay.** That's where you'll get to see—and maybe even hear—the **Holgate** and **Aialik Glaciers.**

For those who prefer to provide the power for their boat, consider a kayaking trip—either a guided day trip or, for experienced paddlers, a multi-day trip. Don't overestimate your paddling experience—these are not calm waters, and the weather and wind change quickly, making for very challenging paddling.

Less demanding is to hire a water taxi to drop you off at a beach or cove. Some of the best camping coves include **Bear Cove**, the **Coleman Bay Area** (near the Aialik Bay Ranger Station), and **McMullen Cove**.

Favorites of both Alaskans and

Some Green Near the Ice

Bears, whales, seals, sea lions, puffins, and mountain goats may draw the most oohs and aahs from visitors but there are impressive— though quieter—life forms living in the park: its trees and plants. Often within eyeshot (or wind-blown chill) of the glaciers and icefield, there are three primary kinds of "plant communities" within Kenai Fjords National Park: coniferous forest, deciduous forest, and alpine plant communities.

The coniferous forest's Sitka spruce is an evergreen that looks slightly gray; mountain hemlocks are brighter green. In their shade grows Alaska blueberry and watermelon berry, which range from orangey-red to a deep shade of purple.

The park's deciduous forest areas grow thick with black cottonwoods and Sitka alders. These trees can tolerate more moisture than can spruce. Look for cottonwoods and alders around Exit Glacier and near streams and rivers.

But, for those who climb above treeline—which sits between 750 and 1,000 feet in the park's mountains—the alpine plants await. The shrubs and grasses here are some of the park's heartiest, able to withstand the higher altitude's harsh winds and short growing season. Here look for thick shrubs, miniature flowers, and, for the truly lucky hiker, herds of grazing mountain goats.

visitors, the state's network of public-use cabins offers good (bear-safe) base camps. But don't head out to a **Kenai Fjords cabin** without a reservation (907-644-3661) or camping gear—the bunks are wood and require sleeping pads and sleeping bags. And there's no electricity or running water.

The **Aialik cabin,** which sits at the head of **Aialik Bay,** is accessible by boat or floatplane from Seward. (Note: The cabin is on land leased from the Port Graham Native Corporation, so if you want to hike beyond the 5-acre site, you'll need to get a permit: 907-284-2212. A hike to **Abra Cove,** well outside the 5-acre area, makes that arrangement well worth the time.)

Check in with park rangers to find out about tide times and how many hours you should allow for a given activity. Spend your days kayaking, hiking, or tidepooling—or, thanks to the long summer days, some of each. During blueberry season, bring containers along and stock up—just watch out for the berry-loving big bears (and maybe even their cubs).

Also accessible from Seward by boat or floatplane is the **Holgate cabin.** Sitting on a bluff above a beach, the cabin offers stellar views of the **Holgate glacier.** (Keep that in mind if a giant cracking noise wakes you up in the night, it's just the glacier shedding some of its ice.) Also part of the scenario: lots of mosquitoes. Be sure to pack bug repellent and a head net.

There's one established campground. Backcountry camping is allowed through most of the park, including along the Harding Icefield Trail and in coves and beaches throughout the fjords.

A breaching humpback whale

Information

How to Get There

Take the Seward Highway (AK-1, which turns to AK-9) south from Anchorage. Leave extra time to make the 126-mile trip on the National Scenic Byway, brimming with photo ops. (Watch for surfers taking on the bore tide.) During summer, RV traffic can slow the drive down. There is daily bus and Alaska Railroad service between Anchorage and Seward during the summer months. Charter flights are also available from Anchorage and Homer.

When to Go

Though open year-round, most visitors explore the park during the summer months, when boat trips are offered. Flight-seeing companies run trips year-round out of Seward (subject to cancellation because of harsh weather). The road to Exit Glacier usually opens in late spring; it closes to car traffic with the first snowfall. Once there's enough snow coverage, the 7-mile road opens to those who want to trek, dog-sled, or cross-country ski. Hikers and bicyclists are allowed on the road year-round.

Visitor Centers

The **Kenai Fjords National Park Information Center** at Seward's small harbor is open mid-May to mid-Sept. The **Exit Glacier Nature Center** is at the Exit Glacier trailhead.

Headquarters

500 Adams St., #103
Seward, AK 99664
nps.gov/kefj
907-422-0500

Camping

The park's established campground (12 sites) is first come, first served. The park also offers two summer-use cabins (see p. 466).There's also a winter-only cabin: **Willow Cabin** at Exit Glacier. For cabin reservations, 907-644-3661.

Lodging

In the park there's concessioner-operated **Kenai Fjords Glacier Lodge** (kenaifjords glacierlodge.com). **Seward** (seward.com; 907-224-8051) offers lodging options.

KENAI FJORDS
EST 1980

Kobuk Valley

Alaska

Established
December 2, 1980

1,795,280 acres

In the heart of the Arctic, Kobuk Valley National Park is one of the least visited parks in the system, seeing maybe 5,000 travelers a year. There are neither roads nor entrance gates here. Nearly all is wild. What people miss by passing it by, though, are 100-foot-tall sand dunes, some of the oldest evidence of human settlement in North America, and the chance to experience a quarter-million caribou on the move.

Well above the Arctic Circle, Kobuk Valley is nowhere near the beaten track. Over the course of a busy year, the park will see fewer visitors than Yellowstone's Old Faithful gets in a single hour on a rainy summer Sunday. Most years, Kobuk Valley is listed as the least visited National Park in the entire system; some years, not even a thousand people make their way here.

Seasonally populating the park is the largest caribou herd in the United States. The majestic animals pass through twice a year, heading north in the spring and south in the fall.

A paddler in a folding canoe takes in a Kobuk River view.

More than a hundred species of birds use the park as a flyway and nesting ground. The very remoteness of the park—the very fact so few people come here—is what makes Kobuk Valley one of the most vital areas protected by the National Park Service. Here, it's never been anything but business as usual for nature.

Kobuk Valley is a transition zone, with Gates of the Arctic National Park to the east, the Bering Sea to the west, Noatak National Preserve to the north, and the Selawik National Wildlife Refuge to the south. Within Kobuk Valley, the great birch and spruce forests of central Alaska give way to the tundra of the Arctic.

In general, the farther north you go, the shorter the trees are, having a hard time surviving the cold soil to send roots down past the permafrost. A very tall tree in the Arctic is five or six feet high, and those are usually along riverbanks, where the water helps growth and adds to the visual landscape.

The park does not have the high peaks of the central Brooks Range. The highest mountain in the park is Mount Angayukaqsraq, just 4,760 feet high. Still, the mountains are many and imposing, with the Baird Mountains (a subrange of the Brooks) practically cutting the park in half.

► HOW TO VISIT

This is one of the most remote areas of the United States, a place where those familiar with Arctic travel fare best. Some adventurers float in, paddling the **Kobuk River** (often frozen) or the even more remote **Salmon River** (only for the extremely hardy; you must carry a pack raft up to the headwaters to access the river).

Use the banks as base camps for hiking and the rivers themselves as roads. Plan well, dress for changing weather, and expect a bear around nearly every corner. Welcome to Alaska's Garden of Eden.

River Travel

Most visitors see the park from the vantage of its rivers. The **Salmon River,** designated a Wild River, drops through the park north to south before meeting the **Kobuk River.** Though only about 2 percent of visitors float the Salmon, it is the best place from which to see the landscape change from tundra in the northern reaches to forest in the south. Up at the headwaters, the river is fast, squeezing through a narrow valley, but

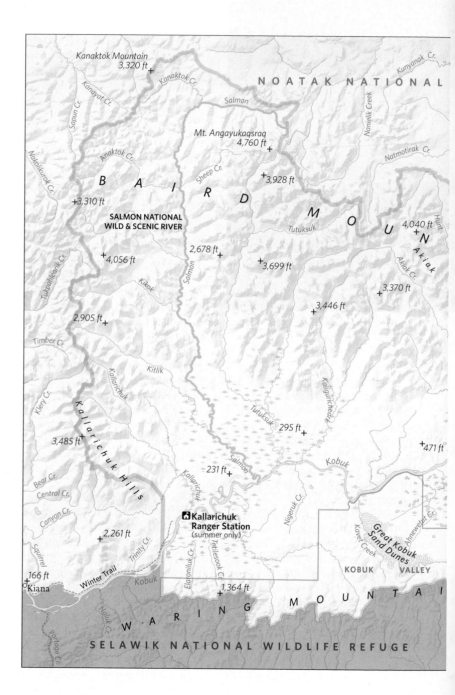

Kanaktok Mountain
3,320 ft

Kanaktok Cr.

Sapun Cr.

Kanavat Cr.

Nokolikurok Cr.

Anaktok Cr.

NOATAK NATIONAL

Salmon

Kunyanak Cr.

Nanielik Creek

Natmotirak Cr.

Mt. Angayukaqsraq
4,760 ft

Sheep Cr.

+3,928 ft

B   A   I   R   D

+3,310 ft

SALMON NATIONAL
WILD & SCENIC RIVER

+4,056 ft

Kikot

Tukpathlearik Cr.

2,905 ft+

Timber Cr.

Kallarichuk

Kitlik

Klery Cr.

Kallarichuk Hills

3,485 ft+

Bear Cr.

Central Cr.

Canyon Cr.

Squirrel Cr.

2,261 ft+

Trinity Cr.

166 ft
+
Kiana

Winter Trail

Kobuk

Nolak Cr.

Portage Cr.

Salmon

2,678 ft+

+3,699 ft

M   O   U   N

Tutuksuk

4,040 ft
+

Hunt

Akiak Cr.

A k i a k

3,370 ft

+3,446 ft

Kaligurichearik

Tutuksuk

295 ft+

Salmon

231 ft+

Kallarichuk

🏠 Kallarichuk
Ranger Station
(summer only)

Elatoniluk Cr.

Tetliesook Cr.

Nigeruk Cr.

Kobuk

+471 ft

Great Kobuk
Sand Dunes

Kovel Creek

Ahnewetut Cr.

KOBUK   VALLEY

Kobuk

1,364 ft+

W   A   R   I   N   G   M   O   U   N   T   A   I

W

SELAWIK NATIONAL WILDLIFE REFUGE

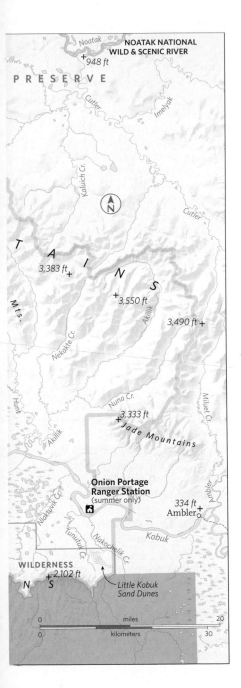

for the final third of the way, it's slow and shallow, with the water forming enchanting turquoise pools.

The Kobuk River cuts across the southern quarter of the park, stretching more than 200 miles in all, 61 of which are inside the park. It's a slow river, barely a current in most places, and clear (unlike so many northern

Bering Land Bridge National Preserve

For thousands of years, North America and Asia were connected by the Bering Land Bridge. The word "bridge" is unfortunate, suggesting something no more than a mile long. But the Bering Land Bridge—an entire ecosystem now called Beringia—once stretched as much as 400 miles north to south. This was the route used by the first humans to come to what is now North America.

And then the ice melted, the sea rose, and the continents became separate entities. Today, the preserve, on the U.S. side of Beringia, is a landscape of tundra and sweeping mountains, musk oxen, and caribou. The preserve's landscape is a jagged array of tors—large freestanding outcroppings—above a miniature forest of tundra. Some of the largest grizzly bears in Alaska walk this territory. The preserve includes the largest maar lake in the world. (A maar is a broad, low-relief volcanic crater that, when filled with water, forms a shallow lake.)

Most visitors who come charter a flight from Kotzebue or Nome into Serpentine Hot Springs. Getting to the preserve is expensive. Being there is unforgettable.

rivers, it's fed by glacier). The river is very popular with salmon, which swim upstream more than 100 miles from the coast to spawn here.

Private operators run canoe trips on the Kobuk River, with camping on beaches filigreed with moose and wolf tracks. Most trips are a week long. The trip route runs between **Ambler** and **Kiana.**

Onion Portage & Sand Dunes

Onion Portage, in the shadow of the Jade Mountains, on the eastern side of the park, is a handy shortcut point for people paddling the Kobuk River. It cuts about 10 very twisting river miles from a journey. The site, though, is notable for its location.

From here, when the time is right, it's easy to watch the approaching caribou come down through the white spruce and birch forest on their migration. What's more, this is an archaeological site with some of the oldest human remains in North America.

Onion Portage features eight distinct layers of stratification—a rarity in the Arctic, where permafrost churns up everything. This piece of land dates back some 10,000 years ago, when there was no such thing as North America (the land was joined to Asia at the Bering Land Bridge; see p. 471).

The people in the Kobuk Valley at the time of the Woodland Culture of Onion Portage were the ones who came across the Bering Land Bridge and found everything they needed here.

The **Onion Portage site,** studied by pioneering archaeologist J. Louis Giddings, was a prime hunting grounds for native peoples during times of migration. Tools found at the site attest to the evolution of hunting techniques. At the time of the earliest settlement, this area would have hosted mammoths, scimitar cats, and beavers the size of coffee tables.

The portage remains an important crossing point for such animals as moose, caribou, and black bear. A highlight of any Arctic trip is watching a massive heard of caribou swim a crossing: they're so well-adapted to the water it's as if they're moving along on a conveyor belt, their heads barely moving.

The archaeological site has been allowed to go wild again, so there's not much to see, except one of the prettiest crossroads in the Arctic.

One of the most unusual features of the park is **Great Kobuk Sand Dunes,** grainy glacial silt covering an area of about 200,000 acres. Most of this terrain is hidden under plant life now, but three "active" dunes remain (about one-tenth of the dune area in all).

These are classically shaped sand dunes, carved into crescents by the constant wind and standing more than 100 feet high. The dunes are accessible via a hike south from the Kobuk River, near where the Hunt River comes in. There are no trails and no markers, so finding one's way in from the Kobuk River is a considerable challenge. The hike involves slogging through boggy tundra at least some of the way to the dunes.

Seen from the air, the dunes look like the product of someone having dropped a chunk of the Sahara down into a bog. Taking advantage of the habitat, birds fill the wetlands surrounding the dune area.

Great Kobuk sand dunes

Information

How to Get There

The only way in is by plane. Alaska Airlines *(alaskaair.com)* flies from Anchorage to the park's city of Kotzebue. The national park website has a list of pilots who have a permit to fly into the park. Visitors who bring collapsible boats can float from Ambler to Kiana.

When to Go

The park is open year-round, but only very experienced wilderness adventurers should consider visiting outside summer months. Any time of year, expect sudden weather shifts. Snowmobile access is permitted in winter.

Visitor Centers

The park's visitor center (907-422-3890), open year-round, is the **Northwest Heritage Center,** in Kotzebue.

Headquarters

P.O. Box 1029
171 Third Ave., Kotzebue, AK 99752
nps.gov/kova
907-442-3890

Camping

There are no developed campgrounds. With a few exceptions, you can camp anywhere in the park. No permit is needed, but for the sake of safety you should register your itinerary with park officials. Observe all bear precautions, and take enough extra food to allow for being weathered-in for a few days—not uncommon.

Lodging

The nearest lodging is in **Kotzebue** *(cityofkotzebue.com)*.

Lake Clark

Alaska

Established
December 2, 1980

4,030,006 acres

The land of the Dena'ina Athabascan people for 14,000 years is just as notable for the home that one man, Richard Proenneke, made here for 30 years. Lake Clark National Park and Preserve offers a diversity of experiences and landscapes that cause even state residents to swoon. Be prepared to revel in the reflections of volcanoes and remain ever ready for bear-viewing opportunities, all the while dreaming of ways to stay for a while.

Though it's just 100 miles southwest of Anchorage, the roadless Lake Clark remains one of America's least visited national parks. But it's worth chartering a floatplane—the taxis of Alaska—to get there (even if just for a day trip). From wildlife viewing and fishing to cultural history and landscapes so majestic—dense forest, far-sweeping tundra, lakes tinted turquoise by glacial silt—it's nearly impossible to capture their grandeur with a camera (though, of course, you should definitely give it a try), the park does justice to a wealth of grand outdoor options.

Telaquana Lake

coastline, and the striking Chigmit Mountains, which rise along the park's center, bridging the Aleutian Range to the south and, to the north, the Alaska Range.

The Chigmit Mountains are home to two active volcanoes, Mount Iliamna and Mount Redoubt. In 2009, Mount Redoubt provided proof that southern Alaska is one of the world's most tectonically active places.

The park's diversity of wildlife also astounds. There of 37 species of mammals. Massive brown bears come to feed on sedge in the salt marshes, dig razor clams, and feast on migrating salmon all along the Cook Inlet coastline. It is harder to spot the elusive lynx. Ground squirrels (a favorite food for grizzlies) are plentiful. Add to that 187 species of birds—and fish, plenty of fish.

▶ HOW TO VISIT

Lake Clark doesn't have very much in the way of developed areas and park-operated services. There are no boardwalks or shuttle-bus services in the park. If you decide to venture into the park solo, keep in mind that this is Alaska—and that help is not always just a cell phone call away.

The park lacks an extensive trail system, which somehow adds to the wild aspect to the park's fine opportunities for great-outdoors experiences: paddling, hiking, camping, and climbing. If you aren't keen on off-trail navigation by yourself, you can take advantage of one of many guide services in the area.

Hiking is best around the lakes—and from lake to lake. Fishing is usually first class. If you have the time, sign up for a guided kayak adventure—or rent

The park protects a giant swath of wilderness in south-central Alaska. The park is just north of Katmai National Park and across Cook Inlet from the Kenai Peninsula. Boats can enter the park via Cook Inlet, but most people arrive by floatplane. Visitors commonly arrange to be dropped off and picked up at the same spot or, in the case of river trips, a spot downstream.

The heart of the park, Lake Clark stretches some 40 miles. Three rivers (of many), the Mulchatna, Chilikadrotna, and Tlikakila, have Wild and/or Scenic designations. The mountains of Lake Clark dominate the views.

Lake Clark's geography includes the tundra of the Turquoise-Telaquana Plateau, forested areas along the

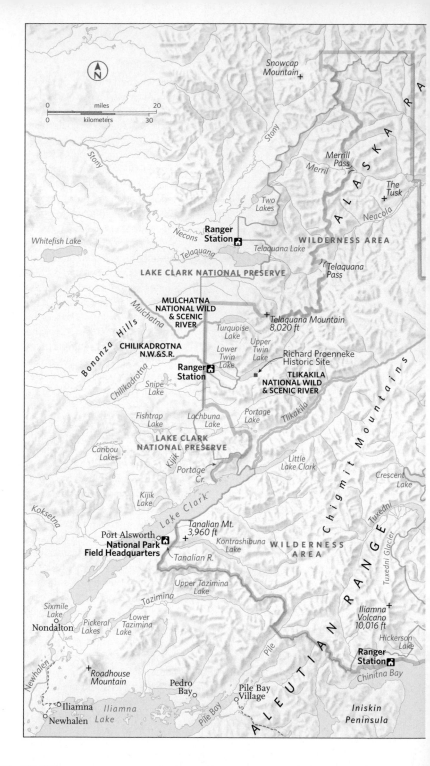

N

0   miles   20
0   kilometers   30

Snowcap
Mountain

A L A S K A

Merrill
Pass

Merril

The
Tusk

Neacola

Stony

Stony

Two
Lakes

WILDERNESS AREA

Necons

Ranger
Station

Telaquana Lake

Whitefish Lake

Telaquana

Telaquana
Pass

LAKE CLARK NATIONAL PRESERVE

MULCHATNA
NATIONAL WILD
& SCENIC
RIVER

Mulchatna

Telaquana Mountain
8,020 ft

Turquoise
Lake

Upper
Twin
Lake

Bonanza Hills

CHILIKADROTNA
N.W.&S.R.

Lower
Twin
Lake

Richard Proenneke
Historic Site

Chilikadrotna

Ranger
Station

TLIKAKILA
NATIONAL WILD
& SCENIC RIVER

Snipe
Lake

Fishtrap
Lake

Lachbuna
Lake

Portage
Lake

Tlikakila

Chigmit Mountains

Caribou
Lakes

LAKE CLARK
NATIONAL PRESERVE

Kijik

Portage
Cr.

Little
Lake Clark

Crescent
Lake

Koksetna

Kijik
Lake

Lake Clark

Tuxedni Glacier

Tuxedni

Port Alsworth
National Park
Field Headquarters

Tanalian Mt.
3,960 ft

Tanalian R.

Kontrashibuna
Lake

WILDERNESS
AREA

A L E U T I A N   R A N G E

Upper Tazimina
Lake

Tazimina

Iliamna
Volcano
10,016 ft

Sixmile
Lake

Nondalton

Pickeral
Lakes

Lower
Tazimina
Lake

Hickerson
Lake

Ranger
Station

Newhalen

Roadhouse
Mountain

Pedro
Bay

Pile Bay
Village

Pile

Pile Bay

Chinitna Bay

Iliamna
Newhalen

Iliamna
Lake

Iniskin
Peninsula

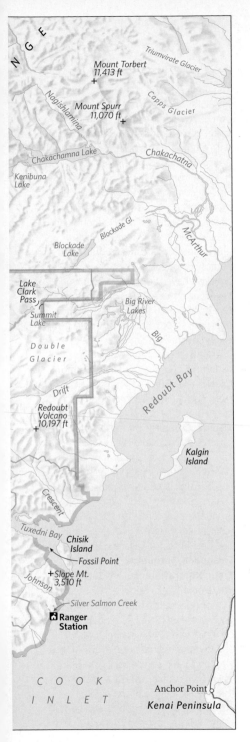

a kayak, raft, or canoe from an independent outfitter outside the park so to experience the park at water level.

The Richard Proenneke Cabin at Twin Lakes

After retiring, Richard Proenneke, a mechanic and amateur naturalist, decided to make **Upper Twin Lake** his home. He spent the summers of 1967 and 1968 building a log cabin by hand, an experience that he wrote about and filmed. This documentation was the basis of books and movies that

Alaska's Jurassic Park

No, dinosaurs will not suddenly pop out movie-style here. This is a gentler—but far more interesting—*Jurassic Park* than the silver screen version. Fossil Point in Tuxedni Bay, on the park's southeastern coast, is known for Jurassic rocks and fossils, collected here since the late 1800s. That's when a Russian mining engineer collected specimens, which he shipped off to St. Petersburg for study. Today, by law, fossils cannot be removed from the park.

Exploration of the area's fossils continues. Most of the fossils are marine life that became extinct more than 145 million years ago, including the very large *Inoceramus* clam. Fossils here include bivalves, ammonites (spiral sea creatures), and belemnites (think squid, but with internal skeletons).

The best way to access Fossil Point is by boat. Charters are available from several towns along the Kenai Peninsula, including Homer.

showcase his craftsmanship and what it takes to live alone in a wild place—something Proenneke did for 30 years. At age 82, he left his cabin and its contents to the National Park Service, then headed to California, where he died at age 86. Now a National Historic Site, the cabin is open to visitors. Guided tours are given throughout much of the summer. During the tour, visitors can sit at his desk and even read his famed journals.

The cabin is accessible by float-plane to Upper Twin Lake. Day-trippers make up the largest portion of the cabin's visitors, Backpackers consider it an excellent spot to begin—or end—a backcountry foray. Three of the best routes are **Hope Creek,** which goes from the cabin into the **Hope Creek Valley,** where you'll trek over alpine terrain; the **Low Pass Route,** which skirts the lake before heading through meadows and along some challenging and steep scree slopes; and, for a good day hike, the 10-mile **Upper to Lower Twin Lakes Route**.

Hike along the south side of the lakes. If possible, bring fishing equipment and some cooking gear. There's a good chance you'll catch something for lunch, perhaps lake trout or arctic char.

Carry bug repellent and, better yet, wear a head net—mosquitoes are especially plentiful in June and July.

On the Water

Lake Clark is a standout on the fishing front, but not the only good site. Throughout the summer, the park's lakes and rivers offer abundant salmon runs as well as rainbow trout, grayling, arctic char, and more. You'll need a State of Alaska fishing license, which can be purchased at any large outfitter in Anchorage or Port Alsworth. Once you have a license, head to **Crescent Lake,** in the **Chigmit Mountains,** along with a guide with a boat. Because of dense brush, park visitors can't access the lake from the land.

A guide is also helpful when it comes to salmon fishing. Running in the waters here are reds (second half of July) and silvers (mid-August to early September). Several guide companies run day trips to the lake; visitors also have the option of spending several days here by booking a trip to a local fishing lodge. Keep in mind that the fish are also very popular with brown bears.

Another spot favored by both fishermen and bears is **Silver Salmon Creek.** Silvers make their run here from August into September. The creek is also a top spot for birders—watch for seabirds on the cliffs and shorebirds, including the black oyster-catcher, with its bright orange beak, dancing around on the mudflats.

The park is also a dream spot for kayaking, rafting, and "pack rafting" (an ideal sport for those who love to combine hiking with a float trip). The best lakes for kayaking include **Telaquana, Turquoise, Twin, Lake Clark, Kontrashibuna,** and **Tazimina.** You can rent a kayak in Port Alsworth.

For rafters, the park's rivers offer take-your-breath-away scenery and, on the broad Tlikakila River, Class II and III rapids. Originating in Lake Clark Pass and fed by a series of glaciers, the brown, fast-moving river runs through the center of the park. In summer, king, coho, and sockeye salmon forge upstream here.

Red fox *(Vulpes vulpes)* on the Cook Inlet coast

Information

How to Get There

There are no roads to Lake Clark National Park. Book a flight from Port Alsworth, Anchorage, or Kenai, or charter a floatplane. It's also possible to get to the park's eastern boundary by crossing Cook Inlet from the Kenai Peninsula by boat.

When to Go

Open year-round, the park's peak season runs June through mid-Sept. June and July are the warmest months, with temperatures between 50°F and 70°F. That's mosquito time too. Wildflowers are best in late June. Aug. and Sept. are the wettest months. Autumn colors peak at higher elevations in early and mid-Sept. After that, be prepared for anything from sunshine to snow.

Visitor Centers

Outside the park, the **Port Alsworth Visitor Center** (907-781-2117) is open June–early Sept. For general visitor information, contact the **Homer Field Office** (907-235-7903).

Headquarters

1240 W. Fifth St.
Anchorage, AL 99501
nps.gov/lacl
907-644-3626

Field Headquarters
Port Alsworth, AK 96653
907-781-2218

Camping

Lake Clark is basically a giant, mostly trail-free, camping site. There's one primitive campground, on **Upper Twin Lakes.** Preparation is key when it comes to camping in Lake Clark National Park. The weather can change quickly, sometimes making it difficult for a floatplane pilot to retrieve you. It's not unusual for a trip to run a few days longer than planned. It's a good idea to pack extra food.

Lodging

There are several lodges on private lands within the park's boundaries. For ideas check out: *nps.gov/lacl/planyourvisit/eating-sleeping.htm.*

LAKE CLARK
EST. 1980

Wrangell–St. Elias

Alaska

Established
December 2, 1980

13,188,000 acres

By far the largest national park—nearly four times the size of Yellowstone—Wrangell–St. Elias National Park could be the closest thing we'll ever have to Shangri-La. It's a landscape protected by mountains, where glaciers flow through streaks of earth, where nature's work—the click of a mountain goat's hoof, the sniff of a bear checking the wind—goes on with almost no one to hear or see it.

One of the park's glaciers, the Malaspina, is larger than Rhode Island. The gigantic park contains four mountain ranges, with nine of the highest peaks in North America, including Mount St. Elias, at 18,009 feet. Wrangell–St. Elias National Park and Preserve, Glacier Bay National Park, Canada's Kluane National Park, and the trans-border Tatshenshini-Alsek parks, make up a 24,300,000-acre UNESCO Heritage Reserve site.

▶ **HOW TO VISIT**

The best way to see the park depends on time, experience, and budget. The easy way in is on the **McCarthy Road** or the **Nabesna Road.** Both go a little

Wildflowers and Nizina Glacier

a backwoods-Alaska movie, with buildings in every state of repair, antler decor, dogs that seem to own the streets, and people who have chosen to live a long way from "civilization" and are willing to fight to keep things that way.

The old **Kennecott Mine** is 5 miles deeper into the park. Hike, or rent a bike in McCarthy. The Kennecott Mines were once one of the richest digs in the world. In just over 30 years of operation, nearly 600,000 tons of copper and close to a million ounces of silver were brought out. What's truly amazing is the sheer size of the operation: The main building is 14 stories high. Until they got their railway working, every single bit of equipment either had to be made on site, floated downriver, or brought in by horses. The mine is a National Historic Site.

A 2-mile trail leads from McCarthy to beautiful views of the **Kennicott Glacier**—feeder of the Kennicott River—and the **Root Glacier.** For a more challenging hike, keep going past the Root to the 9-mile **Erie Lake/ Stairway Icefall trail.** This hike takes you back to the **Stairway Icefall** and may be the only chance you'll ever have to see a 7,000-foot vertical wall of ice shining its glacier blues.

The other main route into the park is the Nabesna Road, which goes back 42 miles into the **Wrangell Mountains.** Check road conditions before heading out; this is not a place to get stuck. The biggest draw here is simply going where few others go. On view is the spine of Alaska, along the divide between two rivers, the **Copper** and **Nabesna,** which ends at the Bering Sea, on the far end of Alaska.

ways into the park. To see the deeper country, you'll need a horse, a guide, or a pilot. Flight-seeing here is one of the great Alaska experiences.

McCarthy & Nabesna Roads

Most people enter the park via the McCarthy Road, which comes into the park at **Chitina.** A few trails split off from the road, including the **Nugget Creek Trail,** which leads 15 miles to the foot of **Mount Blackburn.** A more challenging trail is the 14-mile **Dixie Pass,** with a steep climb to panoramic views.

The McCarthy Road ends at the **Kennicott River;** just across is **McCarthy,** which looks like a set from

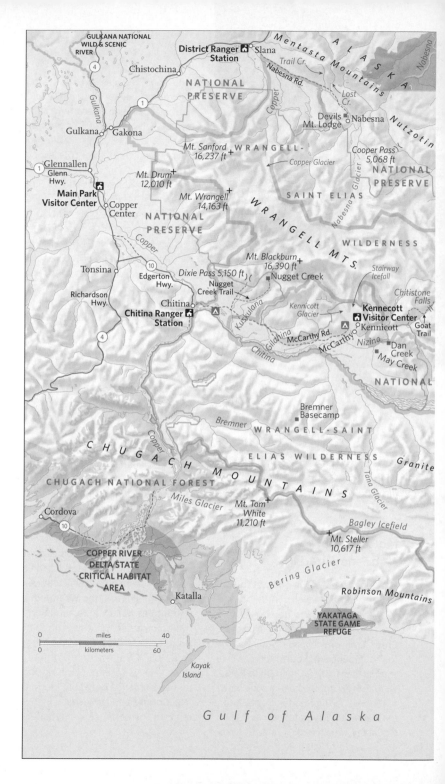

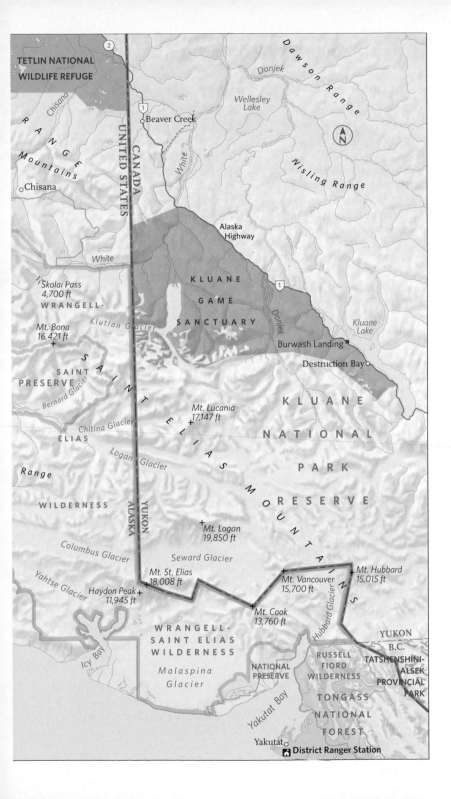

TETLIN NATIONAL
WILDLIFE REFUGE

R A N G E
Mountains

Chisana

Chisana

Skolai Pass
4,700 ft

WRANGELL-

Mt. Bona
16,421 ft

Klutlan Glacier

SAINT
PRESERVE

Bernard Glacier

Chitina Glacier

ELIAS

Logan Glacier

Range

WILDERNESS

Columbus Glacier

Yahtse Glacier

Haydon Peak
11,945 ft

Icy Bay

WRANGELL-
SAINT ELIAS
WILDERNESS

Malaspina
Glacier

UNITED STATES

CANADA

White

White

Alaska
Highway

K L U A N E

G A M E

S A N C T U A R Y

Donjek

Burwash Landing

Destruction Bay

Mt. Lucania
17,147 ft

S A I N T   E L I A S   M O U N T A I N S

YUKON
ALASKA

Seward Glacier

Mt. Logan
19,850 ft

Mt. St. Elias
18,008 ft

Mt. Cook
13,760 ft

Mt. Vancouver
15,700 ft

Hubbard Glacier

Mt. Hubbard
15,015 ft

2

Donjek

Dawson Range

Wellesley
Lake

Beaver Creek

1

N

Nisling Range

1

Kluane
Lake

K L U A N E

N A T I O N A L

P A R K

R E S E R V E

YUKON
B.C.

TATSHENSHINI-
ALSEK
PROVINCIAL
PARK

NATIONAL
PRESERVE

RUSSELL
FIORD
WILDERNESS

TONGASS

NATIONAL

FOREST

Yakutat Bay

Yakutat

District Ranger Station

The Copper River Delta

It's one thing to strike silver or copper but quite another to get it out of the mine and on its way. What made sense at the time was to build nearly 200 miles of railroad track between the mines and the town of Cordova, on Prince William Sound. Over the decades the trains were in operation, they hauled out hundreds of millions of dollars worth of ore.

Trains haven't run here for a very long time. Indeed, most of the route's north-south right of way has been reclaimed by the forest. But some adventurous backpackers willing to walk miles and miles do follow the line down to the scenic wonderland of the Copper River Delta.

For those who don't want to spend a couple weeks in the bush, there's another way to access this part of the park. Drive to Valdez, ferry to Cordova, then drive out past the airport until the road ends at a bridge that seems to barely cling on above the silty Copper River.

The reward of the Copper River Delta, besides glaciers up close (bring crampons if you want to hike the ice) and some of the best salmon anywhere, is one of Alaska's most vital bird flyways. During the peak of migration, from late April into mid-May, the delta hosts one of the largest gathering of shorebirds in the world, including giant trumpeter swans, whose wings seem the same color as the glaciers. All this in a landscape of jagged mountains, ice, and the shallow flow of the river. Hard to beat.

Beyond the Roads

Glaciers get all the publicity in Wrangell–St. Elias, but glaciers turn into rivers, and this corner of Alaska has some of the state's best. In the park, rafting companies work the Nabesna, Kennicott, **Chitina,** and **Nizina** rivers, as well as the granddaddy of them all, the Copper (see sidebar at left). These rivers are truly wild—cold and full of glacial silt that can weigh down a person's clothes so fast there's no swimming out. Park offices can help by providing a list of river guides.

Getting still deeper into the park requires an airplane. Flight-seeing the park is like looking into a hole in time. From high above it isn't hard to get a sense of what the landscape looked like during the last Ice Age, the jagged, scraped-bare peaks of the high mountains thrusting through thousands of feet of ice.

To get closer to the mountains, charter a flight out of McCarthy and try the **Bremmer Basecamp** hike, which leads from a gravel landing strip deep in the park through four or five days of relatively easy-to-walk countryside (Once there were mines tucked away in this part of the park, and traces remain.)

For something more ambitious, fly to the **Goat Trail,** a strenuous route with scree scrambles and cold river crossings. A true wilderness experience, plan on a week to get in and back. Here, as elsewhere in the park, obey all bear-safety precautions.

Wrangell–St. Elias National Park and Preserve is so big that one could travel it over a lifetime and still see only a corner. That's okay. Even the tiniest corner is a wonder of the American park system.

Hikers near Root Glacier

Information

How to Get There

Wrangell–St. Elias has two road access points: the main one, the McCarthy Road, is outside Copper Center. The road is rough but passable. Rougher still though passable in a passenger vehicle, Nabesna Road, the other road access point, can be picked up at the Slana Ranger Station, 75 miles northeast of Copper Center.

When to Go

The park is open year-round; outside summer months, though, it's a destination only experienced winter campers should try. Be prepared for abrupt temperature changes any time of year.

Visitor Centers

The main visitor center and park headquarters is in **Copper Center,** about 200 scenic miles from Anchorage and 250 less scenic miles from Fairbanks. The visitor center (907-822-7250) is open April through Oct. A second visitor center (907-554-1105), in **McCarthy,** is open Memorial Day to Labor Day. Both visitor centers are intermittently staffed.

Headquarters

P.O. Box 439
Mile 106.8 Richardson Hwy.
Copper Center, AK 99573
nps.gov/wrst
907-822-7250

Camping

You can camp almost anywhere in the park except around McCarthy. No permit needed, but it is wise to register your itinerary with park officials. The park's 14 very basic cabins, scattered around the park, are hike- or fly-in.

Lodging

The park's only full-service lodgings, including several concessioner-run B&Bs and the **Kennicott Glacier Lodge** *(kennicottlodge.com;* 800-582-5128), are in **McCarthy.** Around the edges of the park, the towns of **Glennallen** and **Copper Center** offer motels. Visit *nps.gov/wrst/planyourvisit/lodging.htm* for information.

WRANGELL-ST.ELIAS
EST 1980

Skookum Volcano Trail, Wrangell–St. Elias National Park

ACKNOWLEDGMENTS

We are indebted to the many individuals and the federal, state, and private agencies that helped prepare this guide, especially to the National Park Service and the superintendents and chiefs of interpretation and their staffs at each park.

ILLUSTRATIONS CREDITS

Photos by Phil Schermeister unless otherwise noted

NPS = National Park Service

Cover
Tim Fitzharris/Minden Pictures

Back Cover
(UP LE), NPS; (UP RT), iStock.com/Eric Foltz; (LO LE) © Dr. Caroline Rogers/NPS; (LO RT), David Baselt

East
18, iStock.com/Eric Foltz; 26-7, NPS/John Brooks; 29, NPS/Judd Patterson; 31, NPS/Thomas M. Strom; 36, Serge Skiba/Shutterstock; 39, NPS/jt-fineart; 40-41, NPS; 43, NPS; 45, NPS; 66-9 (artwork), Richard Schlecht; 72-3, NPS/John F. Mitchell; 80 (UP), Courtesy of the U.S. Forest Service; 80 (CTR) and 80 (LO), Courtesy of the Virginia Department of Conservation and Recreation; 81 (UP), Robert Hankins; 81 (CTR), Courtesy of the U.S. Forest Service; 81 (LO), Courtesy of the Virginia Department of Conservation and Recreation; 82-3, © Dr. Caroline Rogers/NPS; 86, Jo Ann Snover/Shutterstock; 89, © Dr. Caroline Rogers/NPS

Midwest
94-5, iStock.com/Eric Foltz; 99, NPS; 106-7, Mark Baldwin/Shutterstock; 115, iStock.com/-A1A-; 120 (UP), Bureau of Land Management; 120 (CTR), chuckhaney.com; 120 (LO), iStock.com/lrh847; 121 (UP), Todd Gallion/USFWS; 121 (CTR), Cross Ranch State Park; 121 (LO), Sully Creek State Park; 126, Per Breiehagen/Getty Images; 130-131, NPS

South Central
140-141, Ian Shive/TandemStock.com; 145, iStock.com/nickrlake; 146, iStock.com/David Hughes; 149, iStock.com/Eric Foltz; 157, iStock.com/Peter Mukherjee; 158 (UP), iStock.com/RoseMaryBush; 158 (CTR), Justin Britten; 158 (LO), NPS; 159 (UP), BLM.gov; 159 (CTR), BLM SE New Mexico; 159 (LO), Bernadette Madison; 165, NPS

Southwest
176-7, iStockphoto/RJSorensen; 181, iStock.com/Robert Ingelhart; 183, Ciurzynski/Shutterstock; 189,

Kennan Harvey/Aurora Photos/Alamy; 198-9, NPS/Neal Herbert; 202, NPS/Neal Herbert; 205, NPS/Neal Herbert; 206 (UP), Nick Eason; 206 (CTR), NPS/Bob Moffitt; 206 (LO), Michael Hare/Shutterstock; 207 (UP), George H.H. Huey/Alamy; 207 (CTR), Bill Stevens, BLM Moab Field Office; 207 (LO), SCPhotos/Alamy; 208-9, iStock.com/rwhitacre; 213, iStock.com/Avid Creative, Inc.; 224-5, Bcbounders/Dreamstime.com; 231, NPS; 236, Kenny Tong/Dreamstime.com; 239, NPS; 249, col/Shutterstock; 251, iStock.com/ebettini; 252-3, iStock.com/TexPhoto;; 257, Steven Castro/Shutterstock; 259, NPS

Rocky Mountains
260-261, Danielle Lehle; 279, NPS; 281, Danielle Lehle; 282 (UP), Jaypetersen/Dreamstime.com; 282 (CTR), USDA Forest Service; 282 (LO), NPS/Alamy; 283 (UP), USFWS; 283 (CTR), Sara Domek; 283 (LO), NPS; 291, iStock.com/kojihirano; 292-3, istock.com/kjschoen

Pacific Northwest
316-7, NPS; 319, NPS; 325, iStock.com/Arpad Benedek; 332-3, NPS/Wendy Swee; 337, NPS; 339, idreamphoto/Shutterstock; 340 (UP), iStock.com/Mark Skerbinek; 340 (CTR), C_Eng-Wong Photography/Shutterstock; 340 (LO), Douglas Peebles Photography/Alamy; 341 (UP), Eric Nishibayashi; 341 (CTR), rolphphoto.com; 341 (LO), Kevin Ebi/Alamy; 342-3, NPS; 346, NPS; 349, Dave G. Houser/Alamy; 379, Yongyut Kumsri/Shutterstock

Pacific Southwest
390 (UP), Dave Menke; 390 (CTR), Kevin J. Sperl; 390 (LO), iStock.com/toos; 391 (UP), NPS; 391 (CTR), Oregon Parks and Recreation Department; 391 (LO), WorldFoto/Alamy; 422-3, David Baselt; 429, iStock.com/Eric Foltz

Alaska
442-3, Paxson Woelber, Expedition Arguk; 447, Michael Christopher Brown/National Geographic Creative; 448-9, NPS; 454 (UP), Alan Wu (photo at http://commons.wikimedia.org/wiki/File:One_of_the_many_ocean_inlets_in_Misty_Fjords_National_Monument.jpg and license at https://creativecommons.org/licenses/by-sa/2.0/); 454 (CTR), Design Pics Inc/Alamy; 454 (LO), iStock.com/Jerry Moorman; 455 (UP), Sergey Uryadnikov/Shutterstock; 455 (CTR), M. Cornelius/Shutterstock; 455 (LO), Design Pics Inc/Alamy; 456-7, NPS; 461, NPS; 467, NPS/Kaitlin Thoresen; 468-9, NPS; 473, Design Pics Inc/Alamy; 474-5, NPS/Jeanette Mills; 479, NPS; 480-481, Carl Donohue/Skolai Images; 486-7, Wrangell-St. Elias National Park & Preserve

National Parks | Credits/Index

Index Abbreviations

Bureau of Land Management
- BLM
National Forest - NF
National Historic Park - NHP
National Marine Sanctuary - NMS
National Monument - NM
National Park - NP
National Recreation Area - NRA
National Recreation Trail - NRT
National Wildlife Refuge - NWR
State Park - SP

A

Abbey, Edward, 198
Acadia NP, Me., 15, 16–25
Adams, Ansel, 279, 373
Admiralty Island NM, Alas., 454
Alaska
 Admiralty Island NM, 454
 Alaska Chilkat Bald Eagle
  Preserve, 455
 Chilkat SP, 455
 Denali NP, 4, 433, 434–441
 Gates of the Arctic NP and
  Preserve, 433, 442–447
 Glacier Bay NP, 433,
  448–453
 Katmai NP, 433, 456–461
 Kenai Fjords NP, 433,
  462–467
 Kobuk Valley NP, 433,
  468–473
 Lake Clark NP and Preserve,
  433, 474–479
 Mendenhall Glacier, 454
 Misty Fiords NM, 454
 Russell Fjord Wilderness,
  455
 Wrangell–St. Elias NP, 430–
  431, 433, 480–487
Alaska Chilkat Bald Eagle
 Preserve, Alas., 455
Alatna River, Alas., 443,
 445–446
Albright, Horace, 296
American Samoa
 American Samoa NP, 315,
  316–319
American Samoa NP, American
 Samoa, 315, 316–319
Anacapa Island, Channel
 Islands, Calif., 321, 322–323
Apgar, Mont., 265

Appalachian Trail, U.S., 59,
 73, 80
Arches NP, Utah, 175, 176–183
Arizona
 Glen Canyon NRA, 206
 Grand Canyon NP, 175,
  214–223
 Petrified Forest NP, 175,
  240–245
 Saguaro NP, 175, 246–251
Arizona-Sonora Desert
 Museum, Ariz., 249
Arkansas
 Hot Springs NP, 139, 166–171
Ash River, Minn., 126, 128
Atkins, Chris, 426

B

Badlands NP, S. Dak., 92, 94–99
Balcony House, Mesa Verde NP,
 Colo., 233, 236, 237–238
Bear Lake, Colo., 293, 296–297
Big Bend NP, Tex., 136–137, 139,
 140–149
Big Tree, Redwood NP, Calif.,
 428
Biscayne NP, Fla., 15, 26–31
Bitter Lake NWR, N. Mex., 159
Black Canyon of the Gunnison
 NP, Colo., 175, 184–189
Black River Recreation Area
 (BLM), N. Mex., 159
Booth, John Wilkes, 41
Bosque del Apache NWR,
 N. Mex., 158
Boucher, Louis, 218
Brandywine Falls, Ohio, 101, 104
Brantley Lake SP, N. Mex., 158
Bridger-Teton NF, Wyo., 282
Bright Angel Trail, Ariz., 218,
 219, 222
Brooks Camp, Katmai NP, Alas.,
 457, 460
Bryce, Ebenezer, 190
Bryce Canyon NP, Utah,
 172–173, 175, 190–197
Buckner, William, 412
Burr Trail Loop, Capitol Reef
 NP, Utah, 209, 212
Buzzard, Bill, 412

C

Cades Cove, Tenn., 57, 60–62
California
 Channel Islands NP, 315,
  320–325

Death Valley NP, 312–313,
 315, 326–331
Joshua Tree NP, 315,
 350–355
Lassen Volcanic NP, 383,
 392–397
Pinnacles NP, 315, 356–361
Redwood NP, 2–3, 383,
 422–429
Sequoia & Kings Canyon NP,
 315, 362–369
Yosemite NP, 7, 315,
 370–379
Canyonlands NP, Utah, 175,
 198–205
Cape Royal Road, Grand
 Canyon NP, Ariz., 222
Capitol Reef NP, Utah, 175,
 208–213
Capone, Al, 170
Carbon River, Wash., 404
Carlsbad Caverns NP, N. Mex.,
 139, 150–157
Cascade Canyon, Wyo., 277, 280
Cascade Range, Canada-U.S.,
 393, 407
Cascade River Road, Wash.,
 407, 412
Cassidy, Butch, 212
Cathedral Valley Loop, Capitol
 Reef NP, Utah, 209, 212
Cedar Grove, Kings Canyon NP,
 Calif., 368
Cely, John, 34
Chain of Craters Road, Hawai'i,
 343, 345–346, 347, 348
Champlain, Samuel de, 17, 24
Channel Islands NP, Calif., 315,
 320–325
Chapin Mesa Museum, Mesa
 Verde NP, Colo., 236–237,
 239
Chasm Lake, Colo., 298
Chelan, Lake, Wash., 406, 407,
 409, 410–412
Chief Mountain International
 Highway, Alta., 265, 269–270
Chigmit Mountains, Alas., 475,
 478
Chihuahuan Desert, Mexico-
 U.S., 140–141, 151, 156, 159
Chilkat SP, Alas., 455
Chisos Mountains, Tex., 140–141,
 144–145, 147, 149
Cinder Cone, Lassen Volcanic
 NP, Calif., 393, 395, 396

Cliff Palace, Mesa Verde NP, Colo., 233, 236, 237
Clingmans Dome, N.C.-Tenn., 59–60
Colorado
    Black Canyon of the Gunnison NP, 175, 184–189
    Great Sand Dunes National Park and Preserve, 263
    Great Sand Dunes NP and Preserve, 284–291
    Mesa Verde NP, 175, 232–239
    Rocky Mountain NP, 263, 292–299
Colorado Desert, Calif., 354
Congaree NP, S.C., 15, 32–39
Coolidge, Calvin, 366–367
Coral Bay, V.I., 88
Crater Lake NP, Oreg., 383, 384–389
Cross Ranch SP, N. Dak., 121
Crystal Cave, Calif., 363, 365, 369
Cub Lake, Colo., 293, 297
Cuyahoga Valley NP, Ohio, 90–91, 93, 100–105

D
Dead Horse Point SP, Utah, 206
Death Valley NP, Calif./Nev., 312–313, 315, 326–331
Denali NP, Alas., 4, 433, 434–441
Dog Canyon, Tex., 161, 164, 165
Dry Tortugas NP, Fla., 15, 40–45

E
Everglades NP, Fla., 15, 46–55
Exit Glacier, Alas., 463, 467

F
Fellow, Abraham Lincoln, 186
Fern Canyon, Calif., 423, 427–428
Flanigan, David, 256
Florida
    Biscayne NP, 15, 26–31
    Dry Tortugas NP, 15, 40–45
    Everglades NP, 15, 46–55
Fort Jefferson, Dry Tortugas NP, Fla., 40–42, 43–44, 45
Fossil Butte NM, Wyo., 283
Fremont River, Utah, 208–209, 212
Fruita, Utah, 209–210, 213

G
Garden Key, Fla., 40, 41–44, 45
Gates of the Arctic NP and Preserve, Alas., 433, 442–447
George Washington NF, Va., 80
Giant Forest, Sequoia NP, Calif., 363, 365–366, 369
Glacier Bay NP, Alas., 433, 448–453
Glacier NP, Mont., 263, 264–271
Glacier Point, Yosemite NP, Calif., 371, 373, 375–377, 379
Glen Canyon NRA, Ariz./Utah, 206
Going-to-the-Sun Road, Glacier NP, Mont., 264, 265–269
Gold Bluffs Beach, Calif., 423, 427, 429
Grand Canyon NP, Ariz., 175, 214–223
Grand Teton National Park, 260–261, 263, 272–281
Grand Teton NP, Wyo., 260–261, 263, 272–281
Grant, Madison, 426
Grant Grove, Sequoia NP, Calif., 362–363, 366–368, 369
Great Basin NP, Nev., 175, 224–231
Great Fountain Geyser, Wyo., 303–304
Great Kobuk Sand Dunes, Alas., 472, 473
Great Sand Dunes NP and Preserve, Colo., 263, 284–291
Great Smoky Mountains NP, N.C.-Tenn., 12–13, 15, 56–63
Gros Ventre Range, Wyo., 277
Gros Ventre Wilderness, Wyo., 282
Grosvenor, Gilbert H., 7
Guadalupe Mountains NP, Tex., 139, 160–165
Gulpha Gorge, Ark., 170, 171
Gunnison, John W., 186

H
Haleakalā (volcano), Hawai'i, 332–338
Haleakalā NP, Hawai'i, 315, 332–339
Harding Icefield, Alas., 462, 463–465
Harvey, Fred, 215
Hawai'i
    Haleakalā NP, 315, 332–339

Hawai'i Volcanoes NP, 315, 332, 342–349
Iao Valley SP, 340
Kanaha Pond Wildlife Sanctuary, 341
Keālia Pond NWR, 340
Polipoli Spring SP South Central, 341
Wai'anapanapa SP, 340
Waikamoi Preserve, 341
Hawai'i Volcanoes NP, Hawai'i, 315, 332, 342–349
Hayden, Ferdinand, 186
Hermit Road, Grand Canyon NP, Ariz., 218–219
Hillman Peak, Oreg., 385–387, 388
Hoh Rain Forest, Wash., 416, 420
Holleback, Amelia, 215
Honeywell, Mark, 30
Hoover, Herbert, 77, 170, 285
Horseshoe Canyon Unit, Canyonlands NP, Utah, 199, 204
Hot Springs NP, Ark., 139, 166–171
Howland Hill Road, Calif., 428
Hurricane Ridge, Olympic NP, Wash., 415–419, 421

I
Iao Valley SP, Hawai'i, 340
Idaho
    Yellowstone NP, 9, 263, 300–311
Island in the Sky District, Canyonlands NP, Utah, 198–202, 205
Isle au Haut, Me., 16, 24
Isle Royale NP, Mich., 93, 106–111

J
Jackson Lake, Wyo., 273, 276, 277–278, 280
Jackson National Fish Hatchery, Wyo., 283
Jefferson NF, Va., 81
Jenny Lake, Wyo., 273–277, 280, 281
John D. Rockefeller, Jr. Memorial Parkway, Wyo., 282
Johnson, Lady Bird, 423
Johnson, Lyndon B., 203
Joshua Tree NP, Calif., 315, 350–355

K

Kabetogama Lake, Minn.,
122–123, 127–128, 129

Kanaha Pond Wildlife
Sanctuary, Hawai'i, 341

Karstens, Harry, 434

Katmai NP, Alas., 433, 456–461

Keālia Pond NWR, Hawai'i, 340

Kenai Fjords NP, Alas., 433,
462–467

Kennecott, Alas., 481

Kentucky
Mammoth Cave NP, 15, 64–71

Kīlauea (volcano), Hawai'i,
342–346, 348

Kings Canyon NP, Calif. *See*
Sequoia & Kings Canyon
NP, Calif.

Kīpahulu Valley, Haleakala NP,
Hawai'i, 338

Klamath Marsh Refuge, Oreg.,
390

Kobuk River, Alas., 446,
469–472

Kobuk Valley NP, Alas., 433,
468–473

Kolob Canyons Road, Zion NP,
Utah, 258

L

Lady Bird Johnson Grove,
Redwood NP, Calif., 426

Lafayette NP. *See* Acadia NP,
Me.

Lake Chelan NRA, Wash.,
406–407, 412, 413

Lake Clark NP and Preserve,
Alas., 433, 474–479

Lake Ilo NWR, N. Dak., 121

Lassen Volcanic NP, Calif., 383,
392–397

Lehman, Absalom, 227

Lehman Caves, Nev., 224–227,
231

Lincoln, Abraham, 371

Little Cranberry Island, Me., 20

Little Missouri National
Grassland, N. Dak., 120

Longmire, Martha, 403

Longs Peak, Colo., 292, 297–
298, 299

Lostwood NWR, N. Dak./
Mont., 120

M

Madden, Owney, 170

Maine
Acadia NP, 15, 16–25

Mammoth Cave NP, Ky., 15,
64–71

Mammoth Hot Springs, Wyo.,
301, 307, 308, 310, 311

Manti-LaSal NF, Utah, 207

Many Glacier, Mont., 265, 269,
271

Marble Islands, Alas., 449

Marion, Francis, 33

Mariposa Grove, Yosemite NP,
Calif., 371, 377, 379

Mauna Loa (volcano), Hawai'i,
342–343, 347–348

Mazama, Mount, Oreg.,
384–389

Maze District, Canyonlands NP,
Utah, 199, 203, 204, 205

McDonald, Lake, Mont., 265–
267, 271

McKinley, Mount, Alas., 433,
435–441

McKittrick Canyon, Tex., 161,
163–164

Medano Creek, Colo., 286–290,
291

Mendenhall Glacier, Alas., 454

Merriam, John C., 426

Mesa Verde NP, Colo., 175,
232–239

Michigan
Isle Royale NP, 93, 106–111

Mineral King, Sequoia NP, Calif.,
363, 368, 369

Minnesota
Voyageurs NP, 93, 122–129

Misty Fiords NM, Alas., 454

Moab, Utah, 183, 199, 204, 205

Mojave Desert, Calif., 253, 315,
350, 354

Montana
Glacier NP, 263, 264–271
Lostwood NWR, 120
Upper Missouri River Breaks
NM (BLM), 120
Yellowstone NP, 9, 263,
300–311

Moran, Mount, Wyo., 277–278

Moro Rock, Calif., 363, 366, 369

Mount Desert Island, Me.,
16–25

Mount McKinley. *See* Denali
NP, Alas.

Mount Rainier NP, Wash., 383,
398–405

Mudd, Samuel, 41

Muir, John, 362, 366, 370–371,
377, 378, 395

Muir Inlet, Alas., 449, 452

N

National Bighorn Sheep Center,
Wyo., 283

National Elk Refuge, Wyo., 282

National Park of American
Samoa, 315, 316–319

Needles District, Canyonlands
NP, Utah, 198–199, 202–204,
205

Nevada
Death Valley NP, 312–313,
315, 326–331
Great Basin NP, 175, 224–231

New Mexico
Bitter Lake NWR, 159
Black River Recreation Area
(BLM), 159
Bosque del Apache NWR,
158
Brantley Lake SP, 158
Carlsbad Caverns NP, 139,
150–157
Pecos River Corridor Area
(BLM), 159
White Sands NM, 158

Newberry National Volcanic
Monument, Oreg., 390

Newfound Gap Road, Great
Smoky Mountains NP, N.C.-
Tenn., 57, 58–60, 63

Newhalem, Wash., 409, 413

Nisqually Glacier, Wash., 404

Noatak River, Alas., 446

Nordenskiöld, Gustaf, 238

Norris Geyser Basin, Wyo., 305

North Carolina
Great Smoky Mountains NP,
12–13, 15, 56–63

North Cascades NP, Wash.,
380–381, 383, 406–413

North Dakota
Cross Ranch SP, 121
Lake Ilo NWR, 121
Little Missouri National
Grassland, 120
Lostwood NWR, 120
Sully Creek SP, 121
Theodore Roosevelt NP, 92,
112–119

North Rim, Grand Canyon, Ariz.,
214–215, 221–222, 223, 257

Northern Range, Mont.-Wyo., 308–310
Novarupta (volcano), Alas., 456

O

Ofu Island, American Samoa, 316, 317, 318, 319
Ohio
    Cuyahoga Valley NP, 90–91, 93, 100–105
Ohio & Erie Canal Towpath Trail, Ohio, 101–104
Old Faithful Geyser, Yellowstone NP, U.S., 301–303
Olmsted, Frederick Law, Jr., 19
Olympic NP, Wash., 383, 414–421
O'Neil, Joseph P., 419
Onion Portage, Kobuk River, Alas., 472
Oregon
    Crater Lake NP, 383, 384–389
    Klamath Marsh Refuge, 390
    Newberry National Volcanic Monument, 390
    Oregon Caves NM, 391
    Oregon Dunes NRA, 390
    Prospect State Scenic Viewpoint, 391
    Rogue Wild and Scenic River, 391
Oregon Caves NM, Oreg., 391
Oregon Dunes NRA, Oreg., 390
Ouachita NF, Ark., 171
Ozette, Wash., 420

P

Pago Pago, American Samoa, 316–317
Painted Desert, Ariz., 220, 221, 240, 241, 243–244, 245
Pecos River Corridor Area, N. Mex./Tex., 159
Petrified Forest NP, Ariz., 175, 240–245
Phantom Ranch, Grand Canyon, Ariz., 216, 222, 223
Pike, Zebulon, 285
Pinnacles NP, Calif., 315, 356–361
Polipoli Spring SP South Central, Hawai'i, 341
Ponce de Leon, Juan, 41
Powell, John Wesley, 198, 221, 252

Prairie Creek Redwoods SP, Calif., 427–428
Prospect State Scenic Viewpoint, Oreg., 391

R

Rainier, Mount, Wash., 383, 398–405
Rainy Lake, Minn.-Ont., 126–127, 129
Rapidan Camp, Shenandoah NP, Va., 77, 78
Rapidan Wildlife Management Area, Va., 81
Redwood NP, Calif., 2–3, 383, 422–429
Rio Grande Wild and Scenic River, Big Bend NP, Tex., 148
Rock Harbor, Isle Royale NP, Mich., 106, 107–109, 111
Rockefeller, John D., Jr., 17, 21
Rockefeller, Laurance S., 83, 280
Rocky Mountain NP, Colo., 263, 292–299
Rogue Wild and Scenic River, Oreg., 391
Roosevelt, Franklin D., 42, 77, 209, 415
Roosevelt, Theodore, 112–113, 115, 116, 130, 214, 233, 241, 357, 377, 393, 415
Ross Lake NRA, Wash., 406, 407–409, 413
Ross Maxwell Scenic Drive, Tex., 141, 147–148
Royal Palm, Fla., 51
Russell Fjord Wilderness, Alas., 455
Ruth, Babe, 170

S

Sable Pass, Alas., 439
Saguaro NP, Ariz., 175, 246–251
Sand Flats Recreation Area, Utah, 207
Sangre de Cristo Mountains, Colo.-N. Mex., 285–286, 289, 290, 291
Santa Barbara Island, Channel Islands, Calif., 324
Santa Cruz Island, Channel Islands, Calif., 323–324
Santa Rosa Island, Channel Islands, Calif., 324

Schoodic Peninsula, Me., 16–17, 24
Schulman, Edmund, 229
Scott M. Matheson Wetlands Preserves, Utah, 206
Sequoia & Kings Canyon NP, Calif., 315, 362–369
Sequoia NF, Calif., 368
Seward, William, 433
Shark Valley, Fla., 51, 53–54, 55
Sheldon, Charles, 434, 439
Shenandoah NP, Va., 15, 72–79
Shenandoah River SP, Va., 81
Signal Mountain, Wyo., 277
Sillett, Stephen, 426
Sky Meadows SP, Va., 80
Skyline Drive, Shenandoah NP, Va., 73, 76–78, 79
Snake River, U.S., 230, 272, 273, 278, 279, 280, 282
Sonoran Desert, Mexico-U.S., 246–247, 249, 250
South Carolina
    Congaree NP, 15, 32–39
South Dakota
    Badlands NP, 92, 94–99
    Wind Cave NP, 92–93, 130–135
South Rim, Grand Canyon, Ariz., 214–215, 218–219, 222, 223
Spielberg, Steven, 427
Sprague Lake, Colo., 293, 297
Spruce Tree House, Mesa Verde NP, Colo., 236, 237
St. Helens, Mount, Wash., 383, 384, 393
Stehekin Valley, Wash., 411–412
Stout, Frank D., 427
Stout Grove, Redwood NP, Calif., 428
Sully Creek SP, N. Dak., 121

T

Tall Trees Grove, Redwood NP, Calif., 423
Ta'u (island), American Samoa, 316, 318, 319
Taylor, Michael, 426
Teklanika River, Alas., 435, 438–439, 440
Tennessee
    Great Smoky Mountains NP, 12–13, 15, 56–63
Terrence, William, 186
Teton Glacier, Wyo., 275

Teton Range, Wyo., 273, 276, 277, 308
Texas
Big Bend NP, 136–137, 139, 140–149
Guadalupe Mountains NP, 139, 160–165
Pecos River Corridor Area (BLM), 159
Theodore Roosevelt NP, N. Dak., 92, 112–119
Thurston, Lorrin, 345
Tinkers Creek Gorge, Ohio, 104
Tioga Road, Yosemite NP, Calif., 371, 377–378, 379
Toklat River, Alas., 438
Torres, Francisco, 285
Tucson, Ariz., 246, 250
Tuolumne Meadows, Yosemite NP, Calif., 371, 377–378, 379
Tutuila (island), American Samoa, 316–318

U
Underwood, Gilbert Stanley, 191
United States Virgin Islands Virgin Islands NP, 15, 82–89
Upper Geyser Basin, Wyo., 301
Upper Missouri River Breaks NM (BLM), Mont., 120
Utah
Arches NP, 175, 176–183
Bryce Canyon NP, 172–173, 175, 190–197
Canyonlands NP, 175, 198–205
Capitol Reef NP, 175, 208–213
Dead Horse Point SP, 206
Glen Canyon NRA, 206
Manti-La Sal NF, 207
Sand Flats Recreation Area, 207
Scott M. Matheson Wetlands Preserves, 206
Westwater Canyon Wilderness Study Area (BLM), 207
Zion NP, 175, 252–259

V
Valley of Ten Thousand Smokes, Alas., 456, 457
Vallombrosa, Antoine de, 116
Vancouver, George, 448
Virgin Islands NP, V.I., 15, 82–89

Virginia
George Washington NF, 80
Jefferson NF, 81
Rapidan Wildlife Management Area, 81
Shenandoah NP, 15, 72–79
Shenandoah River SP, 81
Sky Meadows SP, 80
Wilderness Road SP, 80
Voyageurs NP, Minn., 93, 122–129

W
Wai'ānapanapa SP, Hawai'i, 340
Waikamoi Preserve, Hawai'i, 341
Washington
Mount Rainier NP, 383, 398–405
North Cascades NP, 380–381, 383, 406–413
Olympic NP, 383, 414–421
Waterton Lakes NP, Alta., Canada, 270, 271
Westwater Canyon Wilderness Study Area, Utah, 207
Wetherill Mesa, Colo., 233, 238, 239
Wheeler Peak Scenic Drive, Great Basin NP, Nev., 228–230, 231
White, Jim, 150
White Sands NM, N. Mex., 158
Whitney, Mount, Calif., 363, 375
Wild Basin, Rocky Mountain NP, Colo., 298
Wilderness Road SP, Va., 80
Wilson, Bates, 203
Wilson, Woodrow, 7, 456
Wind Cave NP, S. Dak., 92–93, 130–135
Windigo, Isle Royale NP, Mich., 107, 109–110, 111
Wizard Island, Oreg., 384, 385, 388
Wonder Lake, Alas., 440
Wrangell-St. Elias NP, Alas., 430–431, 433, 480–487
Wright, Frank Lloyd, 94
Wyoming
Fossil Butte NM, 283
Grand Teton NP, 260–261, 263, 272–281
Gros Ventre Wilderness, 282

Jackson National Fish Hatchery, 283
John D. Rockefeller, Jr. Memorial Parkway, 282
National Bighorn Sheep Center, 283
National Elk Refuge, 282
Yellowstone NP, 9, 263, 300–311

Y
Yellowstone Lake, Wyo., 300, 301, 308, 310
Yellowstone NP, U.S., 9, 263, 300–311
Yellowstone River, U.S., 300, 309
Yosemite NP, Calif., 7, 315, 370–379
Yosemite Valley, Calif., 370–379

Z
Zahl, Paul, 426, 427
Zion NP, Utah, 175, 252–259

MAP KEY and ABBREVIATIONS

National Park .... N.P.		
National Park and Preserve .... N.P. & Pres.		
National Preserve .... Nat. Pres.		
National Conservation Area .... N.C.A.		
National Historical Park .... N.H.P.		
National Memorial .... Nat. Mem.		
National Monument .... Nat. Mon.		
National Natural Landmark ...... N.N.L.		
National Recreation Area .... N.R.A.		
National Historic Site .... N.H.S.		

National Forest .... N.F., Nat. For.	
National Recreation Area .... N.R.A.	
National Volcanic Monument ..... N.V.M.	
State Forest .... S.F.	

National Wildlife Refuge .... N.W.R.
National Wildlife Range
State Game Refuge
State Game Sanctuary .... S.G.S.
State Wildlife Area
Habitat Area

National Grassland

Bureau of Land Management ...... B.L.M.
National Monument (B.L.M.) ...... Nat. Mon.
National Recreation Area (B.L.M.) ... N.R.A.

State Park .... S.P.
State Historic Site .... S.H.S.
State Primitive Park
State Recreation Area .... S.R.A.
State Wilderness Park .... S.W.P.
Provincial Park .... P.P.
County Park

Indian Reservation .... I.R.
Reserve (Canada)

Built-up Area

Roads and features

U.S. Interstate — 5

U.S. Federal, State or Provincial Highway — 50 33 1

Other Road — J59

Unpaved Road

Trail

Ferry

Railroad / Tram

Continental Divide

Fault Line

Wilderness Area

National Marine Sanctuary

National Wild & Scenic River

Military Reservation

National boundary

State boundary

Scenic route

⊛ State capital / Provincial capital	Intermittent river
🏠 Ranger Station / Visitor Center / Park Headquarters	Intermittent lake
▪ Point of interest	Dry lake
▲ Campground	Sand dunes
⛽ Picnic area	⑃ Falls
🌊 Overlook / Viewpoint	♂ Spring
+ Elevation	○ Geyser
⌣ Pass	Glacier
}--{ Tunnel	Swamp
⟋ Dam	Reef
	Shipwreck

POPULATION

○ **DENVER**	above 500,000
○ **Sacramento**	50,000 to 500,000
○ Helena	10,000 to 50,000
○ Morton	under 10,000

OTHER ABBREVIATIONS

Admin.	Administrative	N.S.T.	National Scenic Trail
Ave.	Avenue	Pk.	Peak
Cr.	Creek	Pkwy.	Parkway
Dr.	Drive	P.P.	Provincial Park
E.	East	PRES.	Preserve
Fk.	Fork	Pt.	Point
ft.	feet	R.	River
Gl.	Glacier	Ra.	Range
Hdqrs.	Headquarters	Rd.	Road
Hwy.	Highway	Rec.	Recreation
I.-s.	Island-s	Res.	Reservoir
L.	Lake	S.	South
M.	Middle	St.	Street
MEM.	Memorial	TERR.	Territory
Mt.-s.	Mount-ain-s	Tr.	Trail
N.	North	U.S.F.S.	United States Forest Service
NAT.	National	W.	West
N.M.S.	National Marine Sanctuary	WILD.	Wilderness

National Geographic Guide to National Parks of the United States, 8th ed.

George Fuller, William R. Gray, Robert Earle Howells, Kathryn Knorovsky, Charles Kulander, Rachael Jackson Moss, Daniel A. Nelson, Edward Readicker-Henderson, Jenna Schnuer, Jeremy Schmidt, Mel White, Joe Yogerst
Authors

Published by the National Geographic Society
Gary E. Knell, *President and Chief Executive Officer*
John M. Fahey, *Chairman of the Board*
Declan Moore, *Chief Media Officer*
Chris Johns, *Chief Content Officer*

Prepared by the Book Division
Hector Sierra, *Senior Vice President and General Manager*
Lisa Thomas, *Senior Vice President and Editorial Director*
Jonathan Halling, *Creative Director*
Marianne R. Koszorus, *Design Director*
Barbara Noe, *Senior Editor*
R. Gary Colbert, *Production Director*
Jennifer A. Thornton, *Director of Managing Editorial*
Susan S. Blair, *Director of Photography*
Meredith C. Wilcox, *Director, Administration and Rights Clearance*

Staff for This Book
Caroline Hickey, *Project Manager*
Sheila Buckmaster, *Editor*
Elisa Gibson, *Art Director*
Kay Hankins, *Designer & Illustrations Editor*
Erin Monroney, *Researcher*
Carl Mehler, *Director of Maps*
Michael McNey, Matthew Chwastyk, and XNR Productions, *Map Research and Production*
Allie Fahey, Marty Ittner, Mark Jenkins, *Contributors*
Marshall Kiker, *Associate Managing Editor*
Judith Klein, *Senior Production Editor*
Katie Olsen, *Design Production Specialist*
Nicole Miller, *Design Production Assistant*
Darrick McRae, *Manager, Production Services*
Rebekah Cain, *Imaging Technician*

The National Geographic Society is one of the world's largest nonprofit scientific and educational organizations. Its mission is to inspire people to care about the planet. Founded in 1888, the Society is member supported and offers a community for members to get closer to explorers, connect with other members, and help make a difference. The Society reaches more than 450 million people worldwide each month through *National Geographic* and other magazines; National Geographic Channel; television documentaries; music; radio; films; books; DVDs; maps; exhibitions; live events; school publishing programs; interactive media; and merchandise. National Geographic has funded more than 10,000 scientific research, conservation, and exploration projects and supports an education program promoting geographic literacy. For more information, visit www.nationalgeographic.com.

For more information, please call 1-800-NGS LINE (647-5463) or write to the following address:

National Geographic Society
1145 17th Street NW
Washington, DC 20036-4688 USA

Your purchase supports our nonprofit work and makes you part of our global community. Thank you for sharing our belief in the power of science, exploration, and storytelling to change the world. To activate your member benefits, complete your free membership profile at natgeo.com/joinnow.

For information about special discounts for bulk purchases, please contact National Geographic Books Special Sales: ngspecsales@ngs.org

For rights or permissions inquiries, please contact National Geographic Books Subsidiary Rights: ngbookrights@ngs.org

Eighth Edition ISBN: 978-1-4262-1651-0

Printed in China
15/RRDS/1